ALAN S. DAV.

THE FUN ALSO RISES
INTERNATIONAL TRAVEL GUIDE

The World's Most Fun Places To Be At The Right Time

L aunched in 1998 as a subsidiary of Capital Values, Inc., San Francisco-based Greenline Publications introduces a list of unique books in its FunGuide series with the 1999 release of *The Fun Also Rises Travel Guide North America: The Most Fun Places To Be at the Right Time*. The culmination of several years of exhaustive research and planning, *The Fun Also Rises* kicks off a series of related titles, including *The Fun Also Rises International Travel Guide*. These companion editions together include itineraries and Hot Sheets for all events and destinations listed on *The FunGuide 100: The 100 Most Fun Places To Be in the World at the Right Time*.

To reach us or for updated information on all Greenline books, visit the Greenline Publications Web site at www.FunRises.com

Front Cover Photo Credits: Bruce Postle, Melbourne Moomba Festival (left); Alan S. Davis (center); Mary Lou D'Auray (right)

Back Cover Photo Credits: Chuck Thompson (top); Mary Lou D'Auray (bottom)

ISBN: 0-9666352-1-3

Library of Congress: Catalog Card Number 99-073373

Distributed in the United States and Canada by Publishers Group West (PGW), Berkeley, California

Printed in Canada

First Edition

All rights reserved

10 9 8 7 6 5 4 3 2 1

Copyright © 1999 Greenline Publications

GREENLINE PUBLICATIONS

10 Lombard St., Ste. 200

San Francisco, CA 94111

ALAN S. DAVIS'

THE *Fun* ALSO RISES

INTERNATIONAL TRAVEL GUIDE

THE WORLD'S MOST FUN PLACES TO BE AT THE RIGHT TIME

Latin America and the Caribbean – Europe – Africa, Asia, and Australia

Edited by Chuck Thompson

First Edition

Special thanks to brother James Marti, whose encouragement got me started on this adventure.

Special thanks to brother Mitch Rofsky, whose help and optimism got me through to the end.

As author, I acknowledge the hundreds of people who have contributed to this book. This includes friends, tourist-board and travel-industry representatives, event organizers, and all those people who help make these events fun. In particular, I'd like to thank Dr. Roger Brunswick (a psychiatrist who helped me develop The Mating Rating), Bob Chirlian (whose travel agency got me where I needed to go), Air France, Carmen McCarty of American Airlines, Jane Watkins and Cheryl Andrews, Fred Farkouh and Richard Faccio, Ann Opara and Joyce Taira, Richard Ross, Jim and Gloria Hassan, Eugene Yee, Jorge Guarro, Elaine Petrocelli, Donald George, Georgia Hesse, Paul McMenamin, and Raul Santiago.

As publisher, I thank Gary Todoroff, our marketing consultant, and our friends at PGW, who helped put our ideas onto bookshelves. I also want to single out Terrance Mark and our inner staff—Saida Benguerel, Michele Powers Glaze, Gerard Gleason, and Aimée Goggins—they were always there when needed.

As author and publisher, I thank Chuck Thompson—there could not have been a person more responsible, effective, and nice to work with, or one from whom I could have learned as much about writing.

Alan S. Davis

To my parents,
with thanks for their support
and for passing on the travel bug

To Jaimee and Paul, who have lovingly accepted
their father's endeavors

And to Emile, whose love, companionship, and humor
have made this one terrific ride

Editor	Chuck Thompson
Associate Editor	Saida Benguerel
Contributing Editor, Chapters	Janet Byron, Heidi Craig, Diane Weipert
Contributing Editor, Junos	Susan Kinsella
Copy Editor	Michele Powers Glaze

Contributors

Deborah Bennett (Destination: Athens, Juno: Sailing), Keith Brickhouse (Montreux Jazz Festival), Tom Bross (Oktoberfest, Stuttgart's Volksfest), Greg Brown (Viña del Mar Song Festival), Sue Buchholz (Nice Jazz Festival), Johanna Campbell (Edinburgh Fringe Festival, Hogmanay), Siri Campbell (Cannes Film Festival, Monaco Grand Prix), Hilary Casey (St. Patrick's Festival), Chris Collins (Juno: Carnivals), Mary Lou D'Auray (Cowes Week, Vienna Opera Ball), Felipe Ferreira (Carnaval Rio), Virginia Ferrero (Feria de San Marcos), Shirley Fong-Torres (Hong Kong Chinese New Year), George Fuller (Juno: Golf), Babs Harrison (Pushkar Camel Fair), David Holt-Biddle (Cape Minstrel Festival), Simon Lee (Trinidad Carnival), Ray March (Feast of St. Anthony), Richard Meyrick (Roskilde Rock Festival), Terin Miller (Fiestas de San Isidro, Juno: Bullfighting), Judy Murphy (Galway Oyster Festival), Gay Myers (Crop Over Festival), Amanda Nowinski (Juno: Discos), Timothy O'Grady (Las Fallas), Laura Randall (Calle San Sebastián), Walter Roessing (Skiing: Zermatt), Mary Simon (Juno: Horse Racing), Amy Spiezio (Junkanoo), David Swanson (Sailing Week), Lesley Tellez (La Tomatina)

Book Design	Terrance Mark Studio
Illustrations	Maureen Radcliffe George
Administration	Gerard Gleason
Research	Aimée Goggins

Jaimee Davis, Paul Davis, Joyce Jones, James Marti

The Fun Also Rises
International Travel Guide

Table of Contents

Table of Contents
cont.

W hen I set out to become a professional fun-seeker five years ago, I envisioned the end product pretty much as a list of the 100 most fun places to be in the world and the right times to be there. Along the way things changed. I realized that travelers could go to world-class events, yet miss some of the highlights—and thus, not get the most out of the experience. Moreover, the destination cities themselves are often the key to having a fantastic trip, and getting the most fun out of a city requires some guidance. This realization led to the three-day itineraries that now make up the bulk of each chapter.

These agendas quickly became the most time-consuming aspect of my work. Nailing down event schedules, setting up timetables, and identifying the hottest hotels, restaurants, and nightlife in 100 cities around the world is a bit like juggling Ginsu knives in a phone booth—room for error is slight, lessons are painful, and you wind up starting over a lot of times before you get it right. The result, I hope, is not only an enjoyable read but a handy planning tool. Many readers have found the Hot Sheets at the end of each chapter to be invaluable quick-reference guides, even for those regrettable trips that don't involve the world's great events.

The magnitude of the information, however, meant we had to separate the *FunGuide 100* destinations into two books. It had to be fun to read, so why overwhelm readers before they'd even gotten started. This book is the companion to *The Fun Also Rises Travel Guide North America*, which provides information and itineraries for the 50 North American events and destinations in the *FunGuide 100* list. In addition to 50 international itineraries, this book includes The *FunGuide100* with updated information.

The aftermath of the launch of the North American edition proved to be almost as much fun as the research had been. I spent nine months touring the country, attending events, visiting bookstores, and appearing on radio and television. It's been rewarding to get media attention, but nothing could be more gratifying than watching a person thumb through the book, and say, "I've been there," or "I've heard of that, and I've always wanted to go," or "I've never heard of that one!" It's also great being told that the book has helped someone plan a really special anniversary or birthday celebration.

Besides positive feedback, I've received a lot of questions. Here are some answers I'd like to share with you.

How did you pick the title *The Fun Also Rises*?

At the time this book was conceived, I was going through a personal transition and looking to get more fun out of life. I remembered the opening scene in *City Slickers*, the one with Billy Crystal running with the bulls at the famous festival in Pamplona, Spain. I must have missed the part where Billy gets a horn up his derrière, because I decided that this event looked like a lot of fun. The difficulty I had getting the necessary information to plan my trip got me thinking about a useful travel book. But it was the extraordinary fiesta and the hope that I could encourage more people to experience it and other events like it that convinced me to write this book. The Fiesta de San Fermín (see page 165) was such a life-changing experience for me that the title of the book it inspired had to pay homage to Ernest Hemingway and his novel *The Sun Also Rises*, which popularized the celebration.

What is your favorite event?

I've rated each event and destination city based on predetermined "fun" guidelines (see page 11). But to pick a favorite would be like trying to decide whether I would rather be hit by tomatoes in Buñol, beads in New Orleans, or chocolate bars in Köln. Do I prefer waltzing in Vienna, "wining" in the Caribbean, or two-stepping in Texas? The answer, of course, is all these parties are fun (especially the four- and five-star events) and which one I like the most depends on my mood at the time you ask.

What is your definition of fun?

I read somewhere that *fun* derives from the Middle English word *fonnen*, meaning "to act foolishly or let loose." (What *is* Middle English anyway? Something between grade school and high school?) Somehow, as we get older, we forget how to do this. I use a number of criteria to evaluate fun (back to page 11), but I particularly enjoy events that make it possible, at least temporarily, to let loose and physically transform ourselves. You won't normally find me in top hat and tails, as I appeared at Royal Ascot, or covered in mud as I was at the Trinidad Carnival's *J'Ouvert*.

Your background as a political activist suggests you've always had an agenda. Do you have one for this book?

I didn't start out with an agenda, but I now have three goals:

1. To help and encourage people to have more fun. These events provide great opportunities for people to interact (see page 13), try something new, be different, and forget about the problems of the world.
2. To improve the quality and quantity of events. Although there are many terrific events out there, my experience in attending so many as a professional fun-seeker gives me a perspective I hope can help festival planners come up with even better events.
3. To create a publishing company that provides products that bring people enjoyment and useful, unique information.

Why did you pick three days for each itinerary?

Limiting visits to three days provides a common denominator for comparing events. These itineraries also suit the trend toward shorter vacations, while allowing travelers to build longer vacations around them. On a flight recently I met a man who was heading to Ibiza, Spain. I told him about La Tomatina (see pages 217 and 251) and he immediately made plans to finish off his vacation in Buñol. These destinations can be enjoyed over a longer period at a more leisurely pace, but the "play hard" itineraries we provide can be a good jumping-off point for many people.

What general advice do you offer fun-seekers?

First, these events are fun to read about but more fun to attend. Second, it helps to be open to new experiences. Third, getting into the spirit of an event (i.e. getting in costume) adds to the fun. Fourth, at these events, always say hello to the person standing next to you. Finally, some of the best and most fun experiences you'll have will be serendipitous—to increase your chances of having them, it helps to be in the right place at the right time. Reading this book should make that easier. The rest is up to you.

—Alan S. Davis
San Francisco, October 1999

About The FunGuide 100

How does one come up with a list of the world's most fun events and destinations? Here are our rules, exceptions, and results.

SELECTION CRITERIA FOR EVENTS

Rule: Events must take place annually in the same city.
Exceptions: San Francisco's biennial Black and White Ball.

Rule: Events in this book must have a total attendance of at least 10,000.
Exceptions: The smallest events are the Napa Valley Wine Auction and Tokyo's Fertility Festival (2,000 each), followed by the Vienna Opera Ball (5,000).

The total attendance at all 92 events (eight of our chapters are destinations without events) is more than 62 million. More than two-thirds of the events have an attendance greater than 50,000. The three most attended events are: Carnaval Rio (10 million), Munich's Oktoberfest (6 million), and Stuttgart's Volksfest (5 million).

Rule: We cannot visit a city twice.
Exceptions: San Francisco, New Orleans, Las Vegas, London, Edinburgh. These world-class cities (★★★★★ or ★★★★) have two world-class events and warrant second visits. For other cities, a second world-class event is listed in the Alternatives section of each itinerary.

Rule: We spend only three days at any event/destination.
Exceptions: We spend a week aboard the Carnival Destiny.

Individual events are judged on:

Participation (The outrageous parades of Trinidad's Carnival are a great example.)

Transformation (During Edinburgh's Fringe Festival, the entire city becomes a stage.)

People-watching (From celebrities in Cannes during the Film Festival to revelers at Cape Town's Cape Minstrel Festival, this is always rewarding.)

Uniqueness (There's nothing like La Tomatina.)

Spectacle (Rio's Carnaval is tough to beat.)

Gorgeous surroundings (The jazz festival in Montreux comes to mind.)

Gorgeous surroundings of a more human variety (At Ascot it is not the horses that have most people's attention.)

Personal release (Events like the Running of the Bulls coax people into being a little more crazy and daring than they normally would be.)

WHAT EVENT RATINGS MEAN

★★★★★ and ★★★★

Must do. These events are worth making a special trip for, even planning your life around.

★★★ and ★★

Should do. These are events you should attend if you're already planning to visit the region or if you are just looking for something fun to do on a given weekend.

★

These events, though not worth a special trip, are the times when it's most fun to be at the destination.

THE WORLD'S TOP EVENTS

★★★★★

Carnaval Rio	Trinidad Carnival
Mardi Gras	Venice Carnival
Munich's Oktoberfest	Vienna Opera Ball
Running of the Bulls	

★★★★

Bike Week	Karneval
Burning Man	Kentucky Derby
Calgary Stampede	La Tomatina
Cannes Film Festival	Las Fallas
Cowes Week	Royal Ascot
Edinburgh Fringe Festival	St. Patrick's Day
Fantasy Fest	Stockholm Water Festival
Fiesta San Antonio	Sundance Film Festival
Galway Oyster Festival	Sydney Gay and
Hogmanay	Lesbian Mardi Gras
Hookers' Ball/Halloween	

DISTRIBUTION OF EVENT RATINGS

	★ (5)	★ (4)	★ (3)	★ (2)	★ (1)	N/A*	Total
NA	1	9	22	9	6	3	50
EUR	4	10	9	3	1	3	30
LAC	2	0	5	2	0	2	11
AASP	—	1	3	4	1	—	9
Total	7	20	39	18	8	8	100

NA—North America (United States and Canada);
EUR—Europe; LAC—Latin America, Caribbean;
AASP—Africa, Asia, South Pacific
*Eight destinations are not tied to specific events.

SELECTION CRITERIA FOR CITIES

Cities are evaluated for the quality and quantity of their night-life, restaurants, attractions, and hotels. We also consider a city's overall aesthetic.

CITY RATINGS

★★★★★ or ★★★★

These world-class fun cities are worth a visit any time but are most fun during the recommended event.

★★★ or ★★

These are nice places to visit, but only worth a special trip during the event.

★

Save going here for the event.

Included in *The FunGuide 100* are eight destinations that are not tied to specific events but must be included on any list of the world's most fun places to be: Acapulco, Athens, Ibiza/Majorca, Lake Tahoe, Zermatt, Hedonism II, the *Carnival Destiny* cruise ship, and Disney World.

TOP CITIES

★★★★★

Barcelona	Monte Carlo
Boston	New York
Cannes	Nice
Chicago	Paris
Edinburgh	Philadelphia
Las Vegas	San Francisco
London	Venice
Los Angeles	Vienna
Madrid	Stockholm
Miami	Tokyo

★★★★

Amsterdam	Munich
Buenos Aires	New Orleans
Cape Town	Rio de Janeiro
Hong Kong	Sydney
Melbourne	Toronto
Montréal	Washington, D.C.

DISTRIBUTION OF CITY RATINGS

	★5	★4	★3	★2	★1	N/A	Total
NA	8	4	22	9	1	3	47
EUR	11	2	5	4	3	3	28
LAC	0	2	2	3	2	2	11
AASP	1	4	2	1	1	—	9
Total	20	12	31	17	7	8	95**

**Five cities with two events are counted once

TOTAL RATINGS

Two events/destinations scored a perfect 10: the Venice Carnival in Italy, and the Vienna Opera Ball in Austria.

DISTRIBUTION OF TOTAL (EVENT + CITY) RATINGS

	★10	★9	★8	★7	★6	★5	★4	N/A	Total
NA	—	2	7	9	11	11	7	3	50
EUR	2	7	3	3	5	7	—	3	30
LAC	0	1	0	0	3	4	1	2	11
AASP	—	0	1	1	4	1	2	—	9
Total	2	10	11	13	23	23	10	8	100

SELECTION CRITERIA FOR THE ITINERARY

Itineraries usually run Thursday through Saturday (when destinations are most lively) unless the high points of an event justify being there on a different day. We typically begin after breakfast on Day 1 and end when nightclubs close on Day 3.

Hotels—When available, we choose only first-class hotels. Selected hotels should (in priority order): fit in with the events (convenient location to recommended events is important); be hip or classy but not stuffy; and capture the character of its city.

Restaurants—The food must be good, but ambience is as important as the meal. Otherwise, the criteria are the same as for hotels.

Nightlife—We cover the hottest places for the over-30 crowd. Our bias is toward Scotch over beer, classy over funky. We generally don't include performing arts.

Sightseeing—We include the best each destination has to offer, but we shy away from zoos, natural-history museums, botanical gardens, and shopping destinations (there's no time for shopping), unless they are unique.

Juno (short for "Did you know?"):
> *Every week of the year there's a fun place to be.*
> *And every fun place to be has a best time to be there.*

Each event in this book is fun, involving many people coming together for a good time. But some events are better than others for meeting someone with whom you can develop a relationship, even if just for a three-day visit. The key ingredients are sexual energy, the number of singles attending, and an opportunity to interact. Although there's no such thing as a sure thing, here are our ratings (medications optional) for the chances of finding a mate at each event.

In alphabetical order by country.

HOPE (VIAGRA)

Event	City	Country	Page	Event	City	Country	Page
Sailing Week	St. John's	Antigua	127	Hedonism II	Negril	Jamaica	63
Sydney Gay and Lesbian Mardi Gras	Sydney	Australia	71	Fun Destination: Acapulco	Acapulco	Mexico	245
Junkanoo	Nassau	Bahamas	36	Ati-Atihan	Manila	Philippines	43
Carnaval Rio	Rio de Janeiro	Brazil	89	Edinburgh Fringe Festival	Edinburgh	Scotland	207
Roskilde Rock Festival	Copenhagen	Denmark	161	Hogmanay	Edinburgh	Scotland	248
Cowes Week	Isle of Wight	England	185	Fun Destination: Ibiza/Majorca	Ibiza/Majorca	Spain	197
Karneval	Köln	Germany	83	Running of the Bulls	Pamplona	Spain	165
Oktoberfest	Munich	Germany	221	Stockholm Water Festival	Stockholm	Sweden	189
Fun Destination: Athens	Athens	Greece	233	Trinidad Carnival	Port of Spain	Trinidad & Tobago	93

HOPE, NO CHANCE (PROZAC)

Event	City	Country	Page	Event	City	Country	Page
Moomba	Melbourne	Australia	97	St. Patrick's Festival	Dublin	Ireland	105
Crop Over Festival	Bridgetown	Barbados	193	Venice Carnival	Venice	Italy	79
Viña del Mar Song Festival	Santiago	Chile	59	Feria de San Marcos	Aguascalientes	Mexico	117
Macau Grand Prix	Macau	China	241	Monaco Grand Prix	Monte Carlo	Monaco	143
Notting Hill Carnival	London	England	213	Queen's Day	Amsterdam	Netherlands	121
Royal Ascot	London	England	155	Feast of St. Anthony	Lisbon	Portugal	151
Cannes Film Festival	Cannes	France	136	Calle San Sebastián	San Juan	Puerto Rico	47
Nice Jazz Festival	Nice	France	175	La Tomatina	Barcelona	Spain	217
Féria de Nîmes	Nîmes	France	147	Fiestas de San Isidro	Madrid	Spain	131
Bastille Day	Paris	France	170	Las Fallas	Valencia	Spain	101
Stuttgart's Volksfest	Stuttgart	Germany	229	Montreux Jazz Festival	Montreux	Switzerland	179
Galway Oyster Festival	Galway	Ireland	225	Skiing Zermatt	Zermatt	Switzerland	55

NO CHANCE (HEMLOCK)

Event	City	Country	Page	Event	City	Country	Page

These events and destinations are fun, really, but they don't exactly lend themselves to mating opportunities.

Vienna Opera Ball	Vienna	Austria	67	Pushkar Camel Fair	Jaipur	India	237
Vendimia	Buenos Aires	Argentina	75	Palio	Siena/Florence	Italy	203
Hong Kong Chinese New Year	Hong Kong	China	51	Cape Minstrel Festival	Cape Town	South Africa	39
Fertility Festival	Tokyo	Japan	109	Songkran Water Festival	Bangkok	Thailand	113

The FunGuide 100

MILLENIUM LIST 2000

		Travel Date	Event Date	Event Official Name (if different)	City, State, Country Host City (if different)	Event/City Rating Origin	Attendance	Pg ✓
Week 1	2000	Jan. 1	Dec. 26-Jan. 1	Junkanoo	Nassau, Bahamas	★★★★★★		36
	2001	Jan. 1	Dec. 26-Jan. 1			c. 1800	10,000	
	2000	Jan. 1	Jan. 1-30	Cape Minstrel Festival	Cape Town, South Africa	★★★★★★		39
	2001	Jan. 1	Jan. 1-30			1898	50,000	
Week 2	2000	Jan. 13	Jan. 14-23	Detroit Auto Show	Detroit, Michigan, USA	★★★★★		NA
	2001	Jan. 11	Jan. 12-21	(North American International Auto Show, NAIAS)		1907	790,000	
	2000	Jan. 14	Jan. 10-16	Ati-Atihan	Manila, Philippines	★★★★★★		43
	2001	Jan. 19	Jan. 15-21		(Kalibo)	1212	200,000	
Week 3	2000	Jan. 20	Jan. 20-29	Sundance Film Festival	Park City, Utah, USA	★★★★★★★		NA
	2001	Jan. 18	Jan. 18-28			1978	18,000	
	2000	Jan. 21	Jan. 20-23	Calle San Sebastián	San Juan, Puerto Rico	★★★★★		47
	2001	Jan. 20	Jan. 20-23			1970	50,000	
Week 4	2000	Jan. 26	Jan. 24-30	Phoenix Open	Phoenix, Arizona, USA	★★★★★★		NA
	2001	Jan. 24	Jan. 22-28		(Scottsdale)	1932	470,000	
	2000	Jan. 28	Jan. 28-30	Super Bowl Weekend	Las Vegas, Nevada, USA	★★★★★★★★		NA
	2001	Jan. 26	Jan. 26-28			1967	200,000	
Week 5	2000	Feb. 4	Jan. 28-Feb. 13	Québec Winter Carnaval	Québec City, Québec, Canada	★★★★★★		NA
	2001	Feb. 2	Jan. 26-Feb. 11	(Carnaval de Québec)		1894	1,000,000	
	2000	Feb 4.	Feb. 5-7	Hong Kong Chinese New Year	Hong Kong, China	★★★★★		51
	2001	Jan. 23	Jan. 24-26			1996	25,000	
Week 6	2000	Feb. 11	—	Skiing Zermatt	Zermatt, Switzerland	—	—	55
	2001	Feb. 15	—	(The Most Fun Place To Ski: Europe)			—	
Week 7	2000	Feb. 19	Feb. 16-21	Viña del Mar Song Festival	Santiago, Chile	★★★★★		59
	2001	Feb. 10	Feb. 7-12	(International Song Festival of Viña del Mar)	(Viña del Mar)	1959	110,000	
Week 8	2000	Feb. 25	—	Hedonism II	Negril, Jamaica	—	—	63
	2001	Dec. 21	—	(The Most Fun Resort)		—	—	

Events are listed according to the week in which the 2000 travel date takes place. Subsequent to January 1, weeks begin on Monday.

NA = Itinerary in companion edition *The Fun Also Rises Travel Guide North America*
Readers' ✓: Been there, Done that, or Plan to

January

Junkanoo
Kick off the new year at 2 a.m with a parade of elaborately costumed dancers, Caribbean music, and enthusiastic crowds that keep the party spirit alive past the break of dawn.

Cape Minstrel Festival
High-energy minstrels begin the year by taking over the streets and coaxing crowds to join them in singing, dancing, and marching in one of the world's most gorgeous and under-appreciated cities.

Detroit Auto Show
Detroit? Dead of winter? The city synonymous with cars revs up for a great weekend during North America's premier auto show (complete with a black-tie preview).

Ati-Atihan
Filipinos take to the streets of Kalibo in a wildly costumed religious festival that celebrates dancing, shaking, foot-stomping, and noise-making.

Sundance Film Festival
The glitterati schmooze, party, ski, and even watch the world's best new films being unveiled at the hottest film festival in the United States.

Calle San Sebastián
Wall-to-wall people mingle, dance, and drink together along the closed-off streets of San Juan at Puerto Rico's biggest fiesta.

Phoenix Open
Phoenix is golf heaven and no pro-golf tournament is more associated with fun, sun, and action than this one. You don't need to be a golfer to enjoy the highlight of Phoenix's social season.

Super Bowl Weekend
Hotels and casinos unfurl red carpets for players who know that the football game is just a sidelight during the world's quintessential gambling weekend.

February

Québec Winter Carnaval
This three-week samba in parkas is fueled by happy throngs and ubiquitous sticks filled with Caribou (a wicked libation made of port and grain alcohol).

Hong Kong Chinese New Year
The biggest holiday in China is most fun in Hong Kong, where a samba party and other Western twists are added to traditional fireworks and dragon dances.

Skiing Zermatt
Zermatt takes the European title for best ski-party town, adding its special touch of Swiss hospitality and gorgeous scenery (the Alps aren't the only things worth looking at).

Viña del Mar Song Festival
A music festival that coincides with Carnaval Rio—the late-night crowd warms up here with beaches and top-name Latin acts before proceeding to Rio.

Hedonism II
This activity-filled Jamaican resort is divided by a walkway that separates the nude side from the prude side—as close to an anything-goes environment as a hotel gets.

		Travel Date	Event Date	Event	City, State, Country	Event/City Rating		Pg
				Official Name (if different)	Host City (if different)	Origin	Attendance	✓
Week 9		2000	Feb. 29	Mar. 2	Vienna Opera Ball	Vienna, Austria	★★★★★★★★★★	67
		2001	Feb. 20	Feb. 22			1877	5,000	
		2000	Mar. 2	Feb. 11-Mar. 4	Sydney Gay and Lesbian Mardi Gras	Sydney, Australia	★★★★★★★★	71
		2001	Mar. 1	Feb. 10-Mar. 3			1978	500,000	
		2000	Mar. 2	Mar. 3-5	Vendimia	Buenos Aires, Argentina	★★★★★★	75
		2001	Mar. 1	Mar. 2-4		(Mendoza)	1936	300,000	
		2000	Mar. 3	Feb. 25-Mar. 7	Venice Carnival	Venice, Italy	★★★★★★★★★★	79
		2001	Feb. 23	Feb. 17-27	(Carnevale di Venezia)		1979	500,000	
		2000	Mar. 4	Mar. 2-7	Karneval	Köln, Germany	★★★★★★★	83
		2001	Feb. 24	Feb. 22-27			1823	1,000,000	
		2000	Mar. 5	Feb. 26-Mar. 7	Mardi Gras	New Orleans, Louisiana, USA	★★★★★★★★★	NA
		2001	Feb. 25	Feb. 17-27			1837	3,500,000	
		2000	Mar. 5	Mar. 4-7	Carnaval Rio	Rio de Janeiro, Brazil	★★★★★★★★★	89
		2001	Feb. 25	Feb. 24-27			1930	10,000,000	
		2000	Mar. 5	Mar. 6-7	Trinidad Carnival	Port of Spain, Trinidad & Tobago	★★★★★★★	93
		2001	Feb. 25	Feb. 26-27			c. 1840	100,000	
Week 10		2000	Mar. 9	Mar. 3-12	Bike Week	Daytona Beach/Orlando, Florida, USA	★★★★★★★	NA
		2001	Mar. 8	Mar. 2-11			1937	500,000	
		2000	Mar. 10	Mar. 3-12	Calle Ocho	Miami Beach, Florida, USA	★★★★★★★★	NA
		2001	Mar. 9	Mar. 2-11	(Carnaval Miami)	(Miami)	1978	1,000,000	
		2000	Mar. 10	Mar. 9-19	Moomba	Melbourne, Australia	★★★★★★	97
		2001	Mar. 9	Mar. 8-18	(The Melbourne Moomba Festival)		1955	1,500,000	
Week 11		2000	Mar. 16	Mar. 15-19	South by Southwest	Austin/Dallas/Ft. Worth, Texas, USA	★★★★★	NA
		2001	Mar. 15	Mar. 14-18	(South by Southwest Music and Media Conference, SXSW)		1987	25,000	
		2000	Mar. 17	Mar. 16-19	St. Patrick's Day Celebration	Savannah, Georgia, USA	★★★★★★	NA
		2001	Mar. 16	Mar. 15-18			1813	300,000	
		2000	Mar. 17	Mar. 12-19	Las Fallas	Valencia, Spain	★★★★★★	101
		2001	Mar. 17	Mar. 12-19			1497	500,000	
		2000	Mar. 17	Mar. 16-19	St. Patrick's Festival	Dublin, Ireland	★★★★★★	105
		2001	Mar. 16	Mar. 15-18			1996	850,000	
Week 12		2000	Mar. 24	Mar. 26	Academy Awards Weekend	Los Angeles, California, USA	★★★★★★	NA
		2001	Mar. 23	Mar. 25			1929	—	
Week 13		2000	Mar. 30	—	Skiing Tahoe	Lake Tahoe, California, USA	—	—	NA
		2001	Dec. 7	—	(The Most Fun Place To Ski: North America)		—	—	

Events are listed according to the week in which the 2000 travel date takes place. Subsequent to January 1, weeks begin on Monday.

NA = Itinerary in companion edition *The Fun Also Rises Travel Guide North America*
Readers' ✓: Been there, Done that, or Plan to

February/March

Vienna Opera Ball	The best formal party in the world—the unparalleled Vienna Opera House is the setting for gorgeous debutantes, ties and tails, and the most elegant evening of the year.
Sydney Gay and Lesbian Mardi Gras	Boas, leather, glitter, G-strings, rubber, and Saran Wrap—lots of people (straights and gays) call one of the world's largest gay-and-lesbian-pride events the best human spectacle on earth.
Vendimia	Unlike most wine festivals, this one is not a laid-back taste test—it turns the town into a party and makes a most convincing argument for the South American wine industry.
Venice Carnival	The world's most beautiful city is transformed into a Fellini-esque world of masked paraders and costumed street performers by day, and a land of elegant balls by night.
Karneval	Not everyone in Köln is dressed like a clown, it just seems like it. One of the world's great pre-Lenten events, this surreal three-day gathering of clowns is about as organized as debauchery gets.
Mardi Gras	The event that's inspired 1,000 imitations could take place only in New Orleans—Mardi Gras launches into a separate universe of costumes, music, and uninhibited revelry.
Carnaval Rio	The world's biggest party features (almost) naked people, outrageous costumes, the best dance music on the planet, and more fun than some continents have in an entire year.
Trinidad Carnival	Steel drums, wild costumes, calypso bands, no sleep, and a 3 a.m. kickoff party that covers participants (there are no spectators here) with mud and music.

March

Bike Week	Thousands of bikers thunder into Florida, and Daytona becomes Harley heaven during an extraordinary week of motorcycle worshiping and partying.
Calle Ocho	While other carnivals are moving into Lent, Miami's is cranking up two weeks of Latin music and dancing in the streets of North America's (still) hottest destination.
Moomba	More than 1.5 million attend Australia's largest outdoor festival, which combines cultural and sporting events with out-of-this-world native-arts displays and performances.
South by Southwest	The world's hippest music festival features 900 bands playing in a city that proudly claims that it has more bars and restaurants per capita than any other US city.
St. Patrick's Day Celebration	An improbable mix of Southern hospitality and Irish moxie makes this two-centuries-old party one of the world's biggest and best St. Patrick's Day celebrations.
Las Fallas	Europe's fireworks capital hosts an incredible spectacle—gorgeous papier-mâché tableaux are constructed, then burned simultaneously while firefighters nervously stand by and fireworks explode overhead.
St. Patrick's Festival	Inspired by the Irish-American celebrations, Dubliners throw the most entertaining parade in the world and follow it up with visits to—what else?—Irish pubs.
Academy Awards Weekend	Los Angeles is the North American destination for glitz and glamour, but with film-biz luminaries, screen superstars, and major media clamoring about, the buzz is deafening.
Skiing Tahoe	The skiing may be fantastic, but it's extraordinary nightlife and scenery that make Lake Tahoe North America's most fun ski resort for skiers and nonskiers alike.

	Travel Date	Event Date	Event Official Name (if different)	City, State, Country Host City (if different)	Event/City Rating Origin Attendance		Pg ✓
Week 14	2000 Apr. 7	Apr. 8-9	Fertility Festival	Tokyo, Japan	★★★★★★		109
	2001 Apr. 13	Apr. 14-15	(Kanamara Matsuri)	(Kawasaki)	c. 1750	2,000	
Week 15	2000 Apr. 13	Apr. 13-15	Songkran Water Festival	Bangkok, Thailand	★★★★★		113
	2001 Apr. 13	Apr. 13-15	(Songkran)	(Chiang Mai)	c. 1300	200,000	
Week 16	2000 Apr. 23	Apr. 22-30	Fiesta San Antonio	San Antonio, Texas, USA	★★★★★★		NA
	2001 Apr. 22	Apr. 20-29			1891	3,500,000	
	2000 Apr. 28	Apr. 14-May 7	Feria de San Marcos	Aguascalientes, Mexico	★★★★		117
	2001 Apr. 27	Apr. 13-May 6	(Feria Nacional de San Marcos)		1848	1,600,000	
Week 17	2000 Apr. 28	Apr. 30	Queen's Day	Amsterdam, Netherlands	★★★★★★		121
	2001 Apr. 28	Apr. 30	(Koninginnedag)		1948	720,000	
	2000 Apr. 30	Apr. 30-May 6	Sailing Week	St. John's, Antigua	★★★★★		127
	2001 Apr. 29	Apr. 29-May 5	(Antigua Sailing Week)		1967	10,000	
Week 18	2000 May 4	Apr. 14-May 7	Kentucky Derby	Louisville, Kentucky, USA	★★★★★★		NA
	2001 May 3	Apr. 20-May 6	(Kentucky Derby Festival)		1875	140,000	
Week 19	2000 May 4	Apr. 28-May 7	New Orleans Jazz & Heritage Festival	New Orleans, Louisiana, USA	★★★★★★		NA
	2001 May 3	Apr. 27-May 6			1970	480,000	
	2000 May 13	May 11-15	Fiestas de San Isidro	Madrid, Spain	★★★★★★		131
	2001 May 15	May 11-15			1622	25,000	
Week 20	2000 May 18	May 12-20	The Preakness	Baltimore, Maryland, USA	★★★★		NA
	2001 May 17	May 11-19	(Preakness Celebration)		1873	90,000	
	2000 May 18	May 18-20	Memphis in May Barbecue	Memphis, Tennessee, USA	★★★★★		NA
	2001 May 17	May 17-19	(Memphis in May World Championship Barbecue Cooking Contest)		1976	80,000	
Week 21	2000 May 18	May 10-21	Cannes Film Festival	Cannes, France	★★★★★★★★		136
	2001 May 10	May 9-20	(Festival International du Film)		1939	31,000	
	2000 May 25	May 6-28	Indy 500	Indianapolis, Indiana, USA	★★★★★		NA
	2001 May 24	May 5-27	(The 500 Festival)		1911	400,000	
	2000 —	—	Black and White Ball	San Francisco, California, USA	★★★★★★★		NA
	2001 May 31	Jun. 2			1956	12,000	
Week 22	2000 Jun. 1	Jun. 1-3	Napa Valley Wine Auction	Napa Valley, California, USA	★★★★★		NA
	2001 Jun. 7	Jun. 7-9		(St. Helena)	1981	2,000	
	2000 Jun. 1	May 26-Jun. 11	Spoleto	Charleston, South Carolina, USA	★★★★★		NA
	2001 May 31	May 25-Jun. 10	(Spoleto Festival USA/Piccolo Spoleto)		1977	72,000	
	2000 Jun. 2	Jun. 1-4	Monaco Grand Prix	Monte Carlo, Monaco	★★★★★★★		143
	2001 May 25	May 24-27	(Grand Prix Automobile de Monaco)		1942	75,000	

Events are listed according to the week in which the 2000 travel date takes place. Subsequent to January 1, weeks begin on Monday.

NA = Itinerary in companion edition *The Fun Also Rises Travel Guide North America*
Readers' ✓: Been there, Done that, or Plan to

April

Fertility Festival

They're not shooting *Attack of the Giant Phallus* in the streets of Kawasaki, it just looks that way when thousands of people fill the streets to celebrate the biggest game in town.

Songkran Water Festival

This wild-and-wet festival commemorates the end of the dry season by staging a monsoon that soaks everybody in sight with pails of flying water.

Fiesta San Antonio

How have the 3.5 million people who annually attend this event kept secret one of the nation's best festivals of music, food, parades, and street parties?

Feria de San Marcos

Hardly a tourist destination, Aguascalientes draws top-name musicians and bullfighters to Mexico's biggest national fair for a nonstop fiesta.

Queen's Day

The world's largest flea market turns into a party for 750,000 at night—fireworks and Amsterdam's infamous pleasures are the calling cards of this unusual event.

Sailing Week

The premier Caribbean race-and-party week is always ranked among the top-five regattas, but it also has the number-one set of beaches.

May

Kentucky Derby

Forget about the 20 horses—it's the 70-event festival, 80,000 mint juleps, and the city that's the crown jewel of Southern style that make the Derby a winner.

New Orleans Jazz & Heritage Festival

Some people consider this the world's best jazz festival because of the daylong talent lineup, but it's the backdrop of New Orleans nightlife that really makes it stand out.

Fiestas de San Isidro

The fiesta is celebrated with music and bullfighting, but this really just makes it the best time of year to visit one of the world's great cities.

The Preakness

The second jewel in horse racing's Triple Crown is really an excuse for Mardi Gras-style fun that combines let-it-all-hang-out revelry with quaint traditions.

Memphis in May Barbecue

When disciples of blues, beer, and barbecue invade Memphis, how could the result be anything less than the world's greatest marriage of down-home food and fun?

Cannes Film Festival

The world's most important film festival transforms this Mediterranean resort into one big nonstop cast party where glamour and attention-getting stunts reign supreme.

Indy 500

The actual race may be "the greatest spectacle in racing," but the days leading up to the main event are geared as much to party fans as to racing fans.

Black and White Ball

Highlighting the city's refined side, this biennial event turns the streets of San Francisco into a set from a glamorous black-and-white movie and the world's largest indoor-outdoor black-tie ball.

Napa Valley Wine Auction

Great food, great wine, great food, great wine, great food, great wine, great food, great wine—the nation's largest charity wine auction.

Spoleto

One of the world's best interdisciplinary arts festivals—neither drunken bacchanal nor hoity-toity gathering—has as its backdrop one of the nation's most beautiful cities.

Monaco Grand Prix

Monte Carlo's streets are so tightly packed that spectators—many of them part of Europe's beautiful-people crowd—can almost touch the racing cars.

	Travel Date	Event Date	Event / Official Name (if different)	City, State, Country / Host City (if different)	Event/City Rating / Origin — Attendance	Pg ✓
Week 23 2000	Jun. 8	Jun. 8-11	Chicago Blues Festival	Chicago, Illinois, USA	★★★★★★★★	NA
2001	May 31	May 31-Jun. 3			1984 — 650,000	
2000	Jun. 9	Jun. 8-12	Féria de Nîmes	Nîmes, France	★★★★★	147
2001	Jun. 1	May 30-Jun. 3	(Féria de Pentecôte)		1952 — 500,000	
Week 24 2000	Jun. 10	Jun. 12-29	Feast of St. Anthony	Lisbon, Portugal	★★★★★	151
2001	Jun. 12	Jun. 12-29	(Festas de Lisboa)		1232 — 300,000	
2000	Jun. 14	Jun. 12-17	Country Music Fan Fair	Nashville, Tennessee, USA	★★★★★★	NA
2001	Jun. 13	Jun. 11-16	(International Country Music Fan Fair)		1972 — 24,000	
Week 25 2000	Jun. 21	Jun. 20-23	Royal Ascot	London, England	★★★★★★★★★	155
2001	Jun. 20	Jun. 19-22	(The Royal Meeting at Ascot Racecourse)	(Ascot)	1711 — 230,000	
Week 26 2000	Jun. 29	Jun. 29-Jul. 9	Summerfest	Milwaukee, Wisconsin, USA	★★★★	NA
2001	Jun. 28	Jun. 28-Jul. 7			1968 — 940,000	
2000	Jun. 29	Jun. 29-Jul. 2	Roskilde Rock Festival	Copenhagen, Denmark	★★★★★★	161
2001	Jun. 28	Jun. 28-Jul. 1	(Roskilde Festival)	(Roskilde)	1971 — 90,000	
Week 27 2000	Jul. 2	Jun. 28-Jul. 4	Boston Harborfest	Boston, Massachusetts, USA	★★★★★★★★	NA
2001	Jul. 2	Jun. 27-Jul. 6			1982 — 2,500,000	
2000	Jul. 3	Jun. 23-Jul. 4	Fourth of July	Philadelphia, Pennsylvania, USA	★★★★★★★★	NA
2001	Jul. 2	Jun. 29-Jul. 4	(Sunoco Welcome America)		1993 — 1,000,000	
2000	Jul. 4	Jun. 28-Jul. 9	Montréal Jazz Festival	Montréal, Québec, Canada	★★★★★★★	NA
2001	Jul. 3	Jun. 27-Jul. 8	(Festival International de Jazz de Montréal)		1979 — 1,500,000	
2000	Jul. 6	Jul. 6-14	Running of the Bulls	Pamplona, Spain	★★★★★★★	165
2001	Jul. 6	Jul. 6-14	(Fiesta de San Fermín)		c. 1600 — 100,000	
Week 28 2000	Jul. 13	Jul. 13-14	Bastille Day	Paris, France	★★★★★★★★★	170
2001	Jul. 12	Jul. 13-14			1789 — —	
2000	Jul. 14	Jul. 14-23	Aquatennial	Minneapolis, Minnesota, USA	★★★★	NA
2001	Jul. 13	Jul. 13-22	(Minneapolis Aquatennial Festival)		1940 — 800,000	
2000	Jul. 14	Jul. 7-16	Calgary Stampede	Calgary, Alberta, Canada	★★★★★★★	NA
2001	Jul. 13	Jul. 6-15			1912 — 1,100,000	
Week 29 2000	Jul. 14	Jul. 9-16	Nice Jazz Festival	Nice, France	★★★★★★★	175
2001	Jul. 13	Jul. 8-15			1948 — 49,000	
Week 30 2000	Jul. 20	Jul. 7-22	Montreux Jazz Festival	Montreux, Switzerland	★★★★★★	179
2001	Jul. 19	Jul. 6-21			1967 — 220,000	
2000	Jul. 27	Jul. 21-30	Cheyenne Frontier Days	Cheyenne, Wyoming, USA	★★★★	NA
2001	Jul. 26	Jul. 20-29			1897 — 400,000	
Week 31 2000	Aug. 2	Jul. 29-Aug. 5	Cowes Week	Isle of Wight, England	★★★★★	185
2001	Aug. 8	Aug. 4-11			1812 — 30,000	
2000	Aug. 3	Jul. 21-Aug. 7	Caribana	Toronto, Ontario, Canada	★★★★★★	NA
2001	Aug. 2	Jul. 20-Aug. 6			1967 — 1,500,000	
2000	Aug. 3	Jul. 26-Aug. 5	Stockholm Water Festival	Stockholm, Sweden	★★★★★★★★	189
2001	Aug. 16	Aug. 12-18			1991 — 1,100,000	
2000	Aug. 5	Jun. 28-Aug. 7	Crop Over Festival	Bridgetown, Barbados	★★★★★	193
2001	Aug. 4	Jun. 27-Aug. 6			1974 — 100,000	

Events are listed according to the week in which the 2000 travel date takes place. Subsequent to January 1, weeks begin on Monday.

NA = Itinerary in companion edition *The Fun Also Rises Travel Guide North America*
Readers' ✓: Been there, Done that, or Plan to

The Fun Also Rises

June

Chicago Blues Festival	Featuring 60 mind-blowing acts on four stages set against the shores of Lake Michigan, the world's largest blues festival amplifies Chicago's musical heritage.
Féria de Nîmes	A completely packed town throws a street party that puts a French twist on everything Spanish, from bullfighting to paella.
Feast of St. Anthony	In every nook and cranny of Lisbon's Old Town, someone is barbecuing sardines, while crowds of people (packed like sardines) dance shoulder-to-shoulder at outdoor concerts.
Country Music Fan Fair	This five-day orgy of fan appreciation pulls in more than 20,000 die-hards for 35 hours of performances and face time with their beloved stars.
Royal Ascot	The premier event of London's social season isn't just about horse racing—it's about royalty, outrageous fashions, and a demonstration that the upper crust can get down.
Summerfest	With 11 stages, about a million spectators, and more than 2,500 local, regional, and international acts. The Big Gig is arguably the world's largest music festival.
Roskilde Rock Festival	Europe's largest annual rock festival is distinguished by precision organization, hearty audiences who brave consistently poor weather, and, of course, lots of music.

July

Boston Harborfest	Bostonians commemorate their city's first party (something about tea being thrown in a harbor) with a celebration that blends history with spectacle.
Fourth of July	The first and last words on Independence Day celebrations have always belonged to the City of Brotherly Love—food fests, parades, concerts, and fireworks keep 2 million patriots coming back each year.
Montréal Jazz Festival	Often called the best jazz festival in the world—2,000 musicians from 25 countries get crowds moving at 400 shows—this event rates as one of Canada's best annual shindigs.
Running of the Bulls	This is it—the world's greatest party! You don't have to run with the bulls to feel the spirit of the crowds who all come together for the same purpose: fiesta, fiesta, fiesta!
Bastille Day	French Independence Day is celebrated with a dramatic parade down the Champs-Élysées and two nights of solid revelry in the most romantic city in the world.
Aquatennial	It's time to come out from the cold—800,000 warm-weather lovers celebrate The 10 Best Days of Summer with food, music, and games.
Calgary Stampede	Calgary, the home of wild chuck-wagon races, becomes one of the world's biggest and best country-style party towns, with a world-class rodeo as its centerpiece.
Nice Jazz Festival	The world's top jazz acts probably come for the same reason the crowds do—nothing beats the French Riviera in summer.
Montreux Jazz Festival	Still the world's premier jazz event, the festival transforms the already beautiful town into one of the most hip spots in the universe.
Cheyenne Frontier Days	Real cowboys and cowgirls still exist and nearly every last one of 'em rides into town for this century-old rodeo, Wild West show, and summertime hoedown.
Cowes Week	The world's largest international yacht regatta transforms the small town of Cowes into a wild gathering of sailors and a frenzied meet market.
Caribana	One of North America's largest and most exuberant street parties—a million revelers celebrate Toronto's Caribbean and Latin populations with dance, music, and food.
Stockholm Water Festival	The beautiful setting and constant surprises by street performers contribute to one of the world's best street fairs and music festivals, which takes place in Europe's most underrated city.
Crop Over Festival	The highlight of the Barbados year, this *Carnaval*-style event is an all-island jubilee that celebrates the end of the sugar-cane harvest with great music and molten energy.

		Travel Date	Event Date	Event / Official Name (if different)	City, State, Country / Host City (if different)	Event/City Rating Origin / Attendance		Pg ✓
Week 32	2000	Aug. 10	—	Fun Destination: Ibiza/Majorca	Ibiza/Majorca, Spain	—	—	197
	2001	Aug. 9	—			—	—	
Week 33	2000	Aug. 15	Aug. 13-17	Palio	Siena/Florence, Italy	★★★★★		203
	2001	Aug. 15	Aug. 13-17	(Palio di Siena)		c. 1600	50,000	
	2000	Aug. 17	Aug. 6-28	Edinburgh Fringe Festival	Edinburgh, Scotland	★★★★★★★★★		207
	2001	Aug. 16	Aug. 5-28	(Edinburgh Festival Fringe)		1947	800,000	
Week 34	2000	Aug. 18	Aug. 20	Concours d'Elegance	Carmel/Monterey, California, USA	★★★★★		NA
	2000	Aug. 17	Aug. 19	(Pebble Beach Concours d'Elegance)	(Pebble Beach)	1950	12,000	
Week 35	2000	Aug. 26	Aug. 27-28	Notting Hill Carnival	London, England	★★★★★★★★		213
	2001	Aug. 25	Aug. 26-27			1965	1,500,000	
	2000	Aug. 30	Aug. 30	La Tomatina	Barcelona, Spain	★★★★★★★★★		217
	2001	Aug. 29	Aug. 29		(Buñol)	1957	25,000	
Week 36	2000	Sep. 1	Sep. 2-3	Big Muddy	St. Louis, Missouri, USA	★★★		NA
	2001	Aug. 31	Sep. 1-2	(Big Muddy Blues & Roots Music Festival)		1992	50,000	
	2000	Sep. 1	Aug. 28-Sep. 4	Burning Man	Reno, Nevada, USA	★★★★★★★		NA
	2001	Aug. 31	Aug. 27-Sep. 3		(Black Rock City)	1986	10,000	
	2000	Sep. 1	Sep. 3	Riverfest	Cincinnati, Ohio, USA	★★★		NA
	2001	Aug. 31	Sep. 2			1977	500,000	
	2000	Sep. 1	Sep. 1-4	Bumbershoot	Seattle, Washington, USA	★★★★★		NA
	2001	Aug. 31	Aug. 31-Sep. 3	(Bumbershoot, The Seattle Arts Festival)		1971	250,000	
	2000	Sep. 7	Sep. 8-10	Street Scene	San Diego, California, USA	★★★★★★		NA
	2001	Sep. 6	Sep. 7-9			1984	85,000	
	2000	Sep. 8	Sep. 7-10	Fiesta de Santa Fe	Santa Fe, New Mexico, USA	★★★★		NA
	2001	Sep. 6	Sep. 6-9			1712	75,000	
Week 37	2000	Sep. 15	Sep. 15-24	Aloha Festival	Honolulu, Hawaii, USA	★★★★★		NA
	2001	Sep. 14	Sep. 14-23			1947	300,000	
	2000	Sep. 15	Sep. 16-Oct. 3	Oktoberfest	Munich, Germany	★★★★★★★★★		221
	2001	Sep. 21	Sep. 22-Oct. 7			1810	6,000,000	
Week 38	2000	Sep. 22	Sep. 21-24	Galway Oyster Festival	Galway, Ireland	★★★★★★		225
	2001	Sep. 28	Sep. 27-30	(Galway International Oyster Festival)		1955	10,000	
Week 39	2000	Sep. 29	Sep. 23-Oct. 8	Stuttgart's Volksfest	Stuttgart, Germany	★★★★★★		229
	2001	Sep. 28	Sep. 29-Oct. 14	(Cannstatter Volksfest)	(Bad Cannstatt)	1818	5,000,000	

Events are listed according to the week in which the 2000 travel date takes place. Subsequent to January 1, weeks begin on Monday.

NA = Itinerary in companion edition *The Fun Also Rises Travel Guide North America*
Readers' ✓: Been there, Done that, or Plan to

August

Fun Destination: Ibiza/Majorca	The Spanish islands are the pick for the world's top beach destinations—fashionable crowds tan on beaches by day and hit the world's best discos by night.
Palio	The tension leading up to and during the world's most incredible horse race—the animals and jockeys speed around the small town square—is released in a centuries-old tradition.
Edinburgh Fringe Festival	You'd have to see it to believe it, but you can't see it all. The world's largest arts festival has hundreds of daily performances of theater, music, opera, dance, and comedy from around the world.
Concours d'Elegance	Champagne flows at the "Super Bowl of auto shows," as prestigious Pebble Beach Golf Course turns into a spectacle of vintage autos and period costumes.
Notting Hill Carnival	Europe's biggest street party, this *Carnaval*-style parade showcases an ethnic side of London that, as a bookend to Royal Ascot, rounds out the picture of one of the world's most happening cities.
La Tomatina	The world's largest food fight lasts just 60 minutes, but where else can you join 10,000 people throwing tomatoes at each other on a hot summer day?

September

Big Muddy	St. Louis knows the blues—this mix of music and food, set on the banks of the Mississippi River, provides the best reason to explore this often-overlooked city.
Burning Man	The world's latest attempt at utopia is a mix of offbeat art and cultural experimentation—free spirits create a perfect (and wild) temporary city in the Nevada desert.
Riverfest	America's biggest farewell-to-summer event includes games, music, food, sun, and one of the world's most outrageous fireworks displays.
Bumbershoot	One of the largest music-and-arts festivals in the United States attracts top international talent to this beautiful city known for its cutting-edge music (and coffee and computers).
Street Scene	Tans, tacos, tequila, and tank tops—at this giant street party, you won't find a shortage of any of the local specialties.
Fiesta de Santa Fe	The festival begins when a 40-foot-tall puppet is burned to banish gloom from the lives of 75,000 assembled partyers—the food, music, and dancing that follow guarantee success.
Aloha Festival	Honolulu is where Hawaiians party and the city rolls out all its (greatest) clichés—hula girls, mai tais, perfect beaches, tropical breezes—for this celebration of island culture.
Oktoberfest	The massive scale of the world's largest beer blowout is stunning—and so is the city—but it's the camaraderie in the huge beer tents that makes this one special.
Galway Oyster Festival	Oysters are simply the excuse for drinking lots of Guinness, which is simply the excuse for starting a party (not ending it) by dancing on the tables.
Stuttgart's Volksfest	Not as famous but almost as large as Munich's Oktoberfest, this beer bash pours the best of German cheer and proves that being number two can still be one heck of a good time.

		Travel Date	Event Date	Event	City, State, Country	Event/City Rating		Pg
				Official Name (if different)	**Host City (if different)**	**Origin**	**Attendance**	✓
Week 40	2000	Oct. 5	Oct. 5-7	Great American Beer Festival	Denver, Colorado, USA	★★★★★		NA
	2001	Oct. 4	Oct. 4-6			1982	35,000	
Week 41	2000	Oct. 6	Oct. 7-9	Taste of DC	Washington, DC, USA	★★★★★		NA
	2001	Oct. 5	Oct. 6-8			1990	1,200,000	
Week 42	2000	Oct. 12	Oct. 7-15	Balloon Fiesta	Albuquerque, New Mexico, USA	★★★★★★		NA
	2001	Oct. 11	Oct. 6-14	(Kodak Albuquerque International Balloon Fiesta)		1972	1,500,000	
	2000	Oct. 19	—	Fun Destination: Athens	Athens, Greece	—	—	233
	2001	Oct. 18	—			—	—	
Week 43	2000	Oct. 26	Oct. 20-29	Fantasy Fest	Key West, Florida, USA	★★★★★★★		NA
	2001	Oct. 25	Oct. 19-28			1979	100,000	
	2000	Oct. 26	Oct. 28	Guavaween	Tampa, Florida, USA	★★★★★		NA
	2001	Oct. 25	Oct. 27			1984	100,000	
	2000	Oct. 27	Oct. 28-31	Hookers' Ball/Halloween	San Francisco, California, USA	★★★★★★★★		NA
	2001	Oct. 26	Oct. 27-31			1978	50,000	
Week 44	2000	Nov. 2	—	Disney World	Lake Buena Vista	—	—	NA
	2001	Nov. 9	—	(Walt Disney World)		—	—	
Week 45	2000	Nov. 9	Nov. 9-11	Pushkar Camel Fair	Jaipur, India	★★★★		237
	2001	Nov. 28	Nov. 27-30	(Pushkar Mela)	(Pushkar)	1976	200,000	
Week 46	2000	Nov. 17	Nov. 18-19	Macau Grand Prix	Macau, China	★★★★		241
	2001	Nov. 16	Nov. 17-18			1954	20,000	
Week 47	2000	Nov. 23	—	Fun Destination: Acapulco	Acapulco, Mexico	—	—	245
	2001	Nov. 22	—			—	—	
Week 48	2000	Nov. 30	Dec. 2-3	Dickens on the Strand	Houston/Galveston, Texas, USA	★★★★★		NA
	2001	Nov. 29	Dec. 1-2			1974	50,000	
Week 49	2000	Dec. 8	Dec. 1-10	Las Vegas Rodeo	Las Vegas, Nevada, USA	★★★★★★★★		NA
	2001	Dec. 14	Dec. 7-16	(National Finals Rodeo)		1985	140,000	
Week 50	2000	Dec. 17	—	Carnival Destiny	Miami Beach, Florida, USA	—	—	NA
	2001	Apr. 1	—	(The Most Fun Cruise)		—	—	
Week 51				Carnival Destiny (cont.)				
Week 52	2000	Dec. 29	Dec. 31	New Year's Eve New York	New York, New York, USA	★★★★★★★		NA
	2001	Dec. 29	Dec. 31			1904	500,000	
	2000	Dec. 29	Dec. 29-Jan. 2	Hogmanay	Edinburgh, Scotland	★★★★★★★★		248
	2001	Dec. 29	Dec. 29-Jan. 1	(Edinburgh's Hogmanay)		1993	400,000	

Events are listed according to the week in which the 2000 travel date takes place. Subsequent to January 1, weeks begin on Monday.

NA = Itinerary in companion edition *The Fun Also Rises Travel Guide North America*
Readers' ✓: Been there, Done that, or Plan to

The Fun Also Rises

October

Great American Beer Festival | The opportunity to taste 1,700 different brews gives the term *mile-high city* new meaning and makes this event the must-do pilgrimage for malt worship and good times.

Taste of DC | One of the world's most important cities shows off with one of the nation's best *Taste* events—more than a million people fill Pennsylvania Avenue for food and music.

Balloon Fiesta | With nearly 1,000 multicolored balloons ascending into the clear Southwestern sky, the world's largest ballooning event transforms Albuquerque into one big fiesta.

Fun Destination: Athens | Mykonos is great, but Greeks know that the action is in Athens, where the clubs are among the best in the world and dance floors give way to table tops.

Fantasy Fest | Relaxing Key West transforms itself for one of the world's most extravagant and wild costume balls, complete with legendary Florida weather and sunsets.

Guavaween | Guavaween is a combination of Halloween and a tribute to Tampa's nickname, The Big Guava— a wild street celebration fills the historic district of Ybor City.

Hookers' Ball/Halloween | San Francisco confirms its liberal reputation when tens of thousands make Halloween night the highlight of their year—the Hookers' Ball and Castro street party blow away any haunted house.

November

Disney World | The world's best theme park and ... party place for adults? Fuzzy cartoon characters may never completely lose their appeal, but often overlooked is this park's grown-up good time.

Pushkar Camel Fair | One of the most enthralling and exotic spectacles anywhere—the sight of thousands-strong caravans arriving from across the desert to the world's largest camel fair defies description.

Macau Grand Prix | Macau is a let-your-hair-down town for the Chinese—probably even after the Portuguese give it back to China in December 1999—and this formula-racing event is the largest of its kind.

Fun Destination: Acapulco | Cancún and Cabo are charging hard, but this is still Mexico's number-one party destination for adults. Great beaches, strolling mariachis, and wild, warm nights.

Dickens on the Strand | Revelers don period clothes and hoist cups of cheer to the literature and culture of 19th-century Britain in one of the nation's top yuletide parties.

December

Las Vegas Rodeo | The Western side of Las Vegas takes over the town during the world championship National Finals Rodeo, where the hootin' and hollerin' is as big as the $4-million purse.

Carnival Destiny | There are sailboats, motorboats, lifeboats, and love boats—but when 2,600 fun-seekers have a week-long party in Caribbean waters, this one becomes the Fun Boat.

New Year's Eve New York | New York has just about the best of everything—restaurants, nightlife, things to do—but the city never gets closer to being the center of the universe than on New Year's Eve.

Hogmanay | Despite the cold, this is New Year's Eve the way you'd like it to be. Europe's largest organized year-end celebration closes off its streets for musical entertainment and partying.

The FunGuide 100

GEOGRAPHICAL INDEX AND WORLD MAPS

Map Locator	Country	City / Host City	Event / Official Name (if different)	Travel Date	Event Date	Event/City Ranking Origin	Attendance	✓
					2000			
					2001			
	North America—United States							
1	Arizona	Phoenix (Scottsdale)	Phoenix Open	Jan. 26 / Jan. 24	Jan. 24-30 / Jan. 22-28	★★★★★★ / 1932	470,000	
2	California	Carmel/Monterey (Pebble Beach)	Concours d'Elegance (Pebble Beach Concours d'Elegance)	Aug. 18 / Aug. 17	Aug. 20 / Aug. 19	★★★★★ / 1950	12,000	
3	California	Lake Tahoe	Skiing Tahoe (The Most Fun Place To Ski: North America)	Mar. 30 / Dec. 7	— / —	— / —	—	
4	California	Los Angeles	Academy Awards Weekend	Mar. 24 / Mar. 23	Mar. 26 / Mar. 25	★★★★★★★ / 1929	—	
5	California	Napa Valley (St. Helena)	Napa Valley Wine Auction	Jun. 1 / Jun. 7	Jun. 1-3 / Jun. 7-9	★★★★★★ / 1981	2,000	
6	California	San Diego	Street Scene	Sep. 7 / Sep. 6	Sep. 8-10 / Sep. 7-9	★★★★★★ / 1984	85,000	
7	California	San Francisco	Hookers' Ball/Halloween	Oct. 27 / Oct. 26	Oct. 28-31 / Oct. 27-31	★★★★★★★★ / 1978	50,000	
7	California	San Francisco	Black and White Ball	none / May 31	none / Jun. 2	★★★★★★★ / 1956	12,000	
8	Colorado	Denver	Great American Beer Festival	Oct. 5 / Oct. 4	Oct. 5-7 / Oct. 4-6	★★★★★ / 1982	35,000	
9	District of Columbia	Washington	Taste of DC	Oct. 6 / Oct. 5	Oct. 7-9 / Oct. 6-8	★★★★★ / 1990	1,200,000	
10	Florida	Daytona Beach/ Orlando	Bike Week	Mar. 9 / Mar. 8	Mar. 3-12 / Mar. 2-11	★★★★★★ / 1937	500,000	
11	Florida	Key West	Fantasy Fest	Oct. 26 / Oct. 25	Oct. 20-29 / Oct. 19-28	★★★★★★★ / 1979	100,000	
12	Florida	Miami	Carnival Destiny (The Most Fun Cruise)	Dec. 17 / Apr. 1	— / —	— / —	—	
13	Florida	Miami Beach (Miami)	Calle Ocho (Carnaval Miami)	Mar. 10 / Mar. 9	Mar. 3-12 / Mar. 2-11	★★★★★★★★ / 1978	1,000,000	
14	Florida	Lake Buena Vista	Disney World (Walt Disney World)	Nov. 2 / Nov. 9	— / —	— / —	—	
15	Florida	Tampa	Guavaween	Oct. 26 / Oct. 25	Oct. 28 / Oct. 27	★★★★★★ / 1984	100,000	
16	Georgia	Savannah	St. Patrick's Day Celebration	Mar. 17 / Mar. 16	Mar. 16-19 / Mar. 15-18	★★★★★★ / 1813	300,000	
17	Hawaii	Honolulu	Aloha Festival	Sep. 15 / Sep. 14	Sep. 15-24 / Sep. 14-23	★★★★★ / 1947	300,000	
18	Illinois	Chicago	Chicago Blues Festival	Jun. 8 / May 31	Jun. 8-11 / May 31-Jun. 3	★★★★★★★ / 1984	650,000	
19	Indiana	Indianapolis	Indy 500 (The 500 Festival)	May 25 / May 24	May 6-28 / May 5-27	★★★★★ / 1911	400,000	
20	Kentucky	Louisville	Kentucky Derby (Kentucky Derby Festival)	May 4 / May 3	Apr. 14-May 7 / Apr. 20-May 6	★★★★★★★ / 1875	140,000	

Index continued on page 28

Readers' ✓: Been there, Done that, or Plan to

The Fun Also Rises

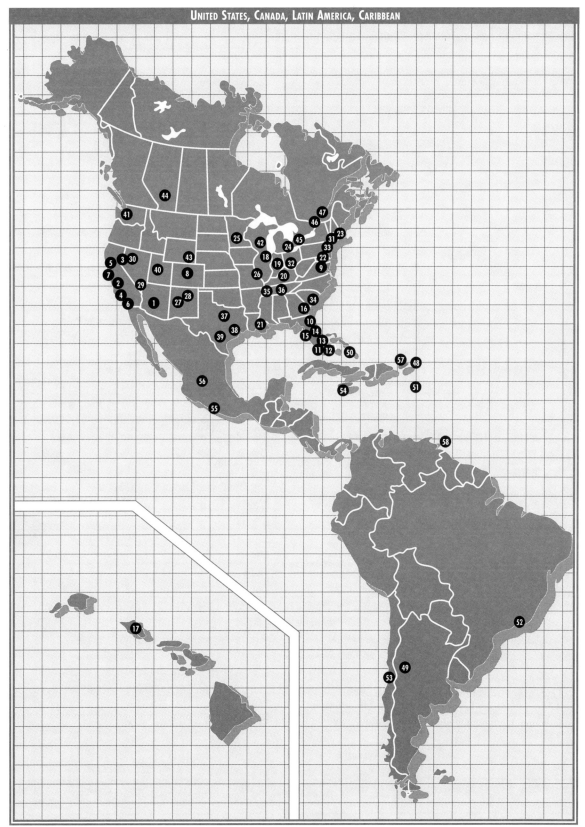

UNITED STATES, CANADA, LATIN AMERICA, CARIBBEAN

Map Locator	Country	City / Host City	Event / Official Name (if different)	Travel Date	Event Date	Event/City Ranking Origin	Attendance	✓
					2000 / 2001			
21	Louisiana	New Orleans	Mardi Gras	Mar. 5 / Feb. 25	Feb. 26-Mar. 7 / Feb. 17-27	★★★★★★★★★ / 1837	3,500,000	
21	Louisiana	New Orleans	New Orleans Jazz & Heritage Festival	May 4 / May 3	Apr. 28-May 7 / Apr. 27-May 6	★★★★★★ / 1970	480,000	
22	Maryland	Baltimore	The Preakness (Preakness Celebration)	May 18 / May 17	May 12-20 / May 11-19	★★★★ / 1873	90,000	
23	Massachusetts	Boston	Boston Harborfest	Jul. 2 / Jul. 2	Jun. 28-Jul. 4 / Jun. 27-Jul. 6	★★★★★★★ / 1982	2,500,000	
24	Michigan	Detroit	Detroit Auto Show (North American International Auto Show, NAIAS)	Jan. 13 / Jan. 11	Jan. 14-23 / Jan. 12-21	★★★★★ / 1907	790,000	
25	Minnesota	Minneapolis	Aquatennial (Minneapolis Aquatennial Festival)	Jul. 14 / Jul. 13	Jul. 14-23 / Jul. 13-22	★★★★ / 1940	800,000	
26	Missouri	St. Louis	Big Muddy (Big Muddy Blues & Roots Music Festival)	Sep. 1 / Aug. 31	Sep. 2-3 / Sep. 1-2	★★★★ / 1992	50,000	
27	New Mexico	Albuquerque	Balloon Fiesta (Kodak Albuquerque International Balloon Fiesta)	Oct. 12 / Oct. 11	Oct. 7-15 / Oct. 6-14	★★★★★★ / 1972	1,500,000	
28	New Mexico	Santa Fe	Fiesta de Santa Fe	Sep. 8 / Sep. 6	Sep. 7-10 / Sep. 6-9	★★★★ / 1712	75,000	
29	Nevada	Las Vegas	Las Vegas Rodeo (National Finals Rodeo)	Dec. 8 / Dec. 14	Dec. 1-10 / Dec. 7-16	★★★★★★★★ / 1985	140,000	
29	Nevada	Las Vegas	Super Bowl Weekend	Jan. 28 / Jan. 26	Jan. 28-30 / Jan. 26-28	★★★★★★★★ / 1967	200,000	
30	Nevada	Reno (Black Rock City)	Burning Man	Sep. 1 / Aug. 31	Aug. 28-Sep. 4 / Aug. 27-Sep. 3	★★★★★★★ / 1986	10,000	
31	New York	New York	New Year's Eve New York	Dec. 29 / Dec. 29	Dec. 31 / Dec. 31	★★★★★★★★ / 1904	500,000	
32	Ohio	Cincinnati	Riverfest	Sep. 1 / Aug. 31	Sep. 3 / Sep. 2	★★★★ / 1977	500,000	
33	Pennsylvania	Philadelphia	Fourth of July (Sunoco Welcome America)	Jul. 3 / Jul. 2	Jun. 23-Jul. 4 / Jun. 29-Jul. 4	★★★★★★★★ / 1993	1,000,000	
34	South Carolina	Charleston	Spoleto (Spoleto Festival USA/Piccolo Spoleto)	Jun. 1 / May 31	May 26-Jun. 11 / May 25-Jun. 10	★★★★★★ / 1977	72,000	
35	Tennessee	Memphis	Memphis in May Barbecue (Memphis in May World Championship Barbecue Cooking Contest)	May 18 / May 17	May 18-20 / May 17-19	★★★★★★ / 1976	80,000	
36	Tennessee	Nashville	Country Music Fan Fair (International Country Music Fan Fair)	Jun. 14 / Jun. 13	Jun. 12-17 / Jun. 11-16	★★★★★ / 1972	24,000	
37	Texas	Austin/Dallas/ Fort Worth	South by Southwest	Mar. 16	Mar. 15-19	★★★★★		
			(South by Southwest Music and Media Conference, SXSW)	Mar. 15	Mar. 14-18	1987	25,000	
38	Texas	Houston/Galveston	Dickens on the Strand	Nov. 30 / Nov. 29	Dec. 2-3 / Dec. 1-2	★★★★★ / 1974	50,000	

Readers' ✓: Been there, Done that, or Plan to

The Fun Also Rises

Map Locator	Country	City / Host City	Event / Official Name (if different)	Travel Date	Event Date	Event/City Ranking / Origin	Attendance	Pg ✓
					2000 / 2001			
39	Texas	San Antonio	Fiesta San Antonio	Apr. 23 / Apr. 22	Apr. 22-30 / Apr. 20-29	★★★★★★★ / 1891	3,500,000	
40	Utah	Park City	Sundance Film Festival	Jan. 20 / Jan. 18	Jan. 20-29 / Jan. 18-28	★★★★★★★ / 1978	18,000	
41	Washington	Seattle	Bumbershoot (Bumbershoot, The Seattle Arts Festival)	Sep. 1 / Aug. 31	Sep. 1-4 / Aug. 31-Sep. 3	★★★★★ / 1971	250,000	
42	Wisconsin	Milwaukee	Summerfest	Jun. 29 / Jun. 28	Jun. 29-Jul. 9 / Jun. 28-Jul. 7	★★★★ / 1968	940,000	
43	Wyoming	Cheyenne	Cheyenne Frontier Days	Jul. 27 / Jul. 26	Jul. 21-30 / Jul. 20-29	★★★★ / 1897	400,000	
	North America—Canada **Province**	**City**						
44	Alberta	Calgary	Calgary Stampede	Jul. 14 / Jul. 13	Jul. 7-16 / Jul. 6-15	★★★★★★ / 1912	1,100,000	
45	Ontario	Toronto	Caribana	Aug. 3 / Aug. 2	Jul. 21-Aug. 7 / Jul. 20-Aug. 6	★★★★★★ / 1967	1,500,000	
46	Québec	Montréal	Montréal Jazz Festival (Festival International de Jazz de Montréal)	Jul. 4 / Jul. 3	Jun. 28-Jul. 9 / Jun. 27-Jul. 8	★★★★★★★ / 1979	1,500,000	
47	Québec	Québec City	Québec Winter Carnaval (Carnaval de Québec)	Feb. 4 / Feb. 2	Jan. 28-Feb. 13 / Jan. 26-Feb. 11	★★★★★★ / 1894	1,000,000	
	Latin America and the Caribbean **Country**	**City**						
48	Antigua	St. John's	Sailing Week (Antigua Sailing Week)	Apr. 30 / Apr. 29	Apr. 30-May 6 / Apr. 29-May 5	★★★★★ / 1967	10,000	127
49	Argentina	Buenos Aires (Mendoza)	Vendimia	Mar. 2 / Mar. 1	Mar. 3-5 / Mar. 2-4	★★★★★★ / 1936	300,000	75
50	Bahamas	Nassau	Junkanoo	Jan. 1 / Jan. 1	Dec. 26-Jan. 1 / Dec. 26-Jan. 1	★★★★★ / c. 1800	10,000	36
51	Barbados	Bridgetown	Crop Over Festival	Aug. 5 / Aug. 4	Jun. 28-Aug. 7 / Jun. 27-Aug. 6	★★★★★ / c. 1790	100,000	193
52	Brazil	Rio de Janeiro	Carnaval Rio	Mar. 5 / Feb. 25	Mar. 4-7 / Feb. 24-27	★★★★★★★★★ / 1930	10,000,000	89
53	Chile	Santiago (Viña del Mar)	Viña del Mar Song Festival (International Song Festival of Viña del Mar)	Feb. 19 / Feb. 10	Feb. 16-21 / Feb. 7-12	★★★★★ / 1959	110,000	59
54	Jamaica	Negril	Hedonism II (The Most Fun Resort)	Feb. 25 / Dec. 21	— / —	— / —	—	63
55	Mexico	Acapulco	Fun Destination: Acapulco	Nov. 23 / Nov. 22	— / —	— / —	—	245
56	Mexico	Aguascalientes	Feria de San Marcos (Feria Nacional de San Marcos)	Apr. 28 / Apr. 27	Apr. 14-May 7 / Apr. 13-May 6	★★★★ / 1848	3,500,000	117
57	Puerto Rico	San Juan	Calle San Sebastián	Jan. 21 / Jan. 20	Jan. 20-23 / Jan. 20-23	★★★★★ / 1970	50,000	47
58	Trinidad & Tobago	Port of Spain	Trinidad Carnival	Mar. 5 / Feb. 25	Mar. 6-7 / Feb. 26-27	★★★★★★★ / c. 1840	100,000	93

Readers' ✓: Been there, Done that, or Plan to

Map Locator	Country	City / Host City	Event / Official Name (if different)	Travel Date	Event Date	Event/City Ranking — Origin	Attendance	✓
					2000 / 2001			
	Europe							
59	Austria	Vienna	Vienna Opera Ball	Feb. 29	Mar. 2	★★★★★★★★★★		67
				Feb. 20	Feb. 22	1877	5,000	
60	Denmark	Copenhagen (Roskilde)	Roskilde Rock Festival (Roskilde Festival)	Jun. 29	Jun. 29-Jul. 2	★★★★★★		161
				Jun. 28	Jun. 28-Jul. 1	1971	90,000	
61	England	Isle of Wight	Cowes Week	Aug. 2	Jul. 29-Aug. 5	★★★★★		185
				Aug. 8	Aug. 4-11	1812	30,000	
62	England	London (Ascot)	Royal Ascot (The Royal Meeting at Ascot Racecourse)	Jun. 21	Jun. 20-23	★★★★★★★★		155
				Jun. 20	Jun. 19-22	1711	230,000	
62	England	London	Notting Hill Carnival	Aug. 26	Aug. 27-28	★★★★★★★		213
				Aug. 25	Aug. 26-27	1965	1,500,000	
63	France	Cannes	Cannes Film Festival (Festival International du Film)	May 18	May 10-21	★★★★★★★★★		136
				May 10	May 9-20	1939	31,000	
64	France	Nice	Nice Jazz Festival	Jul. 14	Jul. 9-16	★★★★★★		175
				Jul. 13	Jul. 8-15	1948	49,000	
65	France	Nîmes	Féria de Nîmes (Féria de Pentecôte)	Jun. 9	Jun. 8-12	★★★★★		147
				Jun. 1	May 30-Jun. 3	1952	500,000	
66	France	Paris	Bastille Day	Jul. 13	Jul. 13-14	★★★★★★★		170
				Jul. 12	Jul. 13-14	1789	—	
67	Germany	Köln	Karneval	Mar. 4	Mar. 2-7	★★★★★★★		83
				Feb. 24	Feb. 22-27	1823	1,000,000	
68	Germany	Munich	Oktoberfest	Sep. 15	Sep. 16-Oct. 3	★★★★★★★★★		221
				Sep. 21	Sep. 22-Oct. 7	1810	6,000,000	
69	Germany	Stuttgart (Bad Cannstatt)	Stuttgart's Volksfest (Cannstatter Volksfest)	Sep. 29	Sep. 23-Oct. 8	★★★★★★		229
				Sep. 28	Sep. 29-Oct. 14	1818	5,000,000	
70	Greece	Athens	Fun Destination: Athens	Oct. 19	—	—	—	233
				Oct. 18	—	—	—	
71	Ireland	Dublin	St. Patrick's Festival	Mar. 17	Mar. 16-19	★★★★★★		105
				Mar. 16	Mar. 15-18	1996	850,000	
72	Ireland	Galway	Galway Oyster Festival (Galway International Oyster Festival)	Sep. 22	Sep. 21-24	★★★★★		225
				Sep. 28	Sep. 27-30	1955	10,000	
73	Italy	Siena/Florence	Palio (Palio di Siena)	Aug. 15	Aug. 13-17	★★★★★★		203
				Aug. 15	Aug. 13-17	c. 1600	50,000	
74	Italy	Venice	Venice Carnival (Carnevale di Venezia)	Mar. 3	Feb. 25-Mar. 7	★★★★★★★★		79
				Feb. 23	Feb. 17-27	1979	500,000	
75	Monaco	Monte Carlo	Monaco Grand Prix (Grand Prix Automobile de Monaco)	Jun. 2	Jun. 1-4	★★★★★★★★		143
				May 25	May 24-27	1942	75,000	
76	Netherlands	Amsterdam	Queen's Day (Koninginnedag)	Apr. 28	Apr. 30	★★★★★★★		121
				Apr. 28	Apr. 30	1948	720,000	
77	Portugal	Lisbon	Feast of St. Anthony (Festas de Lisboa)	Jun. 10	Jun. 12-29	★★★★★		151
				Jun. 12	Jun. 12-29	1232	300,000	
78	Scotland	Edinburgh	Edinburgh Fringe Festival (Edinburgh Festival Fringe)	Aug. 17	Aug. 6-28	★★★★★★★★		207
				Aug. 16	Aug. 5-28	1947	410,000	
78	Scotland	Edinburgh	Hogmanay (Edinburgh's Hogmanay)	Dec. 29	Dec. 29-Jan. 2	★★★★★★★★		248
				Dec. 29	Dec. 29-Jan. 1	1993	400,000	

Readers' ✓: Been there, Done that, or Plan to

The Fun Also Rises

Map Locator	Country	City / Host City	Event / Official Name (if different)	Travel Date	Event Date	Event/City Ranking / Origin Attendance	✓
					2000 / 2001		
79	Spain	Barcelona (Buñol)	La Tomatina	Aug. 30 / Aug. 29	Aug. 30 / Aug. 29	★★★★★★★★★ / 1957 25,000	217
80	Spain	Ibiza/Majorca	Fun Destination: Ibiza/Majorca	Aug. 10 / Aug. 9	— / —	— / — —	197
81	Spain	Madrid	Fiestas de San Isidro	May 13 / May 15	May 11-15 / May 11-15	★★★★★★ / 1622 25,000	131
82	Spain	Pamplona	Running of the Bulls (Fiesta de San Fermín)	Jul. 6 / Jul. 6	Jul. 6-14 / Jul. 6-14	★★★★★★★ / c. 1600 100,000	165
83	Spain	Valencia	Las Fallas	Mar. 17 / Mar. 17	Mar. 12-19 / Mar. 12-19	★★★★★★★ / 1497 500,000	101
84	Sweden	Stockholm	Stockholm Water Festival	Aug. 3 / Aug. 16	Jul. 26-Aug. 5 / Aug. 12-18	★★★★★★★★★★ / 1991 1,100,000	189
85	Switzerland	Montreux	Montreux Jazz Festival	Jul. 20 / Jul. 19	Jul. 7-22 / Jul. 6-21	★★★★★★ / 1967 220,000	179
86	Switzerland	Zermatt	Skiing Zermatt (The Most Fun Place To Ski: Europe)	Feb. 11 / Feb. 15	— / —	— / — —	55

Readers' ✓: Been there, Done that, or Plan to

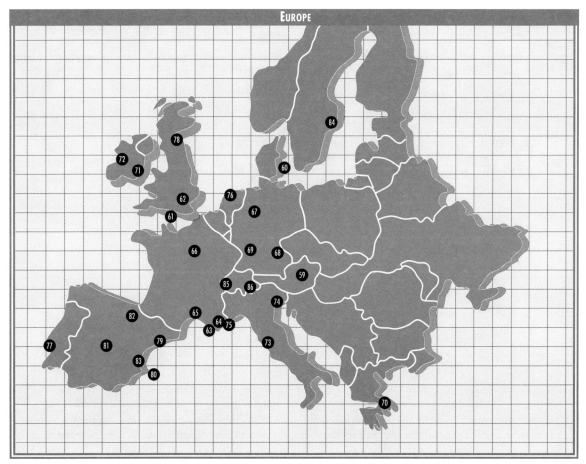

EUROPE

GEOGRAPHICAL INDEX

Map Locator	Country	City / Host City	Event / Official Name (if different)	Travel Date	Event Date	Event/City Ranking Origin	Attendance	✓
			Asia, Africa, South Pacific	▥ 2000 ▢ 2001				
87	Australia	Melbourne	Moomba (The Melbourne Moomba Festival)	Mar. 10 Mar. 9	Mar. 11-13 Mar. 10-12	★★★★★ 1955	1,500,000	97
88	Australia	Sydney	Sydney Gay and Lesbian Mardi Gras	Mar. 2 Mar. 1	Feb. 11-Mar. 4 Feb. 10-Mar. 3	★★★★★★★ 1978	500,000	71
89	China	Hong Kong	Hong Kong Chinese New Year	Feb. 4 Jan. 23	Feb. 5-7 Jan. 24-26	★★★★★ 1996	25,000	51
90	China	Macau	Macau Grand Prix	Nov. 17 Nov. 16	Nov. 18-19 Nov. 17-18	★★★★ 1954	20,000	241
91	India	Jaipur (Pushkar)	Pushkar Camel Fair (Pushkar Mela)	Nov. 9 Nov. 28	Nov. 9-11 Nov. 27-30	★★★★ 1976	200,000	237
92	Japan	Tokyo (Kawasaki)	Fertility Festival (Kanamara Matsuri)	Apr. 7 Apr. 13	Apr. 8-9 Apr. 14-15	★★★★★★ c. 1750	20,000	109
93	Philippines	Manila (Kalibo)	Ati-Atihan	Jan. 14 Jan. 19	Jan. 10-16 Jan. 15-21	★★★★★ 1212	200,000	43
94	South Africa	Cape Town	Cape Minstrel Festival	Jan. 1 Jan. 1	Jan. 1-30 Jan. 1-30	★★★★★ 1898	50,000	39
95	Thailand	Bangkok (Chiang Mai)	Songkran Water Festival (Songkran)	Apr. 13 Apr. 13	Apr. 13-15 Apr. 13-15	★★★★★ c. 1300	200,000	113

Readers' ✓: Been there, Done that, or Plan to

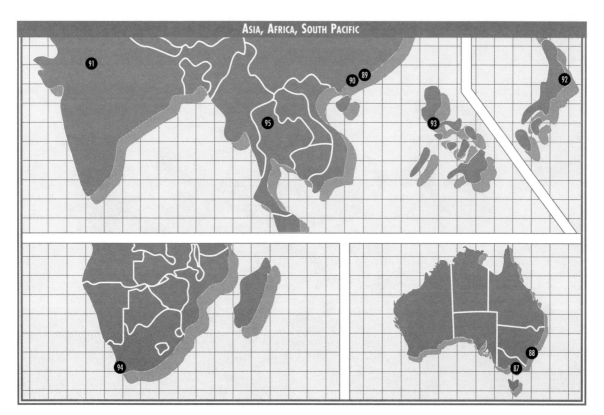

The Fun Also Rises

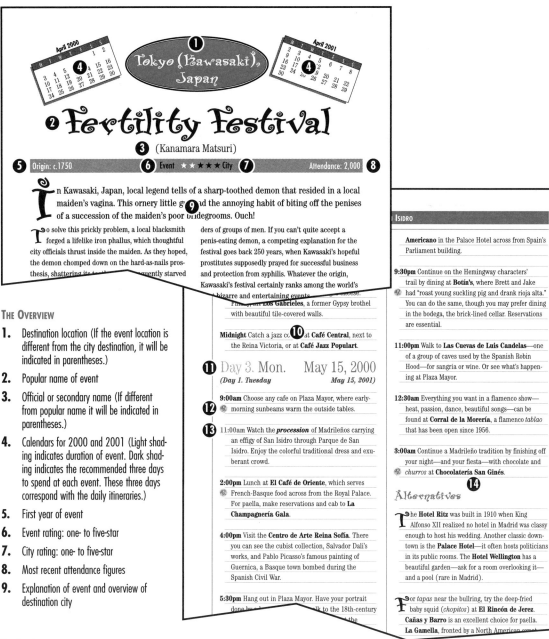

① Tokyo (Kawasaki), Japan

April 2000

April 2001

② Fertility Festival

③ (Kanamara Matsuri)

⑤ Origin: c.1750 **⑥** Event ★★★★ City **⑦** Attendance: 2,000 **⑧**

In Kawasaki, Japan, local legend tells of a sharp-toothed demon that resided in a local maiden's vagina. This ornery little g **⑨** d the annoying habit of biting off the penises of a succession of the maiden's poor bridegrooms. Ouch!

To solve this prickly problem, a local blacksmith forged a lifelike iron phallus, which thoughtful city officials thrust inside the maiden. As they hoped, the demon chomped down on the hard-as-nails prosthesis, shattering its t_____ quently starved

ders of groups of men. If you can't quite accept a penis-eating demon, a competing explanation for the festival goes back 250 years, when Kawasaki's hopeful prostitutes supposedly prayed for successful business and protection from syphilis. Whatever the origin, Kawasaki's festival certainly ranks among the world's bizarre and entertaining events

..., **Los Gabrieles**, a former Gypsy brothel with beautiful tile-covered walls.

Midnight Catch a jazz co **⑩** at **Café Central**, next to the Reina Victoria, or at **Café Jazz Populart**.

⑪ Day 3. Mon. May 15, 2000
(Day 1. Tuesday May 15, 2001)

⑫ **9:00am** Choose any cafe on Plaza Mayor, where early-morning sunbeams warm the outside tables.

⑬ **11:00am** Watch the *procession* of Madrileños carrying an effigy of San Isidro through Parque de San Isidro. Enjoy the colorful traditional dress and exuberant crowd.

2:00pm Lunch at **El Café de Oriente**, which serves French-Basque food across from the Royal Palace. For paella, make reservations and cab to **La Champagnería Gala**.

4:00pm Visit the **Centro de Arte Reina Sofía**. There you can see the cubist collection, Salvador Dalí's works, and Pablo Picasso's famous painting of Guernica, a Basque town bombed during the Spanish Civil War.

5:30pm Hang out in Plaza Mayor. Have your portrait done by ____ k to the 18th-century ____ the

..I ISIDRO

Americano in the Palace Hotel across from Spain's Parliament building.

9:30pm Continue on the Hemingway characters' trail by dining at **Botín's**, where Brett and Jake had "roast young suckling pig and drank rioja alta." You can do the same, though you may prefer dining in the bodega, the brick-lined cellar. Reservations are essential.

11:00pm Walk to **Las Cuevas de Luis Candelas**—one of a group of caves used by the Spanish Robin Hood—for sangria or wine. Or see what's happening at Plaza Mayor.

12:30am Everything you want in a flamenco show—heat, passion, dance, beautiful songs—can be found at **Corral de la Morería**, a flamenco *tablao* that has been open since 1956.

3:00am Continue a Madrileño tradition by finishing off your night—and your fiesta—with chocolate and churros at **Chocolatería San Ginés**. **⑭**

Alternatives

The **Hotel Ritz** was built in 1910 when King Alfonso XII realized no hotel in Madrid was classy enough to host his wedding. Another classic downtown is the **Palace Hotel**—it often hosts politicians in its public rooms. The **Hotel Wellington** has a beautiful garden—ask for a room overlooking it—and a pool (rare in Madrid).

For *tapas* near the bullring, try the deep-fried baby squid (*chopitos*) at **El Rincón de Jerez**. **Cañas y Barro** is an excellent choice for paella. **La Gamella**, fronted by a North American expat

---

THE OVERVIEW

1. Destination location (If the event location is different from the city destination, it will be indicated in parentheses.)

2. Popular name of event

3. Official or secondary name (If different from popular name it will be indicated in parentheses.)

4. Calendars for 2000 and 2001 (Light shading indicates duration of event. Dark shading indicates the recommended three days to spend at each event. These three days correspond with the daily itineraries.)

5. First year of event

6. Event rating: one- to five-star

7. City rating: one- to five-star

8. Most recent attendance figures

9. Explanation of event and overview of destination city

THE ITINERARY

Note: Three-day itineraries generally begin after breakfast on Day 1, but frequently the schedule requires you to be checked in to your hotel the night before.

10. Bold-faced recommendations for where to stay, where to eat, or what to do (More detailed information, such as phone numbers, addresses, and price guides, can be found in the Hot Sheet at the end of each chapter.)

11. Recommended dates of travel for 2000 and 2001 (In some cases, the best three days to attend an event are not the same each year. For example, in Madrid, Day 3 falls on Monday in 2000 and on Thursday in 2001.)

12. ⓡ indicating time to break for a meal (restaurant or eating option)

13. Colored time entries and bold-faced, italicized entries, indicating an activity associated with the event

14. Other significant events or subevents in the area occurring outside the recommended travel dates, and alternative hotels, restaurants, and activities

THE HOT SHEET

15. Telephone country code (left of the /); primary city code (right)

16. The currency conversion rate (one U.S. dollar equivalent, as of September 1, 1999, and the local currency)

17. Numbers indicating the day on which a corresponding description can be found in the itinerary ("A" indicates the Alternatives section.)

18. Indication that city code differs from primary city code, and/or that location lies outside of primary city (See its footnote.)

19. Prices for each hotel's best nonsuite double room during each event

$	Up to $100
$$	$100-$200
$$$	$200-$300
$$$$	$300-$400
$$$$+	More than $400

20. *Rms*, indicating number of rooms in each hotel

21. Best Rooms, indicating rooms to request when making reservations

22. Reservation service and toll-free number in US

23. Restaurant prices indicating average cost of one entree for the recommended meal (Cover and Entry Fee indicating prices at nightspots and attractions)

$	Up to $10
$$	$10-$20
$$$	$20-$30
$$$$	$30-$40
$$$$+	More than $40

24. *Rec*, indicating the recommended meal in the itinerary at each restaurant with a / followed by other suggested meals, if applicable

B	Breakfast
L	Lunch
D	Dinner
T	High tea or snack

25. *Dress*, indicating the atmosphere at each establishment

Kazh	Casual, somewhat elegant, hip
Euro	A more continental take on Kazh, lots of attitude
Dressy	Men in suits, women in cocktail or evening wear
Yuppie	Khakis, button-downs, Ralph Lauren, Gap
FABs	Fraternity-alumni boys (think baseball caps)
Local	What locals wear (varies broadly)

26. *Food*, indicating each restaurant's cuisine

27. *Rec*, indicating the scene at nightspots

G	Gaming
H	Hangout bar
M	Live music
O	Dancing (recorded music, disco)
P	Dancing (live music)
S	Show
F	Food served

28. Type of music featured at nightspot

29. Local tourist office information

30. Detailed information, such as phone numbers, addresses, and prices (CD indicates a charitable donation included) for main events (bold-faced) and subevents (bold-faced, italic) (For alternative events, only contact phone numbers are provided.)

31. Local standard time zone relative to New York

32. Average high and low temperatures during event in Fahrenheit (and Celsius)

33. Local airport name, three-letter airport code, and approximate time (15-minute increments) and taxi fare ($5-increments; if distance is 90 minutes or more, no taxi fare is given) from the airport to our recommended hotel (R indicates recommended rail service from airport to city.)

34. Recommendation on whether or not to rent a car: Yes, No, or Yes/No (could go either way)

35. Primary language spoken

LONDON (ASCOT), ENGLAND — ROYAL ASCOT

The Hot Sheet

☎ 44/171 $ 0.6 Pound

HOTELS	DAY	ADDRESS	PH	PRICE	Fx	RMS	BEST ROOMS
The Halkin	A	5 Halkin St., SW1	333-1000 888-425-5464	$$$$+	333-1100	41	High up, gdn vw
One Aldwych	A	One Aldwych, WC2	300-1000 800-447-7462	$$$$+	300-1001	105	Dlx dbl rm
The Savoy	1	The Strand, WC2	836-4343 800-637-2869	$$$$+	240-6040	202	Thames vw
Sheraton Belgravia	A	20 Chesham pl., SW1	235-6040 800-325-3535		235-3243		

RESTAURANTS	DAY	ADDRESS	PH	PRICE	REC	DRESS	FOOD
Arundel Restaurant	2	Ascot Racecourse	134 487-8599	$$	T/L	Euro	Nuvo European
The Avenue	2	7-9 St. James's St., SW1	321-2111	$$$	D/L	Euro	Nuvo British
Bank	3	1 Kingsway , WC2	379-9797	$$$	L/D	Euro	Nuvo European
The Collection	3	264 Brompton Rd., SW3	225-1212	$$$$	D/L	Euro	Fusion
Fifth Floor Restaurant	A	109 Knightsbridge, SW1 in Harvey Nichols Dept. Store	235-5000	$$	L	Euro	British
The Ivy	2	1 West St., WC2	836-4751	$$$	LD	Euro	Nuvo British
Mezzo	2	100 Wardour St., W1	314-4000	$$$	D/L	Euro	International
Oxo Tower Restaurant, Bar & Brasserie	1	Oxo Tower Wharf Barge House St., South Bank, SE1	803-3888	$$$	D/L British	Euro	Modern, traditional
Quaglino's	A	16 Bury St., SW1	930-6767	$$$	DL	Euro	Nuvo European
The River Restaurant	2	see The Savoy hotel	836-4343	$$	B/LD	Euro	International
Tate Gallery Restaurant	1	Millbank, SW1 Tate Gallery	887-8877	$$	L	Local	British
The Thames Foyer	A	see The Savoy hotel	836-4343	$$	T	Euro	Tea

NITELIFE	DAY	ADDRESS	PH	PRICE	REC	DRESS	
Brigadier Gerard Bar	2	Ascot Racecourse behind the Grandstand	134 487-8555	None		Dressy	
Café de Paris	3	3-4 Coventry St., W1	734-7700	$$	O	Euro	House, garage
Fifth Floor Bar	3	109 Knightsbridge, SW1	235-5000	None	HF	Euro	Harvey Nichols
Garden Bar	2	Ascot Racecourse behind the Grandstand	134 487-8555	None	H	Dressy	
K-bar	2	84-86 Wardour St., W1	439-4393	$$	O	Euro	House, dance
Limelight	A	136 Shaftesbury Ave., WC2	434-0572	$	O	Euro	House, garage
Ronnie Scott's	2	47 Frith St., W1	439-0747	$$	M	Euro	Jazz
Royal National Theatre	A	South Bank, SE1	452-3000	$$$$	S	Kazh	Theater
Shakespeare's Globe Theatre	A	New Globe Walk, Bankside, SE1	902-1500	$$	S	Kazh	Theater
shoeless joe's	1	Temple Place Embankment, WC2	240-7867	None	PF	Euro	Funk, soul, pop
Stringfellows	3	St. Martin's Ln., WC2	240-5534	$$	OP	Euro	Disco
Wag Club	A	35 Wardour St., W1	437-5534	$	OP	Euro	Rock, jazz, Latin, '60s R&B

SIGHTS & ATTRACTIONS	DAY	ADDRESS	PH	ENTRY FEE
Fortnum & Mason	1	181 Piccadilly, W1	734-8040	None
Museum of London	A	London Wall, EC2	600-3699	$
Tate Gallery	1	Millbank, SW1	887-8000	None
Tower of London	3	Tower Hill, EC3	709-0765	$$
Westminster Abbey	3	Broad Sanctuary, SW1	222-5152	$

OTHER SIGHTS, SERVICES & ATTRACTIONS				
Moss Bros.	1	27 King St., WC2	240-4567	None
Tourist Information Centre		Victoria Station, SW1	None	

*134=Ascot

RECommendations: (Restaurants) B—Breakfast; L—Lunch; D—Dinner; T—High tea or snack (Nitelife) G—Gaming; H—hangout bar; M—Live music; O—Dancing (disco); P—Dancing (live music); S—Show; F—Food served. Available but without recommendation. For complete explanation of Hot Sheet format, see p. 34.

EVENT & TICKET INFO

The **Royal Ascot** (Ascot Racecourse): Grandstand and Paddock tickets ($54-$70) can be purchased from *Ascot Racecourse* (44 1344-487-6456) after January 1. Silver (£12-$16.50) and Heath ($3.25) tickets are easy to obtain, but seats aren't assigned unless they're booked for groups of 12 or more.

NYC +5   53°/69° (12°/20°)   London Heathrow (LHR): 45 min./$60 (R) London Gatwick (LGW): 90 min./$75 (R)   No   English

158

The Fun Also Rises

The Fun Also Rises

International
Events & Destinations

December 1999/January 2000

M T W T F S S
26
20 21 22 23 24 25 1 2
27 28 29 30 31 8 9
3 4 5 6 7 15 16
10 11 12 13 14 21 22 23
17 18 19 20

Nassau, Bahamas

December 2000/January 2001

M T W T F S S
25 26 27 28 29 30 31
1 2 3 4 5 6 7
8 9 10 11 12 13 14
15 16 17 18 19 20 21
22 23 24 25 26 27 28

Junkanoo

| Origin: c. 1800 | Event ★ ★ ★ ★ ★ ★ City | Attendance: 10,000 |

The Bahamians have it right. Don't end the year with a bang, start it with cow bells, drums, whistles, trumpets, and just about anything else that makes music! The first great party of the year begins January 1 at 2 a.m. with *Junkanoo*, a Caribbean fete that fills the air with wild beats, and lures 10,000 revelers, many dressed in fantastic crepe-paper costumes. The riotous all-nighter roars up and down the streets of Nassau, the Bahamas' vibrant capital.

Although the celebration runs throughout the city, the prime party spots are along Bay Street, Nassau's main drag. The streets will be packed with spectators cheering, singing, and dancing, so head out shortly after midnight to find an ideal spot for viewing the spectacle that is the *Junkanoo* parade. Liquor sales are prohibited on the streets, but the bars and restaurants do brisk business through the morning.

Some credit the birth of *Junkanoo* to the legendary West African tribal leader John Canu, but its exact roots are unknown. A cultural institution since the days of pirates and slavery, *Junkanoo* has developed from a slaves' holiday to a parade and competition featuring stilt-walkers, dancers, and musi-cians in headdresses that would make a Vegas showgirl proud.

Highlights include costumes, music, and dance competitions, often waged between 500- to 1,000-member groups with names such as Valley Boys, Saxons, Roots, and P.I.G.S. (Progress through Integrity, Guts, and Strength). To best experience the music and party vibe that makes *Junkanoo* special, be sure to follow at least one group for a full "lap," or one wild circuit around the parade route. Judging is held in Rawson Square about 9 a.m.

For natives, the highlight of *Junkanoo* is the closing ceremony—think of it as the Bahamas' answer to the Super Bowl. But most visitors get satisfaction just watching the tropical dawn breaking on a new year that always starts the right way—with a party, instead of a hangover.

Junkanoo

Other than being at *Junkanoo* from 2 until 9 a.m. on New Year's Day, there's no schedule to keep, but you do have some decisions to make.

Hotels

The island's top hotel choice is the **Ocean Club**. The private manse, built in the 1920s, has been turned into a charming, intimate, and elegant resort. Guests can also make use of the facilities at its sister resort, the four-star *Atlantis* hotel on Paradise Island, which, unlike its namesake, is not a mythical utopia. With 18 restaurants, 20 clubs and lounges, a 40-foot water-slide, the world's largest outdoor aquarium, a massive casino, and rooms fit for King Neptune, the Atlantis is a destination event unto itself. Another good resort with every possible need met on-site is **Sandals Royal Bahamian Resort & Spa**, which boasts huge four-poster beds and more statues than many Roman ruins. The **Compass Point Beach Club**, owned by Island Records impresario Chris Blackwell (the man who brought Bob Marley to the world), features 18 cottages, painted every conceivable Caribbean color, and an on-site recording studio.

Restaurants

You don't have to stay at the Atlantis to take advantage of its diverse dining options. Picks of the lot include the brasserie-style **The Café at the Great Hall of Waters**; the Royal Towers' **Five Twins**, with upscale Pacific Rim cuisine and live music; the country-club-style **Bahamian Club**; and the gourmet cuisine and intimate garden setting of the **Courtyard Terrace** at the Ocean Club.

In town, two high-end continental restaurants rate a visit. **Graycliff** has hosted kings and other celebs, with excellent food and a massive wine list. **Sun and ...** serves a fine chateaubriand. For funkier environs, head to **Travellers' Rest** in Gambier Village for seafood, Bahamian-style meats, and banana daiquiris in an open-air dining room or outdoor porch.

Island Attractions

In Nassau, head up Victoria's Steps, all 66 of them (cut into the stone by hand), for a view of the town and Paradise Island beyond. Explore Rawson (Parliament) Square and get a taste of the islands-meet-England architecture. While in town, visit the **Junkanoo Expo** to look at old costumes and pick up recordings of various *Junkanoo* stars. Stop at the **Dolphin Experience**, where you can swim with friendly dolphins in the ocean. Or explore the Exhuma Keys with **Power Boat Adventures**, which will take you on a snorkeling, hiking, shark-feeding, and island-exploring adventure.

Nightlife

Take a turn at the **Atlantis Casino**, the largest casino in the Caribbean and the only one in the world with natural lighting. High rollers can stop at the **Baccarat Lounge** for late-night snacks and music in a sophisticated atmosphere or enjoy a nightcap at **Dragons**, a dance club with live and recorded music. Local favorites before or after *Junkanoo* are **Club Waterloo**, **601**, and **The Zoo**. All are happening nightclubs along Bay Street, where you can dance to live Bahamian bands and recorded stateside hits.

Nassau and Paradise Island, connected by a short bridge, are the two most popular destinations of the Bahamas' 700 islands (29 of which are inhabited). You can recover from the party aboard a fishing boat or flee to one of the more secluded islands.

The *Junkanoo Parade* also takes place on the morning following Christmas Day. Locals debate which parade is more fun—it's a tough call. If you've got time, it might be worth-while doing a whole Christmas/Junkanoo week in the Bahamas and decide for yourself.

The Hot Sheet

☎ US/242

$ 1.0 Bahamian Dollar

HOTELS	ADDRESS	PH	PRICE	FX	RMS	BEST ROOMS
Atlantis	Casino Dr., Paradise Island	363-3000 800- 285-2684	$$$$	363-3524	2300	Royal Towers Imperial Club rm
Compass Point Beach Club	W. Bay St., West Gambier	327-4500 800- 688-7678	$$$	327-3299	18	1-bdrm seafront hut
Ocean Club	Casino Dr., Paradise Island	363-2501 800- 285-2684	$$$$+	363-2424	59	Dlx ocean vw
Sandals Royal Bahamian Resort & Spa	W. Bay St., Cable Beach	327-6400 800- 726-3257	$$$$+	327-6961	405	Grandlux ocean vw

RESTAURANTS	ADDRESS	PH	PRICE	REC	DRESS	FOOD
Bahamian Club	see Atlantis hotel	363-3000	$$$	D	Kazh	Steaks, seafood
The Café at the Great Hall of Waters	see Atlantis hotel	363-3000	$$$$	BL	Kazh	Brasserie-style
Courtyard Terrace	see Ocean Club resort	363-2501	$$$$+	BLD	Euro	Gourmet
Five Twins	see Atlantis hotel	363-3000	$$$	D	Kazh	Pacific Rim
Graycliff	W. Hill St.	322-2797	$$$$	LD	Euro	Continental
Sun and...	Lakeview Dr. off Village Rd.	393-1205	$$$	LD	Euro	Continental
Travellers' Rest	W. Bay St., Gambier Village	327-7633	$$$	LD	Kazh	Seafood Bahamian-style

NITELIFE	ADDRESS	PH	PRICE	REC	DRESS	MUSIC
601	601 E. Bay St.	322-3041	$	P	Kazh	Bahamian, disco
Atlantis Casino	see Atlantis hotel	363-3000	None	H	Local	
Baccarat Lounge	see Atlantis hotel	363-3000	None	H	Dressy	
Club Waterloo	E. Bay St.	393-7324	$	HOP(F)	Yuppie	Bahamian, dance
Dragons	see Atlantis hotel	363-3000	None	P	Euro	Top-40, dance
The Zoo	W. Bay St., Saunders Beach	322-7195	$	O	Kazh	Dance

SIGHTS & ATTRACTIONS	ADDRESS	PH	ENTRY FEE
Junkanoo Expo	Prince George Wharf	356-2731	$

OTHER SIGHTS, SERVICES & ATTRACTIONS

Dolphin Experience	Port Lucaya	373-1244	$$$$+
Power Boat Adventures	Sugar Reef Dock	327-5385	$$$$+
Tourist Information Office	Rawson Sq. near cruise ship dock	326-9772	

EVENT & TICKET INFO

Junkanoo (Nassau, Bahamas): Tickets for seats along the parade route ($10) and for the prime seats in Rawson Square ($25) should be purchased in advance by contacting the *Ministry of Youth, Sports and Culture* (242-394-0445).

RECommendations: (Restaurants) B–Breakfast; L–Lunch; D–Dinner; T–High tea or snack
(Nitelife) G–Gaming; H–Hangout bar; M–Live music; O–Dancing (disco); P–Dancing (live music); S–Show; F–Food served
( )–Available but without recommendation. For complete explanation of Hot Sheet format, see page 34.

🕐 NYC +1   ☀ 59°/78° (15°/25°)   ✈ Nassau (NAS); 30 min./$10   🚗 Yes/No   🗣 English

The Fun Also Rises

Cape Town, South Africa

Cape Minstrel Festival

Origin: 1898   Event ★ ★ ★ ★ ★ City   Attendance: 50,000

In a blur of banjos and body paint the minstrels arrive, decked out in gaudy costumes of silk and satin in every color of the rainbow. It's the glorious *Cape Minstrel Festival Parade*, when Cape Town lets go of its Old World reserve for a rocking, African-style New Year's bash.

The roots of the *Cape Minstrel Festival* go back at least two centuries, when slave laborers were granted a brief New Year's rest. During the first two days of the year, overworked men and women filled the streets of Cape Town wearing vibrant, improvised outfits in the styles of their homelands.

Today, the minstrels who dominate the festival come from the "colored" community of Cape Town. Troupes of 300 to 1,000 people march through the streets. Each group wears unique uniforms and sings and dances to different theme songs. Since many tribal traditions have been lost to South Africa's tumultuous past, elements of American Mardi Gras have been integrated—some troupes bear names such as the Beach Boys, Red Indians, and New Orleans Chiefs.

New Year's Day (*Eerste Nuwejaar's*) begins with the masses gathering on Cape Town's shoreline for a celebration of song and dance. Dozens of competitions are held in an array of categories, assuring some kind of prize for almost everyone. On the second day of the new year (*Tweede Nuwejaar*), troupes weave through the streets of Cape Town in an endless parade of sound and color.

Like the models that flock here during the fashion season, Cape Town is drop-dead gorgeous and, although firmly attached to Africa, very Mediterranean. Nestled in the shadow of Table Mountain, it's one of the oldest European settlements south of the Sahara. Surrounded by both mountains and sea, the city (population 250,000) is rich in culture and astonishing natural beauty. It may be the most magical place in the world to see the birth of the new millennium—as light breaks on the horizon, the air rings with song and the sun rises over Mother Africa.

Cape Minstrel Festival

Day 1. Sat.   Jan. 1, 2000
(Day 1. Monday   January 1, 2001)

5:00am Start your year with a bottle of bubbly from the **Victoria & Alfred Hotel** in the heart of Cape Town's famous Victoria & Alfred Waterfront. The classic hotel overlooks the harbor and Table Mountain on one side, and the Victoria & Alfred Waterfront on the other. Cab across the peninsula to Fish Hoek or one of the other beaches on the eastern side (where the water is warmer) to toast the first sunrise of the new year.

6:30am Don't rush it (and don't leave the hotel's ice bucket on the beach), but take a slow ride through Simon's Town, Kommetjie, Noordhoek, and along the famous Chapman's Peak Drive to Hout Bay.

8:00am Breakfast on the veranda of **Chapman's Peak Restaurant**. Afterward, stroll around this working harbor, then get a cab to take you slowly along Atlantic Drive back to your hotel.

10:30am You may want some downtime at this point. If not, explore one of the city's biggest and best tourist attractions, the Victoria & Alfred Waterfront, named for the area's Victoria and Alfred (Queen Victoria's second son) basins on whose quaysides the development is located.

12:30pm For a taste of California or continental cuisine, go to **Café Faro** near the hotel. Arrive no later than 12:30 p.m.; South Africans tend to eat at exactly 1 p.m. and eateries fill up quickly.

2:30pm Hit the *Cape Minstrel Festival*! Intensity has been building since the 2 p.m. kickoff at Green Point Stadium. Thousands of minstrels and support crews pack into the stadium all day long, prepping for the serious business of singing and dancing. Various competitions will last all afternoon, with

the culmination and final celebrations coming in the early evening. Stand up, tap your feet, clap your hands, and enjoy!

6:30pm Drag yourself away from the minstrels and head for **Fat Boys**, also in Greenpoint, to catch your breath and a martini.

7:00pm Make your way to Bloubergstrand, a beach area up the coast with stunning views of the sun setting over Table Mountain and Table Bay.

8:00pm Have dinner at the up-market **Blue Peter**, where you can continue to marvel at the majestic beauty of Table Mountain and Table Bay. The menu leans in the direction of South African seafood.

10:00pm Cab back to the city and the **Drum Café** for a drink and a uniquely African experience—yes, you can beat your own drum here!

Midnight Nearby is **East City Cafe**, one of Cape Town's hot restaurant/bars. The cigar bar provides a high-class club atmosphere for a nightcap. Also within striking distance is the glitzy **Klub Kapital**. You'll need a little attitude to get into this dance spot.

Day 2. Sun.   Jan. 2, 2000
(Day 3. Wednesday   January 3, 2001)

10:00am Have breakfast in the hotel before setting out to visit the Cape's oldest wine-producing region, Constantia. Four wine estates operate in the vicinity. Start with **Groot Constantia**, which has, among many choices, the sweet whites of the European settlers of the 1600s. The place is also a national monument. The other estates are **Klein Constantia**, **Constantia Uitsig**, and **Buitenverwagting**. Apart from fine wines, they also boast great restaurants. But have lunch at the famous **Jonkershuis** on the Groot Constantia estate. It serves traditional Cape cuisine and fresh seafood.

3:00pm Cape Town and its peninsula have some of the finest beaches in Africa. Start at Noordhoek with a horseback ride on the beach. Then head to Clifton Beach, where Cape Town's pretty people are considered overdressed if they're wearing a bikini! If you prefer a dress code that's even less formal, ask for directions to Sandy Bay—it's the ultimate allover-tan beach. Take a dip in the Atlantic but be warned —the sun may be hot but the water is definitely not!

8:00pm For dinner, go to **Blues**, one of the city's hottest restaurants. The fashionable Camps Bay eatery adds a California touch to some interesting South African dishes.

10:00pm Back in the city, the dance floor at **The Fez** should be heating up. If the aptly decorated club isn't open, meander around the innumerable watering holes on the waterfront—try South Africa's first and most famous boutique brewery, **Ferryman's Freehouse**, for a pint of their best bitter.

Day 3. Mon.   Jan. 3, 2000
(Day 2. Tuesday   January 2, 2001)

9:00am Enjoy breakfast in the Table Bay hotel's **Conservatory** restaurant. The buffet and views of Table Mountain are both excellent.

10:00am Catch one of the regular shuttles to the city center. On foot, explore Adderley Street, the Gardens, and the Houses of Parliament, then take in Tuynhuys, the South African president's Cape Town residence.

Noon When the noonday gun is fired, hit the deck (veranda) of **Cycle's on the Square** in the Holiday Inn-Greenmarket Square. From here you can get a drink and check out the buskers (street performers) in the square's flea market.

1:30pm Walk or cab to the **Kaapse Tafel Restaurant** for a lunch of traditional South African cuisine.

3:00pm Digest some of South Africa's colorful and turbulent past at the **Slave Lodge** cultural and historical museum opposite the restaurant.

4:00pm Today is *Tweede Nuwejaar*, the second day of the *Minstrel Festival* (Sundays don't count). It's even more exuberant than the first one. Watch or, better yet, join the parade through the streets of the fascinating Bo-Kaap area before heading to Green Point Stadium.

9:00pm It's an easy jaunt to **Mano's**, a particularly trendy restaurant with a light, late-night menu.

11:00pm End your evening at the **Green Dolphin** jazz club, a Cape Town institution that will provide a provocative ending to your *Cape Minstrel* visit.

Alternatives

The **Cape Grace** hotel is just a swinging bridge over the harbor away from the Victoria & Alfred. Consider the **Cape Sun Inter-Continental**, always a good choice in the city. You can't beat the venerable **Mount Nelson**, one of Africa's classic hotels.

Two Oceans Restaurant, cut into a cliff face at Cape Point, serves great seafood and grill items. Go to **Tobago's** for spicy Mediterranean food overlooking the harbor. The **Blue Plate** has some of the area's best South African cuisine. The **Bonthuys** is one of Cape Town's top restaurants. The **Paradise Peak Bistro** sits atop Table Mountain—arrive via the **Table Mountain Cableway**.

For nightcaps and live music, **Club Georgia** in the city plays '70s- and '80s-era music. The trendy **Jet Lounge** has DJs playing funk and Latino-house.

Robben Island Museum, Nelson Mandela's place of imprisonment, makes for an interesting three-hour excursion. The **Two Oceans Aquarium** is a waterfront highlight. Or fly above "the fairest Cape in all the circumference of the earth," as Sir Francis Drake described it, with a **Court Helicopters** tour.

The Hot Sheet

☎ 27/21

$ 6.1 Rand

HOTELS	DAY	ADDRESS	PH	PRICE	FX	RMS	BEST ROOMS
Cape Grace	A	West Quay Rd., Waterfront	410-7100 800- 525-4800	$$$$+	419-7622	122	Supr rm w/ mtn or harbor vw
Cape Sun Inter-Continental	A	Strand St.	488-5100 800- 465-4329	$$$	423-8875	364	30th fl w/ mtn or sea vw
Mount Nelson	A	76 Orange St.	423-1000 800- 223-6800	$$$$+	424-7472	226	Lux rm w/ city vw
Victoria & Alfred Hotel	1	Pierhead, Waterfront	419-6677 800- 297-3373	$$$	419-8955	68	Mtn or waterfront vw

RESTAURANTS	DAY	ADDRESS	PH	PRICE	REC	DRESS	FOOD
Blue Peter	1	Popham Rd. in Blue Peter Hotel	554-1956	$	D/L	Euro	Grill, seafood
Blue Plate	A	35 Kloof St.	424-1515	$	LD	Local	South African, seafood, game
Blues	2	Victoria Rd., Promenade Centre	438-2040	$$	D/L	Kazh	Nuvo Californian
Bonthuys	A	121 Castle St.	426-2368	$	D	Euro	Nuvo Cape, meats
Café Faro	1	121 Beach Rd., Mouille Point	439-5260	$	L/BD	Kazh	Continental
Chapman's Peak Restaurant	1	Main Rd., Hout Bay	790-1036	$	B/LD	Kazh	Seafood, steaks
Conservatory	3	Quay 6 in Table Bay hotel	406-5000	$	B/LD	Kazh	Buffet, continental
Jonkershuis	2	see Groot Constantia	794-6255	$	L/D	Euro	South African
Kaapse Tafel Restaurant	3	90 Queen Victoria St.	423-1651	$	L/D	Kazh	Traditional South African
Mano's	3	39 Main St.	434-1090	$	D/L	Local	Healthy fast-food
Paradise Peak Bistro	A	Table Mountain	424-8181	$	BLTD	Local	Bistro
Tobago's	A	Villa Via Hotel in Granger Bay	418-5729	$$	BLD	Euro	Mediterranean
Two Oceans Restaurant	A	Cape Point	780-9200	$	L	Kazh	Grill, seafood, South African

NITELIFE	DAY	ADDRESS	PH	PRICE	REC	DRESS	MUSIC
Club Georgia	A	30 Jamieson St.	422-0261	$	M	Kazh	Jazz, '70s, '80s
Cycle's on the Square	3	10 Greenmarket Sq., in Holiday Inn	423-2040	None	H(F)	Local	
Drum Café	1	32 Glynn St.	461-1305	$	MSP	Local	African drums
East City Cafe	1	72 Barrack St.	461-9988	None	H(F)	Euro	
Fat Boys	1	9 Alfred Rd.	421-1760	$	O	Local	Top-40
Ferryman's Freehouse	2	East Pier Rd., Waterfront	419-7748	None	H(F)	Local	
The Fez	2	13 Hout St., Greenmarket Sq.	424-0250	$	O	Euro	House
Green Dolphin	3	Pierhead, Waterfront	421-7471	$	M(F)	Kazh	Jazz
Jet Lounge	A	Long St.	424-8831	$	O	Kazh	Latin, house
Klub Kapital	1	6 Pepper St.	423-9188	$	O	Euro	Dance

SIGHTS & ATTRACTIONS	DAY	ADDRESS	PH	ENTRY FEE
Buitenverwagting	2	Klein Constantia Rd.	794-5190	None
Constantia Uitsig	2	Spaanschemat River Rd.	794-1810	$
Groot Constantia	2	Main Rd.	794-5128	$
Klein Constantia	2	Klein Constantia Rd.	794-5188	None
Robben Island Museum	A	Waterfront	419-1300	$$
Slave Lodge	3	49 Adderley St.	461-8280	$
Two Oceans Aquarium	A	Dock Rd., Waterfront	418-3823	$

OTHER SIGHTS, SERVICES & ATTRACTIONS

Court Helicopters	A	Helipad, Waterfront	425-2966	$$$$+
Table Mountain Cableway	A	Lower Station on Tafelberg Rd.	424-8181	$$
Cape Town Tourism		Castle and Burg sts.	418-5214	

EVENT & TICKET INFO

Cape Minstrel Festival (Green Point Stadium and Bo-Kaap area of Cape Town): Tickets ($6) for stadium events can be purchased through *Computicket* (27/21-918-8950). All other events are free. For information, contact *Mr. Carelse*, the event organizer (27/829-20-4954).

RECommendations: (Restaurants) B–Breakfast; L–Lunch; D–Dinner; T–High tea or snack
(Nitelife) G–Gaming; H–Hangout bar; M–Live music; O–Dancing (disco); P–Dancing (live music); S–Show; F–Food served
()–Available but without recommendation. For complete explanation of Hot Sheet format, see page 34.

🕐 NYC +7   ☀ 56°/69° (13°/91°)   ✈ Cape Town (CPT); 30 min./$25   🚗 Yes/No   👥 English

The Fun Also Rises

Manila (Kalibo), Philippines

Ati-Atihan

Origin: 1212	Event ★ ★ ★ ★ ★ City	Attendance: 200,000

A *ti-Atihan*'s incessant party cry—*Hala Bira, Puera Pasma!*—literally means "Keep on going, no tiring!" Some devotees claim the noise and energy at the "Mardi Gras of the Philippines" rivals the unmitigated madness of the annual New Orleans blowout. While that may be a slight exaggeration, no one observes this tropical blast from the sidelines.

Visitors to Kalibo, on Panay Island, invariably find a higher state of consciousness during the three days and nights of uninhibited carousing. Throughout the weekend, crowds gyrate in a frenzied, drunken mass of dancing and shaking, stamping feet, beating bongos and cans, and general noisemaking. There are parades, beauty contests, concerts, and outrageous costumes made of coconut shells, feathers, and palm fronds. Everyone stuffs themselves on roasted pig and lobster.

The event probably began in the 13th century in commemoration of a peace pact between warring tribes of Atis—the region's aboriginal Negrito inhabitants. (*Ati-Atihan* literally means "to make like Atis.") When the Spaniards arrived in the Philippines in the 1600s, they tried to eliminate the "savage" celebration but wound up simply rededicating the unstoppable festival to the infant Jesus. *Ati-Atihan* had a new raison d'être but didn't gain much religious virtue from the transition, although, when the dancing is over, exhausted revelers do troop to the cathedral for Mass and *patapak*, a priest's blessing with the healing symbol of the infant Jesus.

Kalibo is less than an hour's flight from Manila, the Philippine capital with nine million residents. Once called the Pearl of the Orient Seas, Manila is a bit rundown these days, but lush areas such as Rizal Park and historic Intramuros (the old Spanish settlement) remain charming. A blossoming nightclub and restaurant scene make Remedios Circle the hippest area in the evening—perfect for warming up or cooling down from the gargantuan party effort demanded by *Ati-Atihan*.

Day 1. Fri.   Jan. 14, 2000
(Day 1. Friday   January 19, 2001)

8:00am The Peninsula is your residence in the Philippine capital. Located in Makati, Manila's commercial center, the ultramodern Peninsula has a huge lobby and large marble bathrooms in every room.

9:00am A day trip to **Pagsanjan Falls** is a good way to see the dramatic, palm-stuffed Philippine countryside. Trails and bamboo rafting trips at Pagsanjan take visitors through an awesome jungle gorge and a series of falls. You could rent a car, but, with Manila's horrible traffic, an inexpensive guide service is better. Tours include lunch.

4:00pm On the way back to Manila, visit the **Manila American Cemetery and Memorial**, where more than 17,000 American service men and women who died in the Pacific (mostly during World War II) are buried. The 152-acre grounds are immaculate and 25 gargantuan tile maps illustrate the war in the Pacific.

7:00pm Kalde-Kaldero, a.k.a. The Singing Cooks and Waiters, ATBP, is a restaurant unlike any in the world. A completely singing staff—cooks, waiters, busboys, cashiers, janitors, security guards, manager— serenade customers while serving Filipino dishes. Downstairs you'll hear traditional Filipino songs, upstairs a blend of the international, from Russian folk songs to "Babe" by American dinosaur rockers Styx. Make reservations for this exuberant experience.

9:00pm Cab to Remedios Circle, Manila's best bar-hopping area. Have a tropical drink at the crowded **Café Havana**, a trendy bar where workers wear black shirts and revolutionary berets. One bearded waiter is a dead ringer for Che Guevara!

10:00pm Walk to the intimate but buzzing **Larry's Bar on the Remedios Circle**. Or check out **Tia Maria's Remedios** around the corner, where American pop

or a live band will have the dance floor packed with a younger crowd.

11:30pm Cab to **Zu**, in the Shangri-La hotel. The hip disco stays crowded past 2 a.m.

Day 2. Sat.   Jan. 15, 2000
(Day 2. Saturday   January 20, 2001)

9:00am Do the breakfast buffet at **Nielsen's**, an airy, sunlit restaurant in your hotel.

10:00am Cab to Intramuros, the sprawling fortress town that was the hub of Old Manila during much of Spain's 300-year rule of the Philippines. Spanish colonial architecture is preserved at this biggest and best Manila attraction. Start your wandering at the **Intramuros Visitors Center**.

Noon Walk to lunch at **Kamayan**. Utensils are provided, but the idea is to eat with your fingers— *kamayan* means "hands." The native-style food— rice, beef, fish, fruit—is served on banana leaves. *Lechon de leche*, a national pork favorite, is the house specialty.

1:00pm Nearby, enjoy the shade around lush Rizal Park, one of the best urban parks in Asia.

2:30pm Head to the hotel and shuttle to the domestic terminal for your flight to Kalibo.

5:00pm From Kalibo airport, cab through the costumed crowds and check into the **Beachcomber Inn**, the best hotel available in this rural town of 61,000. Though not luxurious, it's air-conditioned and within walking distance of the festival action.

6:00pm Walk 10 minutes to the main plaza, which is dominated by the Kalibo Cathedral, ground zero for most *Ati-Atihan* celebrations. Along the way, you'll rub shoulders with thousands of partyers. Several vendors will probably press cold beers or rum drinks into your hands.

7:00pm For dinner, try the informal **Kalibo Food Plaza** ® in the center of town.

8:00pm Follow the thumping drums of the nightly *snakedancing* to Magsaysay Park—also within walking distance—party central for the nighttime crowd.

11:00pm A pretty good *fireworks display* caps off the evening at Magsaysay Park. Much of the crowd will remain until sunrise, but tomorrow's partying will be even more intense, so get some rest.

Day 3. Sun. Jan. 16, 2000
(Day 3. Sunday   January 21, 2001)

10:00am Breakfast at the Beachcomber's **Molave** ® **Room**. The traditional Filipino breakfast should be familiar—eggs, bacon, toast, and coffee.

11:30am Wander toward the cathedral amid thousands of revelers gearing up for the final and wildest day of a weeklong street party. You might see a demonstration of *pahilot*, the faith-healing tradition many Filipinos practice.

1:00pm People begin gathering at the plaza for the *Torch Parade and Procession*, an all-out spectacle of native tradition, Christian zeal, showy costumes, and there's-no-tomorrow partying.

3:30pm Follow the *procession*, dedicated to Santo Niño, as it winds through the streets. Grab food from ® vendors along the way—everything from grilled chicken and calimari to pineapple ice cream. When the sun sets, watch the spirit of the *parade* transform as thousands of bamboo torches carried by the outrageously costumed devotees light the way.

6:00pm If you need to sit down, **Mary's Refreshment** in ® the middle of town is a clean spot for cold drinks, hamburgers, and authentic Filipino fare.

7:00pm Head back to the *snakedancing* for more drinking, mingling, and people-watching. The celebration can last until 3 a.m., so if you've not already done so, cover your face with soot (a favorite, readily available costume) and "make like the Atis" for as long as you can.

Alternatives

A way from the Makati bustle, **The Heritage** hotel on famed Roxas Boulevard, which rims Manila Bay, has an assortment of terrific restaurants, a disco, and a flawless staff. Favored by Douglas MacArthur, the **Manila Hotel** is a gorgeous landmark overlooking Manila Bay. In Kalibo, plans for a top-level hotel have been announced to accommodate *Ati-Atihan* visitors, but as of this printing, nothing is definite. Check with the Philippine Department of Tourism.

N ear your hotel in Manila, **San Mig** and **The Blarney Stone** are good pub-style places. **Patio Guernica** offers refinement and Spanish cuisine in Remedios Circle. Also in the Remedios area, the **Endangered Species** restaurant-bar has safari-themed decor.

M uch of Manila's nightlife centers around The Fort, a bustling entertainment zone in the Fort Bonifacio complex. **Fat Willy's Bar & Restaurant**, which converts to a dance place after dinner, is The Fort's most popular spot.

F ollowing *Ati-Atihan*, a large portion of the crowd takes the two-hour bus-and-ferry trip to Boracay, one of the world's most beautiful tropical islands. The water is mild, sand like powdered sugar, beach bars plentiful, and sunsets the dream of every overworked nine-to-fiver. Two top resorts on very affordable Boracay are **Pearl of the Pacific** and the **Boracay Regency Beach Resort**.

T he Philippines is a fantastic place, but more than any other country in this book (possibly excepting India), it can be difficult to negotiate for first-time visitors. A good guide service, such as **Rajah Tours Philippines**, can simplify your stay.

The Hot Sheet

☎ 63/2

$ 39 Philippine Peso

HOTELS	DAY	ADDRESS	PH	PRICE	FX	RMS	BEST ROOMS
Beachcomber Inn	2	476 N. Roldan St.	K36 262-4846	$	268-4765	19	Dlx
Boracay Regency Beach Resort	A	Station 2, Balabag	B36 288-6111	$$	288-6777	48	Dlx
The Heritage	A	Roxas Blvd. and EDSA, Pasay City	891-8888	$$$	891-8833	547	8th and 9th fls
Manila Hotel	A	One Rizal Park at Roxas Blvd.	527-0011 800- 966-5485	$$$	527-0022	500	Supr dlx Manila Bay vw
Pearl of the Pacific	A	Balabag	B36 288-3220	$$$	288-3961	60	Ocean vw
The Peninsula	1	Ayala and Makati aves., Makati	887-2888 800- 223-6800	$$$$	810-4348	500	Dlx crnr gdn vw

RESTAURANTS	DAY	ADDRESS	* PH	PRICE	REC	DRESS	FOOD
Endangered Species	A	1834 M.H. del Pilar, Malate	524-0167	$$$	D	Local	European, American, Filipino
Kalde-Kaldero	1	Santa Monica St. and Roxas Blvd.	831-5015	$$	D/L	Kazh	Filipino
Kalibo Food Plaza	2	Pastrana Park	no phone	$	D/BL	Local	Fast-food
Kamayan	2	47 Pasay Rd.	843-3604	$$	L/D	Kazh	Filipino
Mary's Refreshment	3	Pastrana St.	K36 268-5105	$	D/L	Kazh	Filipino, American
Molave Room	3	see Beachcomber Inn	K36 262-4846	$	B	Local	Continental, American, Filipino
Nielsen's	2	see The Peninsula hotel	887-2888	$$	B/LD	Kazh	International
Patio Guernica	A	1856 Jorge Bocobo St., Malate on Remedios Circle	521-4417	$$	D/L	Local	Spanish

NITELIFE	DAY	ADDRESS	PH	PRICE	REC	DRESS	MUSIC
The Blarney Stone	A	115 C. Palanca St., Makati bsmnt. Glass Twr. Bldg.	867-1488	None	H(F)	Kazh	
Café Havana	1	1903 M. Adriatico St., Malate at Remedios Circle	521-8097	None	MP(F)	Local	Cuban
Fat Willy's Bar & Restaurant	A	Unit A, The Fort, Taguig in Fort Bonifacio	555-1208	None	P(F)	Local	Rock, disco
Larry's Bar on the Remedios Circle	1	1911 M. Adriatico St., Malate on Remedios Circle	524-3795	None	M(F)	Local	Jazz, R&B
San Mig	A	Legaspi St., Makati in Greenbelt Park	819-3745	None	H(F)	Kazh	
Tia Maria's Remedios	1	532 Crnr. Madre Ignacia St., Malate	522-0429	None	MOP(F)	Kazh	Rock, disco
Zu	1	Ayala and Makati aves. in Shangri-La hotel	813-8888	None	OP(F)	Local	Disco

SIGHTS & ATTRACTIONS	DAY	ADDRESS	* PH	ENTRY FEE			
Intramuros Visitors Center	2	Baluartillo de San Francisco Javier Fort Santiago	527-2961	$			
Manila American Cemetery and Memorial	1	EDSA, 6 mi. SE of Manila at Fort Bonifacio	844-0212	None			
Pagsanjan Falls	1	62 mi. SE of Manila	524-1969	None			

OTHER SIGHTS, SERVICES & ATTRACTIONS

Rajah Tours Philippines	A	533 United Nations Ave., Physicians' Tower, 3rd fl.	522-0541	$$$$+			
Philippine Dept. of Tourism		T.M. Kalaw St., Ermita	524-1703				
Philippine Dept. of Tourism Boracay Field Office		Balabag	B36 288-3689				
Tourism Office of Kalibo		Kalibo Municipal Hall, 2nd fl.	K36 268-4110				

> ## EVENT & TICKET INFO
>
> **Ati-Atihan Festival** (various locations around Kalibo): All events are free, including the **snakedancing** (Magsaysay Park). The **Torch Parade and Procession** takes place on Kalibo's main streets, beginning at M. Laserna. For more information, contact the *Philippine Department of Tourism* (415-956-4060) in San Francisco.

*B=Boracay, K=Kalibo

RECommendations: (Restaurants) B–Breakfast; L–Lunch; D–Dinner; T–High tea or snack
(Nitelife) G–Gaming; H–Hangout bar; M–Live music; O–Dancing (disco); P–Dancing (live music); S–Show; F–Food served
()–Available but without recommendation. For complete explanation of Hot Sheet format, see page 34.

🕐 NYC +13   ☀ 69°/86° (20°/30°)   ✈ Ninoy Aquino, Manila (MNL); 30 min./$15   🚗 No   👥 Pilipino/Tagalog/
Kalibo (KLO); 30 min./$15   English

The Fun Also Rises

Calle San Sebastián

Origin: 1970   Event ★ ★ ★ ★ City   Attendance: 50,000

Old San Juan is the backdrop to a party every weekend, but the blowout of the year is the *Calle San Sebastián* festival. So few locals skip this party—which takes over San Juan's seven-square-block historical district—that residents either make alternative lodging plans for the weekend or wholeheartedly join in the festivities that wind down just before dawn every morning.

The event schedule varies from year to year, but fun unfolds in a predictable pattern: a parade honoring Puerto Rico's cultural scions kicks off *Calle San Sebastián* and quickly segues into celebratory chaos, much of it tinged by salsa and other Latin music. In the bars and on the sidewalks, bands play everything from merengue to Van Morrison, while throngs shuffle from one end of San Sebastián Street to the other, rum drink in one hand, fingers snapping in the other.

Like most events in Puerto Rico, *San Sebastián* is a showcase for national pride. Fiercely patriotic, Puerto Ricans devote as much attention to celebrating their love of country as to having a raucous time.

Old San Juan's beautifully preserved Spanish colonial architecture—pastel houses, cobblestone streets,

wrought-iron balconies—is the perfect setting for a street party that jams long into the warm evenings. The pounding surf of the Atlantic and the calm ripples of San Juan Bay sandwich the old city, which was built as a fortress by Spanish settlers in 1521 and remains partially enclosed by thick stone walls. Old San Juan is best explored on foot especially in January when temperatures hover at a perfect 70 degrees. T-shirt shops, flocks of pigeons, and massive cruise ships barely detract from the Old World wonder of the city's neat façades, military history, and tree-shaded plazas.

During *Calle San Sebastián*, though, it's the concentration of some of the Caribbean's best nightlife, most fun-loving people, and a world-class party that makes Puerto Rico shimmer late into the night.

Calle San Sebastián

Day 1. Fri. Jan. 21, 2000
(Day 1. Saturday *January 20, 2001)*

9:00am Check into **Hotel El Convento**, former site of a 17th-century Carmelite convent, a brothel, a flop-house, and now a luxury hotel. In the heart of Old San Juan, it's just a block from San Sebastián Street.

10:30am Stop by the tourist information center in **City Hall** for a map of Old San Juan and the most up-to-date information on the festival. Check out the courtyard and staircase of this gorgeous building.

11:00am Head north a block to get first dibs on the hand-carved masks, Puerto Rican paintings, and other items featured at the ***Artisans' Fair*** in the courtyard of the **Museum of Art and History**. The museum is also worth a look.

12:30pm Join San Juan's professional set for a lunch of conch salad, fried plantains, *asopao* (a hearty stew), and other Puerto Rican fare at **La Fonda del Jibarito**. The ambience is set by bright table-cloths, and windows opened onto the noisy side-walk. A more elegant spot for typical fare is **La Mallorquina**.

2:00pm Visit the Spanish empire's most powerful legacy in Puerto Rico—**Castillo San Felipe del Morro**. Known simply as El Morro, this 16th-century fort perches powerfully over the Atlantic Ocean.

4:00pm Lounge by El Convento's small rooftop pool, then head to the second-floor dining terrace for complimentary wine and hors d'oeuvres. Or check out **El Picoteo**, the hotel's terraced *tapas* bar.

6:00pm Stake out a spot on San Sebastián Street for the ***Parade of the Cabezudos***, a music-filled march of local VIPs, musicians, dancers, and cos-tumed revelers who don larger-than-life foam-

rubber masks depicting Puerto Rico's cultural icons. Many Puerto Ricans consider the Cabezudos parade the most significant event of the festival.

9:00pm Find a table at the **Parrot Club**, a wildly popu-lar bar and restaurant that serves nouveau-Latino cuisine amid tropical decor. Favorite dishes include blackened tuna in a dark-rum sauce.

11:00pm Return to ***Calle San Sebastián***, grab a rum with pineapple juice or a Medalla (the locally made beer) from a vendor and squeeze yourself into the throngs of people making their way to ... not neces-sarily anywhere.

Day 2. Sat. Jan. 22, 2000
(Day 3. Monday *January 22, 2001)*

9:00am Order a cup of strong Puerto Rican *café con leche* and a *mallorca* (sweet roll) at the counter of **La Bombonera**, a bustling diner straight out of the 1950s.

10:00am Beyond Old San Juan's cobblestones lies the brilliant green jungle of the Caribbean National Forest (the only rainforest in the U.S. National Park Service), also known as **El Yunque**. Take Route 3 east and turn right on Route 191.

1:00pm Head to azure waters, cheap piña coladas, and fried snacks at Luquillo Beach, five miles past the Route 191 turnoff on Route 3. Luquillo is one of the island's best stretches of palm trees and sand.

5:00pm Back on San Sebastián Street, stroll through the lush gardens of **Casa Blanca**, once the home of the Ponce de León family. Exit the gardens from the gate at Sol Street and walk down the stone steps toward Paseo de la Princesa, a meticulously kept walkway that winds between the thick sand-stone walls and San Juan Bay—this is a good place to watch the sun set over the distant ocean.

7:00pm The revelry continues at **El Patio de Sam**. Dine ℞ on seafood crepes, lobster tail, and local drinks.

8:30pm Dancers in 19th-century costume perform Puerto Rico's national dance at the **Dominican Convent**, a white-domed structure on Plaza San José that was built by Dominican friars in 1523.

11:30pm Cab to **Babylon** in the elegant El San Juan Hotel and Casino in Isla Verde. This popular disco, which attracts a 25-and-up crowd, features international dance music on Saturday night. For merengue, hop to **El Chico Lounge** in the same hotel. Then try your hand in the hotel's elegant **Casino**.

Day 3. Sun.   Jan. 23, 2000
(Day 2. Sunday   January 21, 2001)

9:00am Have coffee at **Kiosko 4 Estaciones** at a table ℞ on the sun-drenched Plaza de Armas. The food here is basic (croissants, muffins), but the people-watching is sublime.

10:00am Tucked between the cruise ships is the small **Old San Juan-Cataño Ferry** terminal. Take the short ride to Cataño, home of the **Bacardi Rum Distillery**. Take the Bacardi tour and enjoy a rum-spiked *limonada*.

Noon Have sandwiches or the lunch buffet in the relaxed ℞ atmosphere of the Wyndham hotel's **Darsenas**.

1:30pm Watch the smooth gait of the grand horses that were once the pride of the Spanish conquistadors at the ***Parade of the Paso Finos***.

4:30pm Settle into a patio chair and frothy tropical drink at **Amanda's Café**. The view of the blue sea and the Castillo de San Cristobal is spectacular.

6:30pm Walk to Quincentenary Plaza to catch the distinctively Puerto Rican sounds of *plena libre*, music built around hand-held percussion instruments.

8:30pm For top-notch nouveau-Caribbean cuisine, try ℞ **Amadeus**, located in the heart of the festival on San Sebastián Street.

10:30pm Around the corner from Amadeus is **El Batey**, a dive covered in graffiti and framed caricatures of distinguished patrons. Fifty-cent pool games and a jukebox stocked with the Stones and Elvis make El Batey a second home to many American mainlanders living in Puerto Rico.

Midnight Cab to Santurce and check out **Egipto**, a thriving discotheque with techno and pop music and a dressed-to-the-nines 20- and 30-something crowd. The tourist districts of Condado and Isla Verde offer more good nightlife. With its starry ceiling and domed roof, **Area 51** is, as your whole visit to San Juan, like a night out in another world.

Alternatives

Within walking distance of ***Calle San Sebastián*** is the imposing pink **Wyndham Old San Juan Hotel and Casino**, a luxury accommodation with bay or city views. If you don't mind driving or plan to spend extra time at the beach, your top choices are the new **Ritz-Carlton San Juan Hotel & Casino** (near the airport) or the **Hyatt Dorado Beach Resort Hotel** (20 minutes outside San Juan).

Il Perugino serves excellent traditional Italian dishes. Condado is about a 15 minute drive from Old San Juan and has some good restaurant choices. The gourmet Spanish cuisine at **Ramiro's** is worth the trip. **Ajili Mójili** is a pleasant bistro where the house sauce of tomatoes, fresh herbs and garlic goes well with anything from shrimp to *yautía* dumplings. Another good Condado choice is the sophisticated **Urdin**, which serves seafood paella and enormous steaks. For a big breakfast, join San Juan's trendy set at **Village Bake Shop**.

The Hot Sheet

☎ US/787

$ U.S. Dollar

HOTELS	DAY	ADDRESS	PH	PRICE	FX	RMS	BEST ROOMS
Hotel El Convento	1	100 Cristo St.	723-9020 800- 468-2779	$$$$	721-2877	58	Rm 508
Hyatt Dorado Beach Resort Hotel	A	Rd. 693, Dorado	796-1234 800- 233-1234	$$$$+	796-2022	262	Beach level
Ritz-Carlton San Juan Hotel & Casino	A	6961 Ave. of the Govenors	253-1700 800- 241-3333	$$$$+	253-1777	419	Ocean vw
Wyndham Old San Juan Hotel and Casino	A	100 Brumbaugh St.	721-5100 800- 996-3426	$$$$	721-1111	240	Top fl rms w/ city vw

RESTAURANTS	DAY	ADDRESS	PH	PRICE	REC	DRESS	FOOD
Ajili Mójili	A	1052 Ashford Ave.	725-9195	$$$	LD	Yuppie	Puerto Rican
Amadeus	3	106 San Sebastián St.	722-8635	$$$	D/L	Yuppie	International, Puerto Rican, seafood
Darsenas	3	see Wyndham hotel	721-5100	$$	L/BD	Local	International, Latin
El Patio de Sam	2	102 San Sebastián St.	723-1149	$$	D/L	Local	Seafood
El Picoteo	1	see Hotel El Convento	643-1597	$$	T/LD	Euro	Spanish, tapas
Il Perugino	A	105 Cristo St.	722-5481	$$$	D	Kazh	Traditional Italian
Kiosko 4 Estaciones	3	Pl. de Armas	no phone	$	B/LT	Local	Coffee, pastries
La Bombonera	2	259 San Francisco St.	722-0658	$	B/LD	Local	Puerto Rican
La Fonda del Jibarito	1	280 Sol St.	725-8375	$	L/D	Kazh	Puerto Rican
La Mallorquina	1	207 San Justo St.	722-3261	$$	L/D	Kazh	Puerto Rican
Parrot Club	1	363 Fortaleza St.	725-7370	$$$	D/L	Yuppie	Nuvo Latino
Ramiro's	A	1106 Magdalena Ave.	721-9056	$$$	L/D	Kazh	Spanish gourmet, international
Urdin	A	1105 Magdalena Ave.	724-0420	$$	LD	Euro	International, Spanish
Village Bake Shop	A	105 De Diego Ave.	724-8566	$	B/T	Kazh	American

NITELIFE	DAY	ADDRESS	PH	PRICE	REC	DRESS	MUSIC
Amanda's Café	3	424 Norzagaray St.	722-0187	$$	HF	Local	
Area 51	3	1290 Isla Verde Ave.	728-3780	$	O	Kazh	Disco
Babylon	2	see Casino	791-1000	$	O	Dressy	Dance
Casino	2	6063 Isla Verde Ave. in El San Juan Hotel	791-1000	None	G	Kazh	Casino
Egipto	3	1 Roberto H. Todd Ave.	725-4664	$	O	Euro	Techno, house
El Batey	3	101 Cristo St.	no phone	None	H	FAB	
El Chico Lounge	2	see Casino	791-1000	None	MP	Euro	Latin, oldies

SIGHTS & ATTRACTIONS	DAY	ADDRESS	PH	ENTRY FEE
Bacardi Rum Distillery	3	intersection of Rte. 165 and Rte. 888	788-1500	None
Casa Blanca	2	1 San Sebastián St. Final	724-4102	$
Castillo San Felipe del Morro	1	Norzagaray St.	729-6960	$
City Hall	1	Pl. de Armas	724-7171	None
Dominican Convent	2	98 Norzagaray St.	722-3526	None
El Yunque	2	Rte. 191	no phone	$
Museum of Art and History	1	150 Norzagaray St.	724-1875	None

OTHER SIGHTS, SERVICES & ATTRACTIONS

Old San Juan-Cataño Ferry	3	Pier 2	788-1155	$
Centro de Información		La Casita, Marina St. (near Pier 1)	722-1709	

EVENT & TICKET INFO

Calle San Sebastián (San Sebastián Street, Old San Juan): All events are free. For more information, contact the *Tourism Company of Puerto Rico* (800-866-5829).

RECommendations: (Restaurants) B–Breakfast; L–Lunch; D–Dinner; T–High tea or snack
(Nitelife) G–Gaming; H–Hangout bar; M–Live music; O–Dancing (disco); P–Dancing (live music); S–Show; F–Food served
()–Available but without recommendation. For complete explanation of Hot Sheet format, see page 34.

NYC +1   70°/80° (21°/26°)   Luis Munoz Marin (SJU); 30 min./$15   Yes/No   Spanish

Hong Kong, China

Hong Kong Chinese New Year

Origin: 1996	Event ★ ★ ★ ★ City	Attendance: 25,000

Most of us recognize fireworks and red banners as hallmarks of **Chinese New Year** celebrations, but since when have samba dancing and NFL cheerleaders been part of the act? Since 1996, when some of China's largest corporations began sponsoring New Year celebrations in Hong Kong. Traditionally a family-oriented holiday, the lunar new year in late January or early February has fast become a major festival, with Western touches showing up even in the traditional but spectacular **New Year parade**.

To start out the year right, Hong Kongers gather for family feasts and eat symbolic foods such as abalone (abundance), oysters (good business), and mushrooms (opportunity). But after family obligations have been satisfied, celebrants in this cosmopolitan center take to the streets for a quirky and often hilarious cross-cultural potpourri. To drive away evil spirits, an impressive fireworks display explodes above Victoria Harbour. To bring out partyers, carnival-style music, dance, and food "fiestas" have been added. Even with the new activities, the traditional **Chinese New Year Parade** remains the most fun event, with colorful lanterns, floats, dragon dances, bands, costumed performers, jugglers, and acrobats entertaining the crowds.

The lunar new year presents the perfect excuse to visit Hong Kong, a place that even on a typical day is a swirl of activity and contrasts: skyscrapers and shacks, shopping malls and dim sum carts. You can sample the finest Peking duck (yes, it's better here than in Beijing), ride a tram for dramatic views above the city, and take the Star Ferry to Kowloon to browse through the bustling commercial district.

Great Britain returned Hong Kong to the People's Republic of China in 1997, but the city of six million remains a safe and exotic destination where making money is still at the center of everyday life. In February, it's hardly ironic when local merchants greet Western tourists with the traditional **Chinese New Year** greeting—*Kung hei fat choy!*—which means "Congratulations on being rich."

Hong Kong Chinese New Year

Day 1. Fri.   Feb. 4, 2000
(Day 1. Tuesday   January 23, 2001)

9:00am Upon arriving in Hong Kong, shuttle to **The Regent**, an elegant, modern hotel with spectacular harbor views.

10:00am Adjacent to your hotel is the **Hong Kong Museum of Art**. Its six galleries exhibit vast collections of Chinese antiquities and fine art.

12:30pm Walk a short distance up Nathan Road to the chic and contemporary **Avenue Restaurant & Bar** in the Holiday Inn Golden Mile. The menu includes dishes such as Scottish lobster risotto with leeks, ginger, and coriander.

2:00pm Stroll along the Waterfront Promenade, taking in awe-inspiring sights of the bustling harbor filled with boats, ferries, cargo ships, and traditional Chinese wooden junks.

3:30pm Join the throngs at the massive *Flower Market* in Victoria Park. Shop for peonies, which symbolize prosperity. Plum blossoms and branches of peach trees signify good luck.

5:00pm Have predinner cocktails in The Regent's **Lobby Lounge**. Armani-clad and Chanel-scented couples gather here for the breathtaking views.

7:00pm Dine in the hotel's contemporary seafood restaurant, **Yü**, for dinner. You can watch the beautiful fish in the huge aquarium while enjoying their tasty brethren.

9:00pm For after-dinner drinks, move to the hotel's **Club Shanghai**, which is modeled after a 1930s-style opium den.

11:00pm Taxi to Lan Kwai Fong, an area filled with bistros, jazz clubs, restaurants, and bars. The small,

glitzy **Club 97** has Moroccan decor. The perpetually crowded **Sherman's Bar & Grill** serves drinks and *tapas* into the early morning. Or go to the nearby **Fringe Club**, which caters to Hong Kong's artsy crowd.

Day 2. Sat.   Feb. 5, 2000
(Day 2. Wednesday   January 24, 2001)

8:00am In the **Harbour Side Coffeeshop** at The Regent, enjoy an early breakfast of *jook*, a rice congee soup topped with minced green onion, ginger, and perhaps a thousand-year-old egg.

9:30am Visit the active Taoist **Wong Tai Sin Temple** in New Kowloon. A small fee gets you into the Good Wish Gardens, an area filled with fortunetellers.

10:30am Make the required pilgrimage to Victoria Peak for breathtaking views of the city. Take the free shuttle at the Star Ferry terminal to the **Peak Tram Station** on Garden Road for the eight-minute ride up the hill.

11:00am Stroll around the peak on Lugard and Harlech roads. Check out some of the mansions that make Victoria Peak one of Hong Kong's most fashionable residential areas. Have lunch at the popular **Peak Café**.

2:00pm The always-vibrant *Chinese New Year Parade* on Hong Kong Island will be extravagant for the new millennium. Floats from the four corners of the world will navigate the tight streets. Typical entertainment in past years has included samba dancers from Brazil, cheerleaders from Seattle, and mounted policemen from Canada.

4:00pm Join several of the most lavish floats at the gaily decorated Centenary Garden in Tsim Sha Tsui for the *Chinese New Year Fiesta*. Stay for the food stalls, craft booths, and cultural acts.

5:30pm Stop for live music and a drink at **Someplace Else**, a popular restaurant, bar, and disco.

7:00pm Have dinner at **Vong**, a lively, crowded spot for
Ⓡ people-watching and sublime food—try the *foie gras* with ginger and mango.

9:00pm Get on the world's longest escalator at Central Market (between Des Voeux and Queen's roads) and exit at SoHo (South of Hollywood Road), an up-and-coming restaurant area. Have a drink at **Staunton's Bar & Café**. Then taxi to **Joe Bananas**, a yuppiefied spot for locals and expats, who drink cocktails until all the tables are pushed back to make a dance floor.

Day 3. Sun.   Feb. 6, 2000
(Day 3. Thursday   January 25, 2001)

10:00am Begin your day with the delicious interna-
Ⓡ tional champagne brunch at **The Verandah** (inside The Peninsula hotel).

11:30am Have your concierge arrange a junk cruise to Hong Kong's largest island, Lantau. The 90-minute trip out will give you a chance to take in the mountainous scenery.

1:00pm Walk to the picturesque **Po Lin Buddhist Monastery** to see the world's largest outdoor bronze Buddha. The lotus motif—the name Po Lin means "precious lotus"—symbolizes the ability of every
Ⓡ person to attain enlightenment. Join the stream of diners for a vegetarian lunch at the monastery.

5:00pm To experience a complete 180, head to Hong Kong's Lower Nathan Road, also called The Golden Mile, which boasts shops filled with treasures from around Asia. You are now in the biggest Chinatown in the world!

7:00pm Before the fireworks begin, dine at **Lai Ching
Ⓡ Heen**, The Regent's acclaimed Cantonese restaurant. The menu changes every month, but the quality stays consistently high.

9:00pm The Regent provides the most spectacular views of the *Lunar Fireworks Display*. Guests are invited onto the hotel's private terrace or a terraced suite to watch the magnificent display. A more plebeian experience can be had on crowded Victoria Peak.

Midnight Cross the street to the Phillipe Starck-designed **Felix** disco and restaurant on the 28th floor of The Peninsula. Dance your way into a lucky new year high above the bustle of Hong Kong, the City of Life.

Alternatives

The **Peninsula** hotel, with its throne shape, is a Hong Kong landmark and an ode to more luxurious colonial times. The excellent **Mandarin Oriental** is situated on Hong Kong Island. Also on Hong Kong Island is the **Island Shangri-La**—the sterile exterior hides a posh interior.

Spring **Deer** is popular for an early lunch and well-known for its Peking Duck, or, to be politically correct, Beijing Duck. **Peking Garden Restaurant** at the Star House in Tsim Sha Tsui is excellent for Chinese food—try the diced chicken in chili sauce with two kinds of vegetables. Famous for high tea, **The Lobby** in The Peninsula serves scones, pastries, and finger sandwiches on real Tiffany china. For great dim sum at breakfast or lunch, head to **Luk Yu Tea House**.

SHOP TALK

For couples who argue over how to spend their time—shopping versus having fun—*Chinese New Year* in Hong Kong settles the argument. Virtually all shops in the city close for three days. If you're one of the many who go to Hong Kong for the singular purpose of shopping, however, there's good news—most items go on sale right before the holiday. Stanley Village Market (Stanley Market Road, Stanley, Hong Kong Island), the Night Market (Temple Street, Kowloon), and Nathan Road's Golden Mile are good places for shopping as well as sightseeing.

The Hot Sheet

☎ 852/2

$ 7.8 Hong Kong Dollar

HOTELS	DAY	ADDRESS	PH	PRICE	FX	RMS	BEST ROOMS
Island Shangri-La	A	Supreme Court Rd., 2 Pacific Pl., Central	877-3838 800- 942-5050	$$$$	521-8742	565	Harbor vw
Mandarin Oriental	A	5 Connaught Rd., Central	522-0111 800- 526-6566	$$$$	810-6190	542	Dlx harbor vw
The Peninsula	A	Salisbury Rd., Tsim Sha Tsui, Kowloon	366-6251 800- 223-6800	$$$$	722-4170	300	Dlx harbor vw
The Regent	1	18 Salisbury Rd., Tsim Sha Tsui, Kowloon	721-1211 800- 545-4000	$$$$+	739-4546	508	Supr harbor vw

RESTAURANTS	DAY	ADDRESS	PH	PRICE	REC	DRESS	FOOD
Avenue Restaurant & Bar	1	50 Nathan Rd. inside Holiday Inn Golden Mile	315-1118	$$$	L	Kazh	Modern European
Harbour Side Coffeeshop	2	see The Regent hotel	721-1211	$$	B/LD	Local	International, continental
Lai Ching Heen	3	see The Regent hotel	721-1211	$$$	D/L	Euro	Cantonese
Luk Yu Tea House	A	26 Stanley St.	523-5464	$$	BL	Local	Dim Sum
Peak Café	2	121 Peak Rd.	849-7868	$$	L/BTD	Local	International, Asian
Peking Garden Restaurant	A	227 Nathan Rd.	730-1315	$	LD	Local	North Chinese
Spring Deer	A	42 Mody Rd., 1st fl.	366-4012	$$	LD	Local	North Chinese
The Lobby	A	see The Peninsula hotel	315-3069	$$	T	Euro	Tea
The Verandah	3	see The Peninsula hotel	315-3166	$$$$	B/L	Euro	Brunch
Vong	2	see Mandarin Oriental hotel	522-0111	$$$	D/L	Euro	Contemporary French, fusion
Yü	1	see The Regent hotel	721-1211	$$$$+	D	Euro	Seafood

NITELIFE	DAY	ADDRESS	PH	PRICE	REC	DRESS	MUSIC
Club 97	1	8-11 Lan Kwai Fong, ground fl.	186-1819	$$	O	Kazh	Techno, dance
Club Shanghai	1	see The Regent hotel	721-1211	None	HF	Euro	
Felix	3	see The Peninsula hotel	315-3155	$$	HOF	Euro	Easy listening, disco
Fringe Club	1	2 Lower Albert Rd., South Block	521-7251	None	H	Kazh	
Joe Bananas	2	23 Luard Rd., Wan Chai	529-1811	$$	O	Yuppie	Disco, dance
Lobby Lounge	1	see The Regent hotel	721-1211	None	HM(F)	Euro	Piano bar
Sherman's Bar & Grill	1	34-36 D'Aguilar St., Central	801-4946	None	HF	Kazh	
Someplace Else	2	20 Nathan Rd. in Sheraton hotel	369-1111	None	HOP	Kazh	Easy listening, Latin, dance
Staunton's Bar & Café	2	10-12 Staunton St.	973-6611	None	H(F)	Kazh	

SIGHTS & ATTRACTIONS	DAY	ADDRESS	PH	ENTRY FEE
Hong Kong Museum of Art	1	10 Salisbury Rd. next to Cultural Centre	734-2167	$
Po Lin Buddhist Monastary	3	on Lantau island	985-5426	None
Wong Tai Sin Temple	2	2 Chuckyuen Village, New Kowloon near Wong Tai Sin station	327-8141	$

OTHER SIGHTS, SERVICES & ATTRACTIONS

Peak Tram Station	2	33 Garden Rd., Central	522-0922	$
Hong Kong Visitor Information and Services Centre		Shop 8, Jardine House, Connaught Pl., Central	508-1234	

EVENT & TICKET INFO

Chinese New Year (Hong Kong): All events are free, but bleacher seats ($20) can be purchased for the **parade** (along the waterfront in the Wan Chai district). For more information, contact the *Hong Kong Tourist Association* in New York (212-421-3382).

REcommendations: (Restaurants) B–Breakfast; L–Lunch; D–Dinner; T–High tea or snack
(Nitelife) G–Gaming; H–Hangout bar; M–Live music; O–Dancing (disco); P–Dancing (live music); S–Show; F–Food served
()–Available but without recommendation. For complete explanation of Hot Sheet format, see page 34.

NYC +13   55°/63° (13°/17°)   Hong Kong (HKG); 45 min./$20   No   Cantonese/Mandarin/English

Zermatt, Switzerland

Skiing Zermatt

(The Most Fun Place to Ski: Europe)

Ticktock becomes clip-clop as fun-seekers forget time and settle into this hip but quaint part of Switzerland. **Zermatt** is a Swiss masterpiece that combines a picturesque mountain village, superb snow conditions, one of the longest skiing seasons in the Alps, and lively nightlife. Europe's most fun winter playground, the town has everything that makes a ski resort elite: luxurious lodges, fine restaurants, fashionable boutiques, nonstop nightlife, and exceptional ski facilities.

Switzerland's southernmost ski resort also owes part of its international fame to the Matterhorn. The snaggletoothed 14,690-foot tower is visible from anywhere in **Zermatt**, but the best time to see it is just after dawn, when soft backlighting makes this mass of rock a thing of beauty.

Despite its well-deserved reputation as a chic winter resort, **Zermatt** has retained its original storybook charm. In this century-old mountain village, few streets have names, signs point the way to various hotels and restaurants, and you can walk from one end of town to the other in 15 minutes. Horse-drawn sleighs, oompah bands, yodelers, cozy chalets, and weathered farmhouses provide atmosphere. The only way in or out of town is by train—all motor vehicles must be parked three miles away in Tasch.

Zermatt (most travelers arrive via Geneva) has another advantage over most European resorts. With a base elevation of 5,312 feet, the place is celebrated for its consistently heavy snowfall. While the peak season is December-April, glacial skiing continues into summer.

The area also has downhill, cross-country, and heli-skiing, para-gliding, snowshoeing, curling, ice-skating, sleigh riding, helicopter rides, and indoor tennis and squash. Exhibits at an alpine museum range from Roman artifacts to the equipment used in 1865 by English explorer Edward Whymper when he became the first person to reach the Matterhorn summit. Once the lifts close, the village's 118 hotels and 110 restaurants and bars get crowded and **Zermatt** opens its doors to everyone—skier or not—in search of cosmopolitan parties and the universal urge for fun.

Skiing Zermatt

Hotels

The exquisite **Hotel Monte Rosa**—named for the nearby 14,937-foot peak—has crackling fireplaces, thick rugs, and antique armchairs in the lobby, and rooms decorated with Victorian prints and cabinetry. If you seek no-limits luxury, the historic **Grand Hotel Zermatterhof** (built in 1879) excels with tasteful paneled bedrooms, granite or marble bathrooms, a solarium, pool, and fitness center. The **Hotel Alex** appeals to die-hard skiers—most of its rooms have vistas of the spectacular snow-covered mountains that surround the village. The **Hotel Mont Cervin** has sunny, spacious rooms and picks up guests in a horse-drawn sleigh at the *Bahnhof* (rail station). Its gala dinner each Friday is a popular black-tie affair.

Restaurants

Fondue, raclette, and grilled meats are among the alpine and regional Swiss selections offered at most restaurants.

The elegant **Grillroom**, known for its Italian and Swiss cuisine, is the better of the two restaurants in the Hotel Walliserhof. The street-side restaurant is located in a red-shuttered, balconied building that once was a local farmhouse. More chic, with an alpine decor that includes a stained-glass mural and carved paneling, the **Alex Grill** in the Hotel Alex specializes in rack of lamb, seasonal game, and seafood. The **Tenne Grill** in the Alex Schlosshotel Tenne, also known for its grilled specialties, offers a wide variety of other creative dishes and herb-flavored soups, perfect for wintry evenings. Not to be outdone, **Le Mazot** serves some of the town's tastiest lamb dishes in a rustic, pine-paneled dining room. French and Italian wines are readily available, but the quality and refined taste of many Swiss white wines are a delightful surprise to many visitors. Be sure to sample a few.

Nightlife

Aprés-ski action begins as soon as the lifts close. Many skiers head for a village pastry shop for hot chocolate, tea, or strudel, then sit by a window from 4-6 p.m. to watch crowds stroll past. It's the prime time for jet-set women from South America and Europe to parade through the village in full-length chinchilla and mink coats.

Elsie's Place has long been the village's most pretentious after-skiing watering hole. Irish Coffee—with 80-proof schnapps—is the beverage of choice among the crowds that pack into Elsie's, a refurbished house built in 1879. Not quite as spirited are the hotel bars: **Alex's** in the Hotel Alex; the art nouveau **Tenne-Bar** at the Alex Schlosshotel Tenne; **Daddy's Corner** in the Hotel Bristol; the **Lunar Bar** at the Excelsior Hotel; and the Hotel Monte Rosa's **Montrose Bar**. Try *café fertig*, a local favorite made with coffee and 80-proof schnapps and topped with thick whipped cream.

The intense after-dark fun includes discos; live country, jazz, and rock music; tea dancing; and Swiss folklore performances in local nightclubs. Zermatt's nightlife headquarters is the Hotel Post, whose varied venues include two of the most fun in town—Deep Purple has performed at **Le Village Disco**, built in a 19th-century barn, while a piano-bar/jazz-club ambience is the attraction at **The Pink Elephant**. Bar stools have cowhide seats in **Alex Dancing**, the Hotel Alex's classy disco with a DJ, circular dance floor, and flashing klieg lights. There's plenty of action, but the sound is turned down slightly so you can carry on a conversation.

Ski slopes

Zermatt offers superb downhill schussing for every class of skier. Perpendicular drop-offs as steep as elevator shafts appeal to experts, but nearly half the 153 miles of marked runs cater to intermediate and novice skiers. As in most of the Alps, the vast majority of skiing in Zermatt takes place in open snowfields above the tree line, and many of the slopes are as broad and gentle as football fields.

Three major alpine playgrounds surround Zermatt: Sunnegga, Gornergrat, and Klein (little) Matterhorn. All are connected in a remarkable ski circus by 74 lifts that include cable cars, gondolas, chair lifts, T-bars, Europe's highest open-air railway, and a cable railway that roars under the snow like a subway. Impressive, too, is a single run that takes in 7,221 feet of vertical drop—longer than anything in North America—from the Klein Matterhorn into town. From the latter peak on a clear day, skiers can enjoy a panorama of the Italian and French Alps.

Skiers interested in more than snow are pampered by a remarkable matrix of 38 mountain restaurants, where taste buds are tantalized by all kinds of soups, sausages, fondues, dumplings, raclettes, pastas, trout, and air-dried regional meats. Not only is the restaurant **Kulm Gornergrat** exceptional, its midmountain site offers a vista of the 29 major peaks that ring the resort.

Skiing into Italy

Pure fun and good for lots of bragging back home is skiing across the border from Switzerland into Italy. After riding a series of cable cars to the 12,533-foot summit of the Klein Matterhorn, there's an intermediate run into the land of pasta, prosciutto, and Parmesan cheese. You can stop at midmountain for lunch or ski the entire seven miles into the resort village of Cervinia. But don't tarry too long. A sudden change in the weather or excessive winds occasionally shut down the Italian cable cars, leaving skiers stranded for a night in Italy. As a precaution, carry your passport, traveler's checks, and a lift ticket that's good on the Cervinia lifts. The Italian side of the Matterhorn is called Monte Cervino.

FIVE OTHER FUN SKI DESTINATIONS IN EUROPE

Après-ski fun was invented by the Europeans, whose winter resorts, for the most part, are bigger and much older than the average American ski area. A classic is France's very chic **Courchevel 1850**. It's not only the gateway to The Three Valleys (*Les Trois Vallees*), an incredible complex with 202 lifts linking nine resorts and 200 miles of marked runs, but to hotels, dining, dancing, and world-class classical-music concerts. Serious partying at French resorts doesn't usually begin until midnight.

Kitzbuehel has long been a premier Austrian hotspot, where *Jagertee*—tea blended with 180-proof Austrian Stroh rum— kicks off the evening with a wallop. In the town's casino, you can gamble or dance in a glitzy disco until 4 a.m.

Like Zermatt, charming **Saas-Fee** is a car-free village of narrow streets, small hotels, chalets, and friendly Swiss—some of whom enjoy coed nude saunas. The best hotel is Walliserhof, which has live bands in its nightclub. Smaller than Zermatt, Saas-Fee is ringed by 18 peaks that are 13,000 feet or higher. Skiing is focused in four areas—the most exciting lift is a speedy midmountain train that operates beneath a glacier.

The 800-year-old village of **Madonna di Campiglio** in the Dolomite Alps is special because it hasn't been tainted by hordes of foreigners or fast-food restaurants. You can experience true Italian culture as well as a tremendous ski area serviced by 26 lifts. The food is *mama mia* delicious in 41 restaurants and pizzerias and the fun is centered in discos.

Val d'Isere is a megaresort in the Savoie Alps. Unlike many European resorts, most slopes are a haven for intermediate skiers. The town has 27,000 pillows, 66 restaurants, 12 nightspots, an 11th-century church, and more than 100 lifts, including several beginner lifts that are free to everyone.

General Information Numbers:

Courcheval Tourist Office	33/47-908-0029
Madonna di Campiglio Tourist Office	39/046-544-2000
Kitzbuehel Tourist Office	43/535-662-1550
Saas-Fee Tourist Office	41/27-958-1858
Val d'Isere Tourist Office	33/47-906-0660

The Hot Sheet

☎ 41/27

$ 1.5 Swiss Franc

HOTELS	ADDRESS	PH	PRICE	FX	RMS	BEST ROOMS
Grand Hotel Zermatterhof		966-6600	$$$$+	966-6699	86	Dlx, Matterhorn vw
Hotel Alex		966-7070	$$$$+	966-7090	75	South-facing
Hotel Mont Cervin		966-8888 800- 223-6800	$$$$+	966-2878	143	SW crnr residence
Hotel Monte Rosa		967-3333 800- 223-6800	$$$$+	967-1160	47	Dlx, Matterhorn vw

RESTAURANTS	ADDRESS	PH	PRICE	REC	DRESS	FOOD
Alex Grill	in Hotel Alex	966-7070	$$$	LD	Euro	International
Grillroom	in Hotel Walliserhof	966-6555	$$$	LD	Euro	Italian, Swiss
Kulm Gornergrat	in Kulm Hotel, Gornergrat	966-6400	$$$	L	Local	Swiss
Le Mazot		967-2777	$$$	D	Local	French
Tenne Grill	in Alex Schlosshotel Tenne	967-1801	$$$$	D	Euro	International

NITELIFE	ADDRESS	PH	PRICE	REC	DRESS	MUSIC
Alex Dancing	in Hotel Alex	966-7070	None	O(F)	Kazh	Disco
Alex's	in Hotel Alex	966-7070	None	H(F)	Kazh	
Daddy's Corner	in Hotel Bristol	966-3366	None	M(F)	Kazh	Pop, rock
Elsie's Place	Church Sq.	967-2431	None	H(F)	Local	
Le Village Disco	in Hotel Post	967-1932	None	P(F)	Local	Disco
Lunar Bar	in Excelsior Hotel	966-3500	None	M	Kazh	Pop, rock
Montrose Bar	in Hotel Monte Rosa	967-3333	None	H(F)	Euro	
The Pink Elephant	in Hotel Post	967-1932	None	MP(F)	Kazh	Jazz
Tenne-Bar	in Alex Schlosshotel Tenne	967-1801	None	H(F)	Euro	

Zermatt Tourist Office		967-0181				

GETTING TO ZERMATT

Zermatt is approximately four hours by train from the Geneva airport, five hours from Zurich. Trains leave directly from the airports about every hour, and you can check luggage and skis straight through from your airport of origin. For rail information, contact *Rail Europe* (800-438-7245). Driving saves about 30 minutes, but you'll be less able to enjoy the scenery and you can't take your vehicle into Zermatt. (You must park in Tasch and take a train or taxi from there.)

Since street names and numbers clash with Zermatt's small-village feel, there are none. In town, road signs point the way.

RECommendations: (Restaurants) B–Breakfast; L–Lunch; D–Dinner; T–High tea or snack
(Nitelife) G–Gaming; H–Hangout bar; M–Live music; O–Dancing (disco); P–Dancing (live music); S–Show; F–Food served
( )–Available but without recommendation. For complete explanation of Hot Sheet format, see page 34.

NYC +6 ☀ 32°/40° (0°/4°) ✈ Geneva (GVA); 180 min./SNA 🚗 No 🗣 Swiss German

Viña del Mar Song Festival

(International Song Festival of Viña del Mar)

Origin: 1959   Event ★★★★★ City   **Attendance: 110,000**

Not many music festivals share a history that includes The Police, Julio Inglesias, and the Backstreet Boys—but then again, not many have as much going for them as the *International Song Festival of Viña del Mar*. This wildly popular event (more than 300 million watch on TV) is considered by many to be the best Latin music festival in the world and the hottest venue for up-and-coming groups to shine in the international spotlight.

For six days each summer, this sleepy beachside town absorbs an exuberant crowd of 20,000 people (affectionately called "The Monster") that swarms through its tree-lined streets, quaint cafes, and discos. The mass of revelers infuses the city with the high spirits and nonstop energy of any good South American fiesta.

Festivities take place in an open-air amphitheater on the manicured grounds of the Quinta Vergara. An extensive lineup of hopeful amateurs, current celebs, and music-biz veterans share the stage to celebrate the songs of the Americas. Many soon-to-be-popular acts, such as Ricky Martin, have enthralled the throngs of fans at *Viña* festivals of the past. The quality of performances is always high.

Before heading to the beautiful Chilean coast, spend some time in the nation's capital of Santiago, a city of European architecture, fascinating museums, and bohemian enclaves.

A short drive from Viña del Mar (known as the "vineyard of the sea") sits Valparaíso, a lovely port town built into the coastal hills. A labyrinth of narrow streets winds through the town's carefully preserved colonial buildings and widens onto quaint terraces with panoramic views.

Professionals in the tourist industry say, "Adventure-travel in Chile, party in Argentina." But once a year, during the Southern Hemisphere's summer months and the *Viña Song Fest*, the hottest musical event south of the equator makes everything possible —including a party that doesn't end till the llamas come home.

Viña del Mar Song Festival

Day 1. Sat.　Feb. 19, 2000
(Day 1. Saturday　　　February 10, 2001)

8:00am Wake up at the elegant **Hyatt Regency**, located in the upscale Santiago neighborhood of Las Condes. Here you'll find excellent service and sleek rooms with nice views and private terraces.

9:00am Wander through the tree-lined streets of Bellavista, a charming neighborhood full of small cafes, fashionable restaurants, and residential homes. Take the funicular to the top of Cerro San Cristóbal for magnificent views of the city and the giant statue of the Virgin Mary.

1:00pm Ride the bus down the mountain for lunch at **La Esquina al Jerez**, a crowded Spanish-style restaurant with legs of ham hanging from the ceiling and a lively atmosphere.

2:30pm Head downtown to a majestic neoclassical building called La Moneda. Used as a royal mint in colonial times, La Moneda was the site of Chilean president Salvador Allende's last stand against the violent coup of 1973. Cross the street to the Plaza de la Constitución. The large square, bordered by government buildings, sits just above the giant bunker built by General Pinochet during his dictatorial reign. Cut over to La Ahumada, the wide pedestrian street that's always active.

4:00pm Watch passersby as they stroll among the gardens of the Plaza de Armas, where street artists display paintings, musicians play for tips, and a parade of Santiaguinos marches by. Three blocks from the plaza stands the **Museo Chileno de Arte Precolombino**. After a quick look at its display of pre-Columbian arts and crafts, make your way to the indigenous art fair at Cerro Santa Lucía. Interwoven plazas and gardens line the winding pathways to the summit. At the top, take in the sunset and a 360-degree view of Santiago.

8:00pm Have dinner at **Aquí Está Coco** in Providencia, a trendy neighborhood for young professionals. One of the most popular restaurants in Santiago, this creative eatery has the best fish and shellfish in the city.

10:00pm Hop around the noisy, upbeat bars of Providencia. **El Club** is always fun and friendly.

Day 2. Sun.　Feb. 20, 2000
(Day 2. Sunday　　　February 11, 2001)

9:00am Order room service and enjoy the sight from your terrace.

10:00am Take off for the shady Parque Forestal along the Mapocho River and walk to the **Museo Nacional de Bellas Artes**. This fantastic museum, styled after the Petit Palais in Paris, houses a permanent collection of Italian, French, Dutch, and Chilean paintings.

Noon Have lunch across the river at **El Venezia**, where television celebrities mingle with regular folk over cold beer and grilled meats.

2:00pm Drive to Valparaíso and stroll through this charming port town. Start at the Congress building, which houses the Chilean senate and Lower House. Next, take a look into the soul of Chile by visiting **La Sebastiana** museum, a former home of the Nobel Prize-winning Chilean poet Pablo Neruda.

5:30pm By car, explore back streets and hillside neighborhoods, eventually arriving at **Cafe Turri**, one of Valparaíso's finest restaurants. Have a glass (or bottle) of Chilean wine with dinner. The view of the harbor is excellent.

8:00pm After dinner, set out for Viña del Mar. Check into the worn-down but classic European-style **Hotel O'Higgins**.

9:00pm Walk five minutes to the Quinta Vergara for the ***International Song Festival***. Buy a glowing light from a souvenir vendor to use later in a giant human "wave," and enjoy a show that encourages audience participation. Each night there's a perfor-mance of two of the ten songs competing for the best international song, along with a short dance presentation, a comedian, and two or three big-name acts. After the festivities are over, the O'Higgins is the official party hotel of the festival.

Day 3. Mon.   Feb. 21, 2000
(Day 3. Monday   February 12, 2001)

9:00am After breakfast at the hotel, take a carriage ride around Viña del Mar. Stop at the cultural cen-ter, **Palacio Carrasco**, where the paintings of Dalí, Miró, and Chilean surrealist Roberto Matta have been featured.

Noon Have lunch at **Delicias del Mar**. They serve a wide variety of fish and shellfish, with Chilean twists.

2:00pm Walk through the **Museo Arqueológico Fonk**, which features an important collection of artifacts from indigenous Chilean cultures including Easter Island's Rapa Nui.

4:00pm If you're not drawn to the beach, drive along the coast toward the Abarca fishing launch, where you'll find Wulff Castle perched on a rocky crag over the sea. Proceed up Avenida Marina to the Presidential Palace, a small gray castle where the sitting Chilean president vacations in the summer. Set above the water below is the Hotel Cap Ducal—its architec-ture is meant to suggest a boat at sea.

6:00pm End the afternoon on the Vergara Pier, a fishing spot known for its lively collection of restaurants and bars. The **Cristóforo Restaurant**, located on the pier, has excellent seafood.

8:00pm Make your way back to the Quinta Vergara to cheer on your favorite competitors and groove to the hottest Latin groups at the ***International Song Festival***. After the show, return to the hotel for more all-night festivities. Party until first light hits the unfamiliar stars of the southern sky.

Alternatives

In Santiago, the **Hotel Kennedy** offers first-class amenities. The chic **Hotel Plaza San Francisco** has an art gallery in the basement. The **Hotel Regal Pacific** is a modern tower building with a timeless elegance. In Viña del Mar, the **Hotel Oceanic** overlooks the surf along the rocky coast. The centrally located **Hotel Alcazar** provides mod-ern facilities with traditional decor.

In Santiago, sample the exquisite cuisine served in the Hyatt Regency's **Anakena**, a cheerful Thai restaurant that offers creative, spicy dishes. Or try dinner at the innovative **Balthazar Restaurant**—this highly acclaimed bistro is housed in a restored adobe stable and features an elaborate buffet of continental cuisine with flavors from Asian and Arab countries. In Viña del Mar, have dinner at the **Cafe Brighton** and watch the sun set over the bay.

For a bohemian evening in Valparaíso, enjoy live Chilean folk music at **La Colombina Pub and Restaurant**. Then hit the conventional dance-and-drink stops, which include **Cinzano**, **Tanguería Imperio**, **La Puerta del Sol**, and the innumerable bars along the Subida Ecuador. For daytime fun in Valparaíso, walk along picturesque Cerro Alegre, an authentic Chilean neighborhood dedicated to conserving traditional architecture. Wander down Paseo Yugoslavo, a popular hangout for artists. Take the Artillerma elevator to the **Naval Museum**, where you can get another spectacular view of Valparaíso Bay. In Viña del Mar, the **Casino Municipal de Viña del Mar** makes for a fun escape, with gaming rooms, a disco, and a cabaret.

The Hot Sheet

☎ 56/2

$ 510 Chilean Peso

HOTELS	DAY	ADDRESS	*	PH	PRICE	FX	RMS	BEST ROOMS
Hotel Regal Pacific	A	5680 Av. Apoquindo		229-4000 800- 365-1992	$$$	229-4005	104	Regal dlx rm
Hotel Alcazar	A	646 c/ Alvarez	M32	68-5112	$$	88-4245	75	4th fl supr rm w/balc
Hotel Kennedy	A	4570 Av. Kennedy		290-8100 800- 448-8355	$$	218-2188	133	Kingsize rm w/mtn vw
Hotel O'Higgins	2	Pl. Vergara	M32	88-2016	$$	88-3537	235	Supr gdn and pool vw
Hotel Oceanic	A	12925 Av. Borgoño	M32	83-0006	$$	83-0390	28	Pool and sea vw
Hotel Plaza San Francisco	A	816 Alameda		639-3832 800- 223-5652	$$$	639-7826	160	11th fl rm w/mtn vw
Hyatt Regency	1	4601 Av. Kennedy N.		218-1234 800- 233-1234	$$$	218-2279	310	14th fl rm w/mtn vw

RESTAURANTS	DAY	ADDRESS	*	PH	PRICE	REC	DRESS	FOOD
Anakena	A	see Hyatt Regency hotel		218-1234	$$	LD	Kazh	Thai, Chilean grill
Aquí Está Coco	1	236 La Concepción		251-5751	$$$$	D/L	Euro	Seafood
Balthazar Restaurant	A	10690 Av. las Condes		215-1090	$$	D	Kazh	International, seafood
Cafe Brighton	A	151 Paseo Atkinson	V32	22-3513	$	LD	Kazh	Chilean, seafood
Cafe Turri	2	147 Templeman	V32	25-2091	$$	D/BL	Kazh	International, seafood
Cristóforo Restaurant	3	Meulle Vergara	M32	68-8968	$	D	Kazh	Seafood
Delicias del Mar	3	459 Av. San Martín	M32	90-1837	$$	L/D	Kazh	Seafood
El Venezia	2	200 Pío Nono		737-0900	$$	L/D	Kazh	Chilean meat specialties
La Esquina al Jerez	1	0192 Dardignac		735-4122	$$	L/D	Kazh	Spanish

NITELIFE	DAY	ADDRESS	*	PH	PRICE	REC	DRESS	MUSIC
Casino Municipal de Viña del Mar	A	199 Av. San Martín	M32	68-9200	$$	GHMS(F)	Dressy	Latin, jazz, floor show
Cinzano	A	1182 Anival Pinto	V32	21-3043	None	M	Kazh	Latin
El Club	1	0380 Av. El Bosque N.		246-1222	None	H(F)	Kazh	
La Columbina Pub and Restaurant	A	77 Pasaje Apolo	V32	23-6254	None	HM(F)	Kazh	Folk
La Puerta del Sol	A	2033 Av. Pedro Montt	V32	23-5158	None	H	Kazh	
Tanguería Imperio	A	1459 Condell, 3rd fl.	V32	23-4217	$	M	Kazh	Latin

SIGHTS & ATTRACTIONS	DAY	ADDRESS	*	PH	ENTRY FEE
La Sebastiana	2	692 c/ Ferrari, Cerro Bellavista	V32	25-6606	$
Museo Arqueológico Fonk	3	784 "4" N.	M32	68-6753	$
Museo Chileno de Arte Precolombino	1	361 c/ Bandera		688-7348	$
Museo Nacional de Bellas Artes	2	c/ José Miguel de la Barra		633-0655	$
Naval Museum	A	Subida Artillería	V32	28-1845	$
Palacio Carrasco	3	250 Av. Libertad	M32	68-9481	None
National Tourist Office		507 Av. Valparaíso, #303	M32	88-2285	
Santiago Tourist Office		860 Merced		632-7785	

EVENT & TICKET INFO

Viña del Mar International Song Festival (Quinta Vergara, Viña del Mar): Tickets ($12-$50) are handled by the television station that produces the event. Contact *Canal 13* (56/2-251-4000).

*M= Viña del Mar, V=Valparaíso

REcommendations: (Restaurants) B–Breakfast; L–Lunch; D–Dinner; T–High tea or snack
(Nitelife) G–Gaming; H–Hangout bar; M–Live music; O–Dancing (disco); P–Dancing (live music); S–Show; F–Food served
()–Available but without recommendation. For complete explanation of Hot Sheet format, see page 34.

NYC +1   53°/84° (12°/29°)   Santiago (SCL); 30 min./$20   Yes   Spanish

The Fun Also Rises

February 2000

M	T	W	T	F	S	S
	1	2	3	4	5	6
7	8	9	10	11	12	13
14	15	16	17	18	19	20
21	22	23	24	25	26	27
28	29					

December 2001

M	T	W	T	F	S	S
					1	2
3	4	5	6	7	8	9
10	11	12	13	14	15	16
17	18	19	20	21	22	23
24	25	26	27	28	29	30
31						

Negril, Jamaica

Fun Destination: Hedonism II

The Most Fun Resort

A FunGuide 100 Destination

Every so often you have to choose sides. The path that cuts through the beach at *Hedonism II* neatly divides the Nude side from the Prude side, and the first decision of your vacation at this infamous resort is which side to pick. A word of advice—the singles action is generally better on the Prude side, but the Nudes have more fun. Happily, there's no paperwork involved in joining one side, then spontaneously switching to the other. It's just a matter of being in the proper uniform at the proper time.

Such is the scene at *Hedonism II*, the Garden of Eden resort set on 22 acres of manicured jungle and beachfront property at the end of seven-mile-long Negril Beach on Jamaica's west coast. *Hedonism II* is like the bizarro world for regular folk, where the socially unacceptable is expected and the acceptable is often disdained. Alcohol flows day and night and, after a few hours, even the most uptight skeptics are often seen hurling their swimsuits into the Caribbean and letting the warm waters gently carry them out to sea. The rumors of open sex in the hot tubs and frequent foursomes among swinging couples may or may not be true—it seems to depend on whom you ask. But everyone agrees that,

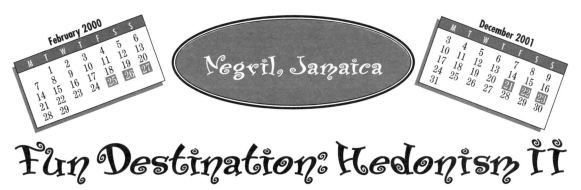

with nonstop activities and the wildest theme parties this side of the silver screen, *Hedonism II* is incomparable in the world of fun.

This sybaritic haven was launched in 1976 as Negril Beach Village, Jamaica's first all-inclusive resort. In 1981, it joined the SuperClubs group and became *Hedonism II*, a place where money is as useless as the pockets of your abandoned pants—all drinks, meals, and activities are included in one prepaid price. As the name suggests, *Hedonism II* is about pleasure—guests are encouraged to leave their inhibitions at home, kick off their shoes (and whatever else they like), and run wild.

The unconventional focus on fun and unusual activities puts **Hedonism II** at the top of the world's most fun resorts list. The spirited theme parties at **Hedo** are legendary. During Pajama Night, most guests arrive in their underwear or other creative (and minimal) attire. With its No Underwear policy, Toga Night is unique. These parties begin in an on-site disco (which rages nightly until the last dancer staggers out) and proceed in any number of directions. One of the most notorious sites for action is the nude hot tub, which holds up to 80 people and is a bit of a legend in itself. Liberal socializing and erotic encounters take place here, especially late at night.

Strolling naked on Prude Beach is not allowed, but walking clothed through Nude Beach is an even greater offense. Your best course of action as a Prude is to be respectful, avoid ogling the birthday suits, and eventually switch teams. Test the waters by shedding your clothes and hitting the Nude beach for a barbecue lunch. It might take some getting used to, but it's a good way to "size up" the scene.

Active types can revive the childhood fantasy of running away to join the big top by checking out **Hedo**'s Circus Workshop, which has clinics for the flying trapeze and more. There are also water sports, tennis, and aerobics. The infamous nude volleyball games provide endless entertainment for players and spectators. And by all means go off property to watch a sunset from Rick's Café.

A few warnings about **Hedonism II** are in order. The accommodations are far from luxurious, with occasional power outages and shared rooms for single visitors (although mirrors have been thoughtfully placed on the ceilings). The food, though copious, is by no means ambrosia for the gods—beach fare may be the culinary highlight. There's nightly entertainment, but you may have to go to a club in town to hear the reggae music that Jamaica made famous. Women usually enjoy the advantage of being outnumbered. However, first-timers are often disappointed to discover that, despite the exceptionally attractive world portrayed on the glossy brochures, **Hedonism II** typically attracts a crowd that is, well, typical.

Many of these problems may have been solved with the inauguration of **Hedonism III**, a luxury version of the resort, scheduled to open in the fall of 1999. On Runaway Bay along Jamaica's north coast (35 miles from the Montego Bay Airport), **Hedo III** offers everything the original does, but with newer and finer facilities. Rooms are air-conditioned and have large marble bathrooms with Roman-style Jacuzzi tubs. Jamaica's first "swim-up" rooms are in place and a transparent water-slide tube provides unique entertainment for the folks in the disco. Once again, it's a matter of making a choice—drink or swim!

For information about **Hedonism**, call 800-467-8737.

CLOSE CALL: CLUB MED

There was a time when you could easily call **Club Med** one of the world's most fun resort operations. In the good old days it was cool to pay for things with beads instead of cash. Some singles continue to think that "villages" such as those in Turks and Caicos and Martinique are as good as it gets, but others are convinced that **Club Med** has lost its edge.

Whether at a village designated for families, couples, singles, or faraway adventure, visitors get the reliable **Club Med** philosophy—fun equals a carefree environment, good facilities, entertainment, and plenty of opportunities to interact with others. **Club Med** makes the staff/guest distinction nearly invisible—employees play and eat with guests. Dinner, with the focus on variety and quantity rather than quality, is buffet style. Guests sit with "new friends" at tables of eight. A staff member sees to it that the conversation flows. Village life follows a routine that guests come to expect—drinks at 6:30 p.m., pre-dinner entertainment, after-dinner dancing and/or a show put on by the staff, and then off to the disco.

For information about **Club Med**, call 800-258-2633.

☎ US/876　🕐 NYC +1　🌗 69°/87° (21°/31°)　✈ Montego Bay (MBJ); 90 min./SNA　🚗 No　🗣 English　💲 39 Jamaican Dollar

White Tie and Tales

There's something undeniably odd about the fact that today's formal man is still dressing in clothes barely changed from 18th-century English foxhunting attire. Despite the proverbial penguin look, however, formal dress is part of the fun in nearly twenty *The Fun Also Rises* events. The **Monaco Grand Prix**, San Francisco's **Black and White Ball** (North American edition), and the **Vienna Opera Ball** are just three that ask participants to dress a part they might not normally play.

White-tie or full-dress events are the most formal, but the requisite black tail coat with silk lapel facings was not always as frivolous as it might appear today. Because men in the late 1700s needed to keep their clothes from rumpling up on the saddle as they rode, the tail coat was cut sharply at the waist, ran straight across the front with no buttons, and had two deeply vented tails falling from the back. The two buttons on the back of the coat once held up the tails, which had buttonholes at the ends, to keep them from impeding the rider. Thoroughbreds have since been traded in for Beemers and Benzes, but the coats have remained.

Hats have traditionally signified status, with the leaders of society often choosing very tall ones to denote their positions "above" the unwashed canaille. Top hats as formal wear, however, were originally designed for safety—crash helmets for the equestrian set, so to speak. Still, these silk top hats were considered shocking when first introduced. History records that one James Heatherington was arrested for disturbing the peace, in 1797, when he strolled through the streets of London wearing the newly invented headpiece. He was fined £50 for creating a near riot, which left women fainting, dogs barking, horses shying, children screaming, and one boy with a broken arm.

Despite their rocky introduction, top hats soon became essential sporting gear, then normal street attire, and, finally, a requirement for evening dress. The collapsible opera version was designed to save space in cloakrooms. Nowadays, lamentably, the silk top hat is fading quickly. In 1975, the world's largest top-hat manufacturer, Spoorenberg of Eindhoven, Holland, went out of business after 160 years. Not only did the company face drastically reduced demand, prices had risen dramatically for the secret shellac ingredient— insect droppings imported from India—that gave the hats their gloss and rigidity.

You may wonder how men could have been enticed to wear insect manure on their heads. Although today it's generally women who are regarded as slaves to fashion, in times past, "fashion plate" was considered a serious and worthy avocation for men, and if the trendsetter was a royal, entire nations often followed. When the future King Edward VII of England decided that the folds in newly made pants looked elegant rather than disheveled, he wore a pair right out of the box. Evening trousers have been creased ever since. And men might still be wearing their tresses long and flowing had a snowball fight not gotten out of hand in the 1500s. When the locks of King François I of France were cut to treat a nasty head wound he'd received from a particularly icy snowball, prudent courtiers followed suit. England's Henry VIII soon felt out-of-date and, in 1535, ordered his attendants to cut their hair along with his.

Blame neckties on the military. In the 1600s, French officers who fought beside Croatian mercenaries in the Thirty Years' War brought home the distinctive bandannas that Croats knotted around their necks. The French king, unable to pronounce *Croat*, called them cravats and men have had nooses around their necks ever since. Perhaps the height of fascination with the necktie came with Beau Brummell, the 18th-century dandy who joined the Prince of Wales (England's future King George IV) in a lifelong devotion to wardrobe. Brummell reputedly spent nine hours each day changing clothes, with mornings spent discarding cravat after cravat until he achieved the perfect effect. Following World War II when narrower neckties came into fashion, the Duke of Windsor (the English monarch who abdicated the throne) designed his own with an extra thickness of lining to produce what we know today as the Windsor knot.

Some formal events allow men a bit more sartorial freedom by specifying "black tie" dress, which largely reduces matters to the penguin look that has been a standby for more than 100 years—tuxedo, black bow tie, and cummerbund. (Cummerbunds, by the way, are always worn with pleats facing up, because when trousers had no pockets, gentlemen tucked their theater tickets into the folds.) But even this "relaxed" look experienced some resistance at first. When tobacco tycoon Griswold Lorillard attended a society ball wearing a short, black-worsted smoking jacket instead of a tail coat, he created quite a stir. Ladies were shocked, gentlemen were offended, and Lorillard was ridiculed—after which he was, of course, copied by millions.

Formal-dress rules address even the minutest details, such as flowers. Only blue cornflowers, coral or red carnations, or white gardenias are considered proper for male evening peacockery. Many tuxedos still have a loop under the left lapel, a remnant of Victorian days when it held a tiny vial of water for the boutonniere.

If men's formal-clothing options are narrow and codified, women's are wide-open and draw from just about every era in history. Female clothing traditionally has been regarded as expressive art, and one of its major themes has always been seduction. What's considered sexy and unmention-able, though, has varied by culture and time. In ancient China, the sight of the female foot was forbidden. The back of a woman's neck was off-limits in Japan. Naughty ladies in 18th-century France flashed shocking glimpses of shoulders and elbows, while a century later no well-bred man would utter the word *leg* in a woman's presence.

For thousands of years, women have used fabrics to entrance and entice. One of the earliest and most erotic of these was diaphanous, clingy silk, with a sensual (and monetary) draw so great it drove many of history's most heroic and adventurous men to brave perilous mountains, deserts, and bandits on the Silk Road in pursuit of its enchantment. Legend says it all began when a Chinese empress in the third century B.C. was investigating a parasite on her mulberry trees and found white worms eating the leaves. When she accidentally dropped one of their cocoons into hot water, more than 4,000 yards of thread unraveled.

As with men's fashions, women's clothes have been used to indicate rank and social status. Hundreds of years ago, women demonstrated their importance by the length of the cloaks trailing behind them. Many of today's most formal gowns still feature elaborate trains. One might even argue that centuries of human commerce have been dedicated to the pursuit of status through formal dress. Men have launched armadas, conquered continents, and ravaged resources in the quest for gold, jewels, and fur. Today, such symbols of wealth are increasingly hidden in safes and bank vaults to protect them from thieves, or spurned as vestiges of outdated environmental rapaciousness.

Even if you never get the chance to shout "Tally-ho!" on an English country ride, elegant dress can enhance your world. Just ask anyone who's jumped for beads at a **Mardi Gras** Krewe Ball in New Orleans, jumped for joy at the finish line at **Royal Ascot**, or jumped at the chance to let someone else seductively undo a perfectly knotted bow tie at the end of an exquisitely fashionable evening.

February/March 2000

M	T	W	T	F	S	S
	1	2	3	4	5	13
7	8	9	10	11	19	20
14	15	16	17	18	26	27
21	22	23	24	25	3	4	5
28	29	1	2			

Vienna, Austria

February 2001

M	T	W	T	F	S	S
5	6	7	8	1	2	3	4
12	13	14	15	9	10	11
19	20	21	22	16	17	18
26	27	28	29	23	24	25

Vienna Opera Ball

Origin: 1877   Event ★ ★ ★ ★ ★ ★ ★ ★ ★ City   Attendance: 5,000

it's enough to make your head spin and spin and spin. In the city of music and romance, the ball of all annual balls, the ***Vienna Opera Ball***, sparkles with chandeliers, music, celebrities, politicians, and beautiful dancers, transforming the Vienna State Opera into the world's most shining example of life as art.

The waltz twirls to life when the State Opera orchestra strikes its first chord and 180 white-gloved debutante couples execute a perfect quadrille across the 160-foot ballroom floor. Cinderella fantasies become reality when the words *Alles Walzer* beckon 5,000 paying guests, dressed in long gowns and white ties, to begin whirling in three-quarter time.

Though the waltz is the ball's raison d'être, various floors of the Opera pulsate with live disco, jazz, and country music. Roulette wheels roll in the casino. Champagne, wine, and buffets serving international cuisine nourish the dancers.

On the main floor, two orchestras alternate all evening. One plays waltzes and polkas, the other swing music. The evening concludes at 5 a.m., when the orchestra plays Strauss' "Blue Danube" and 20,000 pink carnations rain slowly on the remaining couples. Party survivors welcome the day with a traditional breakfast of goulash at nearby restaurants.

The ball season in Vienna begins in November, followed by a cluster of events during the weeks before Ash Wednesday that includes The Magician's Ball, Bonbon Ball, and Ball of the Viennese Coffee House Owners. Of the 300 or so balls, though, the only rival to the ***Opera Ball*** is the ***Imperial Ball*** on New Year's Eve.

Set in the heart of Europe, the Austrian capital (with about 2 million residents) entices visitors with world-famous pastries, Bohemian cuisine, palatial buildings, century-old coffeehouses, and new restaurants. This imperial city is a world center of culture, art, and politics, but it's the ***Opera Ball***, with its magical pomp and circumstance, that compels lovers of class and culture to return year after year.

Vienna Opera Ball

Day 1. Tue. Feb. 29, 2000
(Day 1. Tuesday   *February 20, 2001)*

9:00am Check into the century-old **Hotel Bristol** located across from the Vienna State Opera House. Your room will be decorated with original art and rich, dark wood furniture.

10:30am Take a taxi to **Lambert Hofer Köstume** to ensure that your rented white tie and tails fit properly. If you've arrived dress-ready, visit the **Museum of Applied Arts (MAK)**, which is known for its collection of decorative interior furnishings. Get a cup of strong Viennese coffee at the chic **MAK Café**.

12:30pm Cab to the popular **König von Ungarn** for a tra-
ⓡ ditional Viennese lunch of *Tafelspitz* (boiled beef) in a clublike atmosphere. Mozart once lived upstairs.

2:00pm After lunch, go to the **Austrian Gallery**, where you'll see works by Gustave Klimt and Kokoschka. There's also a great view of the city center here.

4:30pm Catch a cab to **Demel**, a picture-perfect
ⓡ Viennese pastry house. The tea, coffee, and pastries are excellent in this world-famous cafe.

6:00pm Walk back to the hotel along Kärntnerstrasse, the main shopping street though Old Town. Stephandsdom cathedral is a short detour off the route.

8:30pm Have an Italian dinner at **Cantinetta Antinori**
ⓡ with a lively, well-dressed crowd.

10:30pm Cab to **Planter's Club**, where palm trees and eclectic furniture enliven the atmosphere. A DJ plays American oldies for bankers and green-haired creatives until 2:30 a.m.

Midnight Try your luck at European 7-11 (craps) in the elegant **Casino Wien**, located in a former palace in the heart of downtown Vienna.

Day 2. Wed. Mar. 1, 2000
(Day 2. Wednesday   *February 21, 2001)*

9:00am Have breakfast in your hotel room. Dress for a
ⓡ day of walking and dancing lessons.

10:00am For a look at the beauty and grandeur of Old Vienna, tour the royal apartments and baroque library of the **Imperial Palace**.

12:30pm Lunch at **Ofenloch**, a 250-year-old beer house
ⓡ where traditionally clad waitresses serve seasonal Austrian food.

2:00pm You might be a dance champion at home, but doing the Viennese waltz is another story. Head to the **Elmayer Dance School** and learn how to execute proper and perfect turns.

3:30pm Taxi to **KunstHausWien**, a modern-art museum designed by local painter/environmentalist Hundertwasser. The place is an architectural marvel with a colorful, artistic ambience.

5:00pm No trip to Vienna is complete without looking at the Danube, so cab along the majestic river before heading back to the hotel.

7:30pm Relax at the **American Bar**, where you can gaze at the original Adolf Loos mahogany-glass-and-onyx interior from the early 1800s.

9:00pm Taxi to **Motto**, an ultrahip restaurant. The own-
ⓡ ers take pride in hosting fashion designers, singers, and politicians into the morning hours.

Midnight Don't show up at **Eden Bar** until after midnight. That's when the rest of Viennese high society turns up at this classy nightclub to dance to a live band. For a less-formal evening, head to the high-class **Queen Anne** disco, where beautiful people and VIPs dance on two marble dance floors.

Day 3. Thu.   Mar. 2, 2000
(Day 3. Thursday   February 22, 2001)

9:00am Breakfast at the legendary **Café Hawelka**.
℞ Have coffee *melange*, an espressolike coffee with whipped cream and cinnamon. *Buchteln* are delicious plum-jam-filled sweet buns.

10:00am Take the metro to **Schönbrunn Palace**, a treasure-trove of rococo design, Napoleonic memorabilia, and Imperial Hapsburgs information.

Noon Taxi to one of the oldest eateries in town, **Zu den**
℞ **Drei Hacken**. The 200-plus-year-old establishment serves traditional Viennese lunches.

1:30pm Take a final waltz lesson.

> Formal evening attire, hair appointments, and dance lessons should be reserved about a month ahead of time—contact your hotel concierge.

2:45pm Ladies can get their hair done alongside celebrities at **City Coiffeur**. Gents can keep busy with father Sigmund at the **Freud Museum**.

4:30pm Begin your journey into the elegant past by donning your most formal attire, a ritual that may take a little time.

5:45pm Taxi to the epicurean shrine **Steirereck**, one of
℞ the best restaurants in Europe. Book two months in advance for the special Opera Ball dinner.

9:00pm Travel by cab to the ball. Avoid the crowd by using the side entrance or check out the major scene at the main entrance. The elegance of the setting and the people is overwhelming. Find your seat or a spot on the side of the dance floor.

9:30pm Following a short performance, the debutante couples make their spectacular grand entrance and fill the floor for the opening dance. Afterward, all attendees are invited to begin the quick-paced Viennese waltz. The very crowded dance floor may preclude you from showing your stuff, but you'll have plenty of opportunities later.

11:00pm If you haven't prepurchased a seat, stake out a table at one of the buffets scattered around the opera house. Otherwise, you'll be standing all night.

Midnight After a five-minute performance of the cancan, a thousand people jam the main floor for a quadrille lesson. Then it's back to the waltz, polka, and swing.

3:00am Return for another, even wilder quadrille lesson after you've toured the opera house. The caller speeds up the pace to the point where nobody has a clue what to do—it's all great fun.

5:00am The remaining crowd goes back to the main ballroom to dance the last waltz of the evening under a cascade of falling pink carnations.

5:30am Head to the **Café Sacher**, behind the State Opera,
℞ for the traditional post-***Ball*** meal—hearty goulash and cold beer. Everyone is still dressed up but winding down. Although even the greatest of evenings must end, at least your memories will last forever.

Alternatives

The **Hotel Imperial** is an original Württemberg palace inaugurated by Emperor Franz Joseph I. The **Hotel Sacher**, across from the State Opera, is elegant but more noted for its chocolate torte. **Das Trieste** brings chic hotel design to an old riding stable.

Engländer Brasserie is a new international restaurant in a beautiful setting. Enjoy *tapas*-style sandwiches and a frosty beer or vodka at **Trzesniewski**. **Korso** restaurant has a splendid setting and nouveau-Austrian food.

If you like prints and watercolors, visit the **Albertina**, which houses more than a million pieces, including prints by Da Vinci and Rubens.

The Hot Sheet

☎ 43/1

$ 11 Schilling

HOTELS	DAY	ADDRESS	PH	PRICE	FX	RMS	BEST ROOMS
Das Trieste	A	12 Wiedner Hauptstr.	58-9180 800- 448-8355	$$$	589-1818	270	Inner rm or tower vw
Hotel Bristol	1	1 Kärntner Ring	51-5160 800- 325-3589	$$$	5-151-6550	141	Rm 47
Hotel Imperial	A	16 Kärntner Ring	50-1100 800- 325-3589	$$$$+	5-011-0410	128	Imperial rm
Hotel Sacher	A	4 Philharmonikerstr.	51-4570 800- 223-6800	$$$$+	5-145-7810	108	Dlx front rm w/ vw

RESTAURANTS	DAY	ADDRESS	PH	PRICE	REC	DRESS	FOOD
Café Hawelka	3	6 Dorotheergasse	512-8230	$	BLT	Kazh	Cafe, *Buchteln*
Café Sacher	3	see Hotel Sacher	512-1487	$	T/BLD	Kazh	Goulash
Cantinetta Antinori	1	3-5 Jasomirgottstr.	533-7722	$$	D/L	Euro	Italian
Demel	1	14 Kohlmarkt	533-5516	$	T/BL	Kazh	Pastry shop, sandwiches
Engländer Brasserie	A	15 Wiedner Hauptstr.	5-035-9031	$$	BLD	Euro	Viennese, Italian
König von Ungarn	1	10 Schulerstr.	512-5319	$$	L/D	Euro	International, Viennese
Korso	A	2 Mahlerstr.	5-151-6546	$$$	LD	Euro	Viennese, international
MAK Café	1	see Museum of Applied Arts	714-0121	$$	T/BLD	Euro	Cafe, nuvo Viennese
Motto	2	30 Schönbrunnerstr.	587-0672	$$	D	Euro	Austrian, Italian
Ofenloch	2	8 Kurrentgasse	533-8844	$$	L/D	Kazh	Traditional Viennese
Steirereck	3	2 Rasumofskygasse	713-3168	$$$	D/L	Dressy	Viennese, international
Trzesniewski	A	1 Dorotheergasse	512-3291	$	LD	Kazh	Sandwiches
Zu den Drei Hacken	3	28 Singerstr.	512-5895	$$	L/D	Kazh	Austrian, international

NITELIFE	DAY	ADDRESS	PH	PRICE	REC	DRESS	MUSIC
American Bar	2	10 Kärntnerstr.	512-3283	None	H	Euro	
Casino Wien	1	41 Kärntnerstr.	512-4836	None	GH	Dressy	Casino, bar
Eden Bar	2	2 Liliengasse	512-7450	None	P	Euro	Popular
Planter's Club	1	4 Zelinkgasse	533-3393	None	H	Kazh	
Queen Anne	2	12 Johannesgasse	512-0203	None	O	Euro	Oldies, dance

SIGHTS & ATTRACTIONS	DAY	ADDRESS	PH	ENTRY FEE
Albertina	A	3 Makartgasse in Akademiehof	5-3483	$
Austrian Gallery	1	27 Prinz-Eugen-Str. in Upper Belvedere	79-5570	$
Freud Museum	3	19 Berggasse	319-1596	$
Imperial Palace	2	Kaiserhof, Kaisertor	533-7570	$
KunstHausWien	2	13 Untere Weissgerberstr.	712-0491	$
Museum of Applied Arts (MAK)	1	5 Stubenring	71-1360	
Schönbrunn Palace	3	47 Schönbrunner Schloss-Str.	8-111-3224	$

OTHER SIGHTS, SERVICES & ATTRACTIONS

City Coiffeur	3	see Hotel Imperial	50-1100	$$$$+
Elmayer Dance School	2	13 Braunerstr.	512-7197	$$$$+
Lambert Hofer Köstume	1	28 Simmeringer Hauptstr.	74-0900	$$$$+
Viennese Tourist Office		38 Kärntnerstr.	513-8892	

EVENT & TICKET INFO

Vienna Opera Ball (State Opera House, Vienna): Admission ticket ($250) plus table seat ($175) can be ordered from *Österreichischer Bundestheaterverband* (43/1-51-444-2606). For more information, call the *Viennese Opera Ball* in Washington, D.C. (202-237-5202).

Alternative Event

Imperial Ball: Hofburg Congress Centre Vienna, 43/1-58-736-6623

RECommendations: (Restaurants) B–Breakfast; L–Lunch; D–Dinner; T–High tea or snack
(Nitelife) G–Gaming; H–Hangout bar; M–Live music; O–Dancing (disco); P–Dancing (live music); S–Show; F–Food served
( )–Available but without recommendation. For complete explanation of Hot Sheet format, see page 34.

NYC +6   30°/40° (0°/5°)   Vienna (Schwechat) (VIE); 30 min./$45   No   German

February/March 2000

February/March 2001

Sydney, Australia

Sydney Gay and Lesbian Mardi Gras

| Origin: 1978 | Event ★★★★★★★★ City | Attendance: 500,000 |

Raunchy street theater, dykes on bikes, male cheerleaders, body-worshipping "gym fags"—everything about this visual explosion of costumes, music, and in-your-face attitude is sheer spectacle on an Australian scale. Set in a country already noted for audacity, the ultimate "Mom, I've got something to tell you" party for the gay world celebrates homosexual and lesbian humor, creativity, politics, and verve. But don't be fooled by the name, this festival is stuffed with outrageous thrills for straights and gays alike.

A cross between a picnic, political rally, and burlesque show, the *Sydney Gay & Lesbian Mardi Gras* presents a month of events designed to be controversial and titillating while creating a world where queer is the norm. The festivities last all month, but the final three days are always the best. The "If I miss it, I'll just die" event is the world-famous parade, where thousands of overheated extroverts, decked out in the most fantastic costumes this side of San Francisco, march to a gay drummer down stately Oxford Street.

The madness climaxes in an all-night party that starts with the parade and rages deep, hard, and long into the night with rampant public displays of desire and sensuous excess. To keep things interesting, dozens of workshops, parties, and performances that lead up to the final Saturday carry tongue-in-cheek (among other places) titles—"A Family Outing," "Fruit Loops," and "Ten Cubicle Suckatorium" are just a few examples.

Away from the throbbing center of the gay world, Sydney offers the entertainment, food, and architecture you'd expect from one of the world's great cities. Its 3.5 million inhabitants are passionate about food, drink, and late nights. Visit the city's famed landmarks—you can't go down under without seeing Sydney Harbour and the Opera House—but remember that Sydney is a nighttime city filled with some of the world's best clubs. Whatever your sexual preference, getting out this weekend in Sydney is sure to be a most marvelous time.

Sydney Gay and Lesbian Mardi Gras

Day 1. Thu.   Mar. 2, 2000
(Day 1. Thursday   March 1, 2001)

9:30am Set in the hip cafe-and-boutique district of Darlinghurst, **The Kirketon** hotel is a bastion of urban glamour with comfortable, modern rooms.

10:30am Start your exploration of the city with a trek around its skyline-dominating Sydney Opera House. Take the **Opera House Tour** for the inside scoop on this gorgeous yet convoluted and cantilevered icon of architectural excess.

Noon Walk around The Rocks area—this is the birthplace of modern Australia. What remains of the brick buildings that were warehouses during the thriving port years of the Victorian era have been transformed into restaurants, shops, and galleries.

1:30pm Whether you're looking for cool ambience or delectable seafood, **Rockpool** never disappoints. After lunch, walk to the **Harbour Bridge** and climb to the Pylon Lookout for magnificent views.

3:30pm Take a **Sydney Harbour Cruise** from the hub area of Circular Quay. The Harbour Highlights Cruise, which takes a little more than an hour, will give you good looks at attractions such as the Opera House, Harbour Bridge, and Darling Harbour.

6:30pm Join the after-work crowd for a pre-dinner drink at **Wine Banc**. Set in a contemporary grotto, its 22-page wine list is impressive.

8:30pm In the Kings Cross neighborhood are many restaurants, bars, and clubs that cater to the hip crowd. For dinner, insiders flock to the glamorous **International** restaurant for ModOz (modern Australian) cuisine.

10:30pm Taxi to the **Embassy**, an upscale bar-cum-restaurant-cum-nightclub-cum-cigar-lounge in the posh Double Bay area.

Midnight Come on out or just sit back and watch as drag queens whoop it up all over town. The **Imperial Hotel** and the **Albury Hotel** will be staging drag shows that make Ru Paul look like a child playing dress-up.

Day 2. Fri.   Mar. 3, 2000
(Day 2. Friday   March 2, 2001)

8:30am For breakfast, sit at a communal table and try the ricotta pancakes at **bill's**.

10:00am Take a ride on the elevated **Monorail**, which buzzes through downtown and Darling Harbour. Ride the full circuit or jump off at Darling Park to explore the entertainment district of Darling Harbour.

12:30pm Located on the roof terrace of the Cockle Bay Wharf complex at Darling Park, **Ampersand** provides incredible views of the water. The restaurant serves modern French and fusion food in a setting that couples natural beauty with man-made style.

2:00pm Sydney's largest museum, located in Darling Harbour, is a testament to man's imagination. The interactive exhibits at the **Powerhouse Museum** demonstrate how technology can be as inspirational as artistry.

3:30pm Check out the **Museum of Sydney**. Set in the city's original Government House, the museum details the founding of Sydney, including its convict past and the colonization of the continent's aboriginal people.

5:00pm Walk up Bridge Street to the stunning Royal Botanic Gardens. Wander around the lush greenery—look into the trees to see hundreds of large fruit bats hanging upside down. On the way out, circle through The Domain and head toward the **Amp Tower**—the gold-colored spike and tallest building in Sydney. Have a drink in the lounge and enjoy its 360-degree view.

8:00pm One of the few restaurants in the world requiring, the **Grand Pacific Blue Room** is the hippest place in Paddington. The food is modern Australian as are the music and fashion-industry clientele.

10:00pm Taxi to the Darling Harbour area and live the high-roller life at **Star City Casino**.

11:30pm Hit the **Cave** nightclub in the basement of the casino. This top-end disco hosts celebrities and beautiful people who make the scene until the morning hours dancing to funk, soul, and house music.

Day 3. Sat. Mar. 4, 2000
(Day 3. Saturday   March 3, 2001)

9:00am You can have a breakfast fit for a Bedouin prince at **Fez Cafe**. Try the minced-lamb sausages and breakfast couscous.

10:00am Bondi Beach is the most popular and famous beach in metropolitan Sydney. Loll on the sand, take in the surfers, or go for a swim—the beach is easy to get to from downtown by car or bus.

1:30pm For seaside charm in chic, modern surroundings, the restaurant known simply as **56** fits the bill. The food is good enough to draw many off-duty waiters and chefs—a sure sign that a restaurant has arrived.

3:30pm Explore the suburb of Paddington. The **Hogarth Galleries** are credited with starting the aboriginal-art collecting movement.

6:00pm Check out the staging area for the *Sydney Gay and Lesbian Mardi Gras Parade*, the world's largest uninhibited evening parade, where last-minute touches to costumes and final rehearsals of routines build the anticipation.

7:00pm Park yourself at the **MG Garage** restaurant in Surrey Hills. Greek food among vintage automobiles

might seem odd, but with a top chef behind the wheel, the place is a winner.

9:00pm With engines roaring, breasts bared, and pride flags waving, the Dykes on Bikes contingent reaches the viewing stands to start the three-hour parade extravaganza. (You can't cross the parade route, which will be packed five-persons deep, so plan the course to your seat.)

Midnight The *Mardi Gras Party* is an epic dance party—20,000 people, food booths, vendors, and live entertainment. For many this is the greatest party on earth, which is why they stay the course until 8 or 9 a.m.!

Alternatives

Sheraton on the Park is a contemporary glass-and-steel structure with large rooms overlooking the park. At the end of The Rocks area, the distinguished **Park Hyatt** has great views, luxurious rooms, and sophisticated amenities (such as butler service). **The Ritz-Carlton, Sydney** is a five-star hotel that offers rooms with French-door balconies and views of the Opera House.

In The Kirketon hotel, **Salt** has a reputation for providing glamour along with great surf and turf. For superior modern Italian cooking in a cool, re-done warehouse, **Bel Mondo** is the place. Try **Morans**, a fine-dining destination for lunch or dinner. Another nice spot for dinner is **Darley Street Thai**, where the outrageous decor (gold leaf and bright green is the color scheme) is as hot as the curry.

More than 2,000 gay and straight patrons nightly find a home away from home at **Home**, a trilevel, multiclub venue. **Fix** is a fashionable watering hole and cigar lounge. The **Slip Inn** is a prestigious and versatile nightlife venue with six separate bar, food, and lounge areas. In Darlinghurst, **DCM** plays house music for a beautiful, mixed clientele.

The Hot Sheet

☎ 61/29

$ 1.5 Australian Dollar

HOTELS	DAY	ADDRESS	PH	PRICE	FX	RMS	BEST ROOMS
The Kirketon	1	229 Darlinghurst Rd.	332-2011 800- 552-6844	$$	332-2499	40	Premium rm
Park Hyatt	A	7 Hickson Rd.	241-1234 800- 233-1234	$$$$+	256-1555	158	Opera House vw
The Ritz-Carlton, Sydney	A	93 MacQuarie St.	252-4600 800- 241-3333	$$$	252-4286	105	Dlx harbor vw
Sheraton on the Park	A	161 Elizabeth St.	286-6000 800- 325-3535	$$$	286-6686	557	Parkside rm

RESTAURANTS	DAY	ADDRESS	PH	PRICE	REC	DRESS	FOOD
56	3	56 Campbell Parade, Bondi	365-6044	$$	D/L	Euro	Modern Australian
Ampersand	2	Roof Terrace, Cockle Bay Wharf in Darling Park	264-6666	$$$	L/D	Euro	Modern French, fusion
Bel Mondo	A	18-24 Argyle St., level 3, The Rocks	241-3700	$$$	LD	Euro	Nuvo Italian, international
bill's	2	433 Liverpool St.	360-9631	$$	B/L	Kazh	Modern Australian
Darley Street Thai	A	28-30 Bayswater Rd.	358-6530	$$$	D	Kazh	Thai
Fez Cafe	3	247 Victoria St.	360-9581	$	B/LD	Kazh	Middle Eastern, North African
Grand Pacific Blue Room	2	Oxford and S. Dowling sts.	331-7108	$$	D	Euro	Modern Australian, European
International	1	227 Victoria St., 14th fl.	360-9080	$$	D	Euro	Modern Australian
MG Garage	3	490 Crown St.	383-9383	$$	D/L	Kazh	Modern Australian, Greek
Morans	A	61-63 Macleay St.	356-2223	$$$	LD	Euro	Modern Australian
Rockpool	1	107 George St.	252-1888	$$$	L/D	Kazh	Modern Australian, seafood
Salt	A	see The Kirketon hotel	332-2566	$$	LD	Euro	Modern Australian

NITELIFE	DAY	ADDRESS	PH	PRICE	REC	DRESS	MUSIC
Albury Hotel	1	2-6 Oxford St.	361-6555	None	OS	Kazh	Drag, disco, pub
Cave	2	see Star City Casino	566-4755	$	O	Euro	Dance, R&B
DCM	A	31-33 Oxford St., level 1	267-7380	$$	O	Euro	House
Embassy	1	16-18 Cross St., Double Bay	328-2200	$$	HO(F)	Euro	Dance
Fix	A	see The Kirketon hotel	360-4333	None	H(F)	Euro	
Home	A	101 Cockle Bay Wharf, Wheat Rd.	266-0600	$$	O	Kazh	House
Imperial Hotel	1	35-37 Erskineville Rd.	519-9899	None	OS	Local	Drag, disco, pub
Slip Inn	A	111 Sussex St.	299-1700	None	HO(F)	Euro	
Star City Casino	2	80 Pyrmont St.	777-9000	None	GHS	Euro	Casino
Wine Banc	1	53 Martin Pl.	233-5300	None	H(F)	Euro	

SIGHTS & ATTRACTIONS	DAY	ADDRESS	PH	ENTRY FEE
Amp Tower	2	100 Market St.	229-7444	$
Harbour Bridge	1	Cumberland Stairs, Cumberland St.	247-3408	$
Museum of Sydney	2	Bridge and Phillip sts.	251-5988	$
Opera House Tour	1	Bennelong Point	250-7111	$$
Powerhouse Museum	2	500 Harris St.	217-0444	$

OTHER SIGHTS, SERVICES & ATTRACTIONS				
Hogarth Galleries	3	7 Walker Ln.	360-6839	None
Monorail	2	Darling Park or City Centre	552-2288	$
Sydney Harbour Cruise	1	Wharf 6, Circular Quay	206-1111	$$
Sydney Visitors' Centre		106 George St., The Rocks	255-1788	

EVENT & TICKET INFO

Sydney Gay and Lesbian Mardi Gras Parade (Oxford Street to Moore Park Road and Driver Avenue): Reserved Grandstand seating ($50) is limited and should be ordered well in advance. There's no charge to see the parade from the sidewalk, but the large crowd can make viewing difficult. For Grandstand tickets, contact the *Bobby Goldsmith Foundation* (61/29-283-8666).

Mardi Gras Party (Fox Studio, Old Showgrounds, Moore Park): Tickets ($64) sell out months in advance and are restricted to Mardi Gras members. Obtain an International Membership ($27) and order a party ticket at the same time by contacting *Sydney Gay and Lesbian Mardi Gras* (61/29-557-4332).

RECommendations: (Restaurants) B–Breakfast; L–Lunch; D–Dinner; T–High tea or snack (Nitelife) G–Gaming; H–Hangout bar; M–Live music; O–Dancing (disco); P–Dancing (live music); S–Show; F–Food served ()–Available but without recommendation. For complete explanation of Hot Sheet format, see page 34.

🕐 NYC +14   ☀ 63°/76° (17°/24°)   ✈ Kingsford Smith (SYD); 30 min./$20   🚗 No   🗣 English

The Fun Also Rises

ᎦVendimia

Origin: 1936	Event ★ ★ ★ ★ ★ City	Attendance: 300,000

With fireworks, music, and dancing in the streets, it's the largest celebration honoring wine in the world. No, it isn't Bordeaux, France, or even Napa Valley, California—it's the national festival of *Vendimia* in Argentina, where wine is considered as sacred as the country's beloved tango.

During this week-long event, colorful costumes, antique cars, and all-night parties take over the streets as up to 300,000 people from Argentina and around the world converge on the small Andean town of Mendoza. Beautiful young queens are elected, traditional processions wind through town, and wine flows like the Rio de la Plata. The week culminates with an elaborate show, featuring hundreds of performers beneath the glow of thousands and thousands of lights. As if being one of the largest public wine festivals on the planet isn't enough, *Vendimia* takes place only a stone's throw from Buenos Aires, the unofficial party capital of Latin America.

Known as the Paris of the Americas, Buenos Aires is a cultural oasis amid the windswept pampas, forbidding mountains, and arid desolation of the Patagonia. With an area population of about 10 million, the city blossoms like a desert flower, with wide avenues and extravagant architectural styles brought from Europe by its immigrant population. Sidewalk cafes line the streets; French doors and wrought-iron balconies abound. There's even a replica of Big Ben in front of the train station.

One thing that's unmistakably Argentinean is the mournful, erotic sound of the tango, which emerged from the city's bordellos at the beginning of the 20th century. Don't leave Buenos Aires without checking out one of the shows. Argentina is also the land of some of the best beef steaks in the world, so forget about cholesterol, and indulge. The idea of *Vendimia*—and Argentina, in general—is to eat, drink, and be merry, at least as long as the wine holds out.

Vendimia

Day 1. Thu.   Mar. 2, 2000
(Day 1. Thursday   March 1, 2001)

9:30am Check into **Caesar Park Hotel**, conveniently located in the Recoleta District, a trendy, upscale neighborhood of European-style shops and sidewalk cafes. The hotel has spacious rooms with period furniture and marble bathrooms.

10:00am Visit the **Museo Nacional de Bellas Artes**, possibly South America's finest museum. Housed in an elegant *belle-époque* building, there are 34 halls, with an impressive collection of Rodin sculptures, French impressionist paintings (five rooms are devoted to Degas alone), and modern Argentine art.

12:30pm Back in the Recoleta, try the French-inspired continental cuisine at **Lola**. One of the trendiest places to be seen in Buenos Aires, it has a vivacious crowd and an outdoor terrace.

2:15pm Stroll down Avenida Quintana, the Recoleta's main thoroughfare, and take in the French- and Spanish-style mansions. Then head across the street to **Recoleta Cemetery**, an aristocratic necropolis where Argentina's wealthiest residents have been laid to rest. Among the elaborate mausoleums lies the comparatively simple tomb of Argentine legend Evita Peron, beloved by the country's poor for defending the indigent and working class. The tomb is marked with her maiden name, Eva Duarte.

4:30pm Back across the street have a drink and a snack at **La Biela**, the city's most fashionable cafe, where models and millionaires linger over coffee.

8:00pm For a taste of Argentina's famous corn-fed beef, dine at **Spettus Steak House**, which has a great buffet and an excellent selection of Argentine wines.

10:00pm Check out the tango show at **Casa Blanca**. The performance features a combination of traditional Argentine music and dance, and displays of the tango, including numbers by the great singer Hugo Marcel.

Midnight Venture into the thick of Buenos Aires' nightlife at **Divino**. With its glowing, futuristic façade, it's one of the slickest discos in the country.

Day 2. Fri.   Mar. 3, 2000
(Day 2. Friday   March 2, 2001)

9:00am Start with breakfast on the Avenida de Mayo at the famous **Café Tortoni**, a historic gathering place for some of the greatest poets, writers, and artists of the 20th century, including Argentina's Jorge Luis Borges. Today, it's a favorite with intellectuals and elite politicians, such as King Juan Carlos of Spain.

10:15am Investigate the shady Plaza de Mayo, the first square marked for Buenos Aires by founder Juan de Garay in 1580. The old Town Hall still stands here, flanked by the legendary Casa Rosada, home of the residing Argentine president and site of Evita Peron's most famous speeches. Much to the chagrin of the Argentine population, it was Madonna who more recently took her place at the balcony to sing "Don't Cry for Me, Argentina," for the 1997 Hollywood musical, *Evita*.

Noon Walk to Puerto Madero. The city's oldest port now sports a trendy boardwalk with fashionable restaurants and cafes. Have lunch at the festive Cuban restaurant, **Tocororo**.

2:00pm A long walk or short cab ride away is San Telmo. Enjoy this charming and lively Buenos Aires neighborhood while browsing through the shops on Calle Defensa.

4:15pm Check out of the hotel and head for the airport to catch your 6:05 p.m. flight to Mendoza.

7:15pm Settle into the **Hotel Huentala** in Mendoza. The design features a unique fusion of modern and Spanish colonial-style architecture.

7:30pm It's dinnertime, so head to **Marchigiana** ® **Restaurant**. For a change of pace in this beef capital, try a plate of pasta or paella.

9:00pm Watch the *Via Blanca* parade. Restored antique cars roll by, each with a queen representing her province. Enjoy the music and festive air in the streets. When the fun dies down, check out the dance scene at **Treinta y Pico**, or try **Al Diablo** in the bustling Chacras de Corea zone, about 20 minutes away by car.

Day 3. Sat.   Mar. 4, 2000
(Day 3. Saturday   March 3, 2001)

10:00am After continental buffet breakfast at the hotel, ® join the happy masses on San Martín Avenue at the *Carrusel*, an all-day parade of gauchos, horses, *cueca* dancers, musicians, and cars decorated with the ubiquitous queens. This symbolic march resurrects Mendoza's beginnings as a winemaking region.

Noon Take a hiatus and lunch at **Don Mario**, one of ® Mendoza's finest grills.

1:30pm Celebrate Mendoza's exquisite wine by taking a free tour of the area's various bodegas (wine houses), such as **Sociedad Anónima Escorihuela** and **Bodega Lagarde**. You can get a list of addresses from the tourist office on Avenida San Martín.

5:30pm Rejoin the partying in the streets, where the wine is flowing and the excitement is building.

8:00pm Have dinner on the sidewalk terrace at **Alto de** ® **Chacras**, a traditional Argentine grill on Aristides Villanueva.

9:00pm Head to the Frank Romero Day amphitheater for the final *Vendimia* event, the *Coronación de la Reina de Vendimia*. Under 45,000 dazzling lights, more than 800 performers move about the giant stage. At midnight the queen of *Vendimia* is elected, stirring pride in the crowd. As a fitting end to your Argentine stay, graciously turn to your neighbor and offer a toast to the new queen, the celebrated wine, and the splendor of Argentina.

Alternatives

Excellent accommodations abound in the Argentine capital. The French Empire-style **Alvear Palace Hotel**, built in 1932, is the grande dame of Buenos Aires hotels. The centrally located **Libertador Kempinski** has lovely marble- and mahogany-studded rooms. Madonna's favorite is the **Park Hyatt**—it has a 13-floor marble tower and a multimillion-dollar art collection. Choices are limited in Mendoza. One alternative is the comfortable and modern **Hotel Aconcagua**.

For dinner in Buenos Aires, check out **Tago Mago** in the Puerto Madero. It offers Mediterranean cuisine in a chic setting with an animated crowd. Or spend a full evening in the Recoleta area. The trendy Soho-style **Harper's** serves international cuisine to an upbeat crowd of Buenos Aires hipsters. With a wait staff of acting students, the festive **Negroni** is one of the liveliest places to eat in the Recoleta. Make a reservation in advance and stick around for the dinner show, which can include belly dancing and a Michael Jackson impersonator, followed by dancing until 4 a.m. **Sahara** has three floors, two dance clubs, and a stylish restaurant. In Mendoza, **1884 Francis Mallman** is one of the finest restaurants in town. For more action, let loose at **La Mejicana**, in the Palmares Mall, where Mexican food is served during a fun dinner show. Afterward, there's music and dancing until 4 a.m.

A good way to spend an afternoon in Buenos Aires is at the **Museo de Arte Moderno**, which has rotating exhibits of local painters and sculptors. Or check out Plaza San Martín. Once a haven for vagrants, it's now an elegant square with native as well as imported plants and an equestrian monument to the great Argentine general José de San Martín.

The Hot Sheet

☎ 54/114

$ 1.0 Argentine Peso

HOTELS	DAY	ADDRESS	*	PH	PRICE	FX	RMS	BEST ROOMS
Alvear Palace Hotel	A	1891 Av. Alvear		808-2100 800- 448-8355	$$$$	804-9246	100	River vw
Caesar Park Hotel	1	1232 Posadas		814-5150 800- 223-6800	$$$$	819-1121	172	Dlx river or gdn vw
Hotel Aconcagua	A	545 San Lorenzo	261	420-4499	$$	420-2083	159	Front rm w/ mtn vw
Hotel Huentala	2	1007 Primitivo de la Reta	261	420-0766	$$$	420-0766	88	Mtn vw
Libertador Kempinski	A	690 Av. Córdoba		322-8800 800- 325-3535	$$$$	325-5492	200	Dlx rm
Park Hyatt	A	1086 Posadas		321-1234 800- 233-1234	$$$$	321-1235	115	Rm 335

RESTAURANTS	DAY	ADDRESS	*	PH	PRICE	REC	DRESS	FOOD
1884 Francis Mallman	A	1188 Belgrano-Godoy Cruz	261	424-2698	$$$	LD	Dressy	International
Alto de Chacras	3	Aristides Vallanueva y Olascoaga	261	423-6595	$$	D/L	Euro	International
Café Tortoni	2	829 Av. de Mayo		342-4328	$	B/LD	Local	Cafe
Don Mario	3	1324 "25 de Mayo"	261	431-0810	$$	L/D	Kazh	Grilled meats
Harper's	A	1763 Junín		801-7140	$$$$	LD	Euro	International
La Biela	1	600 Av. Quintana		804-4135	$	B/LD	Local	Cafe
Lola	1	1805 R.M. Ortiz		804-3410	$	L/D	Euro	Continental
Marchigiana Restaurant	2	1550 Patricias Mendocinas	261	420-0212	$$	D/L	Euro	Continental
Negroni	A	1769 Junín		806-9309	$$$	D	Euro	Traditional Argentinian
Spettus Steak House	1	876 Av. Alicia Moreau de Justo		334-4126	$$$$	D/L	Euro	Steaks
Tago Mago	A	R. Obligado and J. Salguero		804-2444	$$$	LD	Euro	Mediterranean
Tocororo	2	1050 Av. Alicia Moreau de Justo		342-6032	$$	L/D	Euro	Cuban, international

NITELIFE	DAY	ADDRESS	*	PH	PRICE	REC	DRESS	MUSIC
Al Diablo	2	5505 Lujan	261	no phone	$$	O	Kazh	Dance, house, disco
Casa Blanca	1	668 Balcara		343-5002	$$$$	SF	Euro	Flamenco
Divino	1	225 Cecilia Grierson		316-8400	$$	O	Euro	Disco
La Mejicana	A	2650 Ruta Panamericana in Palmares Mall	261	439-9346	$$	OSF	Euro	Disco
Negroni	A	1769 Junín		806-9309	$$	OS	Euro	Cabaret, dance
Sahara	A	13335 Junín		801-7544	$	O	Euro	Disco
Treinta y Pico	2	318 "25 de Mayo"	261	no phone	$	O	Kazh	Dance

SIGHTS & ATTRACTIONS	DAY	ADDRESS	*	PH	ENTRY FEE
Bodega Lagarde	3	1745 San Martín	261	498-0011	None
Museo de Arte Moderno	A	350 San Juan		361-1121	$
Museo Nacional de Bellas Artes	1	1473 Av. del Libertador		803-4691	None
Recoleta Cemetery	1	Vicente López at Junín		no phone	None
Sociedad Anónima Escorihuela	3	898 Belgano	261	424-2282	None
General Tourist Information Office		237 Av. Callao		372-3612	
Mendoza Visitor Information		1143 San Martín	261	420-2800	

EVENT & TICKET INFO

Via Blanca and *Carrusel* parades (San Martín Avenue, Mendoza) are free.

Coronación de la Reina de Vendimia (Frank Romero Day Greek Theater, Parque General San Martín, Teatro Griego): Tickets ($35) must be purchased no later than January. For tickets and information, contact *PACSEM* (54/261-420-1911).

---

*261=Mendoza

RECommendations: (Restaurants) B–Breakfast; L–Lunch; D–Dinner; T–High tea or snack
(Nitelife) G–Gaming; H–Hangout bar; M–Live music; O–Dancing (disco); P–Dancing (live music); S–Show; F–Food served
()–Available but without recommendation. For complete explanation of Hot Sheet format, see page 34.

NYC +2   60°/79° (16°/26°)   Buenos Aires (Ezeiza) (EZE); 30 min./$50; Mendoza (MDZ) 30 min./$20   Yes/No   Spanish

The Fun Also Rises

Venice, Italy

Venice Carnival

(Carnevale di Venezia)

| Origin: 1979 | Event ★ ★ ★ ★ ★ ★ ★ ★ ★ ★ City | Attendance: 500,000 |

*C*arnevale in Venice isn't so much a fixed event as it is an electrifying escape route to a time and world far away. During the days preceding Lent, the narrow streets of mist-veiled Venice (Venezia) teem with celebrants in opera-quality costumes. Glittering confetti reflects the passions of these surreal time travelers, who dance through the city's ancient pathways and ballrooms.

The *Carnevale* dream world recalls centuries of Venetian glory, especially the period from the Renaissance through the mid-1700s. The former city-state's Byzantine, Gothic, and Renaissance structures present a spectacular backdrop for street entertainers popular in bygone times—fire-eaters, musicians, mimes, dancers, stilt-walkers, magicians, singers, acrobats, and heckler poets. Concerts, theatrical productions, and operas are scheduled throughout town. Piazza San Marco, perhaps Europe's most famed plaza, pulses with a giddy crowd fueled by espresso, grappa, *prosecco*, and wild imagination. Even the damp, cold weather contributes to the magical ambience.

When elaborately (and expensively) costumed partyers aren't wandering like antique envoys through fog and moonlight, they're attending lavish balls in renovated palaces, dancing the minuet, polonaise, and other classical steps. Don't fret if you can't minuet or if you thought polonaise was a sauce—most balls also include modern moves and music.

It's possible that in another galaxy far away there's a place as enchanting as Venice, but you're not likely to see it in your lifetime. Canals carve this unique city into a puzzle built atop more than 100 miniature islands. The soothing sound of water lapping against quays and buildings permeates the Venetian air. In the absence of automobiles, canals function as thoroughfares navigated by private boats, water taxis, and public ferries.

Tourism tops the list of industries in this unique city, and its high-end hotels push grace and luxury—along with your credit card—to the limit. Known to Italians as *La Serenissima* (the most serene), Venice holds some of Europe's finest treasures in its museums and churches. But more importantly, the city itself is a spellbinding work of art made almost unimaginably exquisite during *Carnevale*.

Day 1. Fri.   Mar. 3, 2000
(Day 1. Friday   February 23, 2001)

10:30am Descend the four-story grand staircase at the deluxe **Hotel Danieli**. Built in the 14th century as a showplace for the Doge (leader of the Venetian Republic), the Danieli has been the "hotel for kings" since 1822. Walk to the Ponte dei Sospiri (Bridge of Sighs), where prisoners let out their last breaths before succumbing to grotesque acts of medieval "justice." Skirt the Piazza San Marco and head for the Ponte di Rialto, a beautiful bridge more than 400 years old.

11:30am Near the Ponte di Rialto, find **Nicoloa Atelier**, where you'll be fitted for your 18th-century costume. The best in the business, Nicoloa makes authentic reproductions of period attire.

1:00pm Near Piazza San Marco have lunch at **Da Ivo**. The food is Tuscan, but this rustic restaurant is packed with Venetians, who come for the home-style cooking and friendly atmosphere.

3:00pm On Piazza San Marco, the magic of **Venice Carnival** is just getting started. Confetti from the passing **Venice Carnival Society Parade** blankets the square.

3:30pm Filling the piazza with precision movements, hundreds of masked dancers execute a quadrille for the free, outdoor **Gran Ballo delle Maschere** (Great Ball of the Masks). Afterward, at 5 p.m., a parade of the most beautiful masks rings the elegant piazza.

6:30pm Walk to Calle del Caffettier for a glass of Italian wine or grappa (distilled liquor made from grape must) at the popular wine bar **Vino Vino**.

8:00pm Return to Piazza San Marco for an unforgettable meal at **Quadri**. The views onto the piazza are as magnificent as the seafood specialties.

9:30pm Every night, **Venice Carnival** provides fantastic entertainment. Whether moving real pawns, knights (sans horses), and rooks around a giant chess board or enjoying an open-air concert, **Carnevale** is always intoxicating.

Midnight Step back into the present with a spin of the roulette wheel at **Vendramin-Calergi Palace** on the Grand Canal. German composer Richard Wagner died in this 15th-century building in 1883, so even the casino is steeped in history! Afterward, head for the **Martini Scala Club**, one of the only places to grab a late-night bite. Enjoy piano music while sipping a Bellini cocktail.

Day 2. Sat.   Mar. 4, 2000
(Day 2. Saturday   February 24, 2001)

10:00am After breakfast in the hotel, take a water taxi to the wooden Ponte dell'Accademia. Just off Campo San Vidal is Campo San Stefano and the Venetian **mask bazaar**. Masks play an important role in **Carnevale**, hiding flirtations and illicit affairs, even, reputedly, between men of the cloth and women of the flesh.

11:30am Walk to the **Palazzo Grassi**, a gorgeous, privately owned 18th-century building that has rotating exhibits of modern art and architecture.

1:30pm Make your way to Campo San Fantin and lunch on the beautiful courtyard terrace at **Antico Martini**. The food and decor are classic Venetian.

3:00pm Walk to Piazza San Marco in the heart of the city. **Basilica di San Marco** dominates the piazza with its gaudy and eclectic ornamentation. Go inside (dress conservatively) to view religious icons, sarcophagi, and golden riches. For a panoramic view of the city, climb the nearby bell tower. Next door, the **Palazzo Ducale**, the Doge's palace, is filled with classic oil paintings and frescoes.

5:30pm Before the big night, relax with an English-style tea served at the 8th-century **Caffè Florian** between 3 and 6 p.m. This fashionable cafe has catered to the likes of Lord Byron and Goethe since 1720. When the *Marangona* in the bell tower chimes the coming of night, return to the hotel to begin your transformation into regal courtier.

8:30pm Step out in your starch-stiffened lace-and-brocade masterpiece and join the cream of Venetian society at the grand *Il Ballo del Doge*. After a dinner of regional specialties, you can dance the minuet to a live orchestra or find a DJ spinning disco.

Day 3. Sun.   Mar. 5, 2000
(Day 3. Sunday   February 25, 2001)

9:00am Travel by water taxi to the prestigious Gritti Palace hotel. Have breakfast at **Ristorante Club del Doge** on the hotel's terrace.

10:00am Jump on a *traghetti gondola*, the quickest way across the reverse *S*-shaped Grand Canal to the **Galleria dell'Accademia**, the great repository of paintings by the Venetian masters.

Noon Lunch at nearby **Locanda Montin**. Original art painted by patrons adorns the walls of this charming inn, where regulars sit under an outdoor arbor and let waiters order Italian dishes for them.

1:30pm Walk through the tranquil district of Dorsoduro, the historic Jewish neighborhood, until you find **Collezione Peggy Guggenheim**, considered by some to be the greatest collection of modern art in the world.

3:00pm Take a water taxi to the Ponte di Rialto for a *gondola* ride. While this is *the* romantic and touristy thing to do in Venice, it's also a nice way to explore the city—you'll see Renaissance bridges, towering palaces, and winding canals.

5:30pm Return to Piazza San Marco for the watery *Corteo Acqueo di Carnevale*. Watch as boat after boat of opulently dressed sailors and passengers row by, and gondoliers in traditional costumes pole around singing and carrying on. This is *Venice Carnival* at its most flamboyant.

8:30pm Walk in the misty evening air toward the Ponte di Rialto and the venerable **Trattoria alla Madonna**, which has been pleasing Venetians with regional food and a convivial atmosphere for more than 45 years.

10:00pm Return to any of the outdoor concerts that you might have passed on your way to dinner. Musical entertainment can vary from stringed trios to tango acts—other spectacles include jugglers, tumblers, magicians, and clowns.

Midnight Round out the evening at **Harry's Bar** on Piazza San Marco, which enjoys an international reputation as the best restaurant and bar in the city. While the simple decor may not be anything to write home about, the drinks are good enough to have made the place a favorite of Hemingway. Savor *la dolce vita* and the final moments of your masked fantasy.

Alternatives

Overlooking the Grand Canal, the luxurious **Hotel Europa & Regina** boasts a gorgeous inlaid-marble foyer. The deluxe **Hotel Monaco & Grand Canal**, within a mile of Piazza San Marco, has artfully decorated rooms with crystal chandeliers. The newest hotel address in Venice is the stately "design-hotel" **Ca' Pisani**—in the quiet Jewish quarter, it offers comfortable, modern rooms.

The newly reconstructed **Ca' d'Oro** museum is housed in a late-Gothic building so gorgeous that it shames the great works within.

Another worthwhile masquerade ball on Saturday is the *Gran Gala a la Belle Epoque*. After dinner, various troupes, including mimes, magicians, and jugglers, show their stuff, followed by traditional dances—the polonaise and waltz.

The Hot Sheet

☎ 39/041

$ 1,800 Lira

HOTELS	DAY	ADDRESS	PH	PRICE	FX	RMS	BEST ROOMS
Ca' Pisani	A	Rio Tera' Antonio Fascalini, Dorsoduro 979A	241-7560 800- 337-4685	$$$	520-5858	30	Front facing rm
Hotel Europa & Regina	A	San Marco 2159	520-0477 800- 325-3535	$$$$+	523-1533	185	Dlx canal vw
Hotel Danieli	1	Riva degli Schiavoni, Castello 4196	522-6480 800- 325-3535	$$$$+	520-0208	240	Lagoon vw
Hotel Monaco & Grand Canal	A	Calle Vallaresso, San Marco 1325	520-0211 800- 457-4000	$$$$+	520-0501	70	Grand Canal vw

RESTAURANTS	DAY	ADDRESS	PH	PRICE	REC	DRESS	FOOD
Antico Martini	2	Campo San Fantin, San Marco 1983	522-4121	$$$	L/D	Euro	Venetian, international
Caffè Florian	2	Piazza San Marco 56-59	528-5338	$	T/LD	Euro	Tea, Venetian
Da Ivo	1	Calle dei Fuseri, San Marco 1809	528-5004	$$$	L/D	Euro	Tuscan
Locanda Montin	3	Fondamenta di Borgo, Dorsoduro 1147	522-7151	$$	L/D	Euro	Italian, international
Quadri	1	Piazza San Marco 120-124	522-2105	$$$$	D/L	Euro	Italian, international
Ristorante Club del Doge	3	Campo S. Maria del Giglio, San Marco 2467, in Gritti Palace hotel	79-4611	$$$	B/LD	Euro	Buffet
Trattoria alla Madonna	3	Calle della Madonna, San Polo 594	522-3824	$$	D/L	Euro	Venetian, Italian

NITELIFE	DAY	ADDRESS	PH	PRICE	REC	DRESS	MUSIC
Harry's Bar	3	Calle Vallaresso, San Marco 1323	528-5777	None	H(F)	Euro	
Martini Scala Club	1	Campo San Fantin, San Marco 1983	522-4121	None	MF	Euro	Piano
Vendramin-Calergi Palace	1	Strada Nuova, Cannaregio 2040	529-7111	$	G	Euro	
Vino Vino	1	Calle del Cafetier, San Marco 2007A	523-7027	None	H(F)	Euro	

SIGHTS & ATTRACTIONS	DAY	ADDRESS	PH	ENTRY FEE
Basilica di San Marco	2	Piazza San Marco	522-5205	None
Ca' d'Oro	a	Calle Cadolo, Cannaregio 3934	523-8790	$
Collezione Peggy Guggenheim	3	Calle San Cristoforo, Dorsoduro 71	520-6288	$
Galleria dell'Accademia	3	Campo della Carità, Dorsoduro	522-2247	$
Palazzo Ducale	2	Piazzetta San Marco	522-4951	$
Palazzo Grassi	2	Campo San Samuele, San Marco 3231	523-1680	$

OTHER SIGHTS, SERVICES & ATTRACTIONS

Gondola	3	Ponte di Rialto	522-4904	$$$$+
Nicoloa Atelier	1	Cannaregio 5565	520-7051	$$$$+
Azienda di Promozione Turistica		Piazza San Marco 71F	529-8711	

EVENT & TICKET INFO

Venice Carnival (various locations around Venice): All street events are free. For more information, contact *Club Culturale Italiano* (39/041-71-7065).

Il Ballo del Doge (Palazzo Pisani-Moretta): For tickets ($250) and information, contact the *Murano Art Shop* (39/041-523-3851).

Gran Gala a la Belle Epoque (Palazzo Albrizzi): For tickets ($250) and information, call *Associazone Culturale Italo-Tedesca* (39/041-523-2544).

RECommendations: (Restaurants) B–Breakfast; L–Lunch; D–Dinner; T–High tea or snack
(Nitelife) G–Gaming; H–Hangout bar; M–Live music; O–Dancing (disco); P–Dancing (live music); S–Show; F–Food served
()–Available but without recommendation. For complete explanation of Hot Sheet format, see page 34.

⏰ NYC +6 | ☀ 34°/47° (1°/8°) | ✈ Milan (Malpensa); (MPX) 180 min./SNA Marco Polo (VEC); 30 min./$35 | 🚗 No | 🗣 Italian

Karneval

Köln, Germany

Origin: 1823　　　　　　Event ★ ★ ★ ★ ★ ★ City　　　　　Attendance: 1 million

Clowns traditionally get away with lots of crazy behavior and nowhere is it more fun to the test the limits of clowning around than at *Karneval* in Köln (Cologne). The event transforms this city on the Rhein into a three-day circus of beer consumption, embodied by tens of thousands of exuberant merrymakers dressed in elaborate clown attire.

You'll quickly learn why Köln's greatest draw is its jovial people (Kölners). Everybody at *Karneval* gets into the spirit. Most revelers contribute to the carnivalesque atmosphere by donning colorful costumes. The majority of celebrants run around in clown garb. Others come as virgins, farmers, and Prussian soldiers, which sounds like the setup to a bawdy joke and is just as much fun. Hundreds of songs are recorded especially for *Karneval* and crowded sing-alongs add to the excitement. Other excuses for imbibing include parties, balls, and nonstop tavern hopping (beer at breakfast is nothing to be ashamed of during *Karneval*).

On the Monday before Ash Wednesday, more than a million bedecked partyers walk a five-mile route through town as part of the *Rosenmontagzug* (Rose Monday Parade). Candy, flowers, and bottles of cologne, first manufactured in Köln in the 18th century, are tossed into the crowds. When Kölners aren't heating up cold winter nights at dances and parties, they're singing and laughing inside local bars, whose owners don't even bother trying to observe legal closing hours during *Karneval*.

Germany's fourth-largest city (90 percent of which was destroyed by bombs in World War II) is as picturesque as it is historic. Constantine and Charlemagne both passed through the city, which today is an important economic center and known to Germans as one of their country's best party towns—Köln claims to have more bars than any other city in Germany. The pedestrian zone around the *Hauptbahnhof* (main train station) puts visitors within walking distance of the city's top attractions including Germany's most impressive cathedral, Kölner Dom, and right in the heart of *Karneval*'s hypercharged antics.

Day 1. Sat.   Mar. 4, 2000
(Day 1. Saturday   February 24, 2001)

9:30am Check into your spacious room at the stately **Dom-Hotel**. With a view of Köln's celebrated cathedral, the hotel is next to the festival hub—Domplatz—and within chocolate-throwing distance of just about all the **Karneval** fun.

10:30am After making arrangements with the hotel concierge for this evening's costume, walk to the nearby **Gaffel Haus** and enjoy a traditional *Frühschoppen*, an early-morning drink to kick off **Karneval**. The Altes Rathaus, located on this handsome square as well, is the oldest town hall in Germany (but was entirely rebuilt after World War II).

Noon Head to the **Funkenbiwak** party at Neumarkt Square. You'll find **Karneval** societies dressed in uniform (mostly red), the square noisy, and the crowd full of clowns.

1:30pm Just off the nearby Rudolfplatz, have lunch at **Die Tomate**, a unique restaurant with international dishes all appropriately starring the tomato. *"Klein aber fein!"* (small but excellent) is the quote that applies to this must-try eatery.

3:00pm Explore the **Roman-Germanic Museum**, built atop a Roman villa. It boasts the famous Dionysus mosaic uncovered during a 1941 air raid.

4:00pm Just a step away on Am Hof, experience the true Germanic atmosphere at **Coellner Hofbrau Früh** (note the old spelling of Köln). Steins of frothy Kölsch beer are sure to put you in a festive mood.

7:00pm After getting into your costume, cab to the noble **Grande Milano** for dinner. House specialties include Italian risottos with truffles. The marble and cherry-wood interior is fantastic.

8:30pm Arrive by taxi at one of **Karneval**'s most popular festivities, the **Rote Funken Kostümball**. In addition to all the clowns, you'll take in a host of other colorful and extravagant costumes. Live bands play a range of sounds from ballroom to modern dance music.

Midnight All around Friesenplatz, on both sides of Hohenzollernring, taverns fill up with people singing, dancing, and drinking. Take a taxi there and share the **Karneval** energy or go to the bright, friendly, Tex-Mex-style **Peppermint** pub for a final drink or snack.

Day 2. Sun.   Mar. 5, 2000
(Day 2. Sunday   February, 25, 2001)

10:00am Enjoy brunch in the shadow of the cathedral at the hotel's casual **Atelier am Dom** restaurant.

11:30am Spend time inside the spectacular **Dom Kirche**, the purest, most perfect example of High Gothic architecture. Begun in 1248 but not completed until 1880, the cathedral contains the heaviest bell in the world. Across the way, the ultramodern **Museum Ludwig** houses impressive 20th-century paintings and an outstanding Picasso collection. Located in the same complex is the Agfa-Foto-Historama, perhaps the world's finest photography collection.

1:00pm Have a lunch of modern continental cuisine with a great Rhein River view at **Bastei**, which is built on top of an old fortification.

3:00pm Just past the Zoobrücke, take the **Kölner Rhein-Seilbahn** for a scenic cable car ride across the river to the Rheinpark. With more than 100 acres, you won't be able to explore it all, but you're sure to enjoy the botanical gardens and modern-sculpture park. Wander toward the Tanzbrunnen (Dancing Fountain)—a 30,000 seat open-air auditorium and stage—to find a crowd and music. Near the Hohenzollernbrücke, you can catch a boat and shuttle back to the other side of the river.

6:00pm It's a short hop to **Papa Joe's Klimperkasten**, which has atmosphere galore, live jazz, and piano music. The square outside should be pulsing with celebrants.

8:30pm Taxi to the southern part of the city center for dinner with a panoramic view. Enjoy your meal 11 stories above Köln at the spectacular, glassed-in
Ⓡ **Restaurant im Wasserturm**. French-influenced cuisine and decor top off the experience.

10:30pm The Südstadt neighborhood has the most stylish bars and attracts the biggest crowds at any time of year. **Chlodwig-Eck** is the starting point where everyone gathers for a beer to begin the evening. Afterward, follow the crowd from place to place.

Day 3. Mon.   Mar. 6, 2000
(Day 3. Monday   February 26, 2001)

10:00am Don clown regalia this morning. You may feel silly at first, but that'll change once you're surrounded by throngs of jesters. Go for a hearty breakfast at
Ⓡ **Café Reichard**. With tables in a glass pavilion, it's one of Köln's most grand and popular meeting places.

11:00am Be on the street for the ***Rosenmontagzug***, ***Karneval***'s official parade. From the floats, brightly costumed members of ***Karneval*** societies toss sweets by the ton and flowers by the bushel. Shouting "*Kamelle!*" or "*Strüssjer!*" will encourage them to lob items in your direction.

1:00pm Lunch at the rustic **Ratskeller** in the Altes
Ⓡ Rathaus. Rheinland specialties such as Sauerbraten will warm you up.

2:30pm In honor of all the candy sailing through the air, go to the **Imhoff-Stollwerck-Museum**, an unusual building dedicated to chocolate.

4:00pm Visit Köln's most famous address, **Glockengasse 4711**, a perfume boutique and exhibition center, home of the "wonderful water" also known as eau de cologne.

5:00pm Taxi to nearby **Stadtgarten** on Venloerstrasse for some afternoon refreshment. This modern building complex has a restaurant, beer garden, concert hall, and jazz club.

7:30pm Dine at the prominent **Restaurant Keule** on
Ⓡ Heumarkt. Two floors of rustic ambience make the regional German food even tastier.

9:00pm Take a taxi to the Belgisches Viertel neighborhood. **Alcazar** is just one popular bar that'll be packed during ***Karneval***. On nearby Zulpicherstrasse, the stylish **Umbruch** offers DJ tunes and a great whiskey selection.

Midnight Head a little farther south along Hohenstaufenring to the see-and-be-seen **Aceton**. The interior alone is worth the trip, but the crowd and music are fun, too. Clown around on the dance floor before bidding *Auf Wiedersehen* to ***Karneval***.

Alternatives

The modern **Renaissance Köln Hotel** is close to the ***Karneval*** action. Also ideally located, the **Hotel Europa Am Dom** makes guests feel at home. The luxurious **Hotel im Wasserturm** is a monumental creation in a spectacularly re-designed old water tower.

At **Rosebud**, one of the most beautiful bars in Köln, you can choose from among 150 cocktails. The disco at **Alter Wartesaal** in the old *Hauptbahnhof* is a sure bet for nighttime entertainment.

If you need to give your feet a break, take a scenic boat trip up the Rhein with **Köln-Düsseldorfer Rheinschiffahrt**, near the Deutzer Brücke.

On the Friday of ***Karneval*** weekend, the doctors' ***Meditziner Kostümball*** is a fun event where scrubs and nurse costumes prevail. If you can't get tickets to the ***Rote Funken Kostümball***, the equally worthy ***EhrenGarde Mummenschanz Kostümball*** takes place on Saturday night as well.

The Hot Sheet

☎ 49/221

$ 1.8 Deutschmark

HOTELS	DAY	ADDRESS	PH	PRICE	FX	RMS	BEST ROOMS
Dom-Hotel	1	2A Domkloster	2-0240 800- 543-4300	$$$	202-4444	124	Supr rm w/ cathedral vw
Hotel Europa Am Dom	A	38-46 Am Hof	2-0580 800- 448-8355	$$	258-2032	92	Cathedral vw
Hotel im Wasserturm	A	2 Kaygasse	2-0080 800- 337-4685	$$$$	200-8888	88	Duplex rm w/ city vw
Renaissance Köln Hotel	A	20 Magnusstr.	2-0340 800- 872-6338	$$	203-4777	236	5th fl w/ cathedral vw

RESTAURANTS	DAY	ADDRESS	PH	PRICE	REC	DRESS	FOOD
Atelier am Dom	2	see Dom-Hotel	2-0240	$$$	B/LD	Kazh	International
Bastei	2	80 Konrad-Adenauer-Ufer	12-2825	$$$$	L/D	Euro	International
Café Reichard	3	11 Unter Fettenhennen	257-8542	$$	B/LT	Kazh	Cafe
Die Tomate	1	11 Aachenerstr.	257-4307	$$	L/D	Local	International, continental
Grande Milano	1	29-37 Hohenstaufenring	24-2121	$$$	D/L	Dressy	Northern Italian
Ratskeller	3	1 Rathausplatz	257-6929	$$	L/D	Kazh	International, German
Restaurant im Wasserturm	2	see Hotel im Wasserturm	2-0080	$$$	D/BL	Dressy	International
Restaurant Keule	3	56-58 Heumarkt	258-1159	$$	D/L	Kazh	International, regional

NITELIFE	DAY	ADDRESS	PH	PRICE	REC	DRESS	MUSIC
Aceton	3	46 Luxembergerstr.	42-6112	None	O	Euro	Hip-hop, funk, '60s
Alcazar	3	39 Bismarckstr.	51-5733	None	H	Euro	
Alter Wartesaal	A	11 Johanisstr., Am Hauptbahnhof	912-8850	$$	O	Kazh	House, dance
Chlodwig-Eck	2	1-3 Annostr.	32-7595	None	H(F)	Kazh	
Coellner Hofbrau Früh	1	12-14 Am Hof	258-0397	None	H(F)	Kazh	
Gaffel Haus	1	20-22 Alter Markt	257-7692	None	H(F)	Local	
Papa Joe's Klimperkasten	2	50 Alter Markt	258-2132	None	M(F)	Kazh	Jazz, piano
Peppermint	1	23 Hohenstauffenring	240-1929	None	H(F)	Kazh	
Rosebud	A	20 Heinsbergerstr.	240-1455	None	H(F)	Euro	
Stadtgarten	3	40 Venloerstr.	952-9946	None	H(F)	Kazh	
Umbruch	3	11 Zulpicherstr.	240-6622	None	H	Euro	

SIGHTS & ATTRACTIONS	DAY	ADDRESS	PH	ENTRY FEE
Dom Kirche	2	3 Domkloster	9-258-4720	None
Glockengasse 4711	3	4711 Glockengasse	572-8520	None
Imhoff-Stollwerck-Museum	3	Rheinauhafen	931-8880	$
Kölner Rhein-Seilbahn	2	180 Riehlerstr., Rheinpark	547-4181	$
Museum Ludwig	2	1 Bischofgartenstr.	2-212-2379	$
Roman-Germanic Museum	1	4 Roncalliplatz	2-212-4438	$

OTHER SIGHTS, SERVICES & ATTRACTIONS

Köln-Düsseldorfer Rheinschiffahrt	A	15 Frankenwerft	208-8318	$$$$
Cologne Tourist Bureau		19 Unter Fettenhennen	2-212-3345	

EVENT & TICKET INFO

Karneval Köln (various locations around Köln): All street events are free.

Rote Funken Kostümball (Maritim-Hotel Köln, 20 Heumarkt)

EhrenGarde Mummenschanz Kostümball (Sartory Säle, 44-48 Friesenstr.)

Meditziner Kostümball (Gürzenich, 27-31 Martinstr.)

Rosenmontagzug parade (grandstand seats)

Tickets (about $30 for each) can be purchased at the Carnival Committee's Box Office on Neumarkt square. Tickets and information are also available from the *Carnival Committee* (49/221-57-4000).

RECommendations: (Restaurants) B–Breakfast; L–Lunch; D–Dinner; T–High tea or snack
(Nitelife) G–Gaming; H–Hangout bar; M–Live music; O–Dancing (disco); P–Dancing (live music); S–Show; F–Food served
()–Available but without recommendation. For complete explanation of Hot Sheet format, see page 34.

NYC +6   31°/42° (0°/5°)   Frankfurt (FRA); 120 min./SNA (R) Cologne/Bonn (CGB); 30 min./$30   No   German

The Fun Also Rises

Worldly Processions

Isn't it funny that it's taken a century of psychotherapy to show us what "primitive" cultures had figured out long ago—that releasing inhibitions is actually a good thing? The Roman Catholic Church gets credit for inventing the name *carnival* sometime around the Italian Renaissance. The Latin roots *valle* and *carne* mean "farewell" and "flesh," respectively, and modern carnivals build to an eruption of wild energy on the days just before Ash Wednesday, the solemn first day of Lent when Catholics say goodbye to meat. But little else connected with the carnival feast of abandonment, pleasure, and reverie belongs to the Catholics.

Egyptians recorded the first carnival more than 4,000 years ago as the five days of "time outside of time," an annual chronological hiccup and party that completed their 360-day calendar. By the time the Catholics got involved, it was more or less to call a truce after failing to stop the ancient pagan festivals highlighted by masks, costumes, and dance. To anyone living under the restrictive rule of medieval Catholicism, liberating internal repression and sinning boldly no doubt was a decent trade-off for having to pray regularly and abstain from eating meat during the forty days leading to Easter.

The grand masked balls of the French may have been the most influential carnival tradition, but the mayhem of *entrudo* from Portugal and Spain still influences many Latin American carnivals. For African slaves, who were typically given short holiday periods just once a year, carnivals were an ideal forum for their ancient traditions of song, dance, and percussion. The opportunity to parody members of high society no doubt also held special appeal. In the Americas, exuberant African rhythms have dominated the syncretic festival evolution process.

Pre-Lenten carnivals, such as **Mardi Gras** and **Carnaval Rio**, take place all over the world. If you can't get to one of the *FunGuide100* destinations in late February or early March, don't

worry. Here are some other cities that host outstanding carnivals every year.

Nice, France
Viareggio, Italy
Basel, Switzerland
Aruba, Netherlands Antilles
Vera Cruz, Mexico
Panama City, Panama
Baranquilla, Columbia
Salvador, Brazil
Recife/Olinda, Brazil

African-flavored Caribbean and Brazilian festivals have emerged as the world's two favorite carnival styles. With its trademarked steel-pan, calypso, and soca music and limbo dancing, Trinidad and Tobago's annual carnival has become a model for celebrations around the world. These include *FunGuide100* events such as Toronto's **Caribana**, Barbados' **Crop Over**, and the **Notting Hill Carnival** in London, as well as dozens of others in North America and the Caribbean.

The appeal of carnival has proven so universal that new carnivals and carnival-style festivals have proliferated all over the globe. Not fixed by the Christian calendar, dates for these new events are often based on weather and tourist seasons. Here are some of the best Caribbean-style and multicultural carnivals not mentioned in *The FunGuide 100*:

BEYOND THE FUNGUIDE 100 CARNIVALS				
NAME	CITY	COUNTRY	MONTH	ATTENDANCE
Caribbean-style carnivals:				
Brooklyn West Indian Carnival	Brooklyn, New York	USA	Sep.	4 million (second-largest parade in the world)
Miami Caribbean Carnival	Miami, Florida	USA	Oct.	1 million
DC Caribbean Carnival	Washington, DC	USA	Jun.	400,000
Multicultural carnivals:				
Carnaval-San Francisco	San Francisco, California	USA	May	400,000 (largest Brazilian-style parade outside Brazil)
Solero Summer Carnival	Rotterdam	Holland	Jul.	800,000
Karneval de Kulteren	Berlin	Germany	May/Jun.	250,000
Karneval I Aalborg	Aalborg	Denmark	May	150,000

Though differentiated by time of year (pre-Lent or not) and type of music, parades, and costumes, carnivals connect everyone in a spirit of joy. Visitors of all ages are welcomed and encouraged to participate. Four of the *FunGuide100*'s seven five-star events are carnivals—in Venice, Rio de Janeiro, Trinidad and Tobago, and New Orleans (**Mardi Gras**). Carnivals have most of the elements that contribute to our idea of fun and, most importantly, they transform the people who participate in them as well as the cities in which they are held. This is why 11 *FunGuide100* events fall into this category.

AT A GLANCE: THE WORLD'S MOST FUN(GUIDE 100) CARNIVALS (in order of attendance)						
Name	City	Country	Month	Weather	Attendance	Characteristics
Carnaval	Rio de Janeiro	Brazil	Feb./Mar.	hot	10 million	lavish floats, sequins and skin, samba
Mardi Gras	New Orleans, Louisiana	USA	Feb./Mar.	cool/warm	3.5 million	lavish floats and costumes, bead- and doubloon-throwing
Caribana	Toronto	Canada	Aug.	warm	1.5 million	steel-pan and sound-truck parade, mas bands, sequins and flash, lavish floats and costumes, bead- and doubloon-throwing
Notting Hill Carnival	London	England	Aug.	warm	1.5 million	steel-pan and sound-truck parade, mas bands, sequins and flash
Carnival	Venice	Italy	Feb./Mar.	cold	500,000	no parade, but many people dressed in Renaissance costumes
Sydney Gay and Lesbian Mardi Gras	Sydney	Australia	Feb.	warm	500,000	parade, mostly marching in leather, gold lamé, and outrageous colors
Karneval	Köln	Germany	Feb./Mar.	cold	100,000	lavish floats, costumes, candy- and cologne-throwing
Carnival	Port of Spain	Trinidad and Tobago	Feb./Mar.	warm	100,000	steel-pan and sound-truck parade, mas bands, sequins and flash, J'Ouvert
Fantasy Fest	Key West, Florida	USA	Oct.	warm	60,000	parade, mostly marching; lavish costumes; body paint
Crop Over	Bridgetown	Barbados	Aug.	hot	10,000	steel-pan and sound-truck parade, mas bands, some sequins
Junkanoo	Nassau	Bahamas	Dec./Jan.	warm	10,000	2 a.m. steel-pan and sound-truck parade, mas bands, sequins and flash

Carnaval Rio

Origin: 1930	Event ★ ★ ★ ★ ★ ★ ★ ★ City	Attendance: 10 million

Forget everything you've heard about *Carnaval Rio*—no words have been created to adequately describe the awesome spectacle that takes place in Rio de Janeiro during the four days of festivities prior to the beginning of Lent. The only way to really understand this convulsion of beauty, rhythm, song, dance, and craziness is to go!

Carnaval Rio has rightly become famous for its explosion of feathers, glitter, floats, (practically) nude beauties, pulsating rhythms, and deliriously happy crowds. When 50,000 people in matching costumes come together to dance and sing to drum orchestras and samba bands, you'll think you've died and gone to tropical heaven. The toughest decision is what to do about sleep—the unceasing spectacle created by Cariocas (as natives here are called) will leave you no time to waste on such trivial activities.

But *Carnaval Rio* is not restricted to the *Samba Schools Parades* that are central to the wild marches through the city. During the weekend before Lent, the city also swarms with *bandas*, the different types of musical groups and their devoted legions of party followers. Spontaneous parades, music, and dances erupt all over the city at *blocos*. Along with a variety of outdoor activities, many *Carnaval balls* at clubs and hotels also help make *Carnaval Rio* famous worldwide. During *Carnaval*, Rio is at the same time relaxing and frenetic—the nonstop party vibe makes it easy to leave everyday worries at home. The best way to do Rio is to "have it the nice way," as Cariocas are fond of saying. English translation: Go with the flow.

With a population of about six million, Rio de Janeiro is Brazil's second-largest city, but it's considered the country's cultural and emotional center. Famous for parties and beaches, Rio is an Atlantic beach destination any time of year. But before each Lent, one must wonder what Rio's most famed landmark—the giant statue of Jesus Christ perched atop Corcovado Mountain— must be thinking as it overlooks *Carnaval!*

Day-By-Day Plan For

Carnaval Rio

Day 1. Sun.   Mar. 5, 2000
(Day 1. Sunday   February 25, 2001)

8:30am The **Copacabana Palace** is a Mediterranean-style jewel from the 1920s. Be prepared to bump into actors, rock stars, and international politicians.

10:00am For heart-stopping aerial views of The Wonderful City (as Rio is often called), go to the **Sugar Loaf Cable Car Station**, located in Praia Vermelha. At the station, take the cable car to Urca Mountain, then a second cable car to Sugar Loaf.

1:00pm Taxi to the Flamengo district to have the famous shrimp- or beef-filled *pasteis* at the charming and refined **Alcaparra**.

2:30pm Go back to the hotel and take in the sun and surf of the Atlantic Ocean, right across the road.

5:30pm From **Corcovado Railroad Station**, take the small train through a tropical forest to the famous statue of Christ—Cristo Redentor—atop Corcovado Mountain. Stick around for the gorgeous sunset views.

8:30pm Have dinner at the impeccable **Cipriani** and find out why Francesco Carli is one of the most celebrated chefs in Rio. Or sit on the terrace at **Maxim's** on Copacabana beach, and enjoy the buzz and international cuisine.

10:00pm The ***Samba Schools Parade*** defies description. Just show up at the Sambadrome and prepare to be completely overstimulated. Don't worry if you arrive after the parade has started—the action gets progressively louder, wilder, and more erotic from the third samba school on.

Midnight If you want to participate, head to a ***Carnaval Ball***. The best are held at Scala or Copacabana Palace. Don't be put off by the almost total nudity of some women. This is Rio. This is ***Carnaval***. This is inevitable.

Day 2. Mon.   Mar. 6, 2000
(Day 2. Monday   February 26, 2001)

8:30am Sleeping in is expected, but if you can manage, begin your day at **Ao Ponto**, one of the most famous breakfast spots in town.

9:30am Go to Praca 15, the heart of the old center of Rio, and take a look at the Paco Imperial, where Portuguese royalty lived when they fled to Brazil during Napoleon's occupation of Portugal. Nowadays, it houses contemporary-art exhibitions. Around the square, check out the Church of Our Lady of Carmo, the former cathedral of Rio. Next door is the ornate Church of the Ordem Terceira do Carmo. Follow the Travessa do Comercio, walking under the Arch of Teles for a glimpse of the charm of 19th-century Rio. Finish your stroll along Ouvidor Street.

11:00am At the trolley-car station Bondinhos de Santa Teresa, take the car marked "Paula Matos" for a round trip through the Brazilian Montmartre.

1:00pm Lunch with Cariocas at **Guimas**. The steak with Boursin cheese and pears is delicious.

3:00pm Rent a helicopter at **Helicopter Sightseeing** (at Rodrigo de Freitas Lagoon). Choose Tour Number 4 and fly over the lagoon, Ipanema, Copacabana, Sugar Loaf, Maracana Soccer Stadium, and the statue of Christ.

5:00pm Join the hoopla surrounding the ***Bloco de Segunda***, one of the most lively happenings of the ***Carioca Carnaval***. Buy a can of beer and dance in the streets with the buoyant crowd.

8:00pm Dine on grilled meats as perfected by the gauchos of Brazil. **Mariu's** serves fine marinated barbecued meats, poultry, and fish.

10:00pm People argue over which day is better to see the **Samba Schools Parade**. The solution? Go both days!

Day 3. Tue.   Mar. 7, 2000
(Day 3. Tuesday   February 27, 2001)

10:00am Have breakfast at **Pérgula**, the hotel's poolside restaurant. Or rest on the beach or in your room with room service.

11:30am Taxi to the largest urban forest on the planet, the **Parque Nacional da Tijuca**. Birds, butterflies, and forest animals inhabit its waterfalls, grottoes, lakes, and gardens. It's hard to believe, but this lush forest is located within the city.

1:00pm Follow the Alto da Boa Vista road to Barra da Tijuca, where you'll see the modern side of Rio. Return to Rio's southern zone via the dazzling Niemeyer Avenue, with its scenic seaside road.

2:30pm Have duck with cassis in the informal-chic atmosphere of **Garcia & Rodrigues**, among the books, wine bottles, and kitchen utensils for sale. Don't skip its famous baguette.

4:00pm Walk to Leblon Beach then to Ipanema, stopping for coconut milk at one of the many kiosks along the beach. You could also head to one of the happening cafes or bars along the way.

8:00pm Have dinner while admiring the incomparable views and French cuisine at **Le Saint Honoré**. The shrimp with purée cassava is an excellent choice.

10:00pm Taxi toward the Sambadrome via Avenida Infante Don Henrique de Sagres (a k a Aterro do Flamengo). Ask the driver to stop at the site that marks the founding of the city for yet another unforgettable view of the Bay of Botafogo.

10:45pm Head for the people's party. In the super-popular atmosphere of the **Terreirco do Samba**, a neighborhood square surrounded by small bars near the Sambadrome, shows continue nonstop.

Midnight Join the ***bloco Lira do Delmrio***, which closes the ***Carioca Carnaval***. The parade winds through the streets of Ipanema into the early hours of Ash Wednesday.

6:00am If you're still awake, remember, ***Carnaval*** may be finishing but it's never too early to start planning for next year.

Alternatives

A modern hotel with an awe-inspiring view is **Le Méridien Copacabana**, well known for its French tradition. The **Sofitel Rio Palace** has rooms with balconies overlooking the beach. The beachfront **Hotel Inter-Continental** is a good choice for peace and quiet.

Go to **Margutta** for seafood that's revered throughout Brazil. Have lunch at **Confeitaria Colombo** in downtown Rio for a serving of good food and Old World charm. For lunch, dinner, or just drinks, **Garota de Ipanema** is great—it's reputedly the place of inspiration for "The Girl from Ipanema."

Teeming with beautiful people and good music until sunrise, the **Hippopotamus** is a *club privé*, so it will be necessary to ask your hotel concierge to arrange entry for you. The **Rhapsody** is another late-night dance club for pretty people.

All of Rio shuts down for ***Carnaval***, but if you stick around longer, check out the museums. For kitsch factor, you can't beat the **Carmen Miranda Museum**, a temple to the fruit-laden Latin bombshell of 1940s Hollywood musicals. The **Oscar Niemeyer Foundation** is devoted to Brazil's most famous modern architect. The **Casa do Pontal Folk-Art Museum** showcases Brazilian folk art.

Rio warms up for ***Carnaval*** with the continent's best ***New Year's Eve*** celebration, when more than a million revelers take advantage of the typically warm night for a dress-in-white beach party.

The Hot Sheet

☎ 55/21

$ 1.8 Real

HOTELS	DAY	ADDRESS	PH	PRICE	FX	RMS	BEST ROOMS
Copacabana Palace	1	1702 Av. Atlântica	548-7070 800- 223-6800	$$$$+	235-7330	226	Beach or pool vw
Hotel Inter-Continental	A	222 Av. Prefeito Mendes de Morais	322-2200 800- 327-0200	$$$$	322-5500	431	Club fl ocean vw
Le Méridien Copacabana	A	1020 Av. Atlântica	275-9922 800- 543-4300	$$$$	541-6447	496	Beach vw
Sofitel Rio Palace	A	4240 Av. Atlântica	525-1232 800- 763-4835	$$$	525-1200	388	Beach vw

RESTAURANTS	DAY	ADDRESS	PH	PRICE	REC	DRESS	FOOD
Alcaparra	1	Praia do Flamengo	558-3937	$$	L/D	Local	International
Ao Ponto	2	2964 Av. Atlântica in Hotel Rio Atlântica	548-6332	$$$	B/LD	Local	Cafe, continental
Cipriani	1	see Copacabana Palace	548-7070	$$$$+	D/L	Yuppie	Italian
Confeitaria Colombo	A	32 Rua Gonçalves Dias	232-2300	$	LD	Local	Deli, continental
Garcia & Rodrigues	3	1251 Av. Ataulfo de Paiva	512-8188	$	L	Local	Deli, local goods
Garota de Ipanema	A	49 Vinicius de Moraes	523-3787	$$	LD	Local	Seafood, Brazilian
Guimas	2	5 Rua Macedo Soares	259-7996	$$$	L	Local	Fusion
Le Saint Honoré	3	1020 Av. Atlântica, 37th fl.	546-0880	$$$	D	Yuppie	French
Margutta	A	62 Av. Henrique Dumont	259-3887	$$$$+	D	Yuppie	Italian
Mariu's	2	96 Rua Francisco Otaviano	287-2552	$$$	D/L	Euro	Grilled meats
Maxim's	1	1850-A Av. Atlântica	255-7444	$$	D/L	Local	International
Pérgula	3	see Copacabana Palace	255-7070	$$$	B/LD	Local	Cafe, French

NITELIFE	DAY	ADDRESS	PH	PRICE	REC	DRESS	MUSIC
Hippopotamus	A	354 Rua Barao da Torre	522-8658	$$$$+	O(F)	Yuppie	International, Brazilian
Rhapsody	A	1104 Av. Epitácio Pessoa	247-2104	$$$$+	O(F)	Yuppie	Brazilian, rock

SIGHTS & ATTRACTIONS	DAY	ADDRESS	PH	ENTRY FEE	
Carmen Miranda Museum	A	Aterro do Flamengo and Av. Rui Barbosa	551-2597	$	
Casa do Pontal Folk-Art Museum	A	Estrada do Pontal	490-3278	$	
Oscar Niemeyer Foundation	A	25 Rua Conde Lages	509-1844	None	
Parque Nacional da Tijuca	3	Praça Afonso Viseu	492-2253	None	

OTHER SIGHTS, SERVICES & ATTRACTIONS

Corcovado Railroad Station	1	513 Rua Cosme Velho	558-1329	$$	
Helicopter Sightseeing	2	Av. Borges de Medeiros beside Parque das Taboas	259-6995	$$$$+	
Sugar Loaf Cable Car Station	1	520 Av. Pasteur	541-3737	$$	
Riotur		183 Av. Princessa Isabel	542-8080		

EVENT & TICKET INFO

Samba Schools Parades (Sambadrome, Rua Marques de Sapucai): Tickets ($10-$1,000) should be ordered as far as six months in advance. The most desirable are "tourist" seats, Sector 9 ($200-$400). For information or a list of agencies that handle tickets, contact *Riotur* (55/21-217-7575) or *Riotur, Los Angeles* (310-643-2638).

Bandas, **blocos**, and **street carnivals** (various locations around Rio): Admission is free and participation is encouraged.

Carnaval Ball (Scala, 296 Av. Alfranio de Melo Franco, or the Copacabana Palace): Call *Scala* (55/21-239-4448) or the *Copacabana Palace* (55/21-548-7070) for ticket and ball information.

Alternative Event

New Year's Eve: *Riotur*, 55/21-217-7575

RECommendations: (Restaurants) B–Breakfast; L–Lunch; D–Dinner; T–High tea or snack
(Nitelife) G–Gaming; H–Hangout bar; M–Live music; O–Dancing (disco); P–Dancing (live music); S–Show; F–Food served
()–Available but without recommendation. For complete explanation of Hot Sheet format, see page 34.

⏰ NYC +2   🌓 73°/85° (23°/29°)   ✈ Galeao (GIG); 30 min./$35   🚗 No   👥 Portuguese

March 2000

February 2001

Port of Spain, Trinidad & Tobago

Trinidad Carnival

| Origin: c.1840 | Event ★ ★ ★ ★ ★ ★ City | Attendance: 150,000 |

On the Monday morning before Lent while much of the world sleeps, Trinidad bursts onto the streets of Port of Spain in a riot of musical madness that continues nonstop until midnight Tuesday. This is the mother of all carnivals, a crescendo of creativity driven by ringing steel pans, witty calypsos, turbo-charged soca music, and costumes fit for kings, queens, and commoners.

French planters introduced *Carnival* to Trinidad more than 200 years ago, but their pre-Lenten festival of polite private masked balls was transformed after emancipation in 1838. The freed slaves adopted *Carnival* as their festival of liberation—a time to mock former masters. European-style ballroom dances gave way to the rhythms and vigor of Africa.

Carnival has evolved into a two-month party season, beginning after Christmas and climaxing with two days of street processions on the Monday and Tuesday before Ash Wednesday. On this most cosmopolitan Caribbean island, cultures from around the world—Europe, Africa, South America, Asia, and the Middle East—fly their colors in a vast communal celebration. Joining revelers who daub themselves with mud, paint, and grease for the pre-dawn countdown (*J'Ouvert*) is like nothing you've ever experienced. But you can wait for sunup and watch thousands of party-goers don elaborate costumes that take months to make. All over town, live bands on semitrailers parade through packed streets, while partyers "wine" (locals call it dancing, but it looks more like simulated copulation) to frenzied ultrasonic beats.

All over Trinidad and Tobago, islanders celebrate *Carnival*, but the center of the bacchanal is Port of Spain. Here in Trinidad's capital, as many as 150,000 revelers party and gape at barely clad members of the opposite sex. You don't go to Trinidad for the sights, beaches, nightclubs, or food. You go because Port of Spain, whose carnival has as many participants as spectators, throws the best party in the Western Hemisphere.

Trinidad Carnival

Day 1. Sun.   Mar. 5, 2000
(Day 1. Sunday   February 25, 2001)

9:30am Check into the upside-down **Trinidad Hilton**, where the first floor is at the top of the building. Take in the panoramic view stretching below your window. The hotel overlooks Queen's Park Savannah, the centerpiece of *Carnival*, where all the mas (short for "masquerade") bands will parade tomorrow.

10:30am Taxi or walk to the **Botanic Gardens** on the northern edge of the Savannah. Immerse yourself in the calm, and catch a glimpse of the colonial-style president's residence.

12:30pm Head back to the Hilton for your first taste of local breakfast—black pudding, saltfish, *buljol*, and ® bakes—at brunch on the **Pool Terrace**.

1:30pm The two-day nonstop party is approaching, so take a few hours' rest. If you think you can make it right through, taxi downtown. Stop at the Brian Lara Promenade on Independence Square to mingle with locals and get a blast of soca music. Stroll up Frederick Street, the main drag, to Woodford Square for a look at the Red House, the neo-classical-style parliament building.

4:30pm The ***Trinidad Arts Support Association Fete***—which has live music, food, and drinks—should be in high gear on the grounds of Queen's Hall Auditorium. Taxi over and start your ***Carnival*** with the island's artists, musicians, writers, glitterati, and cognoscenti. They'll be happy to give you the lowdown on the festival.

7:00pm Most businesses and restaurants close from Sunday night through Ash Wednesday. An army of vendors will be feeding revelers on the streets for the duration. But some hotels have excellent food. ® The **Tiki Village** at the top of the Kapok Hotel offers Polynesian, Chinese, and local cuisine.

8:00pm Taxi to the Savannah and grab a seat in the Grandstand for the fabulous ***Dimanche Gras*** show, *Carnival*'s formal curtain-raiser. It'll be midnight by the time the King and Queen of the mas bands have been selected and the Calypso Monarch crowned—but there's no sleeping! Go with the flow until after sunrise.

1:00am The highlight of ***Carnival*** for many, ***J'Ouvert*** (from *jour ouvert*, French for "daybreak") officially begins at 4 a.m., but bands (a band in Trinidad includes the performing group and its devoted followers, not just the musicians) start gathering in the streets from 2 a.m. To get into the crazy ***J'Ouvert*** mood, head to any of the fetes rampaging around town. The vibe is exclusive at the Hilton and Holiday Inn, young and wild at the Boy Scouts Association, and simply massive at the Oval Cricket Ground, probably the best venue from which to hit the streets.

4:00am Just follow a steel band, DJ truck, or mud band. Dance. Drink. Flash an encouraging smile, and you'll be splashed with mud. The idea this morning is to let loose, get covered with a mud costume, and follow whatever music and crowd appeals to you. En ® route, grab corn soup, beer, or *roti* (curried meat and/or vegetables wrapped in soft dough) from a street vendor. Dawn should find you in Independence Square, roaring with a cast of thousands.

8:00am Stumble to the **Olympia** in the Trinidad Holiday ® Inn on nearby Wrightson Road for an American, continental, or local breakfast. Try not to collapse before getting a taxi back to the Hilton. Sleep.

Day 2. Mon.   Mar. 6, 2000
(Day 2. Monday   February 26, 2001)

1:00pm Taxi to **Ali Baba**'s in the Royal Palm Plaza, ® Maraval, and feast on authentic Middle Eastern dishes.

2:30pm Cab or hike to the Maraval roundabout on the Savannah. Walk south past the "Magnificent Seven," a row of large esoteric edifices. The restored Whitehall is the Prime Minister's office and Queen's Royal College, alma mater of writer V.S. Naipaul. The mas bands, with themes ranging from historic to exotic, began massing on the streets at 1 p.m. for their parade through the city. Many of the bands save their full costumes for tomorrow, so today is for savoring the *Carnival* spirit, "jumping up" (doing a lively dance with swaying hips and extended arms) with one of the passing bands, and strolling through town. Be prepared to walk. Don't forget sunblock. Earplugs are also a good idea.

4:00pm Pass the Savannah's handicraft stalls (great for souvenirs) and get a beer at the main entrance to the Savannah, just above Memorial Park. Continue downtown to Independence Square to marvel at the parading bands. There will be lots of human scenery along the way.

7:30pm Whet your appetite with some of the best pepper shrimp in the Caribbean at **Hong Kong City** on Tragerete Road, a short taxi ride away.

9:00pm Walk down French Street to internationally acclaimed designer Peter Minshall's mas camp next to the Mas Camp Pub. Dance up Ariapita Avenue to Adam Smith Square to join the night masqueraders. Round off the night with the crowd in the nearby St. James area.

Day 3. Tues.   Mar. 7, 2000
(Day 3. Tuesday   February 27, 2001)

9:00am Breakfast at The Normandie Hotel's **Café Trinidad**. It's located in the middle of a small market area that specializes in local designer wear and jewelry.

11:00am Costume bands have been out in full finery since 8 a.m. Taxi from The Normandie to the Savannah and snag a shaded seat in the Grandstand to view the spectacle as each band revels in its moment of glory on stage.

1:30pm Sample the al fresco local cuisine. The Savannah is bristling with vendors selling *roti*, corn soup, and barbecued or jerk chicken.

3:00pm The Savannah stage can keep you entranced until sundown, but take a leisurely walk through the crowds to the **Pelican Pub** just below the Hilton on Coblentz Avenue. Though usually quiet during *Carnival*, this English-style drinking establishment is one of the capital's favorite watering holes.

4:30pm Head back across the Savannah and downtown to watch the mounting delirium as music, rum, and dance enhance the magic of the approaching sunset.

7:30pm Taxi to **Buccaneer's Cove** in the Royal Palm Suite Hotel on Saddle Road, Maraval. Chill with Caribbean cocktails, old-fashioned shrimp Creole, and other seafood specialties.

9:30pm You're ready for the *Las' Lap* in St. James, a vibrant mile-long stretch where masqueraders discard their costumes and join the masses in the serious business of drinking and partying in a final farewell to *Carnival*.

Alternatives

The downtown **Trinidad Holiday Inn**, the smaller **Kapok Hotel**, and **The Normandie Hotel** (close to the Queen's Park Savannah) are all within easy walking distance of the main *Carnival* route.

Many of the restaurants that closed for *Carnival* weekend re-open on Ash Wednesday. Try **Rafters** and **Solimar** for international cuisine, **Veni Mange** for vegetarian and Creole cooking, and the **Breakfast Shed** for authentic Creole food.

If you stay on after *Carnival*, **The Anchorage** and **Pier 1** offer live music on the waterfront. In town, you can hit **Upper Level Club** and **Club Coconuts** or listen to Trinidad and Tobago's best calypso at the **Mas Camp Pub**.

The Hot Sheet

☎ US/868

$ 6.1 Dollar

HOTELS	DAY	ADDRESS	PH	PRICE	FX	RMS	BEST ROOMS

Hotel accommodations in Port of Spain are extremely limited during the Carnival period. It's advisable to book rooms and flights as early as the preceding October.

HOTELS	DAY	ADDRESS	PH	PRICE	FX	RMS	BEST ROOMS
Kapok Hotel	A	16-18 Cotton Hill	622-6441	$$	622-9677	94	Pool vw w/balc
The Normandie Hotel	A	10 Nook Ave.	624-1181	$$$	624-0108	53	Mtn vw
Trinidad Hilton	1	Lady Young Rd.	624-3211 800- 445-8667	$$$$	624-4485	394	Exec fl rm
Trinidad Holiday Inn	A	Wrightson Rd.	625-3366 800- 465-4329	$$$	625-4166	225	Gulf vw

RESTAURANTS	DAY	ADDRESS	PH	PRICE	REC	DRESS	FOOD
Ali Baba	2	Royal Palm Pl. Shopping Mall Saddle Rd.	622-5557	$$$	L/D	Local	Middle Eastern
Breakfast Shed	A	Wrightson Rd.	no phone	$	B	Local	Creole
Buccaneer's Cove	3	7A Saddle Rd., Maraval in Royal Palm Suite Hotel	628-5086	$$	L/D	Local	Caribbean
Café Trinidad	3	see The Normandie Hotel	624-1181	$	B/L	Local	Caribbean
Hong Kong City	2	86A Tragerete Rd.	622-3949	$$	D/L	Local	Chinese, seafood
Olympia	2	see Trinidad Holiday Inn	625-3366	$$	B/(LD)	Local	American, Caribbean
Pool Terrace	1	see Trinidad Hilton	624-3211	$$	B	Local	Caribbean
Rafters	A	6A Warner St.	628-9258	$$$	LD	Local	American, European, Caribbean
Solimar	A	6 Nook Ave.	624-6267	$$$$	LD	Local	European, American
Tiki Village	1	see Kapok Hotel	622-5765	$$	D/BL	Local	Chinese, Polynesian
Veni Mange	A	67A Ariapita Ave., Woodbrook	624-4597	$$	L	Local	Creole, vegetarian

NITELIFE	DAY	ADDRESS	PH	PRICE	REC	DRESS	MUSIC
The Anchorage	A	Point Gourde Rd.	634-4334	$	MPF	Local	Caribbean
Club Coconuts	A	Ariapita Rd. in Cascadia Hotel	623-6887	$	OP	Local	Caribbean, hip-hop, techno
Mas Camp Pub	A	French St. and Ariapita Ave., Woodbrock	623-3745	$	MPF	Local	Calypso, comedy, steel-pan
Pelican Pub	3	2-4 Coblentz Ave.	624-7486	$	MPSF	Local	Caribbean, alternative, rock
Pier 1	A	Chaguaramas	634-4472	$	MPSF	Local	Caribbean, Latin
Upper Level Club	A	West Mall, Western Main Rd.	637-1753	$	O	Local	Caribbean, R&B, soul, techno

SIGHTS & ATTRACTIONS	DAY	ADDRESS	PH	ENTRY FEE
Botanic Gardens	1	Zoo Rd.	622-4221	None
Tourism & Ind. Dev. Co.		10-14 Phillips St.	623-1932	

EVENT & TICKET INFO

Dimanche Gras (Carnival Grandstand, The Savannah): Tickets ($25) available in advance from *National Carnival Commission* (868-627-1350).

Carnival Grandstand (Carnival Grandstand, The Savannah): Tickets ($20) available in advance from *National Carnival Commission* (868-627-1350)

Trinidad Arts Support Association Fete (Queen's Hall Auditorium): Tickets ($30) are handled through different venues each year. Check the *Trinidad Guardian* or *Trinidad Express* newspapers on arrival.

J'Ouvert (streets near Queen's Park Savannah): Tickets are not required and everyone is welcome to follow a band. If you want to join a band, just pick a J'Ouvert band from listings in the *Trinidad Guardian* or *Trinidad Express* (or ask the locals) and drop by the Mas Camp (in the same building as the Mas Camp Pub) to sign up.

Las' Lap (St. James): No tickets required.

RECommendations: (Restaurants) B—Breakfast; L—Lunch; D—Dinner; T—High tea or snack (Nitelife) G—Gaming; H—Hangout bar; M—Live music; O—Dancing (disco); P—Dancing (live music); S—Show; F—Food served ()—Available but without recommendation. For complete explanation of Hot Sheet format, see page 34.

🕐 NYC +1   ☀ 75°/92° (21°/33°)   ✈ Piarco Airport (POS) 45 min./$40   🚗 No   👥 English

The Fun Also Rises

March 2000

M	T	W	T	F	S	S
	1	2	3	4	5	
6	7	8	9	10	11	12
13	14	15	16	17	18	19
20	21	22	23	24	25	26
27	28	29	30	31		

March 2001

M	T	W	T	F	S	S
5	6	7	1	2	3	4
12	13	14	8	9	10	11
19	20	21	15	16	17	18
26	27	28	22	23	24	25
			29	30	31	

Melbourne, Australia

Moomba

(The Melbourne Moomba Festival)

Origin: 1955	Event ★ ★ ★ ★ ★ City	Attendance: 1.5 million

The fun-loving Aussies have never needed an excuse to party, but they've outdone themselves at this end-of-summer three-day blowout. The mixture of exotic art, water sports, Formula 1 racing, one-of-a-kind multimedia exhibits, perfect temperatures, and, of course, laid-back Aussie hospitality makes Australia's largest outdoor festival an irresistible stop on the international fun circuit.

Set on the banks of the picturesque Yarra River, Melbourne shimmers with happy throngs of festival-goers who collectively answer the event's most frequently asked question—*Moomba* is an Aboriginal word meaning "to get together and have fun." Although details of the program and schedule are in flux, you can count on several crowd favorites to remain the same. Many activities will make use of the lush Alexandra Gardens, from which you can watch the trick-water-skiing competition and the *Moomba River Spectacular*, a stage show that ends with a burst of fireworks reflecting off the river.

Both the water-skiing championships and the prestigious *Quantas Australian Grand Prix* races are independent events that conveniently coincide with *Moomba* weekend. The *Official Grand Prix Ball*, which precedes the auto race, is considered one of the city's most elegant annual evenings.

If you expect to see koalas or kangaroos, you'll be disappointed unless you go to the zoo. It'll take more than a three-day visit to squeeze in day trips that put you in range of stunning coastal scenery along the Great Ocean Road, and reserves such as Phillip Island and Healesville Sanctuary, which are home to penguins, koalas, platypuses, and Tasmanian devils. These sights are 40 or 50 miles outside the city.

With 3.3 million residents, Melbourne is Australia's most culturally diverse city, as well as the second-largest port in the Southern Hemisphere. More importantly, though, Melbourne is a hip city, especially during *Moomba* when the combination of events brings together large numbers of tourists and locals who keep the city's always excellent restaurants, pubs, and nightclubs humming.

Moomba

Day 1. Fri. Mar. 10, 2000
(Day 1. Friday   March 9, 2001)

9:30am The neo-modern **Adelphi Hotel**, in the heart of Melbourne, is all sharp angles and bright primary colors. Rooms are spacious and comfortable. The glass-bottomed swimming pool that hangs over the roof is just one of the hotel's architectural touches.

10:30am Step around the corner to the **Rialto Towers**. Take the speedy elevators to the observation deck of this lofty office building—it's the tallest in the Southern Hemisphere.

12:30pm Walk down Collins Street and Princes Bridge until you get to the Southgate Complex. Inside, **Walter's Wine Bar** keeps people coming back (like the notorious Aussie boomerang) for food and wine.

2:30pm Finish lunch in time to make the guided tour of the **Victorian Arts Centre**, Melbourne's landmark performing-arts center.

4:00pm The **National Gallery of Victoria**, which exhibits the best of Australian and international art, is a short walk away and worth a visit.

6:30pm Walk along the Yarra River to the Crown Entertainment Complex. Have a pre-dinner drink at **Club Odeon** and relax on plush, velveteen couches with other hipsters who have come to see and be seen.

8:30pm Taxi to the St. Kilda neighborhood for dinner at **Circa, The Prince**, with trendy Eames chairs and art. The food is also up-to-date—nouveau twists on classic French fare.

11:00pm Tour vibrant St. Kilda with a stop at the **Stokehouse**, a restaurant-cum-bar with great views of the beach. Enjoy a glass of Australian wine at the **Melbourne Wine Room**. Then finish off the night at the Russian-inspired **Mink** bar.

Day 2. Sat. Mar. 11, 2000
(Day 2. Saturday   March 10, 2001)

9:00am Have breakfast at **Cafe Segovia**, a short walk from the hotel. Make sure to grab a side booth to catch all the morning-after action.

10:30am For more than a century, **Queen Victoria Market** has been a shopping destination. Filled with fruit and vegetable stands, importers, craftsmen, and artisans, the market offers a slice of local history.

11:30am Move from exercising your economic independence to appreciating your personal freedom with a tour of **The Old Melbourne Gaol**—a testament to the country's wild pioneer days. This old hoosegow now houses museum-quality exhibits, dioramas, and wax figures.

1:00pm Walk to Georges department store on bustling Collins Street for lunch at the popular **Brasserie at Georges**. The lunchtime *prix fixe* menu of inspired continental faves lives up to this restaurant's hype.

3:00pm Wander around Fitzroy Gardens toward the Yarra River. Cross at the Swan Street Bridge and follow the crowds to Alexandra Gardens. Find a comfortable, grassy spot to view the river competition and the sports-crazy Aussies.

5:00pm From your perch, watch the ***Moomba Masters Ski Competition***, where expert international water-skiers will be slaloming, jumping, and performing tricks in this world-class event.

7:30pm Join hipsters for dinner at **Blake's** in the Southgate Shopping Centre. The food is modern Australian and the atmosphere is laid-back but fun.

9:30pm Return to your grassy spot by the Yarra to see the dazzling ***fireworks show***. With luck, this will be only a prelude for the sparks that will be flying later in the night.

12:15am See what's stirring at the **Gin Palace**. This upscale bar serves an incredibly fine martini. Then move on to **Tony Starr's Kitten Club**, another downtown bar that welcomes the beautiful people. Where you go from here will depend on whom you meet.

Day 3. Sun.   Mar. 12, 2000
(Day 3. Sunday   March 11, 2001)

10:30am Have a made-to-order breakfast at the hotel's
℞ **Adelphi Lounge**. Don't expect emu-egg omelets or kangaroo bacon—despite the outrageous setting, the fare here is wholesome and statisfying.

Noon Get an early start to the racetrack for some pre-race
℞ fun. Grab a bite to eat and a cold Foster's beer—it's never too early to start calling people "mate."

2:00pm The ***Quantas Australian Grand Prix*** is a world-class event that takes place in a world-class setting—Formula 1 race cars zoom around the pristine and beautiful Albert Park Lake at high speeds and high volume.

4:00pm Follow the roving crowd from pub to pub. There's no longer an official after-race party, but who needs "official" when you're hanging with the Aussies.

5:30pm Plunge into the Adelphi's glass-bottomed pool to check out the scene on the street below. Then take advantage of the poolside bar.

8:30pm Taxi to **Langton's**, a real chefs' domain. The
℞ open kitchen of this chic and lively basement restaurant dishes up imaginative rotisserie meats, fish, and locally grown produce.

11:00pm Go to the Crown Entertainment Complex for a multilevel, multithemed nightlife experience. First, it's the Old Havana charm of **Fidel's Cigar Lounge**. Then it's off to the opulent and glitzy **Crown Casino** for blackjack and roulette. Finish off the night by grooving until dawn at **Heat**, a slick dance club, or check out live music at the **Mercury Lounge**. If all

goes as planned, by the end of the night you'll have done justice to the name *Moomba*.

Alternatives

The **Grand Hyatt** is an elegant, modern highrise with art-deco touches. Exuding Old World character with Laura Ashley print wallpaper and rosewood furniture, **The Windsor** hotel remains the grande dame of Melbourne hotels. **The Prince**, a hip, boutique hotel is a young upstart in the bustling St. Kilda area. For elegance and impeccable service, the grandiose **Sheraton Towers** is hard to beat.

Good restaurants abound in Melbourne. People flock to **2BC** for a mix of modern Mediterranean cuisine with North African accents. Hipsters congregate at **Stella** to enjoy modern Australian food and the suave ambience. **Cecconi's** serves fine Italian food in a classy setting. **Becco** dishes up simple Italian food to a cool clientele, while **est est est** offers modern French cuisine in a smart but casual environment.

The internationally acclaimed **Melbourne Zoo** is worth a visit. See exotic and oddly named animals, such as the kangaroo, wallaby, wombat, and koala, in the Bushland Exhibit.

For an elegant evening out, rub shoulders with racing royalty at the ***Grand Prix Ball***, one of the highlights of Melbourne's social season. Another good excuse to journey down under is the ***Melbourne Cup***. The prestigious horse race, run in early November, offers a unique combination of Ascotlike pomp and fun-loving Aussie spirit.

EVENT & TICKET INFO

(continued from page 100)

Official Grand Prix Ball (Palladium at Crown Entertainment Complex, Melbourne Casino): Tickets ($400), including dinner and entertainment, are available by calling the *Australian Grand Prix Corporation Special Events* (61/39-258-7100).

Alternative Event

Melbourne Cup: Victoria Racing Club Marketing Department, 61/39-258-4659

The Hot Sheet

☎ 61/39

$ 1.5 Australian Dollar

HOTELS	DAY	ADDRESS	PH	PRICE	FX	RMS	BEST ROOMS
Adelphi Hotel	1	187 Flinders Ln.	650-7555 800- 552-6844	$$	650-2710	34	Dlx rm
Grand Hyatt	A	123 Collins St.	657-1234 800- 233-1234	$$$$	650-3491	547	City or gdn vw
The Prince	A	2 Acland St.	536-1111 800- 537-8483	$$	536-1100	40	Dlx crtyd vw
Sheraton Towers	A	One Southgate Ave.	696-3100 800- 325-3535	$$$$	690-6581	385	Dlx crnr rm
The Windsor	A	103 Spring St.	633-6000 800- 562-3764	$$$	633-6001	180	Premier dlx

RESTAURANTS	DAY	ADDRESS	PH	PRICE	REC	DRESS	FOOD
2BC	A	177 Greville St.	529-4922	$$	LD	Kazh	Nuvo Mediterranean, Middle Eastern
Adelphi Lounge	3	see Adelphi Hotel	650-7555	$	B/L	Kazh	International
Becco	A	11-25 Crossley St.	663-3000	$$	LD	Euro	Italian
Blake's	2	Southgate, Shop 2, ground fl.	699-4100	$$	L/D	Kazh	Modern Australian
Brasserie at Georges	2	175 Collins St., lower fl.	929-9900	$$	L/D	Euro	Brasserie, international
Cafe Segovia	2	33 Block Pl.	650-2373	$	B/LD	Yuppie	Nuvo Australian
Cecconi's	A	Crown Complex, ground level	292-6887	$$	LD	Kazh	Northern Italian
Circa, The Prince	1	see The Prince hotel	536-1122	$$	D	Kazh	Modern French
est est est	A	440 Clarendon St., South Melbourne	682-5688	$$	D	Kazh	Modern French
Langton's	3	61 Flinders Ln.	663-0222	$$	D/BL	Euro	French
Stella	A	159 Spring St.	639-1555	$$	LD	Kazh	Continental
Walter's Wine Bar	1	Southgate, level 3	690-9211	$$	L/D	Euro	International

NITELIFE	DAY	ADDRESS	PH	PRICE	REC	DRESS	MUSIC
Club Odeon	1	Crown Complex, level 3	682-1888	$	HOMP	Euro	Rock, dance, hip-hop
Crown Casino	3	Crown Complex, multilevel	292-8888	None	G		
Fidel's Cigar Lounge	3	Crown Complex, level B1	292-6885	None	H	Euro	
Gin Palace	2	190 Little Collins St. enter via Russell Pl.	654-0533	None	H	Kazh	
Heat	3	Crown Complex, level 3	699-6555	$	HO	Euro	Dance
Melbourne Wine Room	1	125 Fitzroy St. in George Hotel	525-5599	None	H(F)	Euro	
Mercury Lounge	3	Crown Complex, level 3	292-5480	$$	MP	Euro	Popular, soft rock, soul
Mink	1	see The Prince hotel	536-1199	None	HO(F)	Euro	Funk, house
Stokehouse	1	30 Jacka Blvd.	525-5555	None	H(F)	Kazh	
Tony Starr's Kitten Club	2	267 Little Collins St., level 2	650-2448	None	H	Euro	

SIGHTS & ATTRACTIONS	DAY	ADDRESS	PH	ENTRY FEE
Melbourne Zoo	A	Elliot Ave., Parkville	285-9300	$
National Gallery of Victoria	1	180 St. Kilda Rd.	208-0220	$
The Old Melbourne Gaol	2	Russell St. near La Trobe St.	663-7228	$
Queen Victoria Market	2	Elizabeth and Queen sts.	320-5822	None
Rialto Towers	1	525 Collins St.	629-8222	$
Victorian Arts Centre	1	100 St. Kilda Rd.	281-8000	$
Victoria Visitor Information Centre		Melbourne Town Hall, Swanston St.	658-9955	

EVENT & TICKET INFO

Moomba (various locations around Melbourne): All events are free.

Quantas Australian Grand Prix (Albert Park, Canterbury Road at Albert Road): General admission tickets for Sunday's race ($50) get you into Albert Park to view the action. Grandstand seats ($200-$320) include all four days of racing (Thursday-Sunday). No single-day Grandstand seats are sold. Tickets are usually available on race day, or by calling the Australian Grand Prix Corporation (61/39-258-7100).

(continued on page 99)

RECommendations: (Restaurants) B–Breakfast; L–Lunch; D–Dinner; T–High tea or snack (Nitelife) G–Gaming; H–Hangout bar; M–Live music; O–Dancing (disco); P–Dancing (live music); S–Show; F–Food served ( )–Available but without recommendation. For complete explanation of Hot Sheet format, see page 34.

🕐 NYC +15   ☀ 51°/71° (10°/21°)   ✈ Melbourne (MEL); 30 min./$20   🚗 Yes/No   👥 English

Las Fallas

Origin: 1497	Event ★ ★ ★ ★ ★ ★ City	Attendance: 500,000

If you can't take the heat, you're going to miss one hell of a party because, quite literally, Valencia likes to play with fire. Valencia Hospital's burn unit is reputedly the best in Spain, partly because of all the practice its workers get after the frenzied week of *Las Fallas*, a saturnalia revolving around massive temporary structures (*fallas*) that are set aflame during one of the most imaginative and spectacular festivals in Europe.

Started by medieval carpenters, who celebrated the longer days of spring by burning the candelabras they worked by throughout the winter, the festival has grown more elaborate over the centuries. Today, satirical effigies of local characters fuel the flames and the festivities. Constructed on street corners and in plazas, these immense structures—some up to 75 feet high—are best described as multicolored, multifigured constructions of wood and papier-mâché made in a style that combines surrealism, political satire, and Walt Disney.

Valencians take their festival seriously. Throughout the year, more than 370 neighborhood committees choose queens, maintain marching bands, and raise money for the building of their *fallas*. The structures can cost up to $200,000, but all but one will eventually burn in a spectacular display (a *falla*'s life span is just four days). During festival week, events include paella contests, a procession of 150,000 females of all ages in baroque costumes bringing flowers to a statue of the Virgin, daytime and nighttime fireworks, and all-night drinking and dancing in the streets. Finally, at midnight on the last night of this continuous outdoor party, the biggest blaze of glory you've ever seen takes place. By dawn, there won't be so much as a pile of ash left to remind you of what has happened.

With a population of about 750,000, Valencia is Spain's third-largest city and one of the more seductive old cities in Europe. An attractive Mediterranean seaport and the seat of one of Spain's ancient kingdoms, the city is now renowned by world partyers for giving new meaning to the phrase, "Burning Down the House!"

Las Fallas

Day 1. Fri.   Mar. 17, 2000
(Day 1. Saturday   March 17, 2001

9:00am Wake up at the luxurious **Hotel Meliá Plaza** on Plaza del Ayuntamiento. The original façade belies a completely renovated interior. Have coffee and toast with the regulars at **Cafetería Ateneo**.

10:00am Walk into the old section of town, Ciutat Vella, marveling at its doorways and some of the more than 300 *fallas*.

Noon Have lunch at **Ca'n Bermell**, an unpretentious, traditional Valencian restaurant in the Old Quarter with oak wine casks stacked against the walls.

1:30pm Join 250,000 people who gather at Plaza del Ayuntamiento each day to witness the ***mascletá***, a sound-only fireworks display that shakes your bones and nearby buildings. The fireworks themselves are reminiscent of everything from Wagner to Hendrix, and change each day. It is the feature of ***Las Fallas*** that many Valencians like best.

3:00pm Familiarize yourself with bourgeois Valencia on a walk through the shopping districts and grand boulevards that surround the Old Quarter.

5:00pm It's been said that Spain cannot be known without the experience of attending a ***bullfight***. During the festival, the country's best matadors are in Valencia.

8:00pm Have an *aperitivo* with *tapas* at any of the open-air cafes along Gran Vía Marquís del Turia. One of the best is **Jose Luis**.

10:30pm Have dinner at **El Angel Azul**, an elegant German-owned restaurant with superb food from a contemporary international menu.

1:00am Watch the nightly ***fireworks*** from either side of what was the old river and is now a park. The best viewing is from Punte del Real, a bridge north of the fireworks (the wind blows south), which fills up about an hour before the show.

1:45am Have a pint of Guinness at **Finnegan's**, an Irish bar on the Plaza de la Reina. This is still St. Patrick's Day, even if you are in Spain.

3:00am For a wind-down drink, try **Café de las Horas**, a serene and lovely bar with paintings and a small fountain.

Day 2. Sat.   Mar. 18, 2000
(Day 2. Sunday   March 18, 2001)

9:30am Have hot chocolate and *buñuelos* (deep-fried, sugar-coated pastries) at **Santa Catalina**, a Valencian landmark across the street from the Santa Catalina church. Walk to the Cathedral, where the Holy Grail is said to be. Here you can see the influences of all the ages of the old city— Roman, Arab, Gothic, Baroque, and modern.

11:00am Visit the **Mercado Central**, one of the largest and best in Europe, a cornucopia of seafood, cow noses, fish cheeks, and science-fiction-size vegetables. Grab a bite then cross the street to check out La Lonja, the old silk market, possibly the finest Gothic building in Spain.

1:15pm Head for the Plaza del Ayuntamiento for ***Las Fallas***' most sensational ***mascletá***.

2:30pm A five-minute walk leads you to **Kailuze**, a chic Basque restaurant popular with the mayor of Valencia and neighborhood regulars.

7:30pm After a siesta, have coffee in the Plaza de la Virgen and watch the ***Ofrenda de las Flores***, the dramatic procession of flower-laden women to the huge statue of the Virgin of the Forsaken. This continues until midnight.

9:30pm Cab to **El Canyar** for plate after plate of truly superb seafood, a feast you'll not forget.

11:30pm Valencia's best clubs and bars are along Calle Caballeros, with the majority concentrated around the Plaza de Tossal. Be sure to check out the men's toilets at several bars—at **Fox Congo**, it's a hedge behind some glass; at **Café Bolseria**, it's a one-way mirror looking down on the people in the bar; and at **Johnny Maracas**, it's a pile of TV sets embedded in sand.

1:30am This is *La Nit del Foc*, the most sensational fireworks display of *Las Fallas*. Find a spot amid the huge crowds by the river.

3:00am End your night with a drink at **El Negrito** or **Ghecko**, both in the Plaza del Negrito.

Day 3. Sun. Mar. 19, 2000
(Day 3. Monday   March 19, 2001)

11:00am After enjoying breakfast in the hotel, look at the special category of *fallas*—the ones with the biggest budgets—before they're burned.

1:00pm Take a tram to the beach at Marvalrossa and have paella (said to be a Valencian innovation) at **La Pepica**, where Hemingway once dined.

3:00pm Enjoy the beach, then tram back to the city.

8:00pm Have dinner at **Ocho y Medio**, a lively, glass-fronted restaurant and bar with an exotic international menu and live jazz.

10:00pm Each large *falla* has a smaller children's *falla*, which is burned at 10 p.m. Then you must choose your favorite big *falla* for the ***cremá***, the setting alight of all the *fallas*. The great blaze begins at midnight, moves to the burning of competition winners, and finally to the inferno in the Plaza del Ayuntamiento when the town hall's own *falla*, the festival's largest, is set ablaze.

1:00am Firemen go from square to square hosing down buildings to protect them. Put on a disposable raincoat and go to Plaza del Doctor Collado to get doused as they extinguish the final *falla*.

3:00am At the two-tiered bar **Cervecería Madrid**, have a quiet drink—preferably *agua de Valencia*, made with Spanish champagne (*cava*) and, of course, orange juice.

Alternatives

The **Hotel Astoria Palace**, favored by bullfighters, actors, and politicians, is centrally located and set on a small, leafy plaza. The five-star **Hotel Meliá Valencia Palace** is modern, comfortable, and across the river from the Gran Vía Marquís del Turia. While only a three-star hotel, the **Ad Hoc** has an ideal location at the edge of Old Town and a nice setting in a restored Spanish town house complete with tiled floors and brick walls.

Seu-Xerea boasts a British chef and reputation as one of the best restaurants in the city. Two Michelin-starred restaurants are **Rias Gallegas** and **Oscar Torrijos**. The insiders' favorite is **La Tapineria**, a tiny and inexpensive restaurant with outdoor seating.

Babal (formerly named **Hannax**) attracts the beautiful people. **Boss** and **Plaza** are on Plaza de Cánovas del Castillo. Both play loud dance music, welcome an older clientele, and are open late.

The **Instituto Valenciano de Arte Moderno** (**IVAM**) ranks as one of the best modern-art museums in Spain. The **Museo Fallero** has a collection of the papier-mâché figures not burned during *Las Fallas*. (The falla voted best each year is not burned.) It's close to the attractive City of Arts and Sciences. Or visit the newly restored **Museo Nacional de Cerámica**, which has works by Picasso and the most spectacular baroque doorway you're ever likely to see.

The Hot Sheet

☎ 34/96

$ 150 Peseta

HOTELS	DAY	ADDRESS	PH	PRICE	FX	RMS	BEST ROOMS
Ad Hoc	A	4 c/ Boix	391-9140	$$	391-3667	28	Crtyrd vw
Hotel Astoria Palace	A	5 Pl. Rodrigo Botet	352-6737 800- 448-8355	$$$	352-8078	203	3rd fl
Hotel Meliá Plaza	1	4 Pl. del Ayuntamiento	352-0612 800- 336-3542	$$$	352-0426	100	Plaza vw
Hotel Meliá Valencia Palace	A	32 Paseo de la Alameda	337-5037 800- 448-8355	$$$	337-5532	196	Riverbed vw

RESTAURANTS	DAY	ADDRESS	PH	PRICE	REC	DRESS	FOOD
Ca'n Bermell	1	18 c/ Santo Tomás	391-0288	$$$	L/D	Local	Traditional Valencian
Cafetería Ateneo	1	18 Pl. del Ayuntamiento	no phone	$	B/LTD	Local	Cafe
El Angel Azul	1	33 c/ Conde Altea	374-5656	$$$$	D/L	Kazh	International
El Canyar	2	5 c/ Segorbe	341-8082	$$$$	D/L	Kazh	Seafood
Jose Luis	1	59 Gran Vía Marqués del Turia	351-6105	$	T/LD	Local	*Tapas*
Kailuze	2	5 c/ Gregorio Mayans	374-3999	$$$	D/L	Euro	Basque
La Pepica	3	6 Paseo Neptuno	371-0366	$$	L/D	Local	Paella, Valencian
La Tapineria	A	16 c/ Tapineria	391-5440	$$	D	Local	International
Ocho y Medio	3	5 Pl. Lope de Vega	392-2022	$$$	D/L	Euro	Continental, Valencian
Oscar Torrijos	A	4 c/ Dr. Sumsi	373-2949	$$$$	LD	Kazh	Mediterranean
Rias Gallegas	A	11 c/ Cirilo Amorós	351-2125	$$$$	LD	Kazh	Galician
Santa Catalina	2	6 Pl. Santa Catalina	391-2379	$	B/T	Local	*Buñuelos*
Seu-Xerea	A	4 c/ Conde de Almodóvar	392-4000	$$$	LD	Kazh	Cosmopolitan

NITELIFE	DAY	ADDRESS	PH	PRICE	REC	DRESS	MUSIC
Babal (Hannax)	A	36 c/ Caballeros	391-8101	$$	O	Euro	Dance
Boss	A	6 Pl. Cánovas del Castillo	334-5924	$	O	Euro	Dance, Latin
Café Bolseria	2	41 c/ Bolseria	391-8903	None	O	Euro	Dance
Café de las Horas	1	1 c/ Conde de Almodóvar	391-7336	None	H(F)	Local	
Cervecería Madrid	3	10 c/ Abadia de San Martín	352-9671	None	H	Local	
El Negrito	2	1 Pl. del Negrito	391-4233	None	H	Euro	
Finnegan's	1	19 Pl. de la Reina Abajo	391-0503	None	H(F)	Local	
Fox Congo	2	35 c/ Caballeros	392-5527	None	O	Euro	Contemporary, hip-hop
Ghecko	2	2 Pl. del Negrito	391-0779	None	H	Euro	
Johnny Maracas	2	39 c/ Caballeros	391-5266	None	O	Euro	Latin
Plaza	A	73 Gran Vía Marqués del Turia	no phone	None	O	Euro	

SIGHTS & ATTRACTIONS	DAY	ADDRESS	PH	ENTRY FEE
Mercado Central	2	Pl. de Mercado	382-9101	None
Museo Fallero	A	4 Pl. de Monteolivete	352-5478	$
Museo Nacional de Cerámica	1	2 c/ Poeta Querol	351-6392	$
Instituto Valenciano de Arte Moderno (IVAM)	A	118 c/ Guillem de Castro	386-3000	$
Oficina Municipal de Tourismo		1 Pl. del Ayuntamiento	351-0417	

EVENT & TICKET INFO

Las Fallas (Plaza del Ayuntamiento and various locations around Valencia): All events are free except for **bullfights** (Plaza de Toros, 28 Calle Jativa). Tickets ($40) available by calling *Plaza de Toros* (34/96-351-9315). For more information, contact the *Tourist Office of Spain* in Los Angeles (323-658-7188).

RECommendations: (Restaurants) B–Breakfast; L–Lunch; D–Dinner; T–High tea or snack
(Nitelife) G–Gaming; H–Hangout bar; M–Live music; O–Dancing (disco); P–Dancing (live music); S–Show; F–Food served
()–Available but without recommendation. For complete explanation of Hot Sheet format, see page 34.

NYC +6   40°/57° (4°/13°)   Valencia Airport (VLC); 30 min./$20   No   Spanish

St. Patrick's Festival

Dublin, Ireland

Origin: 1996	Event ★ ★ ★ ★ ★ ★ City	Attendance: 850,000

The encompassing tide of "mighty *craic*" (that's mad fun to you) makes this four-day explosion of music, dance, street theater, fireworks, sport, pageantry, and parades a world-class party. St. Patrick's Day has long been the national holiday celebrated in more countries than any other, but until recently, celebrations actually held in Ireland have paled in comparison with those held abroad. Since 1996, however, that oddity has, as the famed Irish poet William Yeats would say, "All changed, changed utterly."

Rejuvenated by a revived economy, a rising confidence in national identity, and an emerging sense of European modernity, the spirit and excitement of the new Dublin is being reflected in its *St. Patrick's Festival*. The high-energy *St. Patrick's Eve Parade* kicks off the event, followed by the *Grand Parade* at noon the next day. Not to be missed after the parade is the massively popular *Monster Ceili Dancefest*, which may remind you of Riverdance on a Guinness high. The entire festival is a glorious combination of irreverent entertainment, mythology, history, modern spirit, and cultural exposition, with raucous crowds of friendly Irish leading the way.

The holiday originated to honor the patron saint of Ireland, who in the fifth century brought Christianity and the shamrock to the isle and supposedly rid the place of snakes. For the new *St. Patrick's Festival*, the good saint is rumored to banish rain—sunshine in recent years has sent revelers spinning into orbits of bliss.

Dating from about A.D. 988, Dublin today boasts a largely youthful population of 1.5 million. Teeming with musicians, writers, playwrights, filmmakers, and entrepreneurs, the Irish capital has emerged as an energized, revitalized place, quite different from the "dirty Dublin" of some years ago. The food scene, which in years past suffered a glum reputation, has also improved. The trend toward fusion or "modern Irish" cuisine has garnered well-deserved critical acclaim. And, of course, there's no better place for an Irish pub crawl than Dublin!

St. Patrick's Festival

Day 1. Fri.   Mar. 17, 2000
(Day 1. Friday   March 16, 2001)

9:00am Nestled in the Temple Bar area (Dublin's Soho), the **Clarence Hotel** is *the* place to stay. Owned by rock stars, it's decorated in spare, Shaker style and has views overlooking the River Liffey.

10:00am Stroll to the recently refurbished **Bewley's Oriental Café** on Grafton Street. While enjoying great people-watching, have a full Irish breakfast (served all day) of fried eggs, bacon, sausage, tomatoes, beans, hash browns, and buttered toast.

11:30am The best views of the *Parade* can be had on O'Connell Street or St. Stephen's Green. Prepare for battle. Go early and climb the nearest lamppost! At worst you'll be guaranteed a hilarious time just listening to the Irish wisecrack about the lack of views or overpopulation or both.

2:30pm Go to the nearby **Shelbourne Bar** for the best Irish stew in town.

3:45pm Held in the open air at St. Stephen's Green, the *Monster Ceili* is a traditional Celtic, Riverdance-style free-for-all. *Ceilis*, Gaelic for "barn dances," are an essential part of Irish celebrations. This one just happens to be open to all—participation is encouraged and instruction gladly provided.

6:00pm Wander through the lanes and alleys of the bohemian Temple Bar neighborhood. Then continue along the river to the **Brazen Head** on Bridge Street, beyond Christ Church Cathedral. Renowned as Dublin's oldest pub, its history includes the arrests of various ruffians and rebels due to their "loose talk" after a few drinks.

8:00pm Dine in stylish, relaxed comfort at the **Tea Room**. The decor is simple, but the food is excellent.

10:00pm Head back into Temple Bar and take your pick from the assorted bars and clubs. Stop at the **Irish Film Centre** for a drink, before continuing on to Parliament Street, which is full of hangouts. The chic **Front Lounge** has comfortable couches.

Day 2. Sat.   Mar. 18, 2000
(Day 2. Saturday   March 17, 2001)

9:00am Wake up with Irish breakfast tea and a continental breakfast in the common area of the Clarence. Keep your eyes peeled for bleary-eyed celebrity guests.

10:00am Cab to the **National Gallery** and admire the impressive collection of European art. The imposing Shaw Room is adorned with spectacular Waterford crystal chandeliers. The collection of paintings by Jack B. Yeats (younger brother of Ireland's lauded poet William B. Yeats) is a must-see.

Noon Go for lunch at the award-winning **Fitzer's**, which adjoins the museum and serves international and Mediterranean dishes. It's popular with locals, most of whom will be trading views on politics or catching up on local gossip.

1:30pm Spend the early afternoon in "Old Ireland," walking to College Green and **Trinity College**, the university founded by Elizabeth I in 1592. Check out the "Book of Kells," an illuminated manuscript dating from A.D. 800, in the Long Room of the Old Library.

3:00pm If they're not in official use, you can go inside the apartments known as **Dublin Castle**. The elegant building, built around an ancient castle, is used to entertain visiting heads of state.

4:30pm Adjourn to **Cafe Mocha** on South William Street, a three-story coffeehouse with a brightly colored interior and board-game floor. It serves tea, espresso, sandwiches, and desserts.

6:00pm Experience some guerrilla theater in the *Major International Street Theatre Production*, a celebration of hit-and-run and staged street theater that features cutting-edge international talent.

9:00pm Dinner tonight is at **Restaurant Peacock Alley**. This trendy eatery serves New World cuisine.

11:30pm Find the **Gaiety** on King Street. It's a theater by day and disco and movie house by night.

Day 3. Sun.   Mar. 19, 2000
(Day 3. Sunday   March 18, 2001)

9:00am Walk along the north side of St. Stephen's Green to **Café en-Seine** for a croissant and coffee opposite the Lord Mayor's residence (Mansion House on Dawson Street). You can enjoy the outdoor seating or admire the dizzying heights of the ceiling in the upscale cafe/bar.

10:00am Visit the **Dublin Writers' Museum**, which is housed in a magnificent 18th-century mansion. It showcases the lives and works of Dublin's literary celebrities of the last 300 years.

Noon By now you should be ready for the **Duke Pub-Irish Literary Pub Crawl**, a must for anyone forced to read *Ulysses* in school. The two-to-three-hour pub tour is guided by young actors, who give theatrical readings of the works of Irish masters such as Joyce, Beckett, Behan, and Yeats.

3:00pm Finish off the tour at **Davy Byrnes**, famous for its pub grub and the many illustrious writers who've eaten it. Seafood is the specialty, so savor a meal of oysters or fresh salmon with a pint of Guinness.

4:30pm Join in the interactive *Paddy's Big Day Out*, a carnival of street actors, artists, and musical performers plying their trades around College Green and Dame Street.

6:00pm Enjoy a pint in **McDaids**, an authentic pub with a faithful mix of locals and visitors.

7:30pm *Skyfest* marks the end of the *St. Patrick's Festival* with spectacular pyrotechnic flourishes set to Irish-music masterpieces.

9:00pm Sample the garlic mushrooms at the fashionable **Boulevard Cafe**, where the young and trendy repair for the intimate atmosphere and good food.

11:00pm Lillie's Bordello is a favorite club with visiting celebs. Its door policy can be strict, so ask your hotel to get you on the guest list. Then offer a toast to the patron saint of great parties.

Alternatives

New to Dublin's list of hip lodging is **The Fitzwilliam Hotel**—it has a chic, cosmopolitan flavor; "baronial modern" architectural accents; a roof garden; and a Michelin-starred restaurant. Set in four converted town houses, **The Merrion** is elegant, plush, and comfortable. The modern **Westbury Hotel** also has luxurious Victorian accents.

Within the Shelbourne Hotel lies the **Side Door**, a Californian and Mediterranean hybrid with minimalist decor. The Michelin-starred **Patrick Guilbaud Restaurant** is practically a Dublin institution with its exquisite French cuisine. Jump back into modern Dublin with lunch at the stylish **Mao Cafe Bar** on Chatham Row, a trendy lunch venue serving Asian-fusion food. Have tea and recover from the festivities amid the opulent decor of the **Lord Mayor's Lounge** in the Shelbourne Hotel.

Hit the **Chocolate Bar** *before* 11 p.m. when it transforms from a businessman's after-work watering hole to a young nightclubber's disco. Or try **The Kitchen** for all-night partying with the younger set. The **Rí-Rá's** is another club contributing to Dublin's growing reputation as a party town. Nearby is **The Globe**, a hip, artsy bar.

The **Guinness HopStore** in the Guinness Brewery is worth visiting.

The Hot Sheet

☎ 353/1

$ 0.7 Irish Punt

HOTELS	DAY	ADDRESS	PH	PRICE	FX	RMS	BEST ROOMS
Clarence Hotel	1	6-8 Wellington Quay	670-9000 800- 628-8929	$$$	670-7800	50	Upr fl river vw
The Fitzwilliam Hotel	A	St. Stephen's Green	478-7000 800- 448-8355	$$$	478-7878	130	Dlx
The Merrion	A	Upper Merrion St.	603-0600 800- 223-6800	$$$	603-0700	125	Dlx gdn-wing rm
Westbury Hotel	A	Grafton St.	679-1122 800- 223-6800	$$$	679-7078	161	Skyline exec rm

RESTAURANTS	DAY	ADDRESS	PH	PRICE	REC	DRESS	FOOD
Bewley's Oriental Café	1	78 Grafton St.	677-6761	$	B/LT	Local	Cafe
Boulevard Cafe	3	Exchequer St.	679-2131	$$	D/L	Kazh	Continental
Café en-Seine	3	40 Dawson St.	677-4369	$	B/L	Local	Cafe
Cafe Mocha	2	39-40 S. William	679-8475	$	T/BLD	Local	Cafe, international
Davy Byrnes	3	21 Duke St.	677-5217	$$	D/L	Local	Modern Irish, seafood
Fitzer's	2	Merrion Sq.	601-4496	$	L/BT	Kazh	International, Mediterranean
Lord Mayor's Lounge	A	27 St. Stephen's Green in Shelbourne Hotel	676-6471	$$	T/L	Kazh	Modern Irish
Mao Cafe Bar	A	2-3 Chatham Row	670-4899	$$	L/D	Kazh	Asian fusion
Patrick Guilbaud Restaurant	A	21 Merrion St.	676-4192	$$$	LD	Euro	French
Restaurant Peacock Alley	2	see The Fitzwilliam Hotel	677-0708	$$$	D/L	Dressy	Modern Irish, Mediterranean
Shelbourne Bar	1	27 St. Stephen's Green in Shelbourne Hotel	676-6471	$	L	Kazh	Irish stew
Side Door	A	27 St. Stephen's Green in Shelbourne Hotel	676-6471	$$	D/L	Kazh	International, Mediterranean
Tea Room	1	see Clarence Hotel	670-7766	$$$	D/BL	Kazh	International

NITELIFE	DAY	ADDRESS	PH	PRICE	REC	DRESS	MUSIC
Brazen Head	1	Bridge St.	677-9549	None	H	Local	
Chocolate Bar	A	Upper Hatch St.	478-0225	None	H	Kazh	
Front Lounge	1	33 Parliament St.	670-4112	None	H	Euro	
Gaiety	2	King St.	677-1717	$$	P	Kazh	Rock, jazz
The Globe	A	11 S. Great George's St.	671-1200	None	H	Euro	
Irish Film Centre	1	6 Eustace St.	679-5744	None	H	Local	
The Kitchen	A	6-8 Wellington Quay	677-6635	$	O	Kazh	Dance, contemporary
Lillie's Bordello	3	Adam Ct.	679-9204	$$	P	Local	Contemporary
McDaids	3	Harry St.	679-4395	None	H	Local	
Rí-Rá's	A	Dame Ct.	677-4835	$	O	Euro	Jazz, contemporary

SIGHTS & ATTRACTIONS	DAY	ADDRESS	PH	ENTRY FEE
Dublin Castle	2	Dame St.	677-7129	$
Dublin Writers' Museum	3	18 Parnell Sq. N.	872-2077	$
Guinness HopStore	A	Crane St., St. James's Gate	453-6700	$
National Gallery	2	Merrion Sq. W.	661-5133	None
Trinity College	2	College Green	677-2941	$

OTHER SIGHTS, SERVICES & ATTRACTIONS

Duke Pub-Irish Literary Pub Crawl	3	Duke St.	670-5602	$
Dublin Tourism Centre		Suffolk St.	605-7700	

EVENT & TICKET INFO

St. Patrick's Festival (various locations around Dublin): All events are free, but approximately 300 grandstand seats ($35) for the **Parade** are available by phoning the St. Patrick's Festival (353/1-676-3205).

RECommendations: (Restaurants) B–Breakfast; L–Lunch; D–Dinner; T–High tea or snack
(Nitelife) G–Gaming; H–Hangout bar; M–Live music; O–Dancing (disco); P–Dancing (live music); S–Show; F–Food served
()–Available but without recommendation. For complete explanation of Hot Sheet format, see page 34.

🕐 NYC +5   ☀ 36°/51° (2°/10°)   ✈ Dublin (DUB); 30 min./$20   🚗 No   👥 English

The Fun Also Rises

April 2000

M	T	W	T	F	S	S
					1	2
3	4	5	6	7	8	9
10	11	12	13	14	15	16
17	18	19	20	21	22	23
24	25	26	27	28	29	30

Tokyo (Kawasaki), Japan

April 2001

M	T	W	T	F	S	S
2	3	4	5	6	7	8
9	10	11	12	13	14	15
16	17	18	19	20	21	22
23	24	25	26	27	28	29
30						

Fertility Festival

(Kanamara Matsuri)

Origin: c.1750   Event ★ ★ ★ ★ ★ City   Attendance: 2,000

In Kawasaki, Japan, local legend tells of a sharp-toothed demon that resided in a local maiden's vagina. This ornery little guy had the annoying habit of biting off the penises of a succession of the maiden's poor bridegrooms. Ouch!

To solve this prickly problem, a local blacksmith forged a lifelike iron phallus, which thoughtful city officials thrust inside the maiden. As they hoped, the demon chomped down on the hard-as-nails prosthesis, shattering its teeth, and subsequently starved to death. With the villain vanquished, the maiden finally was able to become a wife and mother—certainly a cause for celebration!

Thus, the city's absurdly extravagant *Kanamara Matsuri*, or Festival of the Steel Phallus, was born, paying annual homage to the beloved love pump at Kanamara Shrine. Events include lighting a sacred fire, admiring the city's cherry blossoms, and drinking sacred sake, but the real passion is saved for everybody's favorite male organ. Celebrants eat penis-shaped candy, and phalluses are forged out of everything from steel to huge radishes. The highlight is a parade through town that features huge phalli carried on the shoulders of groups of men. If you can't quite accept a penis-eating demon, a competing explanation for the festival goes back 250 years, when Kawasaki's hopeful prostitutes supposedly prayed for successful business and protection from syphilis. Whatever the origin, Kawasaki's festival certainly ranks among the world's most bizarre and entertaining events.

Kanamara is best when done as a day trip from Tokyo (an hour away by train). Tokyo is one of the world's most manic cities 365 days a year: a place where few thoroughfares have street signs, cups of coffee can cost $10, and teenagers with mohawks stand on crowded train platforms next to stone-faced businessmen and elegant women dressed in kimonos. There's no real "downtown Tokyo," so, much of the fun comes from getting lost in such areas as bar-laden Shibuya, hyperexpensive Ginza, historic Asakusa, and, of course, nearby Kawasaki.

Day-By-Day Plan For

Fertility Festival

Day 1. Fri. Apr. 7, 2000
(Day 1. Friday April 13, 2001)

9:00am Wake up to a room service breakfast at the **Four Seasons Hotel**, your first-class accommodations one magazine described as "travelers' Valhalla."

10:30am Subway to Asakusa, a charming neighborhood with the feel of Old Japan. The gigantic paper lantern hanging near the gorgeous Sensoji Temple is one of Tokyo's most photographed attractions.

12:30pm Have a steaming bowl of sukiyaki at nearby **Imahan Bekkan**. You'll sit on traditional *tatami* mats in an immaculate dining room.

2:30pm Catch the subway to Ueno Station and visit the **Tokyo National Museum**, Japan's largest museum with some 86,000 objects of ancient Japanese and Asian art.

4:30pm Viewing cherry blossoms in the spring is perhaps the quintessential expression of being Japanese. Join locals sipping sake beneath their beloved trees at Ueno Park, one of Japan's most famed places to take in the blossoms.

6:30pm The Roppongi district is famed as a top (and expensive) nightspot in Japan. Near Roppongi Station, the **Gaspanic Club**, a small bar popular with both foreigners and locals, features a rare bargain—300-yen (about $3) drinks during happy hour.

8:30pm Dinner at **Inaka-ya** is a must. Guests sit around a large, open cooking area. Waiters shout orders to cooks who quickly grill a variety of meats, vegetables, and fish and serve them on big wooden paddles.

10:30pm Walk to the **Lexington Queen**, one of Roppongi's best-known dance spots. It frequently attracts celebrities.

12:30am Nearby **Velfarre** has a stiff cover on weekends, but the large disco is one of Tokyo's most fashionable.

Day 2. Sat. Apr. 8, 2000
(Day 2. Saturday April 14, 2001)

8:30am Breakfast on coffee and pastries at **Tim's NY**, a trendy spot in the popular Ebisu area.

10:00am Subway to Ginza Station and wander the Ginza district for a feel of modern, bustling Tokyo. Ginza boasts some of the world's highest property values and many overpriced shops.

Noon Fresh ingredients make the difference at Ginza's elegant **Ten-Ichi Honten**, which serves some of Tokyo's finest tempura.

2:00pm It's a long walk or a short cab ride to the famed **East Garden** (**Higashi Goen**) at the Imperial Palace. The emperor and Japanese royalty still reside at the ancient fortress (you can't go inside the palace itself).

4:00pm Take the subway to Ryogoku Station and visit the **Edo-Tokyo Museum**, an eight-floor museum depicting life in Tokyo from the 17th century through World War II. The incredible building looks as if it might have been lifted off the set of a Japanese version of *Star Wars*.

5:00pm If it's open, take a look in the **Sumo Museum** next door. Hours depend on the current sumo schedule.

8:00pm Have an inexpensive (for Tokyo) dinner at **Yamaga**, a classic *yaki-tori* (grilled chicken) restaurant that also serves soups, veggies, and fish. It's cramped, busy, and authentic.

9:30pm Shibuya has replaced Roppongi as Tokyo's trendiest nightlife area and its choices of bars and streets seem endless. Start at **Sugar High**, a small bar and disco that gets packed.

11:00pm The large, popular **Club Asia** disco has different music (techno, '70s, etc.) every night of the week.

12:30am Trendy clubs in Shibuya often have a shelf life equivalent to the average cherry blossom, so if you see a crowd milling around a bar, don't hesitate to pop in.

Day 3. Sun.   Apr. 9, 2000
(Day 3. Sunday   April 15, 2001)

8:00am Hit the hotel's continental buffet or try a traditional Japanese breakfast of *miso* soup and *onigiri* (rice ball wrapped in seaweed).

9:00am Subway to Shinjuku-Gyoenmae Station and visit the **Shinjuku Gyoen National Garden** and the famed Meiji Shrine. The shrine's giant, green-copper roof is renowned for its beauty throughout Japan.

10:30am The trip to Kawasaki takes about 90 minutes, so catch the train about this time.

Noon From the Kawasaki-Daishi Station, walk two minutes to the Kanamara Shrine, where ***Kanamara Matsuri*** began with a solemn ceremony at 10 a.m. Grab lunch from the small group of vendors—deep-fried octopus, *okonomiyaki* (a kind of Japanese omelet), and beer are prevalent options—and explore the modest grounds. The shrine is not impressive, but the activity is interesting, to say the least. Large radishes are carved into penis replicas, visitors pose for pictures aboard six-foot-long wooden phalli, transvestites rally around a ten-foot-tall, neon-pink you-know-what.

1:00pm A Shinto priest offers benediction and the festival springs to life as various groups (mostly men) hoist portable penis shrines to their shoulders and parade through the narrow streets of Kawasaki. Follow one of the groups through town.

3:00pm Back at the temple, the unconventional festival concludes when all line up for a bowl of sacred

sake, an unfiltered milky variety that looks a tad suspicious as it's poured from a vessel shaped like, you guessed it, the day's most celebrated organ.

6:30pm Gotta have sushi in Tokyo. Roppongi's always-crowded **Fuku Sushi** gets consistently high marks for ambience and very fresh fish.

8:30pm The elaborate costumes alone make a visit to **Kabuki-za Theater** unforgettable. English translations of this dance-and-drama art form are provided on headphones. Sunday is a formal kabuki night.

10:30pm You might find a decent Sunday crowd at **Yellow**, a trendy Roppongi bar. The classy bar at the Four Seasons is also a nice place to ponder the ephemeral charms that make Japan in springtime as lovely as a cherry blossom and as much fun as a festival that celebrates its own kind of fleeting blossom.

Alternatives

The **Century Hyatt** is conveniently located in busy Shinjuku. Visiting rock stars often choose the **Hotel Seiyo Ginza**. The **Tokyo Prince Hotel** is nice and affordable.

With its Tsukuji Fish Market location, **Sushisei** is often cited as Tokyo's most popular sushi restaurant, but lines can be long. **Roy's Restaurant Hiroo**, opened by Roy Yamaguchi of the famed Roy's Restaurant in Hawaii-Kai, offers trend-setting Euro-Asian dishes. **Spago**, with its trademark California cuisine, has become hip in Roppongi.

Blue Note Tokyo is one of the world's top jazz clubs. A must-see for Beatles fans, the **Cavern Club** has tons of Fab Four memorabilia and Japanese bands dressing and sounding remarkably like the originals. The large **Club Quatro** often has top-quality national and international bands. **Castillo** attracts a 30-and-up crowd with its '70s and '80s music.

The Hot Sheet

☎ 81/3 $ 110 Yen

HOTELS	DAY	ADDRESS	PH	PRICE	FX	RMS	BEST ROOMS
Century Hyatt	A	2-7-2 Nishi Shinjuku	3-349-0111 800-233-1234	$$$$	3-344-5575	766	Exec fl
Four Seasons Hotel	1	10-8 Sekiguchi 2-chome, Bunkyo-ku	3-943-2222 800-332-3442	$$$$+	3-943-2300	282	Dlx
Hotel Seiyo Ginza	A	1-11-2 Ginza, Chuo-ku	3-535-1111 800-447-3496	$$$$+	3-535-1110	52	Dlx
Tokyo Prince Hotel	A	3-3-1 Shibakoen	3-432-1111 800-542-8686	$$$	3-434-5551	484	Dlx dbl

RESTAURANTS	DAY	ADDRESS	PH	PRICE	REC	DRESS	FOOD
Fuku Sushi	3	5-7-8 Roppongi	3-402-4116	$$$	D/L	Local	Sushi
Imahan Bekkan	1	2-2-5 Asakusa	3-841-2690	$	L/D	Local	Sukiyaki, shabu-shabu
Inaka-ya	1	7-8-4 Roppongi, Minato-ku	3-405-9866	$$$$	D	Euro	Traditional grilled meats, fish
Roy's Restaurant Hiroo	A	1-4-40 Hiroo, Shibuya-ku at Ebisu Prime Sq. Pl.	3-406-2277	$$$$	L/D	Local	European, Asian
Spago	A	5-7-8 Roppongi	3-423-4025	$$$$	D	Local	California
Sushisei	A	4-13-9 Tsukuji in Tsukuji Fish Market	3-541-7720	$$$	L/D	Euro	Sushi
Ten-Ichi Honten	2	6-6-5 Ginza, Chuo-ku	3-571-1272	$$$$+	L/D	Euro	Tempura
Tim's NY	2	1-10-11 Minami Ebisu, Shibuya-ku	3-793-5656	$$	B/LD	Euro	Coffee shop
Yamaga	2	1-5-9 Dogenzaka, Shibuya-ku	3-461-3010	$$$	D	Local	Grilled chicken skewers

NITELIFE	DAY	ADDRESS	PH	PRICE	REC	DRESS	MUSIC
Blue Note Tokyo	A	6-3-16 Minamiaoyama, Minato-ku	5-485-0088	$$$$+	M(F)	Euro	Jazz
Castillo	A	6-1-8 Roppongi, 5th fl. Dainiaoi Bldg., Minato-ku	3-475-1629	None	O	Local	'70s, '80s
Cavern Club	A	5-3-2 Roppongi	3-405-5207	$$	M(F)	Local	Beatles
Club Asia	2	1-8 Maruyama-cho, Shibuya-ku	5-458-1996	$$$	O	Local	Techno, hip-hop, house
Club Quatro	A	32-13 Udagawa-cho	3-477-8750	$$$	M	Local	Concert hall
Gaspanic Club	1	3-10-5 Roppongi, 3rd fl. Marina Bldg.	3-402-7054	$	H	Kazh	Dance, pop
Kabuki-za Theater	3	4-12-15 Ginza, Chuo-ku	5-565-6000	$$$$+	S	Dressy	
Lexington Queen	1	3-13-14 Roppongi	3-401-1661	$$$	O	Local	Pop, house, dance
Sugar High	2	2-16-3 Dogenzaka, 3rd fl. Yubun Bldg., Shibuya-ku	3-780-3022	$$	O	Local	Techno, house, drum 'n' bass
Velfarre	1	7-14-22 Roppongi, Minato-ku	3-402-8000	$$$$	O	Local	Disco, techno
Yellow	3	1-10-11 Nishi-Azabu, Minato-ku	3-479-0690	$	M	Local	Various

SIGHTS & ATTRACTIONS	DAY	ADDRESS	PH	ENTRY FEE
East Garden (Higashi Goen)	2	1-1 Chiyoda, Chiyoda-ku	3-213-1111	None
Edo-Tokyo Museum	2	1-4-1 Yokoami, Sumida-ku	3-626-9974	$
Shinjuku Gyoen National Garden	3	11 Naitocho, Shinjuku-ku	3-350-0151	$
Sumo Museum	2	1-3-28 Yokoami, Sumida-ku	3-622-0366	$
Tokyo National Museum	1	13-9 Ueno Park, Taito-ku	3-822-1111	$
Japan National Tourist Organization		3-5-1 Marunouchi, B1 fl., Chiyoda-ku	3-201-3331	

EVENT & TICKET INFO

Kanamara Matsuri (Kanamara Shrine, Kawasaki): All events are free. For more information, contact the city of *Kawasaki* (81/44-200-2244).

RECommendations: (Restaurants) B–Breakfast; L–Lunch; D–Dinner; T–High tea or snack
(Nitelife) G–Gaming; H–Hangout bar; M–Live music; O–Dancing (disco); P–Dancing (live music); S–Show; F–Food served
()–Available but without recommendation. For complete explanation of Hot Sheet format, see page 34.

NYC +14   46°/63° (8°/17°)   Narita (New Tokyo) (NRT) 120 min./SNA (R)   No   Japanese

The Fun Also Rises

April 2000

M T W T F S S
1 2
3 4 5 6 7 8 9
10 11 12 **13 14 15** 16
17 18 19 20 21 22 23
24 25 26 27 28 29 30

Bangkok (Chiang Mai), Thailand

April 2001

M T W T F S S
2 3 4 5 6 7 8
9 10 11 12 **13 14 15**
16 17 18 19 20 21 22
23 24 25 26 27 28 29
30

Songkran Water Festival
(Songkran)

| Origin: c.1300 | Event ★ ★ ★ ★ ★ ★ City | Attendance: 200,000 |

Only the good-natured Thais could make getting splashed with buckets of ice water a fun experience, but that's exactly what happens to locals and visitors during ***Songkran***, the Thai New Year celebration. During this sacred time, people around the country sprinkle holy water on images of Buddha in purification ceremonies. But in Chiang Mai, northern Thailand's beautiful 700-year-old city, the solemn ritual has transmogrified into a spirited, citywide water fight.

Beginning on April 13, the ***Songkran*** celebration in Chiang Mai is by far the best in the country. Drive-by drenchings and water-gun ambushes are honored maneuvers. Tourists are favorite targets for Chiang Mai's devotees of *sanuk* (fun), so leave cameras at the hotel. In addition to boisterous water-throwing, parades include drum dances, costumed dancers, colorful floats, blaring bands, and processions of beautiful young women competing for the Queen of Water Festival crown. Food stalls and riverside restaurants selling exotic foods make the whole city fragrant.

The entry point to Thailand is Bangkok, a crowded city of about 10 million (forget the official 5 million count). Bangkok has grand temples and a proud history, but it's become infamous for wide-open prostitution, especially in the Patpong area. You don't have to partake of the flesh trade to observe a scene that's both seedy and intriguing. Tourists from around the world flock to Thailand, some in search of Bangkok's beautiful boy-transvestites (called *katoey* or "lady-men" in local parlance).

As Thailand's second-largest city, Chiang Mai has a small red-light district, but it's known for its 200 temples, especially the golden Wat Phrathat Doi Suthep, which glitters from a mountaintop perch. There's a terrific night bazaar, and rural villages, teak forests, wild rivers, and national parks surround the city. Just don't forget your Super Shooter. You'll need it—and a couple changes of dry clothes—during wild and intense ***Songkran***.

Songkran Water Festival

Day 1. Thu.   Apr. 13, 2000
(Day 1. Friday   April 13, 2001)

9:00am Eat in the **Mae Ping Coffee Shop** at Chiang
Ⓡ Mai's **The Imperial Mae Ping Hotel**. It's within
walking distance of local attractions. Change into
light, quick-drying clothes.

10:00am Walk 15 minutes (or cab and stay dry) to the
bustling **Warorot Market**. The three-story structure is built like a mini-arena. Stand on the top
floor and look on the jammed produce floor below.

11:00am Walk 10 minutes up Chiang Moi Road toward
the center of town, where most of the *Songkran*
action takes place. You'll be thoroughly drenched by
smiling strangers once you near the Old City.

Noon For Thai food, try **Spice Cuisine**. Have the cashew
Ⓡ chicken and watch the mayhem on Sriphum Road.

1:30pm The world's biggest water war is in full throttle,
so submit to constant dousing. Groups toss ice water
(painful!) from moving cars. Others fire mega-size
water guns or draw buckets directly from the canal.
Main roads will be clogged with water warriors.

3:30pm Watch the *Phra Sing Parade* pass through
Tha Pae Gate. Costumed revelers, bands, and
beauty queens file through the streets and, like
everyone else, get soaked.

4:30pm Follow the parade to the spiritual center of the
festival, **Wat Phra Singh**, Chiang Mai's ornate central temple built in 1345. Inside, check out one of
the country's most revered statues of Buddha.

6:00pm Rachdamnorn Road runs through the center
of Old Town, and during Songkran it's jammed with
food stalls. You can comfortably sample the food—
water generally isn't thrown after sunset—before
thoroughly drying out at the hotel.

7:30pm Cab to **Ban Khun Mae** restaurant for northern
Ⓡ Thai specialties. The slightly upscale atmosphere
makes for a nice change from the wild afternoon.

9:30pm Cab to the **Night Bazaar**, an exotic maze of
stalls, shops, and tents that sell everything from
teak carvings to silk underwear to trinkets.

11:30pm For dancing amid flashing lights and a buoyant crowd, walk to **The Fantasy Discotheque**. You
can walk back to your hotel from here.

Day 2. Fri.   Apr. 14, 2000
(Day 2. Saturday   April 14, 2001)

7:00am Have breakfast in the hotel coffee shop before
Ⓡ shuttling to the airport for your flight to Bangkok.

10:00am Check into **The Oriental**. Its blend of Asian
grace and Western comforts makes it one of the
world's famed hotels.

10:30am Taxi to Thailand's top tourist attraction, the
Grand Palace, which combines classic Thai and
Italian Renaissance architectural styles. Inside
you'll find the stunning Wat Phra Keo, the country's
most famous temple. Don't miss the **Wat Po** next
door. It houses an enormous, five-and-a-half-ton
reclining Buddha covered in gold leaf.

1:00pm Cab to **Vijit Restaurant**. The menu features
Ⓡ excellent Thai, Chinese, Japanese, and continental
dishes, and the atmosphere is casual.

2:30pm For traditional handicrafts, visit the government-
run **Narayana Phand** on the fourth floor of a shopping mall across the street.

3:30pm Cab to **Jim Thompson's House** and tour the
treasure-packed Thai-style home of the American
adventurer credited with reviving the Thai silk
trade after World War II.

5:00pm Cab back to The Oriental for tea in the palatial
® **Authors' Lounge**. The ambience of luxury, history,
and architectural beauty makes it a must.

6:30pm Taxi to **The Barbican**, known for its large beer
selection, Long Island iced tea, and happy-hour
prices from 5:30-7 p.m.

8:30pm Thai cuisine is served in a traditional wooden
® house at **Baan Khanitha**. Try the green curry with
coconut tips.

10:30pm Walk through infamous Patpong, ground zero
for Thailand's notorious sex trade. Bars with topless
dancers and prostitutes are numerous, but the
street is also crammed with cut-rate merchandise
vendors. Absorb it all at the legit **Bobby's Arms**,
which has pub food and good beers.

Midnight End the evening with a drink in The Oriental's
famed **The Bamboo Bar**, whose bartenders reportedly can mix any cocktail perfectly.

Day 3. Sat. Apr. 15, 2000
(Day 3. Sunday   April 15, 2001)

9:00am Have the buffet breakfast on the terrace over-
® looking the Chao Phya River in **The Verandah** at
The Oriental.

10:00am Cab to the **National Museum**. The huge
museum (26 buildings and halls) chronicles Thai
history from 5600 B.C. Along the way, stop at the colorful and bustling **Pak Klong Talad** flower market.

Noon Near the hotel, lunch at **Harmonique**, which has
® a patio and indoor area filled with antiques. It's
popular for old-style Thai cuisine.

1:30pm A boat tour of the muddy Chao Phya River is
an essential Bangkok experience. Arrange a tour
with The Oriental's concierge or at the landing outside the hotel. Cruise to the **Royal Barge Museum**
for a look at ornately designed boats used during
royal processions.

3:15pm Head to the hotel for a Thai massage poolside.

6:00pm Take in a blazing red sunset and Bangkok's
best skyline view at the **Compass Rose Lounge** in
the Westin Banyan Tree hotel.

8:00pm Combining traditional and modern Thai
® cooking, the **Celadon Thai** in the Sukhothai Hotel
provides an elegant meal in a setting to match.

10:00pm Cab to **CM² Bangkok**, a multithemed club
with various entertainment areas, including a disco.

11:30pm Dance to Western rock at the Grand Hyatt's
upscale **Spasso**, which one local magazine
described as "an up-market pick-up joint."

1:00am Cab to **Narcissus**, a disco for Bangkok's young
elite, with stiff prices and a massive sound system.
In the morning, prepare for your flight and next
year's *Songkran* with a cold splash of water.

Alternatives

In Chiang Mai, the **Suriwongse Hotel** is a luxury hotel
near the *Songkran* action. The **Westin Riverside
Plaza** is the best area hotel, but it's a bit out of town.
In Bangkok, the **Grand Hyatt Erawan** and **The
Peninsula** are at their reliable, luxurious best.

In Chiang Mai, **The Smiling Monkey Pub &
Restaurant** serves good food in a historic teak
house. With decent pub food and Night Bazaar location, **The Red Lion English Pub & Restaurant** is a
popular expat hangout.

In Bangkok, the elegant set meal includes a Thai
dance show at **The Sala Rim Naam**, which has
been called the best Thai restaurant in the country.
Le Café Siam is a good spot for a French-Thai
blend. The **Hard Rock Cafe**'s live music makes for
a good alternative nightspot.

The Hot Sheet

☎ 66/2 $ 37 Baht

HOTELS	DAY	ADDRESS	*	PH	PRICE	FX	RMS	BEST ROOMS
Grand Hyatt Erawan	A	494 Rajdamri Rd.		254-1234 / 800- 233-1234	$$	254-6308	337	Regency Club rm
The Imperial Mae Ping Hotel	1	153 Sridonchai Rd.	53	27-0160	$$	27-0181	371	11th-13th fls
The Oriental	2	48 Oriental Ave.		236-0400 / 800- 526-6566	$$$	237-8284	393	Rms 11 and 12
The Peninsula	A	333 Charoennakorn Rd.		861-2888 / 800- 448-8355	$$$	861-1112	370	River vw
Suriwongse Hotel	A	110 Chang Klan Rd.	53	27-0051	$	27-0063	168	Rm 808
Westin Riverside Plaza	A	318/1 Chiang Mai-Lampoon Rd.	53	27-5300 / 800- 937-8461	$$	27-5299	526	Dlx

RESTAURANTS	DAY	ADDRESS	*	PH	PRICE	REC	DRESS	FOOD
Authors' Lounge	2	see The Oriental hotel		236-0400	$$	T	Local	Tea
Baan Khanitha	2	36/1 Sukhumvit 23		258-4181	$	D/L	Kazh	Thai
Ban Khun Mae	1	6/8-9 Chiang Mai-Sankampaeng Rd.	53	26-0171	$	D/L	Local	Northern Thai
Celadon Thai	3	13/3 S. Sathorn Rd. in Sukhothai Hotel		287-0222	$$	D/L	Local	Thai
Harmonique	3	22 Charoenkrung 34		630-6270	$	L/D	Local	Thai
Le Café Siam	A	4 Soi Akson, Chuaploeng Rd.		671-0031	$	LD	Dressy	Cafe
Mae Ping Coffee Shop	1	see The Imperial Mae Ping Hotel	53	27-0160	$	B/LD	Local	Coffee shop
The Red Lion English Pub & Restaurant	A	123 Loi Kroh Rd.	53	81-8847	$	LD	Kazh	Pub food
The Sala Rim Naam	A	see The Oriental hotel		437-6211	$$$$	LD	Kazh	Thai
The Smiling Monkey Pub & Restaurant	A	40/1 Bumroongburi Rd.	53	27-7538	$	BLD	Kazh	Thai, pub food
Spice Cuisine	1	Sriphum Rd.	53	41-8312	$	L/D	Kazh	Thai
The Verandah	3	see The Oriental hotel		236-0400	$$	B/LD	Local	Buffet
Vijit Restaurant	2	World Trade Cntr., Rajdamri Rd.		255-9529	$	L/D	Local	Thai, international

NITELIFE	DAY	ADDRESS	*	PH	PRICE	REC	DRESS	MUSIC
The Bamboo Bar	2	see The Oriental hotel		236-0400	None	H	Kazh	
The Barbican	2	9/4-5 Soi Thaniya, Silom Rd.		234-3590	None	H	Kazh	
Bobby's Arms	2	Patpong 1 Rd.		233-6828	None	H(F)	Kazh	
CM² Bangkok	3	Soi 6 Siam Sq. in Novotel Bangkok hotel		255-6888 ext. 2549	$	MOP(F)	Local	Jazz bar, disco
Compass Rose Lounge	3	21/100 S. Sathorn Rd. in Westin Banyan Tree hotel		679-1200	None	H(F)	Local	
The Fantasy Discotheque	1	100 Chang Klang Rd. in Chiang Inn Hotel	53	81-9053	$	O	Local	House, hip-hop, techno, pop
Hard Rock Cafe	A	424/3-6 Siam Sq., Soi 11		254-0830	None	MP(F)	Local	Rock
Narcissus	3	112 Sukhumvit 23, Soi Prasarnmitr		258-4805	$$	OP	Kazh	Dance
Spasso	3	see Grand Hyatt Erawan hotel		254-1234	None	MP	Kazh	Rock, jazz

SIGHTS & ATTRACTIONS	DAY	ADDRESS	*	PH	ENTRY FEE			
Grand Palace	2	Maharat and Sanam Chai rds.		612-3741	$	enter on Na Phra Lan Rd.		
Jim Thompson's House	2	6 Soi Kaseman 2, Rama I Rd.		215-0122	$			
Narayana Phand	2	127 Ratchadamri Rd.		255-4328	None			
National Museum	3	4 Na Phra That Rd.		224-1396	$			
Night Bazaar	1	104/1 Changklan Rd.	53	27-0066	None			
Pak Klong Talad	3	Maharat Rd., near Memorial Bridge		no phone	None			
Royal Barge Museum	3	Klong Bangkok Noi		424-0004	$			
Wat Phra Singh	1	Samlan Rd.	53	27-6221	None			
Wat Po	2	2 Maharat Rd.		222-0933	$			
Warorot Market	1	Chiang Moi Rd. at Chang Klan Rd.	53	no phone	None			

	ADDRESS		PH
TAT Information Counter	Arrival Hall Donmuang Airport, Terminal 1 or 2		523-8972
TAT Northern Office- Chiang Mai	105/1 Chiang Mai-Lamphun Rd. S. of Nawarat Bridge	53	24-8604

RECommendations: (Restaurants) B–Breakfast; L–Lunch; D–Dinner; T–High tea or snack   *53=Chiang Mai
(Nitelife) G–Gaming; H–Hangout bar; M–Live music; O–Dancing (disco); P–Dancing (live music); S–Show; F–Food served
()–Available but without recommendation. For complete explanation of Hot Sheet format, see page 34.

🕐 NYC +12   ☀ 77°/95° (25°/35°)   ✈ Bangkok Int'l Airport (BKK); 60 min./$20   🚗 No   👥 Thai
                                                         Chiang Mai (CNX); 15 min./$10

Feria de San Marcos

(Feria Nacional de San Marcos)

Origin: 1848	Event ★ ★ ★ ★ City	Attendance: 1.6 million

Mexico's wild nightclubs and beauty-packed beaches provide plenty of opportunities to party. But year in and year out, the country's largest and most famous fiesta, *Feria de San Marcos*, wins new converts with three rowdy weeks of dancing, carousing, and tequila baptisms.

Music fills every side street and blasts out of temporary discos and bars, as the event engulfs Aguascalientes' stone-paved pedestrian plazas. Street-food choices abound, and roving mariachi bands spark enthusiasm on corners throughout town. But music and food aren't the only draws. Makeshift clubs with indoor and outdoor dance floors stay open until dawn. The tequila companies do such a good job of getting everyone *borracho* (drunk) in their tent bars that even confirmed wallflowers drop their inhibitions and become lost in *baile* (dance). Mexico's only legal casino operates during the event.

During the festival, local laws are relaxed, making it legal to stumble through the streets with a spicy *carne asada* taco in one hand and a bottle of tequila in the other. Fireworks extravaganzas flare up nightly along with theater performances, poetry readings, dance shows, and other spectacles. Bullfights, horse shows, and a rodeo highlight the daytime activities. Those who need more than tequila and livestock to get excited can bungee-jump or test the thrill rides in the carnival area.

Named for its thermal springs, Aguascalientes (hot waters) has few city attractions, so the only time you're likely to want to visit is during *Feria de San Marcos*. The capital of the small central Mexico state of the same name isn't normally the place to go to paint the town red—a more appropriate color would be the faded sepia of the worn floorboards at one of the town's few cantinas. Over the course of the festival, however, the town's 900,000 residents play host to some of their country's top musicians, bullfighters, and party animals, making Aguascalientes the ultimate fiesta destination as hot as its name.

Feria de San Marcos

Day 1. Fri.   Apr. 28, 2000
(Day 1. Friday   April 27, 2001)

9:30am Breakfast at your hotel, the first-class, four-story **Fiesta Americana** set conveniently at the edge of the fairgrounds. Its Mexican-colonial architecture features terra-cotta-colored stucco walls, balconies, and stone archways.

10:45am While it's still cool, stroll to the colonial heart of the city. Begin at the fair's *paseo*, the wide avenue that runs north to San Marcos church and garden. Follow Carranza Street—foot traffic only—where you'll find the artists section and folk-art shops.

11:45am At the main square, Plaza de la Patria, admire the newly renovated interior of the **Catedral**. On an adjacent corner, pick up *Feria* programs at the Tourist Information Office in the **Palacio de Gobierno**, the state capitol. The building houses colorful murals by Chilean artist Osvaldo Barra Cunningham, whose mentor was Diego Rivera. Don't miss the humorous one of the fair on the second floor.

1:30pm Opposite the cathedral, in the pink palace (which formerly housed the opulent Hotel Francia), **Sanborn's** provides air-conditioned bliss in its upstairs restaurant—perfect for a cold beer and lunch.

3:00pm Cab to your hotel and do as the locals do—lie low until around 5 p.m. With the mile-high altitude, a siesta will be welcome. Or hang out in a shady corner of the pool terrace and study the fair program.

5:00pm As you head to the plaza, turn back to watch the bull and bullfighter emerge from the hotel clock as it chimes the hour.

6:00pm Don't miss the *voladores de Papantla*, six fearless flying Indians who whirl around and around a sturdy maypole that soars 150 feet above ground. It's best to scout around the fairgrounds before the big crush begins at dusk. Then stop in at **Merendero Don Chendo** for appetizers and drinks.

8:30pm Stake out a table at Fiesta Americana's outdoor patio, **Café Plaza**. It's a great spot to do cocktails and dinner as you watch the parade of humanity go by. When the urge strikes, feel free to join in.

9:30pm Talk about the ultimate sign of a nonstop fiesta—the *Feria* has a daycare center that operates 7 p.m.-7 a.m.! And where are the parents? A good bet is the nearby *Casino*, where gambling is legal only during the fair. It may be the only casino in the world where a priest circles the craps table asking for donations.

11:30pm The city's nightclubs and discos move to temporary quarters at the fairgrounds, and dancing and drinking go on until early morning. Most places are open-air. Mariachi groups and *tambora* (big drum) bands play amid the throngs of partyers, so there's plenty of chances to dance.

Day 2. Sat.   Apr. 29, 2000
(Day 2. Saturday   April 28, 2001)

10:00am Have a room-service breakfast before heading for the fascinating **Hacienda de Chichimeco**, a ranch noted for breeding spirited bulls. Brave souls can even take a crack at bullfighting.

2:00pm If you didn't get lunch at the Hacienda, grab a bite at **VIP's**, across the street from your hotel. Or try one of the restaurants near the fair.

4:00pm Take the 20-minute stroll past the bullring, the carnival, and the cow exhibits to the Lienzo Charro, site of the equestrian events. At the *charreada* (rodeo), dashing *charros* (cowboys) in wide-brimmed sombreros dazzle the crowd with their horseback skills, bronco riding, and roping talents.

6:30pm Take a siesta, or walk around the fairgrounds, stopping for a tequila in preparation for dinner.

8:00pm Dine at the elegant **Los Murales** in the Quinta Real hotel, a colonial-style building furnished with antiques, original art, and Mexican handicrafts. Try the *huachinango a la Veracruzana*, a regional red-snapper specialty.

11:30pm Some of the biggest names in Mexican show-business are scheduled for the ***Headliner Concerts*** at the Palenque. Allow at least half an hour before show time to make your way through the crowd.

1:30am By now the ***Feria***'s discos should be hopping, especially at the Cuervo tent.

Day 3. Sun.   Apr. 30, 2000
(Day 3. Sunday   April 29, 2001)

10:00am Cab to the **Antigua Hacienda de la Noria** for the breakfast buffet. Start with freshly ground coffee and tropical fruit, then choose from the selection of Mexican-style egg dishes with chorizo, beans, and fragrant breads.

Noon Museum-hop, first to the **Museo José Guadalupe Posada**. Guadalupe Posada was a political cartoonist at the turn of the 20th century. Then, hit the **Museo de Aguascalientes**, which houses a permanent exhibition of Mexican modernists. Afterward, peek inside the ornate **Church of San Antonio** across the street.

3:15pm Finish your cultural tour at the De Andrea Alameda hotel with a late lunch at **Los Cisnes**. This palatial hotel is the traditional home away from home for the top bullfighters, and you'll be there when they make an appearance at the restaurant en route to the ring.

5:30pm It's a five-minute walk from your hotel to the Plaza de Toros Monumental, the second-largest bullring in Mexico. Top Mexican and Spanish matadors show off their skills for their adoring fans at the ***bullfight***.

9:00pm Have an Argentine-style barbecued steak at **Rincón Gaucho**, one of the fair's popular restaurants. Or try *cabrito al pastor* (goat) at **La Majada**, across from your hotel.

11:00pm This is your last chance to dance in the ***Feria*** discos, so max out your energy reserves and salsa your way into Mexican heaven.

Alternatives

The **Quinta Real** has Old World charm accented with contemporary Mexican furnishings. **Gran Hotel Hacienda de la Noria** offers a taste of traditional elegance. Bullfighting aficionados can headquarter at the **De Andrea Alameda**, where many matadors make their home during the ***Feria***.

The fair program is loaded with activities. In addition to itinerary listings, there are concerts by jazz groups, rock bands, dance troupes, and the Aguascalientes Symphony Orchestra; mariachi competitions; a circus; and a carnival.

If you arrive earlier in the week, enjoy ***San Marcos Day*** (April 25), celebrated with a lively and colorful parade. Although closed during ***Feria***, the center of nightlife from Wednesday to Saturday is **Ios**, where DJs spin for a full house.

According to legend, the state of Aguascalientes owes its political independence to a torrid kiss. In 1835, Mexican president Antonio López de Santa Anna took time out from a rebellion in Zacatecas to attend a party, where he met the dazzling María Luisa Villa. He promised her anything she wanted in return for a kiss. After passionately kissing Santa Anna, she requested autonomy for her region of Aguascalientes. He agreed. María Luisa's husband not only became the first governor, but his wife encouraged him to place a pair of lips in the state's coat-of-arms.

The Hot Sheet

☎ 52/49
$ 9.5 Peso

HOTELS	DAY	ADDRESS	PH	PRICE	FX	RMS	BEST ROOMS
De Andrea Alameda	A	Av. Tecnológico	18-4417	$$	18-3759	48	Gdn vw
Fiesta Americana	1	c/ Laureles	18-6010 800- 343-7821	$$$$+	18-5118	192	Plaza vw
Gran Hotel Hacienda de la Noria	A	1315 Héroe de Nacozari S.	18-4343	$$$	18-5150	50	Poolside
Quinta Real	A	601 Aguascalientes S.	78-5818	$$	78-5616	85	Gdn vw

RESTAURANTS	DAY	ADDRESS	PH	PRICE	REC	DRESS	FOOD
Antigua Hacienda de la Noria	3	1401 Héroe de Nacozari S.	18-2002	$$	B/LD	Local	International, Mexican
Café Plaza	1	see Fiesta Americana hotel	18-6010	$$	D/BL	Local	International, Mexican
La Majada	3	Arturo J. Pane, Expo Pl. near Fiesta Americana hotel	no phone	$	D	Local	Goat barbecue
Los Cisnes	3	see De Andrea Alameda hotel	18-4417	$$	L/BD	Local	International, Mexican
Los Murales	2	see Quinta Real hotel	78-5818	$$	D/BL	Local	International, regional Mexican
Rincón Gaucho	3	110 Arturo J. Pane N.	15-9313	$	D/L	Local	Argentinian barbecue
Sanborn's	1	Pl. de la Patria	12-4002	$	L/BD	Local	International, Mexican
VIP's	2	c/ Commercial, Expo Pl.	18-4260	$	L/BD	Local	International, Mexican

NITELIFE	DAY	ADDRESS	PH	PRICE	REC	DRESS	MUSIC
Ios	A	1821 Blvd. Miguel de la Madrid	12-6576	None	O	Local	Dance
Merendero Don Chendo	1	130 Arturo J. Pane N.	16-1680	$	HF	Local	

SIGHTS & ATTRACTIONS	DAY	ADDRESS	PH	ENTRY FEE
Catedral	1	Pl. de la Patria	15-1052	None
Church of San Antonio	3	Pedro Parga and Zaragoza	15-2898	None
Hacienda de Chichimeco	2	Carretera Jesús María à Valladolid	18-2295	$
Museo de Aguascalientes	3	505 Zaragoza	15-9043	$
Museo José Guadalupe Posada	3	Jardín del Encino	15-4556	$
Palacio de Gobierno	1	Pl. de la Patria	15-1155	None
Tourist Information Office		in Palacio de Gobierno	15-1155	

EVENT & TICKET INFO

Feria de San Marcos (various locations in Aguascalientes): Admission to see the **voladores de Papantla** (fairgrounds), **Casino** (San Marcos Garden), and parade is free. Tickets are needed for the **Headliner Concerts** ($10-$40, in person at the Palenque), **bullfights** ($20-$30, Plaza de Toros), and the **charreada** ($3-$5, Lienzo Charro). It is recommended to purchase tickets in advance for the Headliner Concerts and bullfights from *Ticketmaster* (52/5-325-9000).

RECommendations: (Restaurants) B–Breakfast; L–Lunch; D–Dinner; T–High tea or snack
(Nitelife) G–Gaming; H–Hangout bar; M–Live music; O–Dancing (disco); P–Dancing (live music); S–Show; F–Food served
()–Available but without recommendation. For complete explanation of Hot Sheet format, see page 34.

NYC -1   35°/99° (1°/37°)   Aguascalientes (AGU); 15 min./$10   Yes/No    Spanish

Queen's Day

(Koninginnedag)

Origin: 1948   Event ★ ★ ★ ★ ★ ★ City   Attendance: 720,000

Once a year, more than 700,000 orange-clad revelers, often with their favorite local beverage in hand, invade the quaint cobblestone streets of Amsterdam for the world's wildest rummage sale. They commemorate the Queen's birthday by donning the luminous hues of her House of Orange. Though technically a royal occasion, most partyers seem more interested in the free-flowing Heineken and rare unregulated street trade, which, for one day only, transforms Amsterdam into the largest flea market in the world.

Musicians (mostly amateur) jam on every corner, and thousands of people haul their surpluses to the streets and attempt to sell them to the parading hordes. There are some good buys, but the point is the party, not the product.

Away from the merriment, the Dutch capital lies waiting to be discovered. The city is one of Europe's great urban treasures and, with a population of 720,000, it feels neither too big nor too small. A vibrant metropolis full of bell-ringing bicycles, beautiful people, and a sensual, creative energy, Amsterdam is a place of fascinating duality—gabled storybook houses along with erotic theater, lax drug laws, and unionized sex workers. Canals ripple out from the city center, connected by quaint narrow streets. It's easy to wander the city while the music of church bells and aromas from ethnic markets fill the air.

Mingling with locals, however, is the only way to discover the true meaning of *gezelligheid*, a famed local expression best defined as "cozy conviviality."

Leave modesty behind and explore every facet of this city where culture, beauty, and erotica are as limitless as lager. Visit the museums and tour the canals, but check out the red-light district's sex shops, erotic shows, and racy lingerie stores, as well.

When asked to suggest fun things to do in Amsterdam, the Dutch Tourist Board replied, "We don't promote fun, we promote tulips." Maybe they know you just can't go wrong in Amsterdam.

Queen's Day

Day 1. Fri.   Apr. 28, 2000
(Day 1. Saturday   April 28, 2001)

9:30am The handsome **Pulitzer** hotel was created by connecting 24 renovated 17th- and 18th-century town houses. Its central location near Dam Square makes it ideal for exploring the city.

10:30am Take in Amsterdam's charming architecture with a leisurely tour of the canals. **Holland International** boats leave every 15 minutes from Centraal Station.

12:30pm Have lunch at **Sama Sebo**, a lively Indonesian restaurant off the Leidseplein.

2:00pm Walk to the large **Rikjsmuseum**, which showcases numerous paintings by Rembrandt and other Dutch masters.

6:30pm "Brown Bars" are as Dutch as tulips and wooden shoes, and provide a great place to meet interesting people from all walks of life. **Café Hoppe** is highly recommended.

8:30pm Unlike their European neighbors to the south, the Dutch prefer to eat early. Find a place such as **Luden Restaurant**, which doubles as a hangout after the kitchen closes. Ask for a table in the stylish back area, where modern art hangs on the walls.

10:30pm In the bustling Spui area, **Café Dante** and **Café Luxembourg** are popular. Engage locals and tourists while downing an after-dinner shot of *genever* (Dutch gin).

1:00am Dance the night (or a good part of the morning) away at **Ministry**, an intimate and classy nightclub with a different style of music each night. Saturday is the most popular night, but it's also the hardest to get past the stringent doormen.

Day 2. Sat.   Apr. 29, 2000
(Day 2. Sunday   April 29, 2001)

9:00am Have a traditional Dutch breakfast of coffee, cheese, and bread at **Café Americain**, one of the most famous cafes in Amsterdam. Located on the ground floor of the American Hotel, this shining example of art-nouveau decor opened its doors in 1902.

10:00am Two neighboring museums, the **Stedelijk Museum** and the **Van Gogh Museum**, take you into the world of modern and contemporary art. Founded on the collection of the artist's brother, Theo, the Van Gogh Museum has more than 200 paintings by Vincent van Gogh. The Stedelijk has pieces by his compatriots and other modern painters.

1:30pm For uncomplicated continental cuisine, have lunch at **Le Restaurant Tout Court**, a casual but smart eatery off the canals.

3:00pm Discover the bohemian charm of the rapidly gentrifying Jordaan District. This laid-back, friendly neighborhood is a great place for listening to music and watching hipsters parade in modern fashions.

6:30pm Check out one of Jordaan's "Brown Cafes." **Café't Smalle** is one of the newest, opening just 204 years ago.

8:00pm Have dinner at **Le Garage**, a local favorite for modern Dutch food and excellent people-watching. The waiters wear crisp white shirts and black aprons, the crowd is good-looking, and the food is adventurous.

10:15pm Join the milling crowds for pre-**Queen's Day** excitement as they wander from Rembrandtplein to Leidseplein.

Midnight Check out the disco **iT**, one of the hippest nightclubs around. Or take in Chemistry Night at

Escape, the largest and loudest club in town, with a capacity of 2,000. For a more sedate night away from the madness of the masses, try **Bourbon Street**, which features great live blues.

2:30am On the way back to the hotel, stop for a late-night snack at **Bojo**, a funky Indonesian eatery. Outside, the streets will still be stirring with people preparing for the big day tomorrow.

Day 3. Sun.   Apr. 30, 2000
(Day 3. Monday   April 30, 2001)

10:00am After breakfast at the hotel, drive 10 miles to Lisse and the 50-year-old **Keukenhof** gardens, which boast the largest bulb show on earth. Almost 7 million flowers bloom around ancient trees and modern sculptures.

1:00pm On your return to Amsterdam, stop for lunch at American import **Café Esprit**, of Esprit clothiers fame. This modern cantina serves California-style fare on a pleasant terrace.

2:30pm Join the parade of people walking across the city and taking in *Queen's Day* activities. Catch impromptu street performances, live bands, and a host of other artistic endeavors. Buy Grandma's 30-year-old hairpin collection or some professor's antique books. Crowds thin out at Vongel Park, where you can enjoy the fresh spring air.

8:00pm Dine at upscale **Beddington's**. The minimalist decor is spiced up with international dishes such as spring lamb with thyme and bisque of clams and lobster.

10:30pm Explore the seedy side of Amsterdam with a trek into the Dam Staat and Oudezijds Achterburgwal areas. In the heart of the red-light district is the **Casa Rosso** theater, which features nonstop erotic acts. At **Bananenbar**, the emphasis is on banana "tricks."

Midnight On the "wrong side of the canal" is the eclectic **Winston Kingdom**. Sip a cocktail at the curved bar with arty overhanging lights and red decor. With DJs, bands, and poetry, the mixture of entertainment is usually quirky—in other words, an appropriate finale to the weekend.

Alternatives

Located in the city center, **The Grand** is a five-star hotel with rooms overlooking the canals or the beautiful inner courtyard. The convenient **American Hotel** on the Leidseplein offers spacious, comfortable rooms. Popular among royals and celebrities, the **Amstel Inter-Continental Hotel** has Persian carpets, expansive rooms, and an attentive staff.

Indonesian restaurants abound in Amsterdam. **Longpura** and **Kantjil en de Tijger** are two that come highly recommended, though neither is open for lunch. For fresh Dutch food, try the **d'Vijff Vlieghen** (The Five Flies), which is located in five adjoining canal-houses—touristy but very good. Near Centraal Station, the popular, intimate **Pier 10** serves modern Dutch cuisine.

Amsterdam's beautiful people gather at the **Seymour Likely Lounge**. **Sinners in Heaven** is a trendy, beautifully decorated disco for the chic crowd. Cafes such as **Wildschut** and **Café De Jaren** are popular places for gearing up or winding down from intense partying.

Visit the **Anne Frank House**, where the young Jewish girl lived with her family while writing her famous diary. The **Museum Het Rembrandthuis** displays 250 Rembrandt etchings in the very house where they were created. If you haven't seen enough of the green cans already, tour the famous **Heineken Brewery**.

Another high time to come to Amsterdam is late November for the *Cannabis Cup*. This annual event, sponsored by American magazine *High Times*, consists of bud bowls, hemp symposiums, sensimilla workshops, and lots of late-night snacking—plus you get to judge the goods.

The Hot Sheet

☎ 31/20

$ 2.0 Guilder

HOTELS	DAY	ADDRESS	PH	PRICE	FX	RMS	BEST ROOMS
American Hotel	A	97 Leidsekade	556-3000 800-327-0200	$$$$	556-3001	188	Dlx canal or sq vw
Amstel Inter-Continental Hotel	A	1 Professor Tulpplein	622-6060 800-327-0200	$$$$+	622-5808	79	Exec rm 4th fl river vw
The Grand	A	197 Oudezijds Voorburgwal	555-3111 800-937-8461	$$$$	555-3222	182	Canal or gdn vw
Pulitzer	1	315-331 Prinsengracht	523-5235 800-325-3535	$$$$	627-6753	224	Dlx gdn or canal vw

RESTAURANTS	DAY	ADDRESS	PH	PRICE	REC	DRESS	FOOD
Beddington's	3	6-8 Roelof Hartstraat	676-5201	$$$	D/L	Euro	International
Bojo	2	51 Lange Leidsedwarsstraat	622-7434	$$	T	Kazh	Indonesian
Café Americain	2	see American Hotel	556-3000	$$	B/LD	Kazh	Brasserie, cafe
Café Esprit	3	10 Spui	622-1967	$	L/T	Kazh	Californian
d'Vijff Vlieghen	A	294-302 Spuistraat	624-8369	$	D	Dressy	Gourmet Dutch
Kantjil en de Tijger	A	291-293 Spuistraat	620-0994	$$$	D	Kazh	Indonesian
Le Garage	2	54 Ruysdaelstraat	679-7176	$$$$	D/L	Dressy	Nuvo Dutch
Le Restaurant Tout Court	2	13 Runstraat	625-8637	$$$	L/D	Kazh	French
Longpura	A	46-48 Rozengracht	623-8950	$$	D	Euro	Indonesian
Luden Restaurant	1	304 Spuistraat	622-8979	$$$	D/L	Euro	French
Pier 10	A	10 De Ruyterkade Steiger	624-8276	$$	D	Kazh	French, international
Sama Sebo	1	27 P.C. Hooftstraat	662-8146	$$$	L/D	Kazh	Indonesian

NITELIFE	DAY	ADDRESS	PH	PRICE	REC	DRESS	MUSIC
Bananenbar	3	37 Oudezijds Achterburgwal	622-4670	$$$$	HS	Kazh	
Bourbon Street	2	6-8 Leidsekruisstraat	623-3440	$	M	Euro	Blues
Café Dante	1	320 Spui	638-8839	None	H(F)	Kazh	
Café De Jaren	A	20-22 Nieuwe Doelenstraat	625-5771	None	H(F)	Kazh	
Café Hoppe	1	18-20 Spui	420-4420	None	H(F)	Kazh	
Café Luxembourg	1	24 Spui	620-6264	None	H(F)	Kazh	
Café't Smalle	2	12 Egelantiersgracht	623-9617	None	H(F)	Kazh	
Casa Rosso	3	106-108 OZ Achterburgwal	627-8954	$$$	S	Kazh	
Escape	2	11 Rembrandtplein	622-1111	$$	O	Kazh	Mellow house
iT	2	24 Amstelstraat	625-0111	$	O	Kazh	Disco
Ministry	1	12 Regulierdwarsstraat	623-3981	$	O	Euro	Dance
Seymour Likely Lounge	A	250 Nieuwezijds Voorburgwal	627-1427	None	H	Kazh	
Sinners in Heaven	A	3-7 Wagenstraat	620-1375	$	O	Euro	House, R&B, dance
Wildschut	A	1-3 Roelof Hartplein	676-8220	None	HF	Euro	
Winston Kingdom	3	123-129 Warmoesstraat	623-1380	$	MOP	Local	Rock, house, disco

SIGHTS & ATTRACTIONS	DAY	ADDRESS	*	PH	ENTRY FEE
Anne Frank House	A	263 Prinsengracht		556-7100	$
Heineken Brewery	A	78 Stadhouderskade		523-9666	$
Keukenhof	3	Hwy. A4 to Lisse	252	46-5555	$
Museum Het Rembrandthuis	A	4-6 Jodenbreestraat		624-9486	$
Rikjsmuseum	1	42 Stadhouderskade		674-7000	$
Stedelijk Museum	2	13 Paulus Potterstraat		573-2911	$
Van Gogh Museum	2	7 Paulus Potterstraat		570-5200	$

OTHER SIGHTS, SERVICES & ATTRACTIONS

Holland International	1	Prins Hendrikkade		622-7788	$
VVV Amsterdam Tourist Office		1 Leidseplein		900-400-4000	

EVENT & TICKET INFO

Queen's Day (various locations around Amsterdam): All events are free. For more information, contact Amsterdam Tourist Information (31/20-551-2512).

Alternative Event

Cannabis Cup: 420 Tours in New York, 212-219-7000

RECommendations: (Restaurants) B–Breakfast; L–Lunch; D–Dinner; T–High tea or snack
(Nitelife) G–Gaming; H–Hangout bar; M–Live music; O–Dancing (disco); P–Dancing (live music); S–Show; F–Food served
( )–Available but without recommendation. For complete explanation of Hot Sheet format, see page 34.

NYC +6   38°/55° (3°/12°)   ✈ Amsterdam (Schiphol) (AMS); 30 min./$45   🚗 Yes/No   👥 Dutch

The Fun Also Rises

Larger Than Life

You're a bird, soaring above the parched serengeti as massive herds of wildebeests ripple across the grasslands below. You're a dolphin, gliding through glittering coral reefs, then shooting up in exhilarating somersaults high above the waves. You're a mountain climber near the top of Mount Everest, watching helplessly as an avalanche of snow and ice roars furiously toward you ... then all goes black.

This is fun? Yes, because you're in the midst of large-format movies, films so huge and crisp they almost literally bring you into the experience. While this book emphasizes participation rather than passive observation, virtually all of our destinations include giant-screen movie theaters that occasionally provide a worthy diversion from the main attractions we suggest.

Projected onto screens as high as eight stories or domes up to 88 feet in diameter, large-format films extend beyond viewers' fields of peripheral vision. Specially designed theaters with steeply raked seating provide a "best" seat for everyone, and multichannel, multispeaker sound systems enhance the effects. In certain theaters, viewers can dive into these three-dimensional films with the aid of electronic liquid-crystal shutter glasses (a far cry from those goofy plastic 3-D glasses of the 1950s). Some film centers add audience motion. The combination of these effects brings viewers into the action so realistically that they often walk out of films such as *Everest* expecting to buckle up their boots and tackle snow and ice outside.

So, what makes these panoramic illusions possible? Basically, it's the larger-size film and a revolutionary projection system pioneered by a group of Canadian filmmakers and entrepreneurs who were inspired by the multiscreen films that amazed audiences at Montreal's Expo '67. Their 15/70 film frames are ten times larger than conventional 35mm frames and three times greater than 70mm ones.

Originally found most often at museums, science centers, world fairs, and expositions,

large-format film theaters are now just as likely to be built at theme parks and, increasingly, as part of commercial developments. Since its opening in November 1994, the SONY IMAX theater at New York's Lincoln Square has been one of the highest-grossing single movie screens in the United States.

Filmmakers who lease special cameras and equipment from companies such as Imax and Iwerks, two leaders in technology and number of theaters, make many of the films shown on these oversize screens. In 1976, MacGillivray Freeman Films thrilled audiences with *To Fly!* at the Smithsonian Institution's National Air and Space Museum in Washington, D.C. Their haunting 1998 film *Everest* has led to an explosion of public interest in large-format films. Destination Cinema, in cooperation with National Geographic Television, produces films specific to its theaters at tourist destinations such as the Grand Canyon and Niagara Falls. For fans of this new technology, the good news is large-format movies should get even better. Imax has teamed up with NASA to develop cameras for launch into space, where astronauts will shoot a 3-D film about the building of the International Space Station.

With public demand increasing, large-format films will continue to develop. As Imax co-founder Graeme Ferguson observes, "One of the things you discover when you invent a medium is that you yourself don't know all of its potential. It's only when a large number of artists start using it that they start to astonish those who invented it."

Buoy Meets Girl

As a mating, or "matey," ritual, few events compare with *Cowes Week* (see page 185) and *Antigua Sailing Week* (see page 127). But there are other great sailing competitions out there.

Arguably, the most prestigious international 'round-the-buoy events—in which competitors sail preset courses around markers—are the America's Cup and the Olympic Games. The *America's Cup* ranks as yachting's premier bigboat match race. If you want to experience the ultimate in blue-blood international sailing, hosted and sponsored by the sport's biggest players, this is it. The America's Cup, held February 19-March 4, 2000, in Auckland, New Zealand, will include up to a dozen syndicates from 10 countries vying for yachting's most coveted trophy. In contrast, the *Summer Olympics*—racing events will run September 16-30, 2000, in Sydney, Australia—provide a chance to see the world's top sailors battle it out 'round the buoys in small sailboats such as Lasers, Finns, Tornadoes, and Stars.

Intrigued by endurance contests? Don't miss a start of the *Volvo Ocean Race* (previously the Whitbread Round the World Race), a grueling nine-month marathon in which crews and million-dollar racing machines from more than a dozen countries challenge the world's most formidable oceans. The arduous course, which begins in Southampton, England, takes in nine international stopovers (including Miami, Baltimore, and Rio de Janeiro) and their subsequent starts, and is best-known for its cold, wild ride through tumultuous seas, 80-knot winds, 50,000-ton icebergs, and around infamous Cape Horn.

In other locales, the prestigious and difficult *Sydney to Hobart Yacht Race* (Tasmania, Australia) brings 300,000 picnickers down under each December to watch the competition begin. Every four years (next held in 2002), *Around Alone*, an epic 27,000-mile global race for solo sailors and their custom-designed ocean speedsters, draws thousands of sailing fans to hospitable Charleston, South Carolina, for the start. Around Alone has three stops—Cape Town, South Africa; Auckland, New Zealand; and Punta del Este, Uruguay—making it possible to follow the race and witness the start in each port.

You can celebrate May 24 at Bermuda's fitted-dinghy races in St. George's harbor. Bermuda is one of the friendliest, most attractive places on earth, and the island-built fitted dinghy is a remarkable craft. Or spend Memorial Day weekend at San Francisco's traditional *Master Mariners Regatta*, an event that features some of the world's most exquisite antique wooden sailboats. Each Labor Day weekend, Newport, Rhode Island, hosts *The Museum of Yachting Classic Yacht Regatta*. Whatever your tastes, whatever the season, there's a race committee in some faraway port preparing to fire the starting gun.

TEN GREAT SAILING EVENTS	
America's Cup	64/9-303-2000
Antigua Sailing Week (see page 127)	268-462-8872
Around Alone	360-629-3114
Bermuda Fitted Dinghy Races	441-295-2214
Cowes Week (see page 185)	44/198-329-5744
The Museum of Yachting Classic Yacht Regatta	401-847-1018
Master Mariners Regatta	415-364-1656
Summer Olympics	61/2-913-6363
Sydney to Hobart Yacht Race	61/29-363-9731
Volvo Ocean Race (previously the Whitbread Round the World Race)	44/148-956-4555

Sailing Week

(Antigua Sailing Week)

St. John's, Antigua

April/May 2000

April/May 2001

Origin: 1967   Event ★ ★ ★ ★ City   Attendance: 10,000

Think of sailing and you think of beautiful water, beautiful beaches, and beautiful people. *Sailing Week* adds the critical missing component to this blend of fantasy visions—10,000 partyers.

Sailing Week is the Caribbean's premier event for the wild and wealthy international sailing community, a tightly knit group that builds its existence around the pursuit of sheer fun. Its infamous beach parties in Antigua bring thousands of rum-guzzlers and crew members from more than 250 yachts to this annual reunion. Parties, cookouts, dances, volleyball games, and live music are scheduled around the gorgeous island, and everybody is on the lookout for port-of-call romance.

After opening races on Sunday, the first official party sets the mood for the week. On the white-sand beaches at Rex Halcyon Cove, a couple thousand people party to reggae, soca, and steel-band music. Hundreds of beach vendors hawk clothing, souvenirs, food, beer, and rum drinks. Beachside restaurants and bars are packed—most set up music and dance floors outdoors. From then on, sun-kissed sailors soak up the tropical revelry until "whenever." You may want to stay an extra day to catch Wednesday's *Lay Day* games at the Antigua Yacht Club. That's where you'll find a one-handed yacht race around the harbor, beer races (a running-and-chugging relay), underwater-obstacle-course-in-murk swimming, a tug of war, and a wet T-shirt contest.

Sailors know the in's and out's of the Caribbean better than anyone, so it's no shock that their best bash is on one of the region's perfect islands. St. John's is Antigua's easy-to-negotiate capital city, but spectacular beaches are what make the island so memorable. Imagine "tropical getaway," and Antigua is what you see. In addition to *Sailing Week* fun, the island has nearly 200 beaches—a bit shy of its popular "one for each day of the year" slogan—and enough rum punch, tanned bodies, and tropical breezes to convince you to stick around until "whenever".

Day 1. Sun.   Apr. 30, 2000
(Day 1. Sunday   April 29, 2001)

10:00am Check in at **Siboney Beach Club**, an intimate 13-room inn wrapped in lush greenery that sits at the south end of Dickenson Bay, one of the island's best beaches and the site of *Sailing Week*'s biggest party. Pick up a rental car, carry a map to help you navigate the maze of unmarked roads, and remember to drive on the left!

10:30am Pass through St. John's and watch for signs pointing to Jolly Harbour, a newer development on the west coast. Bypass Jolly Harbour for now and continue south, passing tiny hamlets and one fantastic, underdeveloped beach after another. Best of these is Dark Wood Beach (just before Crab Hill) where you can stop for a quick swim and a beer. The island on the horizon is Montserrat—you should also spot some of the yachts heading north on the first race. Continue south on the road, where it turns inland, becomes luxuriant Fig Tree Drive, and winds through the closest thing to a rainforest on the island. Bear right as you head downhill and aim for English Harbour. This drive requires about an hour and takes in Antigua's most beautiful scenery.

12:30pm Lunch at the **Admiral's Inn**, a Georgian-era structure long on atmosphere and history. The food is reliable—pan-fried red snapper and pumpkin soup are good—and the setting facing English Harbour is memorable.

1:30pm Begin your tour of **Nelson's Dockyard National Park** at the Dockyard Museum, next to Admiral's Inn. Set on English Harbour—a notable hurricane hole—the site was the Caribbean repair facility for the British Royal Navy in the 1700s. Nelson's Dockyard is the only surviving Georgian dockyard left in the world. Check out Fort Berkeley at the entrance to the harbor, reached by a short nature trail.

3:30pm Drive toward Shirley Heights—skip the Dow's Hill Historical Centre (a disconcertingly Disneyesque spin on slavery and tourism), but explore the military fortifications. Continue to Shirley Heights for a magnificent view of English and Falmouth harbors, as well as neighboring Guadeloupe and Montserrat. Hang out for the late-afternoon barbecue at **Shirley Heights Lookout**. A free steel-band party is held every Sunday to celebrate sunset, followed by reggae until 10 p.m.

7:00pm Head to Dickenson Bay where the first party of *Sailing Week* takes place. With the first race completed, at least 200 boats will be anchored offshore and the beach will be filled with thousands of partyers. Have dinner at **Warri Pier**, a restaurant set over the water that offers a great view of the yachts and beach scene. This is a popular and romantic spot, so make reservations or arrive early.

8:30pm The beach party should be in full swing. The hub of the action is **Rex Halcyon Cove** beach resort (to which Warri Pier is connected), but head down the beach and you'll find other spots percolating, such as **Spinnakers**, **Antigua Village Beach Club**, and **Coconut Grove**. The beach party keeps going until well after midnight.

Day 2. Mon.   May 1, 2000
(Day 2. Monday   April 30, 2001)

9:30am Breakfast at **Coconut Grove**, a romantic, thatched-roofed beachfront restaurant at the Siboney Beach Club.

10:30am Head to the remote east coast, a 45-minute drive from Dickenson Bay. When you arrive at Harmony Hall, ask a worker to take you in the dinghy to their "secret" snorkeling hideout, Green Island. Wear plenty of sunscreen.

Noon Harmony Hall isn't quite a trip to Europe, but the charming managers are Italians who winter on Antigua and serve their native Mediterranean cuisine under a 195-year-old sugar mill on a terrace that offers a 360-degree view. Check out the lobster cage at water's edge and select your crustacean for lunch (pastas and salads are also available). While lunch is being prepared, peruse Harmony Hall's crafts store and surprisingly good art gallery, where regional artists are showcased.

2:00pm For another beach, swing by Half Moon Bay, a sweeping arc of plush white sand and placid, gin-clear water. The ruins of a storm-damaged resort are found at one end. Otherwise this isolated beauty is often deserted.

3:00pm On your way back, stop by **Betty's Hope Estate** (near the village of Pares). Once the largest colonial sugar plantation on Antigua, the estate is being restored and the slave village, also on the site, is currently under excavation. The windmill at this historic landmark is operational and its majestic sails are often in place.

5:30pm Tonight's party takes place at Jolly Harbour. This is a quieter party scene than the first night, so enjoy the sunset and a rum punch and make it an early evening. You'll find the yachting set gathered around the Committee Desk, where official race results are posted.

7:00pm Dinner at **Julian's** in St. John's. This is perhaps Antigua's best restaurant, serving Caribbean-flavored continental cuisine in an 18th-century colonial house. Jerk-spiced chicken breast with jumbo shrimp and rack of lamb are highlights.

Day 3. Tue.   May 2, 2000
(Day 3. Tuesday   May 1, 2001)

9:00am Breakfast at **Hemingway's**, which sits on a West Indian-style veranda overlooking Heritage Quay. Cappuccino, eggs, and pancakes are available, or try a local favorite, saltfish.

10:00am Most of Antigua's shopping is concentrated around Heritage Quay. You can also tour the **Museum of Antigua and Barbuda** in a half-hour—it's a decent repository for the geological and (sanitized) political history of this twin-island nation, as well as its culture. The soaring **St. John's Cathedral** is one of the most imposing in the Caribbean.

12:30pm Just outside St. John's, at Fort James, is **Miller's by the Sea**, a lively outdoor restaurant that sits on a beach. When a cruise ship is in, the dance floor bustles with so many people that the groove spills out onto the sand. Try the curried conch.

4:30pm The third yacht race winds up at Falmouth Harbour (next to English Harbour), and a collection of restaurants, bars, and activities ensures extensive partying. The location of the official *Race End Party* has yet to be determined, but other party places include **Colombo's**, the site of last year's race-end bash; the **Antigua Yacht Club** (though it quiets down early); **Mad Mongoose**, where many of the Brits congregate; and, particularly, **Abracadabra**, a great Italian restaurant, where the party energy really gets hopping after 11:30 p.m. When you leave for the night, listen for the wind whistling through the moored yachts' sails and rigging.

Alternatives

If a big resort is more to your liking, stay at the well-run, midpriced **Rex Halcyon Cove** on Dickenson Bay. **The Inn at English Harbour** is favored by Brits and has a beach facing the harbor near Nelson's Dockyard—next to the action without being engulfed by it. If the island's nautical history holds appeal, stay at **Admiral's Inn**, which has 14 distinctive rooms with beamed ceilings and antiques.

A longer stay allows you to enjoy *Lay Day* on Wednesday. The *Lord Nelson Ball* on Saturday has a strictly enforced dress code (jacket and tie for men, cocktail dresses for ladies), so the event is a tad stuffy, but it's a last chance to cavort.

The Hot Sheet

☎ 268

$ 2.7 East Caribbean Dollar

Hotels	Day	Address	Ph	Price	Fx	Rms	Best Rooms
Admiral's Inn	A	at English Harbour	460-1027 800- 223-5695	$$	460-1534	14	In main bldg
Rex Halcyon Cove	A	on Dickenson Bay	462-0256 800- 255-5859	$$$	462-0271	210	Beachfront
Siboney Beach Club	1	on Dickenson Bay	462-0806 800- 533-0234	$$	462-3356	13	3rd fl
The Inn at English Harbour	A	at English Harbour	460-1014 800- 223-6510	$$$$	460-1603	28	Beachfront

Restaurants	Day	Address	Ph	Price	Rec	Dress	Food
Admiral's Inn	1	at English Harbour	460-1027	$$	L/BD	Kazh	West Indian
Coconut Grove	2	see Siboney Beach Club	462-1538	$	B/LD	Kazh	Continental, West Indian, seafood
Harmony Hall	2	near Freetown	460-4120	$$$	L	Kazh	Italian, seafood
Hemingway's	3	St. Mary's St. in St. John's	462-2763	$	B/LD	Local	West Indian
Julian's	2	Church St. and Corn Alley in St. John's	462-4766	$$$	D	Kazh	Continental
Miller's by the Sea	3	at Fort James	462-9414	$$	L/BD	Local	West Indian
Shirley Heights Lookout	1	at Shirley Heights	460-1785	$	T/LD	Local	Barbecue
Warri Pier	1	see Rex Halcyon Cove	462-0256	$$$	D/(L)	Kazh	West Indian, seafood

Nitelife	Day	Address	Ph	Price	Rec	Dress	Music
Abracadabra	3	at English Harbour	460-2701	None	OF	Kazh	Dance
Antigua Village Beach Club	1	on Dickenson Bay	462-2931	None	P	Kazh	Soca
Antigua Yacht Club	3	at Falmouth Harbour	460-1543	None	MP	Kazh	Soca
Carib Bar	1	see Rex Halcyon Cove hotel	462-0256	None	MP	Kazh	Steelband
Coconut Grove	1	see Siboney Beach Club	462-1538	None	O	Kazh	Dance
Colombo's	3	at English Harbour	460-1452	None	MOPF	Local	Reggae, dance
Mad Mongoose	3	at Falmouth Harbour	463-7900	None	O	Kazh	Dance
Spinnakers	1	on Dickenson Bay	462-4158	None	MPF	Kazh	Steelband

Sights & Attractions	Day	Address	Ph	Entry Fee
Betty's Hope Estate	2	near Pares Village	462-1469	$
Museum of Antigua and Barbuda	3	Long St. near Heritage Quay	462-4930	$
Nelson's Dockyard National Park	1	National Park at English Harbour	460-1379	$
St. John's Cathedral	3	between Long and Newgate sts.	462-4686	None
Antigua and Barbuda Tourist Office		Nevis St. near Friendly Alley in St. John's	462-0029	

Event & Ticket Info

Antigua Sailing Week (various locations on Antigua): Admission to parties is free. Races can be viewed at no charge. **Lay Day** (Antigua Yacht Club, Falmouth Harbour): Tickets at the door ($2). **Lord Nelson Ball** (Admiral's Inn, Nelson's Dockyard): Tickets can be purchased in advance ($40) or at the door ($50). For additional information, call the Antigua Sailing Week Office (268-462-8872).

RECommendations: (Restaurants) B–Breakfast; L–Lunch; D–Dinner; T–High tea or snack
(Nitelife) G–Gaming; H–Hangout bar; M–Live music; O–Dancing (disco); P–Dancing (live music); S–Show; F–Food served
( )–Available but without recommendation. For complete explanation of Hot Sheet format, see page 34.

NYC +1   75°/83° (23°/28°)   V.C. Bird (ANU); 30 min./$20   Yes   English

The Fun Also Rises

May 2000 · May 2001

Madrid, Spain

Fiestas de San Isidro

| Origin: 1622 | Event ★★★★★ City | Attendance: 25,000 |

Late-night, heart-rending flamenco singers. *Churros* frying early in the morning and chocolate, coffee, and beer being served in the afternoon. Women in flouncy dresses and men in checkered suits dancing with passion and precision. Music seeping from doorways and windows. It's all part of the annual *Fiesta de San Isidro*, when revelers jam the streets of Madrid intent on raising the party bar in the already heady atmosphere of Spain's premier city.

The *Fiesta de San Isidro* has become the most important bullfighting festival on earth, and Madrid's Plaza de Toros Monumental de Las Ventas is the world's most acclaimed bullring. But this festival, which has attracted the likes of Ernest Hemingway, Orson Welles, and Ava Gardner, has far more to offer than just *corridas* (bullfights).

On May 15, Madrileños celebrate *Fiesta* by turning out in traditional costumes that scream "Photo op!" to every visitor. Women wear flowing dresses and tie scarves around their hair. Men in tailored suits don Scottish caps and dance the *chotis* to celebrate San Isidro, the city's patron saint. Parks and plazas host a variety of concerts—from classical to rock to jazz—and dances, performances, art exhibitions are held around the city.

Turn-of-the-century Madrid continues to flourish with a post-Franco renaissance that imbues each of its 4 million or so residents with an unsurpassed zest for life. The Spanish capital is one of the world's great nightlife cities. Most Madrileños, or *gatos* (cats) as they call themselves, are not likely to dine before 10:30 p.m. Old Madrid is most active between Calle Huertas and the Plaza de Santa Ana, where dancing and live jazz and flamenco can be found. Open-air cafes dot the *paseo* toward the Museo del Prado, which displays paintings by Francisco de Goya, an ardent bullfight fan and painter of Spanish life. Even if you never see a matador, this is the best time to enjoy vibrant Madrid.

Fiestas de San Isidro

Day 1. Sat. May 13, 2000
(Day 3. Thursday   May 17, 2001)

8:30am Wake up at **Hotel Tryp Reina Victoria**, an art-
Ⓡ deco masterpiece. Have a traditional breakfast of
churros (fried fritters) with chocolate or a *tortilla
española* (potato omelet). Keep your eyes peeled
for matadors and members of the bullfighting community who frequent the hotel.

10:00am From Plaza de Santa Ana, follow Calle Carretas
to Puerta del Sol, where you can stand at Kilometer
0, the geographic center of Spain and, at one time, the
world. You'll also see the symbol of Madrid, a bear and
madrono (strawberry tree). Take Calle Preciados
to Gran Vía and Gran Vía to Plaza de España. Cross
the plaza diagonally to Parque del Oeste, where you
can ride the **Teleférico**—a cable car over the
Manzanares River—for lovely views of the city.

2:00pm Cab to **Viña P.** for lunch. The decor pays homage
Ⓡ to bullfighting. If the place is full, walk to **La Bodeguita
del Caco** for food from Spain's Canary Islands.

3:30pm When in Madrid, do as the locals do: siesta.

5:00pm Have a cold beer at **Cervecería Alemana**, the
"clean, well-lighted place" of Ernest Hemingway's
Madrid days. Then venture to any bar across the
street from the Plaza de Toros for a traditional *Sol
y Sombra* (Sun and Shade), a drink consisting of
half anisette and half cognac.

7:00pm The ***Gran Corrida de Toros*** is the raison
d'être bullfight of the fiesta. If bullfighting isn't
your glass of sangria but you want to see what it's
about, this is as good as it gets. You'll likely see a
top-rated matador and a very spirited crowd.

10:30pm Teatriz, a converted theater redesigned by
Ⓡ Phillipe Starke, is a great place to dine as well as
warm up for a night on the town.

1:00am Hit the clubs. Start at **Joy Eslava** or **El
Palacio Gaviria**. Both are always active. Located in
a 19th-century baroque palace, Gaviria has several
bars. Another popular disco is **Pachá**.

Day 2. Sun. May 14, 2000
(Day 2. Wednesday   May 16, 2001)

9:00am Breakfast at **Café Gijón**, a famous literary
Ⓡ hangout and a good spot for morning *cortado*
(espresso "cut" with milk).

10:00am Walk to the **Museo del Prado** for a look at the
works of Francisco de Goya. See the father of modern art's *Majas*, as well as tapestry cartoons and
tumultuous dark paintings.

Noon Stroll through Parque Retiro, looking at the
Palacio de Cristal and the Cason del Buen Retiro.
There should be a ***noon concert*** at the band shell.
Or rent a rowboat for a romantic interlude.

2:00pm Lunch at **Lhardy**, an Old Madrid institution
Ⓡ since 1839. Reserve a table for the more expensive
sit-down restaurant or eat deli style.

4:00pm Visit the **Museo Thyssen-Bornemisza** for an
easy chronological tour of predominately European
art throughout the ages. Look for the stunning portrait of "Tita" Cervera, a former Miss Spain and wife
of the magnate who founded the museum.

5:30pm The **Real Jardín Botánico**, south of the Prado,
is most pleasant at this time of day. Squeeze in a
late siesta.

8:30pm Take advantage of the perfect evening with an
outdoor concert. Although the ***Fiesta*** schedule
varies from year to year, you should have no difficulty finding a musical venue to suit you.

10:00pm Partake of Madrid's famous *tapas*. With a glass of Manzanilla dry or *fino* sherry, head to Pasaje Matheu for the *patatas bravas* at **Las Bravas**, the originators of this famous *tapa*. Keep moving, as Madrileños do, to **La Taberna Dolores**, for salmon slices on top of soft Burgos cheese. Finally, hit **Los Gabrieles**, a former Gypsy brothel with beautiful tile-covered walls.

Midnight Catch a jazz combo at **Café Central**, next to the Reina Victoria, or at **Café Jazz Populart**.

Day 3. Mon.   May 15, 2000
(Day 1. Tuesday   May 15, 2001)

9:00am Choose any cafe on Plaza Mayor, where early-morning sunbeams warm the outside tables.

11:00am Watch the ***procession*** of Madrileños carrying an effigy of San Isidro through Parque de San Isidro. Enjoy the colorful traditional dress and exuberant crowd.

2:00pm Lunch at **El Café de Oriente**, which serves French-Basque food across from the Royal Palace. For paella, make reservations and cab to **La Champagnería Gala**.

4:00pm Visit the **Centro de Arte Reina Sofía**. There you can see the cubist collection, Salvador Dali's works, and Pablo Picasso's famous painting of Guernica, a Basque town bombed during the Spanish Civil War.

5:30pm Hang out in Plaza Mayor. Have your portrait done by a local artist, then walk to the 18th-century **Royal Palace** on Calle Bailén. Check out the Throne Room and spectacular gardens.

8:30pm Walk to **Museo Chicote** bar, the setting for "The Denunciation" and "The Butterfly and the Tank," Hemingway's stories about Madrid during the Spanish Civil War. Or have a martini, as Jake and Brett did in *The Sun Also Rises*, at **Bar Americano** in the Palace Hotel across from Spain's Parliament building.

9:30pm Continue on the Hemingway characters' trail by dining at **Botín's**, where Brett and Jake had "roast young suckling pig and drank rioja alta." You can do the same, though you may prefer dining in the bodega, the brick-lined cellar. Reservations are essential.

11:00pm Walk to **Las Cuevas de Luis Candelas**—one of a group of caves used by the Spanish Robin Hood—for sangria or wine. Or see what's happening at Plaza Mayor.

12:30am Everything you want in a flamenco show—heat, passion, dance, beautiful songs—can be found at **Corral de la Morería**, a flamenco *tablao* that has been open since 1956.

3:00am Continue a Madrileño tradition by finishing off your night—and your fiesta—with chocolate and *churros* at **Chocolatería San Ginés**.

Alternatives

The **Hotel Ritz** was built in 1910 when King Alfonso XII realized no hotel in Madrid was classy enough to host his wedding. Another classic downtown is the **Palace Hotel**—it often hosts politicians in its public rooms. The **Hotel Wellington** has a beautiful garden—ask for a room overlooking it—and a pool (rare in Madrid).

For *tapas* near the bullring, try the deep-fried baby squid (*chopitos*) at **El Rincón de Jerez**. **Cañas y Barro** is an excellent choice for paella. **La Gamella**, fronted by a North American expat, serves new Spanish cuisine. You can't beat the steaks and Old World ambience at **Casa Paco**. Also highly recommended is dinner at **Zalacaín**, a romantic restaurant that offers ever-changing tasting menus. **Casa Patas** near Plaza de Santa Ana is another flamenco *tablao* for dinner and a show.

The Hot Sheet

☎ 34/91

$ 150 Peseta

HOTELS	DAY	ADDRESS	PH	PRICE	FX	RMS	BEST ROOMS
Hotel Ritz	A	5 Pl. de la Lealtad	521-2857 800- 223-6800	$$$$+	532-8776	158	Prado vw
Hotel Tryp Reina Victoria	1	14 Pl. de Santa Ana	531-4500 800- 448-8355	$$	522-0307	201	Interior rm
Hotel Wellington	A	8 c/ Velázquez	575-4400 800- 448-8355	$$$	576-4164	287	Gdn vw
Palace Hotel	A	7 Pl. de las Cortes	360-8000 800- 325-3589	$$$$	360-8100	440	Grand dlx

RESTAURANTS	DAY	ADDRESS	PH	PRICE	REC	DRESS	FOOD
Botín's	3	17 c/ Cuchilleros	366-4217	$$$	D/L	Euro	Spanish
Café Gijón	2	21 Paseo de Recoletos	521-5425	$	B/LDT	Euro	Cafe, bar
Cañas y Barro	A	23 c/ Amaniel	542-4798	$$	LD	Euro	Paella
Casa Paco	A	11 Puerta Cerrada	366-3166	$$$	LD	Euro	Steaks
Chocolatería San Ginés	3	Pasadizo de San Ginés off c/ Arenal	366-5875	$	T	Euro	*Churros* and chocolate
El Café de Oriente	3	2 Pl. de Oriente	541-3974	$$$	L/D	Euro	French-Basque
El Rincón de Jerez	A	5 c/ Rufino Blanco near Manuel Becerra	355-4745	$	T/LD	Euro	*Tapas*
La Bodeguita del Caco	1	27 c/ Echegaray	429-4023	$$$	L/D	Euro	Spanish island
La Champagnería Gala	3	22 c/ Moratín	429-2562	$$	L/D	Euro	Paella
La Gamella	A	4 Alfonso XII	532-4509	$$$	LD	Euro	Nuvo Spanish, seafood
La Taberna Dolores	2	4 Pl. de Jesús	429-2243	$	T/LD	Euro	*Tapas*
Las Bravas	2	5 Pasaje Matheu	521-5141	$	T/LD	Euro	*Tapas*
Lhardy	2	8 Carrera de San Jerónimo	521-3385	$$$$+	L/DT	Euro	French, Spanish
Los Gabrieles	2	17 c/ Echegaray	429-6261	$	T/LD	Euro	*Tapas*
Teatriz	1	15 c/ Hermosilla	577-5379	$$$	D/L	Euro	Italian, international
Viña P.	1	3 Pl. de Santa Ana	531-8111	$$	L/D	Euro	Spanish
Zalacaín	A	4 Alvarez de Baena	561-4840	$$$$+	LD	Euro	Basque

NITELIFE	DAY	ADDRESS	PH	PRICE	REC	DRESS	MUSIC
Bar Americano	3	see Palace Hotel	360-8000	None	H(F)	Euro	
Café Central	2	10 Pl. del Angel	369-4143	$	M	Euro	Jazz
Café Jazz Populart	2	22 c/ Huertas	429-8407	None	M	Euro	Jazz, blues, soul, folk
Casa Patas	A	10 c/ Cañizares	369-0496	$$$$	SF	Euro	Flamenco
Cervecería Alemana	1	6 Pl. de Santa Ana	429-7033	None	H(F)	Euro	
Corral de la Morería	3	17 c/ Morería	365-8446	$$$	S(F)	Euro	Flamenco
El Palacio Gaviria	1	9 c/ Arenal	526-6069	$$	O	Euro	Disco, Latin, lounge
Joy Eslava	1	11 c/ Arenal	366-3733	$$	O	Euro	Disco, techno
Las Cuevas de Luis Candelas	3	1 c/ Cuchilleros	366-5428	None	H(F)	Kazh	
Museo Chicote	3	12 Gran Vía	532-6737	None	H	Euro	
Pachá	1	11 c/ Barceló	446-0137	$$	O	Euro	Disco, techno

SIGHTS & ATTRACTIONS	DAY	ADDRESS	PH	ENTRY FEE
Centro de Arte Reina Sofía	3	52 c/ Santa Isabel	467-5062	$
Museo del Prado	2	Paseo del Prado	330-2800	$
Museo Thyssen-Bornemisza	2	8 Paseo del Prado	420-3944	$
Real Jardín Botánico	2	1 c/ Claudio Myno	420-3017	$
Royal Palace	3	c/ de Bailén	559-7404	$

OTHER SIGHTS, SERVICES & ATTRACTIONS

Teleférico	1	Paseo del Pinto Rosalles	541-7450	$
Tourist Office of Madrid		2 Duque de Medinaceli	429-4951	

EVENT & TICKET INFO

Fiesta de San Isidro (various locations around Madrid): Events are free, except for the **Gran Corrida de Toros** (Plaza Monumental de Toros de Las Ventas, 237 c/ de Alcalá). Tickets ($7 for a poorly placed seat in the sun to $75 for a good seat in the shade) are available at windows at Las Ventas 10 a.m.-2 p.m. and 5-8 p.m. Or buy tickets in advance at licensed vending booths around the city.

RECommendations: (Restaurants) B–Breakfast; L–Lunch; D–Dinner; T–High tea or snack (Nitelife) G–Gaming; H–Hangout bar; M–Live music; O–Dancing (disco); P–Dancing (live music); S–Show; F–Food served ()–Available but without recommendation. For complete explanation of Hot Sheet format, see page 34.

🕐 NYC +6   ☽ 51°/70° (10°/21°)   ✈ Rarajas (Madrid) (MAD); 30 min./$20   🚗 No   👥 Spanish

The Fun Also Rises

A Lot of Bull

Celebrated in literature, decorated with custom, and condemned by large segments of modern society, bullfighting is more than mere sport: it's equal parts historic spectacle and riveting passion play. By definition, it's undeniably bloody—the purpose, after all, is to kill the animal—and many see it as cruelty to animals (even in Spain, the subject creates controversy). For its defenders, however, bullfighting is an integral part of Spanish culture.

Bullfights and, as importantly, their surrounding pageantry lie at the heart of four events in this book—the **Running of the Bulls** in Pamplona, Spain; **Féria de Nîmes** in Nîmes, France; **Fiesta de San Isidro** in Madrid; and **Feria de San Marcos** in Aguascalientes, Mexico. Each of these events can be enjoyed without endorsing the sport, but to understand what attracted writers such as Ernest Hemingway, James Michener, and Orson Wells to this gory pastime, here's a quick introduction.

For many foreigners, a Spanish fighting bull comes off as a one-ton truck with horns. Somebody's jammed the throttle on full and thrown out the steering wheel. This description might give a pretty good idea of the danger involved in getting into the ring with a mad bull, but for veteran fans the bull is far more significant. Spanish aficionados see fighting bulls as pure animals, moving and living by instinct. Humans, matadors in particular, are viewed as being above animals, possessing art, judgment, and soul.

In a typical *corrida* (bullfight), each matador kills two of six bulls in a rotation. Each contest consists of three stages called *tercios*. In the first *tercio*, the bull is watched to see how aggressively it tries to clear interlopers from its view. Horses, the bull's natural enemies, are brought in. A picador, sitting on a horse that's been padded for protection, holds a long lance, which he uses to poke a gland near the bull's neck that swells as the animal becomes enraged. Slightly piercing the gland prevents the bull from holding its head high enough to gore the matador's head. While the picador's prodding can be bloody, it's intended to simulate damage done by the horns of another bull during battle.

Next, banderilleros stand on tiptoe and run at the bull, thrusting *banderillas* just beneath its hide. These barbed dowels are intended to correct any favoring the animal may have for one side or the other while charging.

In the final *tercio*, matador and bull stand alone in the ring, giving the matador the opportunity to demonstrate his artistry against the animal's power. Using a red cape, the matador attempts to draw the bull in front of him in a series of passes. As the dance progresses, the horns come ever closer to the matador, whose feet barely move. The matador ultimately exposes his back to the horns, making the last pass in the series the most dangerous. A successful series of passes often merits an "Ole!" from the crowd.

Finally, the matador proves his bravery by plunging a sword to its hilt into a small area of the bull's neck, severing the animal's aorta. To accomplish this, the matador must risk death by reaching over the bull's horns. If a matador behaves extremely well and kills the bull swiftly, the crowd waves white handkerchiefs, demanding he be awarded the bull's ear as a trophy. A team of horses then drags the expired bull out of the ring while the crowd stands and applauds the animal's bravery. Gruesome, yes, but unlike the bull you can decide for yourself whether or not to be a part of the action.

May 2000

May 2001

Cannes, France

Cannes Film Festival

(Festival International du Film)

Origin: 1939 Event ★ ★ ★ ★ ★ ★ ★ ★ ★ City **Attendance: 31,000**

Lights! Cameras! Action! As the world's undisputed monarch of film festivals, the *Cannes Film Festival* is proof that wherever celebrities, champagne, and high-stakes deals come together, there's sure to be one helluva party. During the festival's 13-day run, small and sunny Cannes on the French Riviera is recast as a circus of exhibitionism, publicity antics, and parties with guest lists that read like movie credits.

The "grabber" in Cannes is the extravagant atmosphere, but the festival is also strategic. Parties are designed for publicity stunts, pick-up maneuvers, and, most importantly, business deals. Stars and films associated with the festival earn instant cachet. Kazillionaires and their bombshell companions may be hanging to solidify financial deals—or they may just want to bond with Bobby De Niro.

Although mostly insiders and industry people gain entry to *Cannes*' key events, a well-groomed tourist has a good chance of meeting someone who knows someone who knows someone who can find an extra ticket. If schmoozing doesn't get you past the gates of privilege, don't worry—Cannes' top bars throw festival-long parties and welcome the public along with the stars and the glitz. Films show from morning until late at night. Sixty movies, elected from a pool of about 800, compete for the *Palme d'Or* (Golden Palm) award in the bunkerlike Palais des Festivals. The public can attend selected screenings here and at many theaters around town.

During the day, celebs and other platinum-card junkies cruise in and out of the exclusive boutiques and along the main promenade, La Croisette. Temporary billboards and party tents compete for attention with palm trees and white-sand beaches adorned with bare-breasted and buffed bodies. Normally a resort town for those who can afford to drop five figures on a typical shopping trip, *Cannes* has everything a big-time star or stargazer would want, including the world's attention.

The Fun Also Rises

Cannes Film Festival

Day 1. Thu. May 18, 2000
(Day 1. Thursday   May 10, 2001)

8:30am Awake at the luxurious **Hôtel Martinez**. On the main promenade, it's an art-deco hotel with a private beach. Breakfast in one of the cafes or bars surrounding the Forville Marché, a covered market overflowing with dozens of varieties of fish, cheese, paté, olives, and flowers. Walk up the hill to Le Suquet. The oldest part of town, it houses the 12th-century Ste-Anne Chapel and landmark watchtower.

10:00am Proceed to the Palais des Festivals, affectionately called the "bunker" by locals. If your application for an accreditation pass was accepted (see Les Films sidebar), pick up your badge. If not, move on to the **Cannes Forum** for day passes.

1:00pm Lunch on the beach is a **Cannes** tradition. A crowd forming in a particular spot along the boardwalk is a good indication that a celebrity is probably in the midst of a beachside photo op. The **Majestic Beach Restaurant** is a hotspot for festival celebs. You can relax in the water at **L'Ondine**, which is also known for its good food and many celebrity-spotting opportunities.

2:00pm After lunch, take in some movies or stroll down La Croisette, stopping for beach time and a swim. You might also head to Rue d'Antibes, a great shopping street that's packed with scenesters and starlets.

5:00pm It's cocktail time at the **Majestic Terrace Bar** in the Majestic Hôtel across from the Palais. This remains Cannes' number-one stargazing spot and the ultimate see-and-be-seen place at any hour. Don't be intimidated by the security guards. If you don't have a badge, simply say you're meeting with so-and-so at one of the studios that have an office in the hotel. Drinks are very expensive, but remember, this is France, so you can nurse that drink for hours.

7:00pm The major event each evening of **Cannes** is the red-carpet walk into the **Grand Théâtre Lumière**. The big procession starts at 8 p.m., so arrive early and get a prime spot for viewing the stars of the film currently screening. Wave back when they wave to mobs of photographers and onlookers.

9:00pm Dine at highly rated **La Poêle d'Or**. Sample the lobster, braised duck, or soufflés. Make reservations several days in advance to ensure seating. The set menu is the best value at any restaurant.

11:30pm Move on to the **Brasserie Majestic** or **Petit Carlton**. These late-night cafes are destination drinking spots for the wired and the thirsty from every division of the industry. **Le Zanzibar** is the oldest gay bar on the Côte d'Azur—the sidewalk terrace features a mixed clientele of colorful locals and visiting swells.

1:00am The **Cat Corner** is a '70s-revival club, complete with disco music and groovy decor. It's open until dawn.

Day 2. Fri. May 19, 2000
(Day 2. Friday   May 11, 2001)

9:00am Grab an omelet and *une orange pressée* at **Le Claridge** located near the Palais.

10:00am Movies! Movies! Movies!

1:00pm For more stars and lunch, it's a 15-minute drive to Hôtel du Cap Eden Roc. The epitome of elegance—with an exquisite park, pool, and exclusive **Eden Roc** restaurant—this is where the world's elite have met since the hotel's opening in 1870. If you only splurge once, this is the place. Credit cards are not accepted, so bring cash. Ask for a table on the terrace and you'll catch hunks and topless beauties lounging around the pool.

3:00pm After lunch, drive around the Cap d'Antibes and take in the beautiful *belle-époque* villas. Or head for the port in Antibes and check out the super yachts.

5:00pm It's tea time, so head for the **Carlton Terrace Bar** in the Carlton hotel. This is another excellent place to see celebrities.

8:00pm The Eden Roc is a hard act to follow, but **L'Auberge Provençal** is a reasonably priced restaurant with excellent Provençal cuisine. House specialties include *bourride*, bouillabaisse, and aioli.

12:30am As the favorite dive of TV crews filming the festival, **Le Jane's** has become an in place. It's located on the ground floor of the Gray d'Albion Hôtel. Another happening spot, **L'Opéra** disco, attracts top talent until dawn.

Day 3. Sat. May 20, 2000
(Day 3. Saturday   May 12, 2001)

9:00am A block from the Palais, **La Tarterie** carries close to 20 kinds of delicious quiche and tarts. It's also good for a quick bite between films.

10:00am Movie buffs are already at their first screening and have picked at least three other films to see.

Noon On the corner of La Croisette and Andre Commandant, **Le Blue Bar**'s wrap-around windows and terrace make it one of the best spots for people-watching. For drinks, this venerable landmark is less expensive than major hotel terraces.

1:30pm Explore one of the small towns that dot the Riviera—Biot is famous for its glassblowing, Grasse for perfume, and Vallauris for pottery.

5:00pm Drinks at **L'Amiral** in the Hôtel Martinez are a must. Don't be surprised if you find yourself crowded around the piano singing Edith Piaf tunes with movie notables and some not-so-notables.

7:30pm It's a short drive to the medieval village of Mougins. Wander the fascinating streets until you're ready to dine at **La Ferme de Mougins**, a country residence and the perfect hideaway for a romantic dinner on the terrace. For a more formal evening, eat in the elegant dining room.

11:30pm Head back into Cannes for a night out on La Croisette. **Jimmy'z**, an upscale nightclub, has outdoor seating with good views of the bay, the old fort, and, if you're lucky, just a few more stars to round out your weekend.

Alternatives

Getting into any hotel in Cannes during the festival is extremely difficult, so make plans well ahead. Along with Hôtel Martinez, the **Carlton Inter-Continental** hotel is a grande dame of La Croisette. It has a private beach, sea views, and beautiful rooms. Once a haunt of Picasso, **Les Muscadins** in Mougins is at the entrance of the old town. The restaurant specializes in light Italian cuisine. **Auberge de la Vignette Haute** in Auribeau-sur-Siagne is located in a theatrical farmhouse setting only seven miles (11 kilometers) from Cannes. Medieval beams, old stones, and candlelight set the mood in its superb restaurant. **Le Relais Cantemerle** hotel is an art-deco masterpiece with furniture and fixtures from a defunct 1920s hotel.

Moulin de Mougins restaurant is set in a restored 16th-century mill and frequented by movie stars. The food and hospitality are excellent.

If you're still in town on the final Sunday of the festival, **Le Saloon**'s American owner hosts one of the best parties. Starting around midnight, the bash features a dozen Hawaiian Tropic girls and many celebrities.

To complete your picture of the French Riviera, refer to the Hot Sheets for Monte Carlo (see page 146) and Nice (see page 178).

The Fun Also Rises

Les Films

Though frequented by nonindustry people, at the *Cannes Film Festival* most screenings are closed to the general public. You must apply for accreditation by January, pleading your case as a *cinéaste*. You'll receive a form that you must fill out. If accepted, you can pick up your free accreditation badge at the Palais des Festivals. Most of the 4,000 badges available to the public go to film-school students or members of cinema societies. To apply for accreditation, send a letter to: International Film Festival du Cannes, 99 bd. Malesherbes, Paris, France 75008.

Main Competition Major films compete for the *Palme d'Or* or Golden Palm Award. Your accreditation badge allows you to request an invitation—do so downstairs in the Palais des Festivals early in the morning. If you get one of the rare "returned" invitations, you'll need a tuxedo or evening gown to see the red-carpet evening screenings in the Grand Théâtre Lumière.

Un Certain Regard To absorb fringe events, this official section surveys current world cinema. Screenings are held in the Théâtre Debussy and a badge and invitation (as above) are required for entry. Lines begin 30-60 minutes before scheduled screenings.

Critics' Week A panel of international critics selects shorts, features, and documentaries, with an emphasis on first- and second-time directors. These films première in the local Cannes multiplex Les Arcades, as well as the Espace Miramar, with additional screenings at Espace Merimee, Studio 13.

The Directors' Fortnight Feature films are selected independently of all other categories. The Directors' Fortnight office is on La Croisette next to the Noga Hilton and screenings take place in the cinema located in the hotel. Line up alongside the hotel on Rue Amouretti. Arrive at least 30 minutes early for screenings. The public may also purchase tickets to these screenings on a space-available basis for $15 at the Directors' Fortnight office.

The Forum Cannes Festival gives screening access to the general public in conjunction with Cyber Cafe Cinema and Forum Seminars, two cinema societies. To find out what's screening where, pick up one of the major daily trade papers.

Les Parties

Parties are one of the main reasons everyone comes to *Cannes* and just about everywhere—in town, on the beach, in the hills—there's some kind of party going on at any given time during the festival. Studios, magazines, distributors, and P.R. firms throw the big parties. The daily trade papers are the best source of where-when-who information.

Here are two parties you can buy your way into:

The Moving Pictures International Party

Usually held the final Friday of the festival, this legendary bacchanal takes place in a 12th-century castle, three miles down the coast from Cannes in La Napoule. A $40 donation is required (proceeds go to several charities, including children with AIDS). For tickets, inquire at the *Moving Pictures International* office in the Noga Hilton.

The Amfar Benefit

Held at Moulins des Mougins, this blowout attracts the biggest number of movie moguls and celebrities. It also costs $2,500 to get in, but once inside you can rub shoulders with hosts Elizabeth Taylor, Sharon Stone, and Demi Moore. Call *Amfar* in New York for more information (212-806-1600).

The *Cannes* itinerary ensures you'll have a great time whether you manage to crash the parties or not—but getting invitations at *Cannes* is not as tough as it might seem and chances are you'll have plenty of opportunities to show off your best party clothes!

The Hot Sheet

☎ 33/49

$ 6.1 Franc

HOTELS	DAY	ADDRESS	PH	PRICE	FX	RMS	BEST ROOMS
Auberge de la Vignette Haute	A	370 rte. du Village	342-2001 800- 525-4800	$$$	342-3116	15	Valley vw
Carlton Inter-Continental	A	58 La Croisette	306-4006 800- 327-0200	$$$$	306-4025	338	Sea or hill vw
Hôtel Martinez	1	73 La Croisette	298-7300 800- 888-4747	$$$$+	339-6782	393	Exec sea vw
Le Relais Cantemerle	A	258 chemin Cantemerle	358-0818	$$	358-3289	20	Gdn vw
Les Muscadins	A	18 bd. Courteline, Mougins	228-2828	$$	292-8823	8	Sea vw

RESTAURANTS	DAY	ADDRESS	PH	PRICE	REC	DRESS	FOOD
Carlton Terrace Bar	2	see Carlton Inter-Continental hotel	306-4006	$	T	Local	Tea
Eden Roc	2	bd. Kennedy in Hôtel du Cap Eden Roc	361-3901	$$$$+	L/D	Euro	International
L'Auberge Provençal	2	10 rue St-Antoine	299-2717	$$	D/L	Local	Provençal
L'Ondine	1	14 La Croisette	394-2315	$$	L/D	Local	Seafood
La Ferme de Mougins	3	10 av. Ste-Basile, Mougins	390-0374	$$$$	D/L	Kazh	Provençal
La Poêle d'Or	1	23 rue des États-Unis	339-7765	$$$	D/L	Local	Seafood
La Tarterie	3	33 rue Bivouac Napoléon	339-6743	$	B/L	Local	Bakery
Le Blue Bar	3	42 La Croisette	339-0104	$$	L/DT	Kazh	Brasserie
Le Claridge	2	pl. General-de-Gaulle	339-0586	$	B/LD	Local	Snacks, omelets
Majestic Beach Restaurant	1	14 La Croisette on Majestic Hôtel beach	298-7700	$$$$	L	Local	Brasserie
Moulin de Mougins	A	av. Notre-Dame de Vie, Mougins	375-7824	$$$$+	LD	Euro	Provençal

NITELIFE	DAY	ADDRESS	PH	PRICE	REC	DRESS	MUSIC
Brasserie Majestic	1	6 rue Tony-Allard	338-5176	None	H(F)	Local	
Cat Corner	1	22 rue Macé	339-3131	$$	O	Local	Disco
Jimmy'z	3	La Croisette in Casino Croisette	338-1211	$$	O	Euro	Dance
L'Amiral	3	see Hôtel Martinez	298-7300	None	H	Euro	
L'Opéra	2	7 rue Lecerf	399-0901	$$	O	Local	Disco
Le Jane's	2	38 rue des Serbes	299-7959	$$	O	Local	Disco
Le Saloon	A	13 rue Dr-Gerard-Monod	339-4039	None	H	Local	
Le Zanzibar	1	85 rue Félix-Faure	339-3075	None	H	Local	
Majestic Terrace Bar	1	14 La Croisette in Majestic Hôtel	298-7700	None	H(F)	Local	
Petit Carlton	1	93 rue d'Antibes	339-2725	None	H(F)	Local	

| Tourisme Infos Cannes | | in Palais des Festivals | 339-2453 | | | | |

EVENT & TICKET INFO

See preceding page.

RECommendations: (Restaurants) B–Breakfast; L–Lunch; D–Dinner; T–High tea or snack
(Nitelife) G–Gaming; H–Hangout bar; M–Live music; O–Dancing (disco); P–Dancing (live music); S–Show; F–Food served
()–Available but without recommendation. For complete explanation of Hot Sheet format, see page 34.

NYC +6   52°/71°(11°/22°)   Nice/Côte d'Azur (NCE); 45 min./$90   Yes/No   French

Reel Good Times

Rock or roll 'em. It's getting difficult to tell which is more important at today's film festivals: the films or the associated parties. Happily, both are more or less available to the public.

The proliferation of film festivals has made these once industry-only events a public celebration of the art form. It's easy to buy tickets to the screenings, but with a little chutzpah, determined fans can also get into private industry parties. Mingling with Jennifer Lopez or Nick Cage isn't guaranteed, but some movieland fetes such as the **Montréal World Film Festival** are eminently crashable.

Just about every city in the world worth an $8 admission hosts a film festival these days (there are more than 600 worldwide). The three-week-long **Seattle International Film Festival** is one of the world's longest movie showcases and probably the biggest in the United States. It includes a Secret Festival that requires attendees to sign oaths not to discuss the films they see—works in progress and those hung up by legal problems or other situations that preclude distribution. The tone at the **Locarno International Film Festival** is distinguished, proper, and intellectual. Austria's **Viennale** has multilingual moderators at its question-and-answer sessions so that non-German speakers can participate in discussions with actors and directors. The **Edinburgh International Film Festival**, which savors its reputation as champion of the outrageous, makes sure its patrons have enough to do—it unspools at the same time as the city's huge arts festival (see page 207).

Real imitation-butter flavoring wasn't around in time for the world's first film festival—a New Year's Day celebration of early films held in Monaco in 1898. In 1907, the Lumière brothers awarded the first known film-festival prize in Rome. But the real ancestor of the modern film festival, the **Venice Film Festival**, was inaugurated in 1932 in order to extend the tourist season in the city's stylish Lido seaside resort.

The French eventually launched a competing festival in Cannes scheduled to start on September 1, 1939. But only one film was shown before the event was shut down by Nazi Germany's invasion of Poland. The Cannes festival didn't resume until 1946. Today, the **Cannes International Film Festival** (see page 136) is built on high-stakes deal making and glamour and boasts the most prestigious film awards in the world.

Politics has played a part in several other now-legendary film festivals. **The Moscow International Film Festival** began as a showcase for Communist cinema. The **Berlin International Film Festival** (**Berlinale**) started amid bombed-out buildings in 1951. Springing from the hope that it could become a bridge between divided worlds, the festival introduced visionary directors (particularly Eastern European) to the rest of the world. Berlin is now regarded as the first litmus test for the new year's crop of films.

It's hard to believe, but the first North American film festival came years after the concept was well established in Europe. In 1956, the **San Francisco International Film Festival** decided to run with the idea that had done so well across the Atlantic. Why the late start? Mostly it was due to Hollywood's stifling studio system, as well as animosity between Tinseltown executives and the perceived snootiness of European film festivals. The San Francisco Bay Area's reputation as the Hollywood of the North also helped give cachet to the **Mill Valley Film Festival**.

Many filmmakers view the January-to-December festival season as a yearlong procession of marketing opportunities. A well-placed unspooling can attract the interest of critics and global distributors, and bring an unknown film international acclaim. The **Rotterdam International Film Festival** features major international independent films. Not surprisingly, competition at festivals is fierce. Of the 750 new features submitted to the **Sundance Film Festival** (see *The Fun Also Rises Travel Guide North America*, page 43) in 1998, only 32 were chosen for competition (although Sundance and most other festivals feature noncompetitive categories as well). Devoted to work by first- and second-time filmmakers, it's considered the showcase for the best American independent films in dramatic and documentary categories. The summer's **Toronto International Film Festival** is also regarded as one of the festivals that most influence the fate of new films, though in 1997 James Cameron took advantage of the **Tokyo International Film Festival**'s November dates to unveil *Titanic*. **The London Film Festival** winds up with one of the last showings of the year, gathering up the best from all the festivals that have gone before.

Geography often determines the ambience of a film festival. With its January dates, Sweden's **Göteborg Film Festival** may be one of the most frigid, yet it manages to draw 100,000 cinephiles and many top filmmakers from all over the world. Movie fans walk the same streets as Beethoven, Goethe, and Thomas Mann at Czechoslovakia's **Karlovy Vary International Film Festival**, nestled in a centuries-old mountain city near the German border. A former mining town high in the Colorado Rockies hosts the elite and exclusive **Telluride Film Festival**. Since most of the town is built around a single street, celebrities, directors, and the public intermingle. Screenings at the **Jerusalem Film Festival** take place in an outdoor amphitheater on warm summer nights.

Jewish, African, African-American, Native American, Asian, Latino—there's a film festival that represents cinema from just about every ethnic group and nationality. Film festivals exist for women, gays, lesbians, and fans of nearly every genre, including animation, mystery, crime, thriller, documentary, mockumentary, fantasy, and horror. (Are you ready for the **Illinois Insect Fear Film Festival**?) Festivals honor mountains, adventure, wildlife, and anthropology. Italy's **Pordenone-Le Giornate del Cinema Muto** and the **Vancouver International Film Festival** present silent films—Vancouver's event includes a live orchestra.

The **International Festival of Free Flight** features films about hang gliding, skydiving, ballooning, kite-flying, and bungee jumping. And San Francisco's **Short Attention Span Film and Video Festival** screens only films that last two minutes or less—which, of course, leaves more time to hit the parties.

THE WORLD'S TOP TEN FILM FESTS

Name	City	State/Province	Country	Month	# of days	Telephone	# of films shown	attendance (000)
Berlin International (Berlinale)	Berlin		Germany	Feb.	12	49/3-025-9200	250	250
Cannes International Film Festival	Cannes		France	May	12	33/14-561-6600	110	25
Locarno International Film Festival	Locarno		Switzerland	Aug.	11	41/91-756-2121	250	170
Mill Valley Film Festival	Mill Valley	California	USA	Oct.	10	415-383-5256	100	40
Montréal World Film Festival	Montréal	Québec	Canada	Aug.	10	514-848-3883	400	375
Moscow International Film Festival	Moscow		Russia	Jul.	11	7/095-917-2486	310	300
Rotterdam International Film Festival	Rotterdam		Netherlands	Jan.	12	31/10-890-9090	450	300
Sundance Film Festival	Park City	Utah	USA	Jan.	10	801-328-3456	165	18
Tokyo International Film Festival	Tokyo		Japan	Oct.	8	81/33-563-6305	200	152
Toronto International Film Festival	Toronto	Ontario	Canada	Sep.	10	416-968-3456	300	250

June 2000 — May 2001 — Monte Carlo, Monaco

Monaco Grand Prix

(Grand Prix Automobile de Monaco)

| Origin: 1942 | Event ★ ★ ★ ★ ★ ★ ★ City | Attendance: 75,000 |

The dangerous curves along Monaco's cramped downtown race course may be the drivers' biggest worry at the *Monaco Grand Prix*, but it's the thrilling curves and turns in the principality's raging nightclubs that occupy most visitors' minds. Movie stars, jet-setters, and European royalty descend on the world's second-smallest sovereign state over the Ascension Day weekend each year, transforming its *Grand Prix* from an intriguing race into a legendary party.

Whether you arrive by helicopter, boat, train, or bus—with all the main streets closed off for the race, don't even think about bringing a car—race fever is unavoidable from the moment you step into magical Monaco. Rue Grimaldi, one of the town's main drags, becomes a giant street party. Vendors hawk race memorabilia. Restaurants overflow. And along Quai Antoine 1er, hospitality suites hosted by race teams throb with excitement as hard-core racing enthusiasts and casual spectators gear up for the races and parties.

All weekend, in a series of races, Formula 1 cars roar through Monaco's winding streets, on the world's most breathtaking course. Cars begin (and end) the race on Boulevard Albert 1er near the port, careening for 78 laps through a 2.5-mile circuit past hotels, restaurants, and casinos, and speeding on straightaways, through tunnels, and around the famed Grand Chicane turns. It's skill not speed that wins this race.

Most fans see the event unfold on a giant screen erected in the harbor. More-privileged spectators watch from private apartment balconies, hotel rooms, and track-side restaurants. A fortunate few party on fabulous yachts in the harbor while champagne flows and cars hurl past in a deafening roar. But no matter where you catch the action, you're guaranteed an unforgettable party atmosphere.

Monte Carlo lies in the heart of Monaco, a three-mile-long by half-a-mile-wide strip of the Riviera, with 30,000 residents. There's beautiful architecture and lots of great restaurants, but it's the glitz and glamour of the *Monaco Grand Prix* that make this a world-class event.

Casino

Monaco Grand Prix

Day 1. Fri.   Jun. 2, 2000
(Day 1. Friday   May 25, 2001)

7:00am Your bed in the luxurious **Monte Carlo Grand Hotel** may beckon at this hour, but there's no sleeping in—races begin at 7 a.m.! Have breakfast at **Le Pistou**, the hotel's rooftop terrace restaurant.

8:00am Head to your grandstand seat, and don't forget earplugs. Noise and power are a big part of the races. Today's last race ends at 12:30 p.m.

1:00pm For lunch, head to the west side of the port (past the pits and race-team trailers) to **Stars 'n' Bars**. This sports bar and restaurant serves a variety of American-style food. Come back in the evening for live music or disco.

2:30pm Take the stairs at the sea wall and head toward the Monaco Yacht Club. Here you'll find more team trailers and the opportunity to check out the cars close up. Take the escalators and elevators to the world-renowned **Oceanographic Museum**. The short 3-D film, *Invisible Ocean*, is good. For a snack, try one of the area's numerous sandwich shops for traditional baguettes or focaccia.

6:00pm Rejuvenate yourself at the stunning **Thermes des Marins** spa. The seaweed wraps and hydro-massages are a must. Or, take a relaxing cruise and see the sights from the deck of the **Monte Carlo Catamaran**.

9:00pm Dine on the terrace at the **Saint-Benoît**. The harbor view and imaginative fresh-fish specialties are both memorable. If you prefer pasta, try the Italian restaurant row—**Ciao, La Piazza, Rigoletto**, and **Pulcinella** are all good options.

11:30pm For live music, stop by **Cherie's Café**, then continue down Avenue des Spélugues to **McCarthy's Pub**.

Day 2. Sat.   Jun. 3, 2000
(Day 2. Saturday   May 26, 2001)

8:00am Bombay Frigo, with Old India-trading-ship decor, is fast becoming a local hotspot. Grab a continental breakfast, and listen to the racing engines screaming outside.

9:00am There's more racing and qualifying runs, so get a couple hours of motor madness under your belt at the track.

11:30am Enough modern machinery (for now)! Stroll through the medieval Old Town toward the Prince's Palace. The changing of the guard takes place at precisely 11:55 a.m. each day in front of the main gate.

2:00pm A number of smaller track-side restaurants offer lunch and race-watching for the price of a ticket. **La Racasse, Botticelli, Stella Polaris**, and **Venezia** are each worth checking out.

6:00pm Make your way to the famous Place du Casino, and grab a seat at the **Café de Paris**. Dazzling displays of wealth, magnificent cars, and beautiful women are standard distractions. Half a block away is **Flashman's**, an English pub that provides relief from the hectic atmosphere around the casino square.

9:00pm Sass Café is a popular address for well-heeled Euros looking for action. Mainly Italian cuisine with a piano bar, this is a pre- and post-Jimmy'z hangout.

12:30am Jimmy'z is where the elite meet. How elite? For starters, there's no cover charge, but all drinks are $40. Buy a bottle for $350 (mixers are free) and if you don't finish it, they'll put your name on it for the next night. Dancing etiquette here is a bit of a trick in that men generally don't ask women to dance. Single men and women dance solo on the floor—when you make heavy eye contact with a

The Fun Also Rises

target and it's returned, an offer to dance has just been made and accepted.

1:30am Sabor Latino is a salsa club certain to keep you up late. Other fun late-night haunts are **L'X's Club** and **The Living Room**.

Day 3. Sun. Jun. 4, 2000
(Day 3. Sunday   May 27, 2001)

9:00am Start your day in the Condamine open-air market located in the Place d'Armes, just down from the train station. Have a *café au lait* or cappuccino and croissant at one of many cafes or bars.

10:00am Cross the street at the Place d'Armes (going west toward Fontvieille) and take the escalator to the **H.S.H. Prince Rainier III Classic Car and Carriage Collection**. A look at the prince's personal collection of vintage cars is perfect during this car-crazy weekend.

10:45am Get behind the wheel yourself, leave the revving engines and excitement behind, and head to the French countryside. Drive southwest along the coastal road, known as the Lower Corniche. Near the charming French town of Eze Bord de Mer, take the Moyenne Corniche to Eze Village. (Check traffic conditions with your concierge so you're back in time for the races.)

Noon Stop for a gourmet lunch overlooking the sea far below, at the spectacular **Château de la Chévre d'Or**.

1:30pm Return via the winding and somewhat difficult Grande Corniche road. It ends with a breathtaking descent into Monaco.

2:30pm Don't be late for the final race (3 p.m. start), which ends at 5 p.m. Once the winner has been decided, crowds cheer wildly and the week's biggest party is unleashed citywide. This is a ***Monaco Grand Prix*** highlight, so don't miss it.

6:00pm Getting a reservation at **Le Texan** is extremely difficult, but you can have a pitcher of margaritas at its **Alamo Bar**. This top spot is a haven for race-car drivers, movie stars, professional athletes, and royalty.

9:00pm Travel back to the *belle-époque* era by dining on **Le Train Bleu**, an elegant gourmet restaurant modeled after the *Orient Express*. It's located inside of the bustling casino complex.

11:00pm French culture at **Le Cabaret** means the sexiest topless showgirls from the famous Crazy Horse in Paris.

1:00am If you want to gamble, don't forget to bring your passport—**The Monte Carlo Casino** requires it for gaming. After some time at the tables, you'll no doubt discover what the Formula 1 drivers have known all along—there's no more elegant setting for winning or losing than Monte Carlo.

Alternatives

The 1864 **Hôtel de Paris** is synonymous with luxury and perfect service. **Le Méridien Beach Plaza** boasts a private beach and three swimming pools. Unlike Monaco hotels, out-of-town hotels may not require four- to six-night minimum stays. **Le Cap Estel**, the former residence of a Russian prince, is set on the seaside between Monaco and Nice in Eze.

For gourmet Thai cuisine, **Toum** is tucked inside the casino atrium. Another fun stop is **Pinocchio** in the Old Town. Try their wafer-thin Parma ham and melon—it's terrific.

The ***Grand Prix Gala*** is a black-tie soiree that takes place Sunday evening after the races, at the spectacular Salle de Etoiles. You'll be dining with the world's fastest drivers and their entourages.

Check out the Hot Sheets for Cannes (see page 140) and Nice (see page 178) to complete your picture of the Riviera.

The Hot Sheet

☎ 377/9

$ 6.1 Franc

HOTELS	DAY	ADDRESS	*	PH	PRICE	FX	RMS	BEST ROOMS
Hôtel de Paris	A	pl. du Casino		216-3000	$$$$+	216-3849	197	Casino Square track-side vw
			800-	221-4708				
Le Cap Estel	A	Eze sur Mer	33/49	301-5044	$$$$	301-5520	40	Dlx
			800-	203-3232				
Le Méridien Beach Plaza	A	22 av. Princesse-Grace		330-9880	$$$$+	350-2314	308	Sea vw
			800-	225-5843				
Monte Carlo Grand Hotel	1	12 av. des Spélugues		350-6500	$$$$	330-0157	619	Sea vw
			800-	637-7200				

RESTAURANTS	DAY	ADDRESS	*	PH	PRICE	REC	DRESS	FOOD
Bombay Frigo	2	3 av. Princesse-Grace		325-5700	$$$	B/LD	Local	Continental
Botticelli	2	1 av. President J.F. Kennedy		325-3905	$$	L/BD	Local	Italian, seafood
Café de Paris	2	pl. du Casino		216-2020	$$	L/BD	Local	French
Château de la Chévre d'Or	3	rue du Barri, Eze	33/49	210-6666	$$$$+	L/D	Local	French
Ciao	1	7 rue du Portier		325-7868	$$	D/L	Local	Italian
La Piazza	1	9 rue du Portier		350-4700	$$$	D/L	Local	Italian
La Racasse	2	quai Antoine 1er		325-5690	$$	L/D	Local	Classic French
Le Pistou	1	see Monte Carlo Grand Hotel		350-6500	$$	B/LD	Local	Continental
Le Texan	3	4 rue Suffren Reymond		330-3454	$$$	D/L	Local	Tex-Mex
Le Train Bleu	3	pl. du Casino		216-2211	$$$	D	Kazh	Italian, classic French
Pinocchio	A	30 rue Comte-Félix Gastaldi		330-9620	$$	LD	Local	Italian
Pulcinella	1	17 rue du Portier		330-7361	$$	D/L	Local	Italian
Rigoletto	1	11 rue du Portier		325-2428	$$	D/L	Local	Italian
Saint-Benoît	1	10 av. de la Costa		325-0234	$$	L/D	Kazh	Seafood
Sass Café	2	11 av. Princesse-Grace		325-5200	$$	D/L	Local	Italian
Stars 'n' Bars	1	6 quai Antoine 1er		350-9595	$$	L/D	Local	American
Stella Polaris	2	3 av. President J.F. Kennedy		330-8863	$$	L/D	Local	Snack bar
Toum	A	pl. du Casino		216-6363	$$$	D	Kazh	Thai
Venezia	2	27 bd. Albert 1er		315-9727	$$	L/BD	Local	Italian

NITELIFE	DAY	ADDRESS	PH	PRICE	REC	DRESS	MUSIC
Alamo Bar	3	4 rue Suffren Reymond	330-3454	None	H(F)	Local	
Cherie's Café	1	9 av. des Spélugues	330-3099	None	MP(F)	Local	Dance band, salsa
Flashman's	2	7 av. Princesse-Alice	330-0903	None	H(F)	Local	
Jimmy'z	2	Sporting d'Ete	216-2277	None	O	Dressy	Disco
L'X's Club	2	13 av. des Spélugues	330-7055	None	O	Local	Disco
Le Cabaret	3	pl. du Casino	216-3636	$$$$+	S	Dressy	Cabaret
The Living Room	2	7 av. des Spélugues	350-8031	None	MO	Kazh	Piano bar, disco
McCarthy's Pub	1	7 rue du Portier	325-8767	None	M	Local	Jazz, rock
The Monte Carlo Casino	3	pl. du Casino	216-2310	$$	G	Local	
Sabor Latino	2	Galerie Charles III	350-6503	None	MP	Kazh	Latin
Sass Café	2	11 av. Princesse-Grace	325-5200	None	M(F)	Kazh	Piano bar
Stars 'n' Bars	1	see Stars 'n' Bars restaurant	350-9595	None	MOPF	Local	Disco

SIGHTS & ATTRACTIONS	DAY	ADDRESS	PH	ENTRY FEE
H.S.H. Prince Rainier III Classic Car and Carriage Collection	3	Les Terrasses de Fontvieille	205-2856	$
Oceanographic Museum	1	av. St-Martin, Monaco-Ville	315-3600	$$

OTHER SIGHTS, SERVICES & ATTRACTIONS

Monte Carlo Catamaran	1	quai des États-Unis, Harbor	216-1515	$$
Thermes des Marins Spa	1	2 av. de Monte Carlo	216-4040	
Monaco Tourist Office		2 bd. des Moulins	216-6166	

EVENT & TICKET INFO

Monaco Grand Prix (Monte Carlo): Tickets for Thu. ($30-$60), Sat. ($30-$200), and Sun. ($40-$360) can be purchased in advance by contacting the *Monaco Automobile Club* (377/9315-2600). All seats are free on Friday. Ticket information for the 25,000 available seats (maximum of four tickets per person for Sunday's race; checks are payable only in French francs) is available in Dec. from the *Monaco Automobile Club*.

Grand Prix Gala: Tickets ($450) can be purchased through *The Sporting Club* (377/9216-3636).

RECommendations: (Restaurants) B–Breakfast; L–Lunch; D–Dinner; T–High tea or snack (Nitelife) G–Gaming; H–Hangout bar; M–Live music; O–Dancing (disco); P–Dancing (live music); S–Show; F–Food served ()–Available but without recommendation. For complete explanation of Hot Sheet format, see page 34.

🕐 NYC +6   ☾ 56°/67° (13°/19°)   ✈ Nice/Côte d'Azur (NCE); 45 min./$100   🚗 No   👥 French

Féria de Nîmes

(Féria de Pentecôte)

Origin: 1952	Event ★ ★ ★ ★ ★ City	Attendance: 500,000

The only thing that can compete with a year in Provence is three days at the *Féria de Nîmes*, a spectacular event that combines French liqueur, Roman ruins, and the passionate Gypsy sounds of southern Spain. The swaying cypress trees and pastis liqueur of Provence mix with fiery flamenco and fine wines, as this small ancient city in the south of France reinforces its traditional bonds with the Spanish region of Andalusia.

The focus of *Féria* is the afternoon *corrida* (bullfight), in which some of the world's greatest bulls and top *toreros* hash it out in Nîmes' spectacular Roman Arena. Bullfights may not appeal to everyone, but the accompanying parties in the streets certainly will. At this annual fete, friends find each other in the crowd then drift apart; sangria, *vino fino* (dry white wine), and pastis (a licorice-and-aniseed-flavored liqueur) flow between strangers; even love affairs are occasionally sparked. As locals and veterans of the event will tell you, when the spirit of Spain melds with the beauty of France, anything is possible.

The *Féria* was established in 1952, nearly a century after Spanish-style bullfights had become an integral part of the town's culture. As in Pamplona, Spain, young men prove their courage by running with the bulls down the avenues of Nîmes and testing their talent in small-scale, amateur bullfights. For most of the half-million visitors who flood these cobblestone streets each year, however, the theme of *Féria* is fun. Makeshift bodegas and discos pop up in every nook and cranny of town. Impromptu concerts, exhibitions, and dances are held, and flasks of wine are emptied and refilled around the clock.

Don't forget to pack some denim (*de Nîmes*)—the fabric originated here—because you'll want to be comfortable while you explore this city of astonishing history. The amphitheater, where the bullfights are featured, hosted animal and gladiator contests almost 2,000 years ago. You don't have to stay as long as the Romans did, but if you don't have a year to spend in Provence, this wild weekend is the next best thing.

Féria de Nîmes

Day 1. Fri.   Jun. 9, 2000
(Day 1. Friday   June 1, 2001)

9:30am Check into the elegant, centrally located **Hôtel Impérator Concorde**, which has views of both the Quai de la Fontaine and the Jardin de la Fontaine. During *Féria* it's home base for bullfighters.

10:30am Walk through the lovely Jardin de la Fontaine. Take a step back in time at the **Tour Magne** on Mont-Cavalier. The largest tower of the ramparts surrounding Nîmes during Roman times, it was built in 15 B.C. Climb its 140 steps to enjoy a splendid view of the city. Then check out the modern paintings and sculptures in the **Musée d'Art Contemporain**.

1:30pm Have lunch on the garden patio at **Aux Plaisir des Halles**. In the tradition of southern France, all the food is homemade and very fresh.

3:30pm Walk along Boulevard Victor-Hugo to the **Musée des Beaux-Arts** to learn about the old Roman lifestyle and see works by master painters and sculptors. Then visit the **Musée du Vieux Nîmes** to see a display of embroidered garments and original denim from Nîmes' heyday as a fabric production center.

5:30pm Head to the nearby Arènes, Nîmes' astounding stone arena—much like a smaller version of the Roman Coliseum—considered one of the best-preserved Roman amphitheaters in the world. It seats 21,000 spectators for the *bullfight*.

8:30pm Join bullfight aficionados who dine in the garden setting of **L'Enclos de la Fontaine**. The chilled, dill-perfumed langoustine soup is wonderful.

10:30pm Street crowds will be dancing and drinking all night. Lose yourself in the "anything goes" atmosphere.

Midnight Check out the dance scene at **Milton**, one of Nîmes' most popular dance clubs. It keeps swinging until 5 or 6 a.m.

Day 2. Sat.   Jun. 10, 2000
(Day 2. Saturday   June 2, 2001)

10:00am Have *café au lait* and breakfast on the terrace of **Café de la Bourse**.

11:00am Drive north toward the nearby town of Avignon. Along the way, stop and see the magnificent 2,000-year-old Pont du Gard, a 1,000-foot-long former aqueduct that stands as one of the best-preserved Roman monuments in France. For a good photo, try the view from the little town of Castillon-du-Gard.

1:00pm Continue to Avignon and have lunch at **La Cuisine de Reine**, a trendy new bistro with an artsy decor and innovative Provençal dishes such as salmon with eggplant caviar.

3:00pm Stroll through the picturesque streets of Avignon. Stop by the **Palais des Papes**, the forbidding palace where seven exiled popes took refuge in the 14th century.

6:30pm Drive back to Nîmes for another exuberant night of partying and music in the streets.

8:30pm Head to **Chez Edgar** for a Spanish dinner show and an excellent *prix fixe* meal of traditional Provençal cuisine.

11:00pm Join the action in the streets and bodegas (wine shops). Have a glass of sangria and see who's playing on the small stages near the 2nd-century Maison Carrée (in the La Placette square) and the Esplanade Charles de Gaulle.

12:15am Mingle with bullfighters and personalities at the buzzing bodega in the Impérator hotel, possibly the hottest spot for *Féria* action.

Day 3. Sun.   Jun. 11, 2000
(Day 3. Sunday   June 3, 2001)

9:00am The outdoor terrace at **Café Carré** will soothe ℞ your head, and the strong coffee and croissants will restore your body.

10:00am Drive to Arles, a former Roman stronghold that inspired some of Van Gogh's finest work. Check out the old Roman ruins, such as the enormous **Arènes** and **Théâtre Antique**.

Noon Dine on the terrace at the **Brasserie du Nord-Pinus**, ℞ a crowded bistro in the baroque-style Grand Hôtel Nord-Pinus. The restaurant serves traditional regional cuisine. The view may seem familiar— directly across from the terrace is the cafe with yellow awnings depicted in Van Gogh's *The Cafe Terrace on the Place du Forum*.

2:30pm Head to the scenic village of Les Baux-de-Provence. A prosperous town of 6,000 people in the 13th and 14th centuries, it thrives again as one of the most popular tourist destinations in Provence. Walk through the ancient streets to the phenomenal **Château des Baux**, which is built right into mountain stone. Don't miss the exceptional views from the château's 13th-century keep.

5:30pm Drive back to Nîmes for an unforgettable night of festivities. People will be gathering in the streets for music, sangria, and the arrival of the bulls.

8:00pm Join the mass of spectators for the ***Running of the Bulls***, a time-honored tradition in Nîmes. Six bulls are released into the streets in a cordoned-off area. Though these bulls are not raised for the *corridas*—they're returned to the fields after the event—remember, a bull is a bull and those horns are sharp.

9:30pm For fine regional cuisine, have dinner at the ℞ popular **Le Bouchon et l'Assiette**.

11:30pm Hang out in the streets, drinking, dancing, and befriending everyone in sight. Another crowd is enjoying the **Hemingway Bar** at the Impérator.

1:15am Check out the action on the Allée Jean-Jaurès in the Camargue Village, a strip of popular bodegas and restaurants where the ***Féria*** crowd gathers to drink and dance until dawn.

Alternatives

In the suburbs of Nîmes, the **Hotel Mercure** is modern and comfortable. Avignon's **Hôtel de la Mirande** is a beautifully restored town house fit for a pope, offering both elegant rooms and superb Provençal dining in its famed restaurant. In Arles, choose between the atmospheric and highly fashionable **Grand Hôtel du Nord-Pinus** and the more traditional and plush **Hôtel Jules César**.

For a lively, ***Féria***-style restaurant in Nîmes, try the centrally located **La Bodeguita** for *tapas* and Spanish fare. The casual and fun **Au Flan Coco** bistro is known for its fresh produce and local cuisine. Stop at **La Maison Villaret** bakery, popular for creating the famous Nîmes specialty known as *croquants* (hard little biscuits flavored with honey). In Avignon, eat at the **Christian Etienne Restaurant**, well known for its light and contemporary Provençal menu.

La Movida, in the Gypsy quarter, is one of the most fashionable nightspots in Nîmes. It features Spanish music and flamenco shows.

Try a day trip to Aix-en-Provence, the quaint hometown of French painter Paul Cézanne and writer Émile Zola. Wander down the Cours Mirabeau, a lively avenue in the style of the Champs-Élysées. For a good museum in Avignon, check out the **Musée du Petit Palais**, on the Place du Palais des Papes. It has an impressive collection of 13th- to 16th-century Italian religious paintings. The Rocher des Doms park, up the hill, offers an excellent view of the Rhône river and the surrounding countryside.

The Hot Sheet

☎ 33/466

$ 6.1 Franc

HOTELS	DAY	ADDRESS	*	PH	PRICE	FX	RMS	BEST ROOMS
Grand Hôtel Nord-Pinus	A	pl. du Forum	A490	93-4444	$$	93-3400	26	Front facing rm
Hôtel de la Mirande	A	4 pl. de la Mirande	V490 800-	85-9393 525-4800	$$$$	86-2685	20	Dlx rm w/ balc
Hôtel Impérator Concorde	1	15 rue Gaston-Boissier	800-	21-9030 448-8355	$$	67-7025	60	Supr rm facing gdn
Hôtel Jules César	A	bd. des Lices	A490 800-	93-4320 860-4930	$$$	93-3347	55	Gdn or cloister vw
Hotel Mercure	A	46 rue Tony-Garnier	800-	70-4800 221-4542	$	70-4801	100	Gdn vw

RESTAURANTS	DAY	ADDRESS	*	PH	PRICE	REC	DRESS	FOOD
Au Flan Coco	A	rue du Murier d'Espagne		21-8481	$$$	LD	Euro	Provençal
Aux Plaisir des Halles	1	8 rue Littre		36-0102	$$	L/D	Euro	Modern French
Brasserie du Nord-Pinus	3	see Grand Hôtel Nord-Pinus	A490	93-0232	$$	L/D	Euro	Provençal
Café Carré	3	bd. Victor-Hugo next to Maison Carrée		67-5005	$	B/LTD	Kazh	French
Café de la Bourse	2	2 bd. des Arènes		67-2191	$	B/LT	Local	Cafe
Chez Edgar	2	3 rue de la Cité-Foulc		21-5805	$$	D/L	Kazh	Provençal
Christian Etienne Restaurant	A	10 rue de Mons	V490	86-1650	$$$$	LD	Euro	Provençal
L'Enclos de la Fountaine	1	see Hôtel Impérator Concorde		21-9030	$$$	D/BL	Euro	Provençal
La Bodeguita	A	1 pl. d'Assas		58-2829	$$	LTD	Kazh	Spanish, *tapas*
La Cuisine de Reine	2	83 rue Joseph-Vernet	V490	85-9904	$$	L/D	Euro	French
La Maison Villaret	A	13 rue de la Madeleine		67-4179	$	BT	Local	*Croquants*
Le Bouchon et l'Assiette	3	5 rue de Sauve		62-0293	$$	D	Euro	Provençal, traditional French

NITELIFE	DAY	ADDRESS	PH	PRICE	REC	DRESS	MUSIC
Hemingway Bar	3	see Hôtel Impérator Concorde	21-9030	None	H	Kazh	
La Movida	A	La Placette	67-8090	$$$	MS	Euro	Spanish, flamenco
Milton	1	RN 113 direction Montpellier	71-2964	$$	O	Euro	Dance, retro

SIGHTS & ATTRACTIONS	DAY	ADDRESS	*	PH	ENTRY FEE
Arènes	3	Rond-Point des Arènes	A490	96-0370	$
Château des Baux	3	Impasse du Château, Les Baux de Provence	490	54-5556	$
Musée d'Art Contemporain	1	pl. de la Maison Carrée		76-3535	$
Musée des Beaux-Arts	1	rue de la Cité-Foulc		67-3821	$
Musée du Petit Palais	A	pl. du Palais	V490	86-4458	$
Musée du Vieux Nîmes	1	pl. aux Herbes		36-0064	$
Palais des Papes	2	pl. du Palais	V490	27-5000	$
Théâtre Antique	3	rue du Cloître	A490	49-3625	$
Tour Magne	1	Jardins de la Fontaine		67-6556	$
Office du Tourisme, Arles		Esplanade Charles de Gaulle	A490	18-4120	
Office du Tourisme, Avignon		41 cours Jean-Jaurès	V490	82-6511	
Office du Tourisme, Nîmes		6 rue Auguste		67-2911	

EVENT & TICKET INFO

Féria de Nîmes (various locations throughout the city): All street events are free. Tickets to the bullfights ($16-$81) must be purchased at least six months in advance. For information, contact the *Arénes ticket office* (33/466-67-7277).

*A=Arles, V=Avignon

REComendations: (Restaurants) B–Breakfast; L–Lunch; D–Dinner; T–High tea or snack
(Nitelife) G–Gaming; H–Hangout bar; M–Live music; O–Dancing (disco); P–Dancing (live music); S–Show; F–Food served
()–Available but without recommendation. For complete explanation of Hot Sheet format, see page 34.

NYC +6 · 59°/79 (15°/26°) · Aeroport Marseille (MRS); 90 min./SNA · Yes · French

Feast of St. Anthony

(Festas de Lisboa)

Lisbon, Portugal

| Origin: 1232 | Event ★ ★ ★ ★ ★ City | Attendance: 300,000 |

If the **Feast of St. Anthony** on June 13 is a celebration of marriage in Lisbon—the city's unofficial patron saint is said to champion holy wedlock—the night before must be a celebration of the blessed state of singledom. Thoughts of romantic dinners for two and secluded vacations evaporate as masses of people fill the streets for music and dancing to kick off the feast day of their favorite holy man.

In honor of St. Anthony, the evening of June 12 is turned over to parades, parties, and artistic performances. The narrow, winding streets of the Alfama, the old Moorish section of Lisbon, take on a theatrical atmosphere as lacy lanterns pierce the night and throw romantic shadows against the whitewashed walls, flower-laden balconies, and cobblestone alleys. On this night young people from all over the city perform the popular **marchas** (dancing parade) down the Avenida de Liberdade, Lisbon's main boulevard.

When not dancing and laughing, crowds consume mass quantities of grilled sardines, pork, and local red wine. Stages are set up for musicians to play rock, jazz, salsa, and traditional Portuguese music. The party rages until four in the morning.

Though centuries older, Lisbon is reminiscent of San Francisco—it's set on seven hills, the taxi drivers could use some help from St. Anthony, and there's a bridge that's a near twin to the Golden Gate Bridge. With a population of one million, Lisbon is considered a cutting-edge nightlife center, a city that never sleeps. In trying to outdo their Madrileños neighbors, Lisboetas don't begin partying until after midnight and often don't retire until after the sun comes up.

Once the world's most important port, Lisbon offers a fascinating glimpse of a European culture that hasn't completely given in to the hustle of the techno world. There's plenty of fun and romance to be found in this historic city. And even if you're still single when you leave Lisbon, you'll be tempted to come back next year anyway.

Feast of St. Anthony

Day 1. Sat. Jun. 10, 2000
(Day 3. Thursday   *June 14, 2001)*

9:00am Check into the elegant **Tivoli Lisboa Hotel**. It has a striking marble lobby and center-of-town location.

10:00am Walk through the Baixa district and stop at
Ⓡ **Pastelaria Suiça**. It's a local favorite and a nice place to enjoy a pastry while sitting outside. Ask for *uma bica* (strong black coffee, similar to espresso) or *uma meia de leite* (half coffee, half milk).

1:00pm Take the Number 37 bus from the Alfama dis-
Ⓡ trict to lunch at **Casa do Leão Restaurant**. Located in the **Castelo de São Jorge** (a one-time residence of Portuguese royalty), its traditional food and fabulous views have made it an Alfama hotspot.

2:30pm Stroll through the narrow streets of Santa Cruz, a little village packed tightly within the castle walls. Don't miss the views from the battlements and observation terrace.

3:30pm Wander the streets of the Alfama. Be sure to see the Sé, Lisbon's main cathedral. It's been rocked by numerous tremors and rebuilt again and again. Then stop in at the nearby **Igreja de Santo António à Sé**, where St. Anthony was baptized more than 800 years ago.

7:00pm Start your evening at **Solar do Vinho do Porto** in the Bairro Alto. Sample some of the 300 different ports either at the bar or in comfy chairs in a club setting.

9:00pm Dine at **Alcântara Café**, a sophisticated, fash-
Ⓡ ionable restaurant and bar with art-deco accents and a life-size, full-figured Aphrodite behind the bar.

11:00pm Dancers head for **Kapital**, a chic nightclub on three floors with a rooftop veranda. Around the corner is **Kremlin**, a lively hangout for techno music

fans. The wildly popular and cavernous **Frágil** is an airy warehouse turned hipster and rock star hangout.

Day 2. Sun. Jun. 11, 2000
(Day 2. Wednesday   *June 13, 2001)*

9:00am In the Chiado district, find **Á Brasileira**, an art-
Ⓡ deco holdout and traditional spot for coffee or tea.

10:00am Walk five minutes to the tram, which will take you to Belém, a Lisbon neighborhood on the mouth of the Tagus River. Take a look at the **Mosteiro dos Jerónimos**, a monastery built with money made from the spice trade. Also check out the **Torre de Belém**, a fortress built in the middle of the Tagus, now accessible by a footbridge.

1:00pm Taxi to the Docas area and have lunch at **Doca-6**.
Ⓡ You can enjoy Portuguese and international cuisine as you sit at a table overlooking the marina's yachts.

3:00pm Take a cab to the **Museu Nacional do Azulejo**, the national museum devoted to the Portuguese craft of tile painting.

7:00pm After a hotel break, cab back to the Chiado district next to the Bairro Alto. Once a haven for intellectuals and artists, it's now home to upscale boutiques and a great walking area.

9:00pm Do drinks in the Bairro Alto at the converted storefront bar **Pavilhão Chinês**. The list of drinks is as exotic as the decor.

10:30pm Have dinner at **Pap'Açorda**, a popular up-
Ⓡ market, but casual-dress restaurant in the Bairro Alto. *Açorda* means any Portuguese dish cooked with bread, garlic, olive oil, and coriander.

Midnight It's *fado* time! This style of simple, often sad music—some liken it to Southern blues—is thought to have been invented by lonesome seafarers. Head for **Senhor Vinho** where the *fado* connoisseurs congregate for the real stuff.

Day 3. Mon.   Jun. 12, 2000
(Day 1. Tuesday   June 12, 2001)

10:00am After breakfast in the hotel, rent a car and tour the western side of Lisbon. Drive along the Estrada Marginal, which hugs the River Tagus and the Atlantic Ocean. Stop in Estoril, a fashionable Riviera resort area with seaside cafes, and Cascais, once a fishing town and now a village of smart boutiques, discos, and nightclubs.

1:00pm Ask for a window table overlooking the Bay of Cascais at the five-star **Hotel Albatroz** near the old center of Cascais. The paté, ham, Albatroz fish soup, and grilled sea bass are all good lunch bets.

2:30pm Be certain to stop at Sintra, a designated UNESCO World Heritage Site. Visit the beautiful **Palácio Nacional de Sintra** and the **Castelo dos Mouros**, ramparts of an 8th-century Moorish castle. And admire from afar the Palácio da Pena, a pink-and-yellow cakelike palace (closed on Mondays).

6:00pm Drop off the rental car and start the evening with a ride up the **Elevador Santa Justa** to **Chiadomel**, an off-the-beaten-track cafe. It's a cool spot to enjoy the sunset and a drink.

8:00pm Dinner tonight at **Bota Alta** in the Bairro Alto, a somewhat elegant restaurant with original artwork on display. The house specialty, pork cooked with clams, is unforgettable!

9:30pm Watch the **marchas** down Avenida de Liberdade. It's not elaborate, but it's interesting. Young people in colorful costumes come from all quarters of the city to perform the popular *marchas* dances and socialize.

11:00pm All of the old neighborhoods are packed with holiday celebrants. Makeshift bars and restaurants fill every available square and alley. Decorated with glowing paper lanterns, streamers, and garlands of flowers, the Alfama is the most raucous area. The incredibly crowded and festive scene here is what makes this festival stand out.

1:00am A tour of the festival's four **music stages** could keep you going until 4 a.m. (Music starts around 11 p.m.) Take your pick of musical styles, including rock, jazz, and those ubiquitous Andean pan-flute bands. Since this is the marrying saint's festival, clear your dance card, join the fray, and say a little prayer—may St. Anthony be with you!

Alternatives

Across from the gorgeous Edward VII Park, the **Four Seasons Hotel-The Ritz** has elegant and comfortable rooms. Built in contemporary style, **Le Méridien Park Atlantic** offers magnificent views of Lisbon and the River Tagus. **Hotel Lapa Palace**, the most posh hotel in Lisbon, is a converted palace in the diplomatic district. It has panoramic views of the city and the river.

For a traditional "convent" meal, **Conventual** is, literally, in a category all its own. The rustically decorated **Lautasco**—with wagon-wheel chandeliers and all—serves traditional Portuguese cuisine. In the Alfama district, **Faz Figura** is a casual but smart restaurant with seating under a covered terrace and panoramic views of the river and city. A house specialty is *cataplana*, a casserole dish prepared, sealed, and steamed, usually with fish in it.

You can find more of Lisbon's hotspots in the old quarter of the Bairro Alto and in the Alcântara section near the waterfront. If gambling is your goal, head for **Casino do Estoril** in Estoril. In addition to gambling tables, the casino offers dinner, floorshows, and an active bar scene.

Built in neo-Moorish red-brick style in the late 19th century, **Campo Pequeño** is the preeminent bullring in Lisbon. Contests are scheduled during the **Feast of St. Anthony** festivities.

The Hot Sheet

☎ 351/1

$ 180 Escudo

HOTELS	DAY	ADDRESS	PH	PRICE	FX	RMS	BEST ROOMS
Four Seasons Hotel– The Ritz	A	88 Rua Rodrigo da Fonseca	383-2020 800- 332-3442	$$$	383-1783	284	Park vw
Hotel Lapa Palace	A	4 Rua do Pau de Bandeira	395-0005 800- 223-6800	$$$$	395-0665	94	River vw
Le Méridien Park Atlantic	A	149 Rua Castilho	381-8700 800- 543-4300	$$	387-0472	322	River vw
Tivoli Lisboa Hotel	1	185 Av. de Liberdade	319-8900 800- 448-8355	$$$	319-8950	327	City vw

RESTAURANTS	DAY	ADDRESS	PH	PRICE	REC	DRESS	FOOD
Á Brasileira	2	120-122 Rua Garrett	346-9541	$$	B/T	Local	Cafe
Alcântara Café	1	15 Rua María Luisa Holstein	362-1226	$$$	D	Euro	Modern Portuguese
Bota Alta	3	35 Travessa da Queinada	342-7959	$$	D/L	Local	Portuguese
Casa do Leão Restaurant	1	see Castelo de São Jorge	887-5962	$$$	L/D	Euro	Traditional Portuguese
Chiadomel	3	105 Rua de Santa Justa	346-9598	$	T/BLD	Local	Cafe
Conventual	A	45 Praça das Flores	390-9196	$$$	LD	Euro	Continental
Doca-6	2	6 Doca de Santo Amaro, Armazen	395-7905	$$	L/D	Kazh	Portuguese, international
Faz Figura	A	15B Rua do Paraigo	886-8981	$$$	LD	Kazh	Portuguese grilled meats
Hotel Albatroz	3	100 Rua Frederico Arduca	483-2821	$$$	L/BD	Euro	French
Lautasco	A	7 Beco do Azinhal	886-0173	$$	BLD	Kazh	Portuguese
Pap'Açorda	2	57 Rua da Atalaia	346-4811	$$	D/L	Kazh	Portuguese
Pastelaria Suiça	1	Praça Dom Pedro IV	321-4090	$	B/LT	Local	Pastries

NITELIFE	DAY	ADDRESS	PH	PRICE	REC	DRESS	MUSIC
Casino do Estoril	A	Praça José Teodoro dos Santos, Estoril	466-7700	Various	GMPS(F)	Dressy	Floor show
Frágil	1	126 Rua da Atalaia	346-9578	None	O	Euro	House
Kapital	1	68 Av. 24 de Julho	395-7101	$$	HO	Euro	Disco, soul, rock
Kremlin	1	5 Escadinhas da Praia	395-7101	$	O	Euro	House
Pavilhão Chinês	2	89 Rua Dom Pedro V	342-4729	None	H	Euro	
Senhor Vinho	2	18 Rua do Meio a Lapa	397-2681	$$	MS	Euro	*Fado*
Solar do Vinho do Porto	1	45 Rua de São Pedro de Alcântara	347-5707	$$	H	Euro	

SIGHTS & ATTRACTIONS	DAY	ADDRESS	PH	ENTRY FEE
Campo Pequeño	A	Praça de Touros Porta 2	793-2442	$$$$
Castelo de São Jorge	1	Arco de São Jorge, Rua do Chão da Feira	887-7244	None
Castelo dos Mouros	3	Estrada da Pena	923-5116	None
Elevador Santa Justa	3	Rua de Santa Justa at Rua do Ouro	361-3040	$
Igreja de Santo António à Sé	1	1 Rua das Pedras Negras	886-9145	None
Mosteiro dos Jerónimos	2	Praça do Império	362-0034	$
Museu Nacional do Azulejo	2	4 Rua da Madre de Deus	814-7747	$
Palácio Nacional de Sintra	3	Largo Rainha Dona Amélia, Sintra	910-6840	$
Torre de Belém	2	Av. da India	362-0034	$
ICEP Tourist Office		Palácio Foz on Praça dos Restauradores	346-3643	

> ## EVENT & TICKET INFO
>
> **Feast of St. Anthony**
>
> (Avenida de Liberdade and Alfama district of Lisbon): Admission is free. For more information, contact the *Portuguese National Tourist Office* in New York (212-354-4403).

RECommendations: (Restaurants) B–Breakfast; L–Lunch; D–Dinner; T–High tea or snack
(Nitelife) G–Gaming; H–Hangout bar; M–Live music; O–Dancing (disco); P–Dancing (live music); S–Show; F–Food served
()–Available but without recommendation. For complete explanation of Hot Sheet format, see page 34.

NYC +5   60°/76° (15°/24°)   Lisbon (LIS); 30 min./$10   Yes/No   Portuguese

The Fun Also Rises

Royal Ascot

(The Royal Meeting at Ascot Racecourse)

Origin: 1711	Event ★★★★★★★★ City	Attendance: 230,000

Four tons of salmon, 4,500 lobsters, 50,000 bottles of champagne. Sounds like a party—and it is, at the United Kingdom's most glamorous sporting event, the four days of horse racing that begin on the third Tuesday of each June at Ascot Racecourse. Throughout its run, 200,000 rapt fans attend, living out their own versions of the famous *Ascot* scene from *My Fair Lady*.

As important as any of the equine entrants or culinary masterpieces at this event are the spectators in dazzling fashions. Attendees parade in designer attire of all types, but the ladies' hats steal the show. Immense, lavish, demented, stupendous ... any list of superlatives describing *Ascot*'s famed hats pales in comparison with the real thing.

At one point, outfits became so outlandish that Her Majesty's Representative at *Royal Ascot* changed dress protocol to limit the size of hats and specify appropriate colors and fabrics for men's morning coats. Even so, many race-goers still seem to regard the dress code as a personal challenge, dressing as wildly as possible while remaining within proscribed parameters.

London society pages adore *Royal Ascot* and lavish it with attention. Spectators include Her Majesty The Queen, members of the royal family, assorted aristocracy, celebrities, businessmen, and the super-rich (along with many Eliza Doolittles). Each day, they flash smiles and finery for *paparazzi* clustered at the entrance to the Royal Enclosure, where distinguished guests watch the races.

Forever fond of standing on ceremony, the British love *Ascot*'s protocol, royalty, and social pedigree, and this panorama of manners, tradition, and sartorial showboating offers an unforgettable look into a century and a half of British society.

Ascot is an hour's train ride outside London, which offers other distinctly British pleasures. Forget those snide comments you sometimes hear about British cuisine—with influences and residents from all over the world, London has become one of the world's great eating cities. And there are more cultural and historic attractions than could possibly fit inside *two* Ascot hats.

Royal Ascot

Day 1. Wed. Jun. 21, 2000
(Day 1. Wednesday   *June 20, 2001)*

8:30am Check into **The Savoy**. This quintessential British hotel has Victorian grandeur, hand-crafted furnishings, and great views of the Thames.

10:00am Preparing for **Ascot** is half the fun. It's better to reserve an outfit at least a week or two ahead of time, but even if you haven't, stop into London's **Moss Bros.** Rent everything you'll need—morning coats and top hats for men, elegant daywear for women.

11:00am Stand across from **Fortnum & Mason** as the department store's clock strikes the hour and its mechanical Fortnum and Mason come out and bow to each other. Inside the famous establishment, buy gourmet delicacies and splurge on a chapeau that's wearable art, fashion statement, and Ascot souvenir.

12:30pm Cab to the **Tate Gallery Restaurant** for good British fare. Then tour the **Tate Gallery**, which has built its reputation on the world's largest collection of English paintings.

4:00pm Return to The Savoy for the best high tea in London while listening to live harp or piano music in **The Thames Foyer**'s gilded comfort.

7:00pm Cab or walk across the Thames to the **Royal National Theatre**. Sip sherry and listen to a classical recital before watching a performance by one of the world's greatest theater companies.

10:00pm Stroll along the Thames to **Oxo Tower Restaurant, Bar & Brasserie** and dine on French-bent British dishes in the restaurant section while admiring the South Bank area.

Midnight On the way back to your hotel, drop in for a nightcap at **shoeless joe's**. Its famous sports-figure shareholders and their celebrity friends visit regularly.

Day 2. Thu. Jun. 22, 2000
(Day 2. Thursday   *June 21, 2001)*

10:15am In **Royal Ascot** regalia, descend to **The River Restaurant** in your hotel for a late breakfast.

11:45am At Waterloo Station, catch the train to Ascot. You should be able to identify your train by following the sea of enormous hats.

1:00pm All four days at **Ascot** are equally fun, but this is **Lady's Day—Royal Ascot**'s most popular day—when women dress in their most frivolous outfits. In the parking areas, race-goers picnic out of the boots (trunks) of their cars with butlers serving on silver service with crystal glasses. (You may want a snack at an en route pub or at the racecourse.) Enter the racecourse gates by 2 p.m. to see the daily inaugural procession starring Her Majesty The Queen arriving by horse-drawn carriage.

2:30pm All of **Ascot**'s 100-plus bars will be packed, but the climate is most sociable at the **Brigadier Gerard Bar**. The **Garden Bar** is also a good choice. One regular spectator is nicknamed "The Mad Hatter" for her monstrous hats loaded with oddities such as giraffes, dart boards, and apples.

4:00pm Visit **Arundel Restaurant** for afternoon tea (there will be a wait—no reservations).

5:45pm Move near the band in the Grandstand Enclosure to secure a spot for the day-ending sing-alongs, which some revere as **Ascot**'s high point. Even if you don't know the words to the tunes, the spirited crowd will inspire you to fake it.

8:30pm Back in London, **The Avenue** has elegant minimalist decor, with food to match. More casual is **Mezzo** where, like the menu, the crowd is international. As the night progresses, the dance floor downstairs becomes filled.

10:30pm In Soho, **Ronnie Scott's** is one of London's more famous jazz clubs. Get a reservation before visiting. There's also a disco on the second floor.

12:30pm If your dancing feet aren't worn out yet, **K-bar** is the place to go nearby for late-night moves.

Day 3. Fri.   Jun. 23, 2000
(Day 3. Friday   June 22, 2001)

9:00am This is a walking day. Dress comfortably and ℞ order a room-service breakfast.

10:00am Cab to the **Tower of London**, the ancient fortress where yeoman warders (Beefeaters) keep the crown jewels safe.

1:30pm Heading back toward your hotel, try **Bank**, a ℞ bank-turned-restaurant with an "in" following. The chefs spice up traditional British favorites.

3:00pm Walk to **Westminster Abbey**, passing Big Ben as its 14-ton bell strikes 3 p.m. The crowning and burial place of most English monarchs, the abbey is the oldest of London's great churches.

6:00pm Head to the Knightsbridge/Chelsea neighborhood Harvey Nichols department store. Its buzzing **Fifth Floor Bar** is one of London's most active meeting places.

8:30pm Walking to dinner along Sloane, Pont, and Walton streets makes you part of a fashion show. There's a long, catwalklike entrance to **The** ℞ **Collection**, where the stylish clientele prowl the bar and don't seem to care about the good fusion cuisine.

10:30pm After passing the bouncer's inspection at **Café de Paris**, near Piccadilly Circus, have a drink with another perfectly coifed crowd. Or, at **Stringfellows**, you might catch a couple in a semi-erotic dance at the bar stage. And remember Eliza Doolittle's words: "Move yer bloomin' arse!"

Alternatives

Near The Savoy is **One Aldwych**, a hotel in a classy, newly remodeled Edwardian building, featuring up-to-the-moment technology. **The Halkin** has sleek Italian style and an Armani-clad staff. The **Sheraton Belgravia** is a modestly sized hotel in an upscale and convenient neighborhood.

One of the Theater District's most popular restaurants, **The Ivy** serves nouveau Brit cuisine and fine wines. Like Mezzo, **Quaglino's** is another buzzing Sir Terence Conran establishment where the postmodern cuisine is matched by the decor. Not just a bar, Harvey Nichols' **Fifth Floor Restaurant** is said to be the only department-store restaurant with a "scene."

In Soho, try to get into the **Wag Club**. Once inside, you can mix with an attractive, energetic crowd dancing to music on two floors. A short walk away, hang out with Londoners of mixed ages for a dance and drink at the trendy **Limelight**.

Buy a seat, but plan to stand (more fun) and boo the actors at a matinee at the reproduced **Shakespeare's Globe Theatre**. The **Museum of London** will get you up to speed on London's history.

London offers much more than you can pack into three days, so try to schedule a return during the Notting Hill Carnival (see page 213).

The Royal Treatment

By far the best place to see and be seen at *Ascot* is in the Royal Enclosure. This requires that the Queen accept your written request for admittance. To apply, contact your country's embassy in London in January with something like this: "Mr. and Mrs. Finnaeus Bodsworth present their compliments to Her Majesty's Representative and would deem it an honor if they may be allowed the use of the Royal Enclosure for the Royal Ascot meeting from 21-23 June inclusive." You will receive notice a month before the races.

The Hot Sheet

☎ 44/171　　　　　　　　　　　　　　　　　　　　　　　　$ 0.6 Pound

HOTELS	DAY	ADDRESS	PH	PRICE	FX	RMS	BEST ROOMS
The Halkin	A	5 Halkin St., SW1	333-1000 888- 425-5464	$$$$+	333-1100	41	High up, gdn vw
One Aldwych	A	One Aldwych, WC2	300-1000 800- 447-7462	$$$$+	300-1001	105	Dlx dbl rm
The Savoy	1	The Strand, WC2	836-4343 800- 637-2869	$$$$+	240-6040	202	Thames vw
Sheraton Belgravia	A	20 Chesham Pl., SW1	235-6040 800- 325-3535	$$$$	259-6243	89	Gdn vw

RESTAURANTS	DAY	ADDRESS	*	PH	PRICE	REC	DRESS	FOOD
Arundel Restaurant	2	Ascot Racecourse	134	487-8599	$$	T/L	Euro	Nuvo European
The Avenue	2	7-9 St. James's St. , SW1		321-2111	$$$	D/L	Euro	Nuvo British
Bank	3	1 Kingsway , WC2		379-9797	$$$	L/D	Euro	Nuvo European
The Collection	3	264 Brompton Rd., SW3		225-1212	$$$$	D/L	Euro	Fusion
Fifth Floor Restaurant	A	109 Knightsbridge, SW1 in Harvey Nichols Dept. Store		235-5000	$$	L	Euro	British
The Ivy	A	1 West St., WC2		836-4751	$$$	LD	Euro	Nuvo British
Mezzo	2	100 Wardour St., W1		314-4000	$$$	D/L	Euro	International
Oxo Tower Restaurant, Bar & Brasserie	1	Oxo Tower Wharf Barge House St., South Bank, SE1		803-3888	$$$	D/L	Euro	Modern, traditional British
Quaglino's	A	16 Bury St., SW1		930-6767	$$$	DL	Euro	Nuvo European
The River Restaurant	2	see The Savoy hotel		836-4343	$$	B/LD	Euro	International
Tate Gallery Restaurant	1	Millbank, SW1 Tate Gallery		887-8877	$$	L	Local	British
The Thames Foyer	1	see The Savoy hotel		836-4343	$$	T	Euro	Tea

NITELIFE	DAY	ADDRESS	*	PH	PRICE	REC	DRESS	MUSIC
Brigadier Gerard Bar	2	Ascot Racecourse behind the Grandstand	134	487-8555	None	H	Dressy	
Café de Paris	3	3-4 Coventry St., W1		734-7700	$$	O	Euro	House, garage
Fifth Floor Bar	3	109 Knightsbridge, W1		235-5000	None	HF	Euro	
Garden Bar	2	Ascot Racecourse behind the Grandstand	134	487-8555	None	H	Dressy	
K-bar	2	84-86 Wardour St., W1		439-4393	$$	O	Euro	House, dance
Limelight	A	136 Shaftesbury Ave., WC2		434-0572	$	O	Euro	House, garage
Ronnie Scott's	2	47 Frith St., W1		439-0747	$$	M	Euro	Jazz
Royal National Theatre	1	South Bank, SE1		452-3000	$$$$	S	Kazh	
Shakespeare's Globe Theatre	A	New Globe Walk, Bankside, SE1		902-1500	$	S	Kazh	
shoeless joe's	1	Temple Place Embankment, WC2		240-7867	None	PF	Euro	Funk, soul, pop
Stringfellows	3	St. Martin's Ln., WC2		240-5534	$$	O	Euro	Disco
Wag Club	A	35 Wardour St., W1		437-5534	$	O	Euro	Rock, jazz, Latin, '60s R&B

SIGHTS & ATTRACTIONS	DAY	ADDRESS	PH	ENTRY FEE
Fortnum & Mason	1	181 Piccadilly, W1	734-8040	None
Museum of London	A	London Wall, EC2	600-3699	$
Tate Gallery	1	Millbank, SW1	887-8000	None
Tower of London	3	Tower Hill, EC3	709-0765	$$
Westminster Abbey	3	Broad Sanctuary, SW1	222-5152	$

OTHER SIGHTS, SERVICES & ATTRACTIONS

Moss Bros.	1	27 King St., WC2	240-4567	None
Tourist Information Centre		Victoria Station, SW1		None

*134=Ascot

RECommendations: (Restaurants) B–Breakfast; L–Lunch; D–Dinner; T–High tea or snack
(Nitelife) G–Gaming; H–Hangout bar; M–Live music; O–Dancing (disco); P–Dancing (live music); S–Show; F–Food served
()–Available but without recommendation. For complete explanation of Hot Sheet format, see page 34.

EVENT & TICKET INFO

Royal Ascot (Ascot Racecourse): Grandstand and Paddock tickets ($54-$70) can be purchased from *Ascot Racecourse* (44/134-487-6456) after January 1. Silver Ring ($12-$16.50) and Heath ($3.25) tickets are easy to obtain, but seats aren't assigned unless they're booked for groups of 12 or more.

🕐 NYC +5　　☀ 53°/69° (12°/20°)　✈ London Heathrow (LHR); 45 min./$60 (R)
London Gatwick (LGW); 90 min./$75 (R)　　🚗 No　　👥 English

Horsing Around

In their never-ending pursuit to answer the question "Which is faster," people have pitted just about everything they could find against each other. They've raced cars and boats and planes and just about every kind of animal they could drag to a starting line, including frogs, pigs, fleas, and dairy cows. Even human centipedes and kids balancing eggs on spoons have been called upon to outrace the competition!

But no contest ever has equaled the regal drama of horse racing. Horse racing speaks a language that stretches across international boundaries because it embraces so many attributes innate to the human character—love of animals, passion for competition, appreciation of beauty and pageantry, and, most importantly, the urge to back up an opinion with a wager.

From the sporting strongholds of Europe and the Americas to country tracks in obscure villages all over the globe, millions of fans attend horse races each year. The premier events range from the graceful dignity of England's historic English Derby at Epsom Downs to Siena's centuries-old scramble for honor through a medieval Italian piazza (see page 203). The sport has been inextricably woven into the cultural fabric on virtually every continent. (Okay, so there's no Antarctic Stakes, but don't be surprised if someday somebody organizes it.)

Horse racing as we know it was born in England during the 1600s. From Charles II to Queen Elizabeth II, royals have had a three-century fixation on equine competition, both as spectators and participants—thus, the phrase "sport of kings." English noblemen began developing the Thoroughbred racehorse 300 years ago, importing hot-blooded stallions from the deserts of the Middle East and crossing them with their sturdy native mares. Generations of selective breeding have resulted in the sleek-limbed runners that populate the major racetracks of the world today. While other equine breeds, such as the quarter horse and Appaloosa, are matched in tests of speed, the Thoroughbred remains the undisputed king of the track.

For 125 years, the **Kentucky Derby**, often referred to as "the most exciting two minutes in sport," has been North America's foremost horse race. Run at Churchill Downs in Louisville, Kentucky, on the first Saturday of May, it's contested before some 100,000 supercharged spectators. While the Derby has captured the public's imagination, its sister races—the **Preakness Stakes** in Maryland and the **Belmont Stakes** in New York—also draw huge crowds. Together, these races constitute the American Triple Crown—a challenge so demanding that only 11 horses in 12 decades have won the honor.

Despite its fame, the **Kentucky Derby** is neither the oldest, most lucrative, nor most important racing event on the international stage. Some would argue that the *real* Derby is run thousands of miles from Kentucky, in the country where modern horse racing was born. The legendary **English Derby** has been held at Epsom Downs since 1780. Each June, this supreme test of speed and stamina brings together many of Europe's best three-year-olds to run on grass over the trying mile-and-a-half distance. From nobles to commoners, thousands turn out to behold this historic spectacle, a pageant of high fashion and fun, which has been described as "the last genuine folk festival left to the British."

The event synonymous with racing royalty is **Royal Ascot** (see page 155). Established in 1711 by the order of Queen Anne, Ascot has become a national institution and its combination of elegance and excitement has made it an integral part of Britain's social calendar. France's most important horse race, **L'Arc de Triomphe**, held in Paris, has much the same feel, but without the royal patronage.

The Irish enjoy horse racing almost as much as they enjoy Guinness, and they get their fill of both at the **Irish Derby** at The Curragh, Ireland's less stately counterpart to the dignified Epsom Derby. The track in County Kildare has hosted some of the great equine contests of the world over the race's 134-year history.

Australia's famed **Melbourne Cup** offers a more down-to-earth, fun-filled take on the sport. First run in 1861, this two-mile marathon annually draws huge crowds to the magnificent Flemington Race Course in Victoria and a massive, worldwide television audience. For the nine days preceding the event, visitors are treated to the Melbourne Cup Carnival, an extravaganza that includes arts and cultural events as well as world-class shopping. On Cup Day, virtually everything in Victoria comes to a halt in honor of the big race.

The fourth Sunday in November each year, Japan holds its premier event, the **Japan Cup**, at Tokyo Racecourse. Run for the first time in 1981, the $3-million race annually attracts an international crowd—both human and equine—

to experience the Olympiclike festivities that include playing the winner's national anthem. Race organizers bring unsurpassed color and pageantry to Cup Day in the form of mounted police, marching bands, and drill teams. This race also enjoys a well-deserved reputation for sparking one of the sport's great betting spectacles.

The newest entrant on the global racing scene is the $5-million **Dubai World Cup**. Run each March, the race was launched in 1996 by members of the ruling family of the United Arab Emirates. While wagering is not allowed in this devoutly Muslim country, visitors nevertheless are treated to the exotic flavor of the Middle East along with an unforgettable equine spectacle.

Finally, there's the **Breeders' Cup**. Made up of eight races, this North American phenomenon is held in October and November at a different track annually. The Cup was inaugurated in 1984 as the "Super Bowl of Racing," but the "World Cup of Racing" would be more appropriate. Without fail, outstanding equine runners, leading horsemen, and innumerable lovers of the sport from all over the world arrive each fall to take part in this international championship day of racing and to celebrate the universal appeal of horse racing.

HORSE RACING'S GREATEST MOMENTS				
Race	Country	Month	Purse	Phone #
Dubai World Cup	United Arab Emirates	Mar.	$5 million	97/1-432-2277
Kentucky Derby	USA	May	$1 million	502-636-4400
Preakness Stakes	USA	May	$1 million	410-542-9400
Belmont Stakes	USA	Jun.	$1 million	718-641-4700
English Derby	England	Jun.	$1.6 million	44/137-247-0047
Irish Derby	Ireland	Jun.	$700,000	35/34-544-1205
L'Arc de Triomphe	France	Oct.	$1.25 million	33/14-910-2030
Breeders' Cup (eight races)	USA	Oct./Nov.	$1–$4 million	800-722-3287
Japan Cup	Japan	Nov.	$3 million	81/33-503-8221
Melbourne Cup	Australia	Nov.	$2 million	800-775-2000

Roskilde Rock Festival

(Roskilde Festival)

Origin: 1971   Event ★ ★ ★ ★ ★ City   Attendance: 90,000

A thousand years ago, the Vikings headed out from Roskilde to pillage, plunder, drink, and generally party in someone else's backyard. Now it's payback time! Every year, more than 65,000 music fans from around the world descend on this historic Danish town to rock out at the world-famous *Roskilde Festival*, four days and nights of rock, techno music, and excessive consumption of whatever it is that makes them feel good.

Europe's premier outdoor music festival, *Roskilde* delivers the best rock and dance music, as well as a cross section of up-and-coming bands from various countries. During the celebration, some 150 bands play on seven stages, ranging from the comparatively intimate Roskilde Ballroom to the enormous, covered Green Stage and open-air Orange Stage. Nearly three decades of fine-tuning have put this festival in a league of its own—the festival even boasts its own railway station. Filled with food stalls, art installations, bars, restaurants, and crowds of banner-waving fans, *Roskilde* is an unforgettable trip.

In response to public feedback, organizers have been progressively downsizing the event since 1998. This is good news for anyone who has ever attempted to navigate from one end of the grounds to the other without a compass. Fewer people, a more compact site, better food, environmental programs, and improved sanitary facilities have been a hit with the festival-goers.

The town of Roskilde is steeped in Danish heritage and boasts a fine cathedral, Viking ship museum, and compact town center. But only half an hour away lies Copenhagen, Scandinavia's largest city with a population of about one million. A city of green copper spires, lush parks, sparkling harbors, canals, pedestrian streets, and busy outdoor life, the Danish capital is the ideal home port for the festival. Long Scandinavian evenings, summer sun (with luck), and some of the best lager in the world combine to make this the ultimate time to visit Denmark.

Day-By-Day Plan For

Roskilde Rock Festival

Day 1. Thu.   Jun. 29, 2000
(Day 1. Thursday   June 28, 2001)

9:00am With its antique furnishings and Old World charm, Copenhagen's **Hotel d'Angleterre** is your festival base. As you check in, keep an eye out for famous faces—you may see them later on the Orange Stage at *Roskilde*.

10:00am Put off the festival until tomorrow and take the day to explore Copenhagen. A walk along Stroget (a busy pedestrian shopping mall) to the **National Museum** takes in views of the Stork Fountain, Houses of Parliament, and various canals. The museum houses the entire original interior of a Victorian home, among other treasures of Denmark's past.

11:30am At nearby Gammel Strand, join a **Canal Tours Copenhagen**. Jumping ship at the (very) Little Mermaid, head to the impressive steam-blasting oxen of the Gefion statue.

1:30pm Cab via the Royal Palace of Amelienborg to ® lunch at **Cap Horn**. The menu features light, French-style organic cuisine.

3:30pm A stroll up the shopping street of Købermagergade leads you to the **Museum Erotica**. Some might call it the Museum of Pornography—the "electric tabenakel" shows silent skin flicks set to classical music—but it's inarguably an eye-opening part of Copenhagen!

4:30pm Catch quality street performances and have drinks at **Café Klaptræet**, a popular pavement cafe in Kultorvet.

6:00pm Cab to **Tivoli** gardens, which has been called "the world's most famous amusement park." Save the hassle of buying individual tickets and buy a ride pass as soon as you get in the gates.

8:30pm Tivoli is packed with eating places, but ® **Fregatten Sct. Georg III** takes the biscuit. Housed in an old ship on Tivoli's lake, it offers nouvelle cuisine.

11:30pm Head back into town and sample the nightlife. **Club Mantra** pumps out the latest dance beats. For a rock alternative with a crowded dance floor, cab to **Rust Spisehus**.

Day 2. Fri.   Jun. 30, 2000
(Day 2. Friday   June 29, 2001)

10:00am After breakfast at your hotel's **Restaurant** ® **Wiinblad**, cab to the Central Station and catch the train to Roskilde. Buy a yellow *Klippekort* pass—it's less trouble than buying tickets for every journey. Travel light.

11:00am Have a look around the city of Roskilde. Close to the station is **Roskilde Cathedral**. Dating from the 10th century, it houses the remains of 37 of Denmark's monarchs.

Noon Take an early lunch at nearby **Restaurant** ® **Raadhuskælderen**, once an ancient wine cellar. The herring dishes are a Danish treat. Book a table in advance.

1:30pm The **Viking Ship Museum** displays five different vessels and the exhibits are fascinating. If you're feeling adventurous, you can row in a reconstructed ship.

3:00pm Cab to the *Roskilde Festival*. Exchange your ticket for an armband, pick up a beer and a pair of earplugs, and you're ready for action. The rule of thumb is follow your ears, but for decent views, position yourself in front of any particular stage about 30 minutes before performances. Stay clear of the first few rows unless *hyperactive* describes your personality type.

8:00pm *Roskilde* is justifiably proud of its food.
Ⓡ Particularly tasty are the Thai and health-food stalls. Sit at an outdoor table and watch lights illuminate the massive Orange Stage while you eat.

10:00pm New in 1999 were two techno stages that boasted the latest in sound technology. Listen to the sounds of the world to come.

1:00am From the Festival Railway Station, ride to Roskilde Station, then take the next train to Copenhagen.

Day 3. Sat. Jul. 1, 2000
(Day 3. Saturday   June 30, 2001)

10:00am Walk to Gammel Torv where **Café Europa** puts
Ⓡ out a fine breakfast. Or, a brunch at trendy **Café Victor** should put you back together. It opens at 11 a.m.

Noon Walk to Kongens Have and take in the exhibits at the newly refurbished **Museum of Modern Art**.

1:00pm Visit the nearby Rosenborg Castle, which houses the Danish crown jewels and is surrounded by the royal gardens. The in-house restaurant—its
Ⓡ unwieldy name is shortened to **Rosenborg Café**— is known for good lunches.

2:00pm Head for the *Roskilde Festival*, grab a beer, and launch into the stream of revelers flowing from stage to stage. Don't be lured into buying a Viking hat—you'll regret it when you see 500 others later in the day! You won't be familiar with all the bands on the program—check out something from Scandinavia and you'll find there's more to the northern music scene than Abba.

4:00pm It's *Æbleskiver* time! Over the last 20 years, these doughnutlike treats have become the festival's most popular sweet. The stall is always busy, but it's worth the wait.

7:30pm Head to the eatery that smells the best. Use
Ⓡ your cell phone to call a taxi to pick you up in a couple of hours.

10:00pm Exodus! Fifty thousand people go home. The best money you'll have spent all weekend will be the cab fare to the station.

11:00pm Back in Copenhagen, stroll down atmospheric Nyhavn for a nightcap in one of the pavement cafes. The cozy **Elverhøj** is a good choice. Keep what's left of your ears alert for music—this is also the first weekend of the *Copenhagen Jazz Festival*.

Midnight Clink glasses with a friend or stranger, shout *Skål!* and loudly declare that you've seen the future of rock-and-roll and it sounded damn good!

Alternatives

*O*n the harbor sits **Nyhavn 71**, a four-star hotel that boasts fine views. Down the road, the **Hotel Phoenix** is a favorite with Roskilde's visiting rock stars. The top rooms have good views over the Oddfellow Palæet, a beautiful building.

*M*odern Danish and fusion restaurants are hot. In Tivoli, try the new **Restaurant PH**. If there's music on Tivoli's big lawn, **Divan 1** overlooks the show. In town, both **konrad** and **Etcetera** have caused a stir with the in-crowd. **KGB Restaurant & Vodkabar** is a cool place to hang out.

*A*n interesting scene is picking up around Skt. Hans Torv. The square is packed with outdoor tables at **Sebastopol**, a cafe/bar with good late breakfasts. **Pussy Galore's Flying Circus** is a trendy and friendly cocktail bar and restaurant.

*R*ock clubs are rather subdued during *Roskilde Festival*, but keep an eye out for posters or get listings from the free magazines at cafes. Good city venues are **Vega-Idealbar**, **Loppen**, and **Pumpehuset**. For a mellow night, **Copenhagen JazzHouse** is popular with a mixed-age crowd.

*C*openhagen hosts the *Copenhagen Jazz Festival* (late June or early July). The festival features about 500 concerts, many are free.

The Hot Sheet

☎ 45/3

$ 6.9 Krone

HOTELS	DAY	ADDRESS	PH	PRICE	FX	RMS	BEST ROOMS
Hotel d'Angleterre	1	34 Kongens Nytorv	312-0095 800- 223-6800	$$$$	312-1118	130	Nytorv Sq vw
Hotel Phoenix	A	37 Belgrade	395-9500 800- 888-4747	$$$$	333-9833	212	City vw
Nyhavn 71	A	71 Nyhavn	311-8585 800- 843-3311	$$$	393-1585	84	Harbor vw

RESTAURANTS	DAY	ADDRESS	*	PH	PRICE	REC	DRESS	FOOD
Café Europa	3	1 Amagertorv		314-2889	$	B/LD	Kazh	Quality cafe
Café Victor	3	8 Ny Østergade		313-3613	$$	B/LD	Yuppie	French, cafe
Cap Horn	1	21 Nyhavn		312-8504	$$	L/D	Kazh	Organic, international
Divan 1	A	see Tivoli		311-4242	$$$	LD	Kazh	Danish, French, Italian
Elverhøj	3	23 Nyhavn		332-0999	$$$	D/L	Yuppie	Seafood
Etcetera	A	8 Hovedvagtsgade		333-9997	$$$	D	Euro	Fusion
Fregatten Sct. Georg III	1	see Tivoli		315-9204	$$	D/L	Euro	Modern Danish
KGB Restaurant & Vodkabar	A	22 Dronningens Tværgade		336-0770	$$$	LD	Kazh	Modern international
konrad	A	12-14 Pilestræde		393-2929	$$$	LD	Euro	New European, Californian
Pussy Galore's Flying Circus	A	30 Skt. Hans Torv		524-5300	$$	D	Local	International, cafe
Restaurant PH	A	see Tivoli inside Glass House		375-0775	$$$	LD	Kazh	International
Restaurant Raadhuskælderen	2	1 Fondens Bro	46	36-0100	$$$	L/D	Kazh	Traditional Danish, French
Restaurant Wiinblad	2	see Hotel d'Angleterre		312-0095	$$$	B/LD	Euro	International
Rosenborg Café	3	4A Oster Voldgade		315-7620	$	L	Kazh	Modern Danish
Sebastopol	A	2 Guldbergsgade		536-3002	$$	BLD	Euro	French, Danish

NITELIFE	DAY	ADDRESS		PH	PRICE	REC	DRESS	MUSIC
Café Klaptræet	1	11 Kultorvet		313-3148	$	H(F)	Local	
Club Mantra	1	3 Bernstorffsgade		311-1113	$	O	Euro	R&B, soul, house
Copenhagen JazzHouse	A	10 N. Hemmingsensgade		315-2600	$	P	Local	Jazz, dance
Loppen	A	43 Bådsmandsstræde		257-8422	$	P	Kazh	Rock
Pumpehuset	A	52 Studiestræde		393-1960	$	P	Kazh	Rock
Rust Spisehus	1	8 Guldbergsgade		535-0033	$	O	Local	Rock, dance
Vega-Idealbar	A	40 Enghavevej		325-7011	$	P	Kazh	Rock, dance

SIGHTS & ATTRACTIONS	DAY	ADDRESS	*	PH	ENTRY FEE
Museum Erotica	1	24 Købmagergade		312-0311	$
Museum of Modern Art	3	48-50 Sølvgade		374-8494	$
National Museum	1	10 Ny Vestergade		313-4411	$
Roskilde Cathedral	2	Domkirkepladsen	46	36-6044	$
Tivoli	1	3 Vesterbrogade		315-1001	$
Viking Ship Museum	2	Strandengen	46	30-0200	$

OTHER SIGHTS, SERVICES & ATTRACTIONS

Canal Tours Copenhagen	1	26 Gammel Strand	313-3105	$
Copenhagen Tourist Information		1 Bernstorffsgade corner of Tivoli	311-1325	

EVENT & TICKET INFO

Roskilde Festival (Festivalpladsen): Tickets ($145) must be ordered by mail. Tickets are available beginning December 1, and usually sell out by March. Call the Tivoli Billetcenter (45/3-888-7014) for more information.

Alternative Event
Copenhagen Jazz Festival: Copenhagen Jazz Festival, 45/3-393-2013

---

*46=Roskilde

RECommendations: (Restaurants) B–Breakfast; L–Lunch; D–Dinner; T–High tea or snack
(Nitelife) G–Gaming; H–Hangout bar; M–Live music; O–Dancing (disco); P–Dancing (live music); S–Show; F–Food served
()–Available but without recommendation. For complete explanation of Hot Sheet format, see page 34.

🕐 NYC +6   ☀ 55°/85° (12°/30°)   ✈ Copenhagen (Kastrup) (CPH); 15 min./$35   🚗 No   👥 Danish

The Fun Also Rises

The Running of the Bulls

(Fiesta de San Fermín)

| Origin: c. 1600 | Event ★ ★ ★ ★ ★ ★ City | Attendance: 100,000 |

It only makes sense that Saint Fermín, the patron saint of fools, should be the namesake for the craziest, most dangerous, and greatest street party in the world. Even if you don't run with the bulls (you shouldn't—after all, it's the running *of* the bulls, not running *with* them) and are vehemently opposed to bullfighting, the atmosphere and spirit of this fiesta make it a six-star event on a five-star scale.

Capital of the Spanish province of Navarra, the city of Pamplona stages this bacchanalian event within its ancient walls of weathered stone. Most people don't even attempt to sleep as the streets of the Casco Viejo (Old Quarter) reverberate with around-the-clock festivities, each morning's rush of thundering hooves, and the shouts of half-sane thrill-seekers attempting to stay one step ahead of disaster.

While the *Fiesta de San Fermín* features other activities, the event's hallmark is the daily bull run, which creates an excitement and tension found at no other event in the world. Along with bullfights, jai alai matches, singing competitions, a carnival, outdoor dancing, and live music combine to create a continuous frenzy.

In Ernest Hemingway's day, the festival began at the auspicious hour of 7 a.m. on the seventh day of the seventh month. The official blastoff is now at noon on July 6 (opening festivities are a high point of the festival) and the party charges nonstop until midnight on July 14. On July 15, some die-hards not yet ready to believe the thrill is gone make a parody run up Santo Domingo Street in front of the beastly, early-morning bus.

In the foothills of the Pyrenees, Pamplona has about 200,000 people and provides a scenic, Old World backdrop. But it's only during *San Fermín* that the city waves its colors and attracts a pell-mell charge of visitors who come for a once-in-a-lifetime chance to play with the world's original party animals.

The Running of the Bulls

Day 1. Thu.   Jul. 6, 2000
(Day 1. Friday   July 6, 2001)

10:00am Check into the comfortable, luxury-class **Tres Reyes** hotel, where every room comes with a balcony. It's located in a perfect spot between Casco Viejo (Old Town) and the upscale San Juan district.

10:45am You have just enough time to finish picking up your wardrobe for the next 72 hours—white pants, white shirt (a souvenir T-shirt will do), red scarf and waist sash, and comfortable sandals or sneakers. If you haven't already done so, purchase a guidebook (schedule) to *San Fermín*, then head toward the Plaza Consistorial.

Noon In the Casco Viejo, you'll encounter the astonishing sight of thousands of people dressed in white, holding red bandannas over their heads. At precisely noon, the Mayor of Pamplona officially opens the festival with the words, *"Pamplonicos y Pamplonicas. Viva San Fermín!"* He then sets off a rocket signaling the 20,000 celebrants to tie their bandannas around their necks. This frees their hands to carry bottles of champagne and begin seven nonstop days of singing, dancing, and drinking.

2:00pm Walk to the Plaza del Castillo—the heart of activity during the festival—and have lunch at the venerable **Café Iruña**. Popular lore claims this was Hemingway's favorite cafe in Pamplona.

6:00pm Go to the **Windsor Pub**, a hangout for English-speaking bullfight aficionados. Talk with experienced visitors about the pros and cons of running with the bulls early the next morning. Then wander the streets of the Old Town and soak up the party atmosphere.

8:30pm Stroll a few blocks from the Plaza del Castillo to Calle Arrieta and dine at **Rodero**, an elegant, modern restaurant that serves traditional Spanish food.

10:00pm Head to the nearby Parque de la Cuitadela, where you should be able to find a seat on the grass to watch the 30-minute *fireworks display*. Afterward, wander along Paseo Sarasate, Pamplona's main promenade. It's a pretty area lined with trees, street entertainers, and vendors.

Midnight It's time to walk the course the bulls will soon be running. Start at the end, at the Plaza de Toros, traveling in reverse up Calle Estafeta. The street will be filled with revelers doing the same thing—usually *borracho* (drunk) 20-somethings. Along the way check out the action at **La Granja**, a popular bar on this famous stretch of road. End by joining the crowd gathered at the corrals where the bulls spend the night—they seem harmless enough, but then again, they're asleep.

2:00am As with every night of the fiesta, you have a number of options: You could dance in the plaza; lounge at a cafe; hang out at a bar; head to the fairgrounds for food, carnival games, and rides; or get some much-needed sleep.

Day 2. Fri.   Jul. 7, 2000
(Day 2. Saturday   July 7, 2001)

6:00am Whether you run or watch the *encierro*, you'll need to position yourself about an hour beforehand. This means you'll have about 58 minutes to reconsider your decision whether or not to run. At some point during the weekend, try to catch the traditional *dainas*, a daily, 7 a.m. performance in front of city hall by the festival's official brass band.

8:00am At the two blasts signaling the beginning of the run, chaos erupts, and three tons of bull pass by you in a matter of seconds. Your adrenaline, of course, will be pumping for much longer.

8:30am A great way to relax after the morning's excitement is with a dozen *churros* from **La**

ℛ **Mañueta**. You can watch this bakery cooking their *churros* in a wood-burning oven—the same way they've done it for the last 125 years. Take your bag of grub back to Plaza del Castillo, order a coffee, and eat at one of the cafes.

Noon End your stroll through the Plaza Consistorial in time to catch the passing **Procesión de San Fermín** in which *gigantes y cabezudos* (large papiér-mâche figures) join city dignitaries, musicians, and an icon of Saint Fermín in a march through town.

1:30pm Off the Plaza del Castillo on Calle Espoz y
ℛ Mina, have lunch at **Europa Restaurante**. The Spanish cuisine here is traditional and imaginative.

3:30pm Make a trip to the **Catedral**, the 14th- and 15th-century creation James Michener called "the ugliest beautiful church in the world." Through the magnificent French Gothic cloisters you can enter the **Museo Diocesano**. Its carved doorways and chapels are particularly stunning. Just behind the cathedral are the old fortress walls, or ramparts. You can walk along portions and take in an expansive view of the Arga river valley and the Pyrenees beyond.

5:00pm In the shadow of the ramparts, have a drink at **Mesón del Caballo Blanco**, a bar and restaurant with vaulted stone walls and a medieval feel.

6:30pm The whole point of running the bulls is to get them to the bullring for the **Feria del Toro**. Get a seat in the shade to watch this spectacle that's part passion play, part sporting event (see Juno: About Bullfighting, page 135).

9:00pm You've been living off snack food and drinks long enough—enjoy a first-class, Michelin-starred
ℛ meal at **Josetxo**, an extremely attractive and popular restaurant.

11:00pm After dinner, there's still time to make the **fireworks**. A different show is put on every night.

Midnight Head to Calle San Nicolás, where the high concentration of bars per square meter should keep you satisfied. Make an appearance at **Ulzama**, then keep on running for as long you can.

Day 3. Sat.   Jul. 8, 2000
(Day 3. Sunday   July 8, 2001)

7:00am For a complete **encierro** experience, get up early and head to the bullring. Grab a seat in one of the higher-level tiers and watch the grand entrance of the running bulls.

8:00am Inside the arena, the bulls are herded safely away while a crowd cheers on a few brave and/or drunk men who taunt, dodge, and even climb aboard stud steers outfitted with padded horns.

9:00am After the morning's excitement, have breakfast
ℛ at the tranquil and spacious **Café Nixa**.

11:00am Visit the **Museo de Navarra**. The four floors of this regional museum include Gothic and Renaissance art, Roman murals, and important works by Goya. From the windows you can see the corrals where the bulls are kept for the following day's *encierro*.

12:30pm Walk to the nearby **Iglesia de San Saturnino**, where 40,000 pagans were baptized from a well by Saint Saturnino. Stroll down from the Plaza Consistorial to Calle Comedias and have a *tapas*
ℛ lunch at **Roch**. If this 100-year-old establishment is too crowded, try the highly recommended **Baserri** around the corner, where they have exotic dishes such as ostrich with Calvados.

3:00pm The Parque Antoniutti's grass provides a mattress for today's siesta. Tune out or drift off to the sounds of local entertainers, who appear here regularly throughout the day.

5:30pm Back at the Plaza Consistorial, join up with the parade of musical bands and throngs of revelers as they make their ways back to the Plaza de Toros for the second round of the **Feria del Toro**.

9:00pm Dine at the elegant **Hartza**, which serves Navarrese and Basque dishes made with seasonal ingredients. The restaurant is managed by three sisters—their suggested menu is usually worth following.

11:00pm If the bull run hasn't been exciting enough, walk to the Calle Palacio where a young crowd (mostly Australians) hangs out waiting for one of their friends to climb the statue and leap into the crowd in the hopes of being caught. On the square, step into **La Mejillonera**. It's famous for its oysters, but it's also a lively bar. **Mesón de la Navarrería** is popular with expats and locals.

1:00am Head to Calle Jarauta, the heartbeat of San Fermín's unofficial festivities. If you tire of the music on the street, dance at the popular **Café-Bar**

Sai Koba. By now your eyes should match the color of your trademark sash, so stagger back to the hotel and cap off the fiesta of all fiestas with the siesta of all siestas. Hey, even Jake Barnes needed a vacation after this one.

Alternatives

*C*atering to the corporate and luxury traveler, the very modern **Hotel Iruña Park** is a good choice in the San Juan district. In the historic center of town, very close to the *ayuntamiento*, is the three-star **Maisonnave** hotel. At more than 100 years old, it has hosted many famous folk, including Ernest Hemingway and Ava Gardner.

A quiet breakfast over international newspapers, coffee, and homemade tarts can be enjoyed on Parque Taconera at **Alt Wein** (better known as El Vienés).

FOOLS RUSH IN

The fiesta exploded ... It kept up day and night for seven days. ... the things that happened could only have happened during the fiesta ... It seemed out of place to think of consequences during the fiesta. — The Sun Also Rises *by Ernest Hemingway*

Fiesta de San Fermín is the festival Ernest Hemingway made famous in his 1926 novel *The Sun Also Rises*, but you don't necessarily have to read the book (recommended) or risk getting gored (not recommended) to enjoy or understand the event.

With strict punctuality, a gunshot initiates the run of the bulls at 8 a.m. every day from July 7-14. Six bulls are released from their corrals each morning. When all the bulls are out of the corrals, a second shot signals the start of the run. The bulls are supposed to run as a group, which makes the event somewhat safe, but if a third shot is heard, it means a renegade bull is causing trouble and you should do your best to get off the road. The entire **encierro** is over in less than ten minutes.

Bullfights involve the audience to a degree, but the **encierro** can turn spectators into death-defying participants by subjecting them to the caprices of half a ton of horned, hoofed, heaving, hormone-stoked muscle. Along with the Pamplonan *mozos*

(young men) who take part in daily runs, 5,000 visitors—part of the 20,000 or so non-Pamplonans who attend each run—are crazy enough to join in. Terrified and exhilarated, they taunt and/or run with six bulls along a one-and-a-half-mile course leading through the cobbled streets from Plaza Santo Domingo to the city's main bullring.

Both the bulls and the daring young runners encounter steep, uphill climbs; 90-degree curves; narrow passageways; downhill sections; and, finally, a small tunnel that funnels the bulls into a large arena. The animals make the run in less than three minutes, more than twice the speed of the average man. The bulls will go past you, over you, or through you. The experts say that if you fall to the ground (usually the result of being knocked over by other runners), stay down. Most people get back up, which is why every year at least one human is gored or even killed. Take this as an official warning.

If you still plan to run, try for a spot at the top of Calle Santo Domingo. If you end up on Calle Estafeta, you'll be among hundreds of other anxious runners who are invariably disappointed when police clear the entire street just prior to the run—disappointed, but perhaps lucky.

The Fun Also Rises

The Hot Sheet

☎ 34/948

$ 150 Peseta

HOTELS	DAY	ADDRESS	PH	PRICE	FX	RMS	BEST ROOMS
Hotel Iruña Park	A	1 Arcadio María Larraona	17-3200	$$$	17-2387	225	Exterior rm w/ mtn or city vw
Maisonnave	A	20 c/ Nueva	22-2600	$$$	22-0166	138	Interior rm
Tres Reyes	1	Jardines de la Taconera	22-6600	$$	22-2930	168	Balc facing Old Town

RESTAURANTS	DAY	ADDRESS	PH	PRICE	REC	DRESS	FOOD
Alt Wien	A	Parque Taconera	21-1912	$	BLT	Kazh	Cafe
Baserri	3	32 c/ San Nicolás	22-2021	$	L/D	Local	Spanish, *tapas*
Café Iruña	1	44 Pl. del Castillo	22-2064	$	L/BDT	Kazh	Spanish, cafe
Café Nixa	3	2 Duque de Ahumada	22-5958	$	B/LTD	Kazh	Cafe, *tapas*
Europa Restaurante	2	11 c/ Espoz y Mina	22-1800	$$	L/D	Euro	Traditional Spanish
Hartza	3	19 c/ Juan de Labrit	22-4568	$$$$+	D	Euro	Navarrese, Basque
Josetxo	2	1 Pl. Príncipe de Viana	22-2097	$$$$	D	Dressy	Navarrese, Basque
La Mañueta	2	c/ La Mañueta	22-7627	$	B	Local	*Churros*
Roch	3	6 Comedias	22-2390	$	L/TD	Local	Spanish, *tapas*
Rodero	1	3 c/ Arrieta	22-8035	$$$$+	D/L	Dressy	Spanish

NITELIFE	DAY	ADDRESS	PH	PRICE	REC	DRESS	MUSIC
Café-Bar Sai Koba	3	96 c/ Jarauta	21-1586	None	H(F)	Kazh	
La Granja	1	71 c/ Estafeta	22-7911	None	H(F)	Kazh	
La Mejillonera	3	12 Navarrería	22-6636	None	H(F)	Local	
Mesón de la Navarrería	3	15 Navarrería	21-3163	None	H(F)	Local	
Mesón del Caballo Blanco	2	c/ Redín	21-1504	None	H(F)	Kazh	
Ulzama	2	12 c/ San Nicolás	22-2095	None	H(F)	Kazh	
Windsor Pub	1	3 Pl. del Castillo	22-5079	None	H(F)	Local	

SIGHTS & ATTRACTIONS	DAY	ADDRESS	PH	ENTRY FEE
Catedral	2	3-5 c/ Dormitalería	21-0827	$
Iglesia de San Saturnino	3	c/ San Saturnino	22-1194	None
Museo de Navarra	3	Cuesta de Santo Domingo	42-6492	$
Museo Diocesano	2	3-5 c/ Dormitalería	21-0827	$
Tourist Information Office	1	c/ Hilarión Eslava	20-6540	

EVENT & TICKET INFO

Feria de San Fermín (various locations around Pamplona): All events, except for the bullfights, are free. For information, call the *Tourist Office of Spain* in New York (212-265-8822).

Feria de Toro (Plaza de Toros): Tickets ($25-$75) are sold out well in advance but you can: Ask your concierge, try the bullring ticket windows for returns, check with scalpers at the bullring (prices drop after bullfights begin), or ask around at the Windsor Pub.

RECommendations: (Restaurants) B–Breakfast; L–Lunch; D–Dinner; T–High tea or snack
(Nitelife) G–Gaming; H–Hangout bar; M–Live music; O–Dancing (disco); P–Dancing (live music); S–Show; F–Food served
( )–Available but without recommendation. For complete explanation of Hot Sheet format, see page 34.

🕐 NYC +6   ☀ 63°/86° (17°/30°)   ✈ Pamplona (PNA); 15 min./$10   🚗 No   👥 Spanish

Bastille Day

| Origin: 1789 | Event ★★★★★★★ City | Attendance: — |

The French have such a unique way of enjoying life that you can't even describe it in English. Singularly French concepts such as *joie de vivre*, bon vivant, and chic are *de rigueur* for anyone wanting to fully experience Parisian life. This is especially true on July 14, when **Bastille Day**, France's most important national holiday, fans local passions for food, wine, and music, and transforms Paris into civilization's greatest stage for the sensory pleasures of life.

Bastille Day commemorates the common people's 1789 siege of the infamous Bastille prison with cries of *Liberté! Égalité! Fraternité!* But it's modern Parisians' devotion to *Café! Vin! Amour!* that really makes this celebration memorable. On July 13, a dozen Parisian firehouses throw street parties until about 1 a.m. Afterward, most revelers stay out until the lights come up at clubs in the Marais, Pigalle, Left Bank, and Bastille districts (*arrondissements*). Outside, wine-happy crowds dance and sing in the streets throughout the city.

On **Bastille** morning, a huge military parade proceeds down the Champs-Élysées as airplanes swoop over the great avenue. Celebrations spread throughout the city—particularly festive are the Latin Quarter, Montparnasse, St-Germain-des-Prés, and, of course, the Place de la Bastille. Evening fireworks and music and an incredible sound-and-light show, often starring the Eiffel Tower at its spectacular best, mark the beginning of another night of noisy gatherings in streets and clubs.

Paris never fails to leave even veteran travelers awestruck. The City of Light is home to much of the world's greatest art, food, fashion, and architecture. The Louvre, Eiffel Tower, Arc de Triomphe, and Notre-Dame cathedral are just a few of the obvious (and recommended) attractions. But the real Paris hides in small shops down narrow alleys, in cafes along bustling streets, and in the Gaelic faces of its citizens who understand Paris' greatest gift—the ability to celebrate the best of life every day of the year.

Bastille Day

Day 1. Thu.   Jul. 13, 2000
(Day 2. Friday   July 13, 2001)

9:00am Settle into the contemporary elegance of the *beaux-arts* **Hôtel Montalembert**, located in one of Paris' most fun neighborhoods on the Left Bank.

10:00am Acquaint yourself with the St-Germain-des-Prés area and Latin Quarter by strolling from your hotel to **Café de la Mairie** for *café au lait* and a croissant. From the sunny terrace, you can gauge the pulse of the Left Bank as locals circulate past the St-Sulpice church in the Place St-Sulpice, both designed by Louis-Joachim Visconti.

11:00am Wander through the Jardin des Tuileries and relax amid its ponds and fountains.

Noon Just steps from the Tuileries, stop for Mediterranean cuisine at **L'Absinthe**. You can order any wine on the list by the glass, bottle, or half-bottle. Start your meal with a gazpacho of asparagus and langoustine or a terrine of feta cheese, tomato, and aubergine. Get a table outside among the fashionable Parisians and enjoy the magnificent views.

2:00pm Walk to the **Musée du Louvre** for a truly daunting experience. This titanic museum is more than 2,000 feet long on one side and boasts some of the most famous art pieces and antiquities in the world. Built as a fortress in 1200, the structure was turned into a museum in 1793—new halls and the controversial glass-pyramid foyer have been added since. Important pieces such as the *Mona Lisa* and *Venus de Milo* dot the museum, so prioritize your visit and don't expect to see everything.

5:30pm Cross the Pont-Neuf to Île de la Cité. At the eastern end of the island sits the French-Gothic **Notre-Dame de Paris** (of hunchback fame). Check out the splendid views from its famous towers. Behind the cathedral, street performers and musi-cians set up entertainment on the Pont St-Louis. As you stroll over to the Île St-Louis, take note of which ice cream vendor is drawing the biggest crowd and get in line.

8:30pm One of Paris' hottest restaurants, the subterranean **Le Buddha Bar**, meshes East and West with its decor and menu. A mammoth, golden Buddha presides over a dining room of theatrical proportions, where the in-crowd dines while listening to international tunes. Watch celebrities, royalty, and models from the balcony bar before or after your meal.

10:30pm The official party kicks off at the Place de la Bastille, but you'll have more fun at any of the dozen or so parties that the city's fire brigades and paramedics throw in front of fire stations around Paris (check newspapers or ask your hotel concierge for locations).

1:00am Cab to the red-light district and set the dance floor on fire at one of Pigalle's thriving nightspots. On the eve of *Bastille*, the clubs will be packed. Not for the timid, the half-gay-half-straight **Folies Pigalle** has a wild bunch dancing to house music in a former cabaret. You'll find professional types out for cocktails at **Le Dépanneur**. Next door, **Le Moloko** has a small dance floor where you can dance until dawn.

Day 2. Fri.   Jul. 14, 2000
(Day 3. Saturday   July 14, 2001)

9:00am After a room-service breakfast, taxi to the Champs-Élysées, where the French military launches its annual, two-hour *Bastille Day Parade and Air Show*. Many of the choice spots along the avenue are reserved for local dignitaries, so claiming a patch of pavement with a view of the procession can be a challenge. To nab a preferred place, show up well before the 10 a.m. start time.

12:30pm Head for lunch at **Ladurée**, a classic French bistro with *belle-époque* decor that caters to a young, international set. Ask for an outside table, but be sure to check out the pastry display inside.

2:30pm Take a Seine river cruise. Sure, it's touristy, but it's a great way to see this beautiful city. The one-hour **Bateaux Mouches** tour leaves every half-hour.

4:00pm No trip to Paris would be complete without a visit to **Centre Georges Pompidou**, the glass-and-chrome edifice that holds the national modern-art museum. Afterward, stroll through the surrounding Les Halles, once the food-and-flower market.

8:00pm Taking a blanket to the Parc du Champ-de-Mars and dining on a baguette and wine is a dinner option that also provides a good view of the fireworks set behind the Eiffel Tower. Or enjoy a light meal at the quintessential Parisian brasserie, **La Coupole**. Wait for the fun center tables and have oysters or langoustine while seated under beautiful murals by Liger.

10:30pm With luck (the show varies each year), you'll catch one of the most elaborate and beautiful fireworks, music, and laser shows you're likely to see. Choose a spot in the center of the Champ-de-Mars by 10 p.m.

11:15pm Have dinner at **Zébra Square**, a popular restaurant and rendezvous that attracts a well-dressed crowd. The delicate French-Mediterranean cuisine is superb.

12:45am Twirl through the Left Bank, Latin Quarter, Marais, or Champs-Élysées. The Bastille area is especially riotous, along with clubs throughout the city. **Les Bains**, a disco in a converted Turkish bathhouse, is still popular after many successful years. Or try **Barfly**, a cosmopolitan hipster hangout.

Day 3. Sat. Jul. 15, 2000
(Day 1. Thursday July 12, 2001)

9:00am Literary celebrities such as Faulkner, Alberto Moravia, Sartre, Simone de Beauvoir, and Hemingway once gathered under the gaze of **Les Deux Magots**, the statues of two Chinese wise men that give the cafe its name. You could experience the feel of a Parisian day simply by eating all your meals here, but just do breakfast for now. **Le Café de Flore** is another "Lost Generation" haunt that's still going strong. An outside table at either of these cafes is coveted for its views of shoppers and gawkers.

10:30am The art collection at the immense **Musée d'Orsay** concentrates on works created between 1848 and 1914. You'll probably recognize many of the impressionist and post-impressionist pieces at this beautiful, glass-ceilinged onetime railway station.

1:00pm For 40 years, clients have gorged themselves on **Le Dauphin**'s generous helpings of traditional French fare. Don't let the bistro's multilingual menu put you off—the service is attentive, house wine tasty, and food delicious, whether a la carte or *prix fixe*.

3:00pm Cab to the Parc du Champ-de-Mars. At the northwest end, you'll find all 984 feet of **La Tour Eiffel**. Approach through the park and then ascend—through 7,000 tons of steel—to the landmark's third platform for stunning views of central Paris. From the tower, cross the Pont d'Iéna, then veer left toward the Jardins du Trocadéro for another Eiffel view. Head northeast to reach **L'Arc de Triomphe** in the Place Charles-de-Gaulle. For more City of Light viewing, ride the elevator to the top of the Arc, where you can see the great avenues and boulevards of Paris fanning out like spokes on a wheel.

8:00pm After a hotel break, stroll along the Left Bank to **Paul Minchelli**, which lures the likes of Emanuel Ungaro, Pierre Bergé, and Catherine Deneuve, for perfect seafood dishes in a sophisticated setting of leather and chrome.

10:00pm Join in the nightly promenade along Avenue Montaigne and the Avenue des Champs-Élysées. Drop into **Cabaret** for an after-dinner *digestif* and dancing in this former strip joint. Veterans of the nightclub and modeling biz opened this beautiful-people mecca, which is decorated with sensual scarlet, black, and gilt.

12:30am Taxi to the legendary **Moulin Rouge** in Montmartre. Sip champagne and imagine the days of Josephine Baker, when even the hint of a bared breast was scandalous. Today, 60 Doriss Girls enthrall visitors with a blur of plumage, satire, glitter, songs, whirling skirts, bared breasts, and, of course, the very cancan this cabaret made famous.

2:00am After watching the Moulin Rouge action, you can dance next door at **La Locomotive**. You're sure to find music to jostle your caboose on at least one of the three floors. Just don't retire without one last triumphant *Liberté! Égalité! Fraternité!*

Alternatives

From a design perspective, **Hotel Square** is the city's hippest hotel, but its location just west of the Eiffel Tower is somewhat out of the way. The **Hotel Costes** has a popular cafe and is the home away from home for many fashion models. You can never go wrong with the world-famous **Hotel Ritz**, which has bedded the likes of Winston Churchill and Coco Chanel.

The trendiest cafe in Paris, **Le Fumoir**, is across from the Louvre. To enjoy one of the world's greatest views while dining, go to **Altitude 95** in the Eiffel Tower; for the world's greatest meal, it's **Taillevent**. **Au Pied de Cochon** (a polite way of saying pig-trotters) is a lusty brasserie open 24 hours. For a great lunch spot with a bustling terrace, try **La Palette**, a favorite with art dealers. The mirrored walls, faux-leather banquettes, and modern touches at **Les Bookinistes** attract the super-chic. **Régine's**,

a true nightclub, offers swanky dining and dancing, with a decor straight out of a 1960s gangster film.

Often-overlooked, the delightful **Musée Rodin** fills both floors of a grand, 18th-century residence with celebrated bronze and marble sculptures by Auguste Rodin and Camille Claudel. The statues spill out back into a cool, green garden. Both the historically Jewish but now-gay Marais district and the **Musée Picasso** located there are worth a visit.

Throughout France, *La Fête de Musique* celebrates the beginning of summer on June 20. Paris is a special place to be for the event, as musicians take to the streets and play throughout the day all over the city—sometimes awful, sometimes exciting, always fun.

The world's most famous prison

Originally built to protect the palace of King Charles V during France's Hundred Years' War with England, the infamous Bastille, which lends its name to France's top national holiday, was used as a prison. Because so many people were incarcerated without trials and at the whim of the king and his officials, it came to represent the monarchy's arbitrary power. When a mob of citizens seized the hated fortress on July 14, 1789, they struck a blow for the common people (and ultimately for partyers everywhere). They not only executed the governor and freed seven inmates, their actions marked the end of the monarchy and the beginning of the republic. Delegates from all over France flocked to Paris the following year to commemorate the Fête de la Fédération and proclaim their allegiance to one nation. Adoption of a tricolor flag and composition of the beloved "La Marseillaise" anthem of national unity, further strengthened the French national identity. In 1880, the French government proclaimed Bastille Day a national holiday, and Frenchmen and the world have been celebrating ever since.

The Hot Sheet

☎ 33/1 $ 6.1 Franc

HOTELS	DAY	ADDRESS	PH	PRICE	FX	RMS	BEST ROOMS
Hotel Costes	A	239 rue St-Honoré	4-244-5050 800- 448-8355	$$$$+	4-244-5001	83	Dlx crtyd vw
Hôtel Montalembert	1	3 rue de Montalembert	4-549-6868 800- 628-8929	$$$$+	4-549-6949	56	Dlx Louis Phillipe rm
Hotel Ritz	A	15 pl. Vendôme	4-316-3030 800- 448-8355	$$$$+	4-316-3668	175	Dlx gdn vw
Hotel Square	A	3 rue de Boulainvilliers	4-414-9190 800- 525-4800	$$$	4-414-9199	22	Dlx river vw

RESTAURANTS	DAY	ADDRESS	PH	PRICE	REC	DRESS	FOOD
Altitude 95	A	see La Tour Eiffel	4-555-0021	$$$$	LD	Euro	French
Au Pied de Cochon	A	6 rue Coquillière	4-013-7700	$$$	BLTD	Euro	Brasserie
Café de la Mairie	1	8 pl. St-Sulpice	4-326-6782	$$	B/LD	Kazh	Cafe
L'Absinthe	1	24 pl. du Marché-St-Honoré	4-926-9004	$$$	L/D	Euro	French
La Coupole	2	102 bd. du Montparnasse	4-320-1420	$$$$	D/BL	Euro	Classic French
La Palette	A	43 rue de Seine	4-326-6815	$$	L/B	Euro	French
Ladurée	2	75 av. des Champs-Élysées	4-075-0875	$$$	L/BTD	Euro	Classic French
Le Buddha Bar	1	8 rue Boissy d'Anglas	5-305-9000	$$$$+	D	Euro	Asian
Le Café de Flore	3	172 bd. St-Germain	4-548-5526	$$	B/LD	Kazh	Cafe
Le Dauphin	3	167 rue St-Honoré	4-260-4011	$$$	L/D	Euro	Classic French
Le Fumoir	1	6 rue de l'Amiral-de-Coligny	4-292-0024	$	T/LD	Euro	Cafe
Les Bookinistes	A	53 quai des Grands Augustins	4-325-4594	$$$	LD	Euro	Bistro, international
Les Deux Magots	3	6 pl. St-Germain-des-Prés	4-548-5525	$$	B/LD	Kazh	Cafe
Paul Minchelli	3	54 bd. de la Tour Maubourg	4-705-8986	$$$$+	D/L	Euro	Seafood
Taillevent	A	15 rue Lamennais	4-561-1290	$$$$+	D/L	Dressy	Classic French
Zébra Square	2	3 pl. Clément-Ader	4-414-9191	$$$$	D/L	Euro	French, Mediterranean

NITELIFE	DAY	ADDRESS	PH	PRICE	REC	DRESS	MUSIC
Barfly	2	49 av. George V	5-367-8460	None	H(F)	Euro	
Cabaret	3	68 rue Pierre-Charron	4-289-4414	$	O	Euro	Dance
Folies Pigalle	1	11 pl. Pigalle	4-036-7158	$$	O	Euro	House, disco
La Locomotive	3	90 bd. de Clichy	5-341-8888	$$	O	Euro	Rock, techno, disco
Le Dépanneur	1	27 rue Fontaine	4-016-4020	None	H	Euro	
Le Moloko	1	26 rue Fontaine	4-874-5026	None	O	Euro	House, disco
Les Bains	2	7 rue de Bourg l'Abbe	4-887-0180	$$	O	Euro	Techno, disco
Moulin Rouge	3	82 bd. de Clichy	5-309-8282	$$$$+	S(F)	Euro	Cabaret
Régine's	A	49-51 rue de Ponthieu	4-359-2160	$$	P(F)	Dressy	Popular hits

SIGHTS & ATTRACTIONS	DAY	ADDRESS	PH	ENTRY FEE
Centre Georges Pompidou	2	pl. Georges Pompidou near Forum des Halles	4-478-1233	$
L'Arc de Triomphe	3	pl. Charles-de-Gaulle Étoile	5-537-7377	$
La Tour Eiffel	3	Parc du Champ-de-Mars	4-550-3456	$
Musée d'Orsay	3	1 rue de Bellechasse	4-049-4814	$
Musée du Louvre	1	rue de Rivoli	4-020-5317	$
Musée Picasso	A	5 rue de Thorigny	4-271-2521	$
Musée Rodin	A	77 rue de Varenne	4-705-0134	$
Notre-Dame de Paris	1	6 pl. du Parvis	4-234-5610	$

OTHER SIGHTS, SERVICES & ATTRACTIONS

	DAY			
Bateaux Mouches	2	Alma Bridge near Métro Alma-Marceau	4-225-9610	$
Paris Tourism Bureau		127 av. des Champs-Élysées	4-952-5341	

EVENT & TICKET INFO

Bastille Day (various locations around Paris): All official events—firehouse parties, fireworks, and the parade—are free. For information, contact the *Paris Convention and Visitors Bureau* (33/14-952-5395).

Alternative Event

La Fête de Musique: Paris Convention and Visitors Bureau, 33/14-952-5395

REComendations: (Restaurants) B–Breakfast; L–Lunch; D–Dinner; T–High tea or snack
(Nitelife) G–Gaming; H–Hangout bar; M–Live music; O–Dancing (disco); P–Dancing (live music); S–Show; F–Food served
()–Available but without recommendation. For complete explanation of Hot Sheet format, see page 34.

🕐 NYC +6   ☀ 58°/76° (14°/25°)   ✈ DeGalle (CDG); 60 min./$40
Orly (ORY); 30 min./$35   🚗 No   👥 French

Nice Jazz Festival

Origin: 1948   Event ★ ★ ★ ★ ★ ★ City   Attendance: 49,000

It's summertime in the Northern Hemisphere and the sophisticated set knows there's no hotter spot on earth than the French Riviera. And there's no better time to enjoy this legendary playground than during the *Nice Jazz Festival*, the cherry atop the hedonistic sundae served in Nice all summer long.

The *Festival* has hosted the world's best musicians for more than 50 years. Superstars as diverse as Dizzy Gillespie, Nina Simone, the Neville Brothers, James Brown, Jean-Luc Ponty, Tony Bennett, and Chuck Berry come for the same reason the crowds do—nothing beats the French Riviera in summer. Some 200 performers keep the party humming, especially at night, as warm temperatures and seductive music swirl through the Romanesque ruins at Cimiez where the concerts are held.

Days in Nice are for lounging, tanning, swimming, and checking out the scene on the Promenade de Anglais, the crowded stretch along the shore that travel writer Rick Steves has called a "seafront circus" of Europeans at play. The long strand of palm-lined beach, faded pastels of the grand hotels, crowded cafe terraces, white sails against deep Mediterranean blues, beautiful Maritime Alps, chiseled bodies of some of the world's most gorgeous sun worshipers ... these are the sights that keep visitors returning to this gem on the Côte d'Azur.

A notch back from the waterfront, Old Nice reverberates with activity. Narrow passages and crazy, doglegged streets open into bright, irregular piazzas. Merchants offer samples of local olives and cheeses, and restaurateurs lure customers with robust wines and hearty regional fare. In Nice, you don't need a map to know you're only a stone's throw from Italy and a world away from Paris.

With a year-round population of about 450,000, Nice is the largest city along the Riviera. It's a terrific base for exploring the area's many museums (no wonder artists such as Matisse and Picasso were drawn to the area) restaurants, and nightlife that set the standard for the world.

Nice Jazz Festival

Day 1. Fri.   Jul. 14, 2000
(Day 1. Friday   July 13, 2001)

10:00am The comfortable **Hotel Beau Rivage** has two big advantages—a great location on the edge of Old Nice and a private beach (actually, a deck above Nice's rocky beaches).

11:00am Stroll along Promenade des Anglais. The beach and boulevard stretch about four miles along the spectacular Mediterranean. Slip into one of the ℞ irresistible terrace cafes, such as **Le Koudou**, for a typically French lunch.

3:00pm Taxi to Cimiez, where the Romans built thermal baths and arenas on the hilltop in the 1st century B.C. Today, the Roman amphitheater, which seats about 5,000 people, is used for shows including the ***Jazz Festival***. Cimiez is also home to two small but interesting museums, the **Musée Matisse** and the **Musée du Message Biblique Marc Chagall**.

5:30pm The ***Jazz Festival*** doors swing open. As you wander between the three venues within the arena, stop by one of the food stalls for a sampling of local ℞ delicacies. The party atmosphere around the food area makes it a good place for meeting people.

10:30pm The music continues until midnight, but taxi ℞ into Nice for dinner at **La Mérenda**, a bistro famous for its chef, Dominique Le Stanc, and his Provençal cuisine. You'll need to make reservations in person early in the day—the eatery has no phone, takes only cash, and is closed on weekends.

Midnight After dinner, hit the Promenade des Anglais. **Le Relais** and **Le Mississippi** are great piano bars with relaxed atmospheres.

1:00am Make your way to Juan-les-Pins, one of the wildest scenes on the Riviera. About 30 minutes from Nice, the town buzzes with clubs, late-night restaurants, and people (mostly younger) checking out other people. Just wander around and find the place that suits your taste.

Day 2. Sat.   Jul. 15, 2000
(Day 2. Saturday   July 14, 2001)

10:00am Walk west along the Promenade des Anglais. Follow the boulevard to the opera house and turn left on Rue de la Terrasse, then take a right into Cours Selaya, one of the best marketplaces in the south of France. You'll find yourself among happy locals and merchants and row after row of brilliant flowers, produce, cheeses, and freshly baked ℞ breads. Snack on pastry and fruit in the market or have coffee and a croissant at one of the outdoor cafes lining the plaza.

Noon Head west on Rue St-François-de-Paule past the lovely *belle-époque* Opéra. Turn right on Rue de l'Opéra, and check out Place Masséna and Jardin Albert I.

1:00pm Take a taxi to Place Garibaldi for lunch at **Chez** ℞ **René**, where it's mandatory to try the *socca*, a chickpea crepe that's a local specialty. Eat with locals at the picnic tables across the street.

2:30pm Visit the **Musée d'Art Moderne**. The beautiful modern structure houses a fascinating collection of unusual works.

5:00pm Relax on a deck chair or walk through Old Nice and its market.

7:30pm The ***Jazz Festival*** is heating up as it enters prime time. Pick the performance you want to catch, grab a snack, and stake out a spot to enjoy the music and mellow vibe.

11:00pm L'Escalinada, in the heart of Old Town, has a crowded terrace, lively atmosphere, and good food. After dinner, wander through the streets of Old Nice for a look at a hearty culture that is uniquely Niçois.

1:00am Check out the action at **Bar des Oiseaux**, where a young, stylish crowd makes this a popular late-night hangout. Then head to **L'Iguane Café** where you can dance to a Latin beat.

Day 3. Sun.　July 16, 2000
(Day 3. Sunday　　　　July 15, 2001)

8:30am Have coffee and pastries at the hotel, then drive to the nearby village of St-Paul-de-Vence. Since being popularized in the 1920s by painters, sculptors, and other artists, this picturesque town has become one of the most visited in France. Park outside the walled village and walk through the north gate to explore the many art galleries, antiques shops, and artists' studios on the main drag.

Noon Have lunch at **La Colombe d'Or**, where the food is terrific but still plays second fiddle to the museum-quality art on the walls. Many artists, including Picasso and Miró, probably enjoyed the same dishes —rack of lamb, chicken fricassee, and almond tarts among them.

2:00pm Just outside town, visit the **Maeght Foundation**, a modern-art museum with one of the most extraordinary sculpture gardens in the world. You'll see mobiles by Calder and ceramics by Miró.

6:30pm Indulge in a final day of jazz. Bring a picnic and stay through dinner to enjoy the last wistful notes of music, the warm evening air, and the first stars of night twinkling on the ancient ruins of Cimiez.

10:00pm At the **Grand Café de Turin**, a popular spot on Place Garibaldi, you'll see lots of hip and artsy locals. The seafood is great.

Midnight Wind down (or up) at **Le Safari** on Cours Saleya. It's one of the best local spots for people-watching. Observe the crowded market transform into an open plaza and the free-form spirit inspired by the festival's musicians take hold of the crowd.

Alternatives

For the quintessential Riviera experience and a considerably heftier tab, stay at the four-star **Negresco** hotel. This grande dame of Nice offers the most commanding views of the bay. **Château des Ollières**—once the neo-Moroccan palace of Prince Alexi Lobanov-Rostowsky—is now a luxury inn with just eight guest rooms. The restaurant and tropical gardens are delightful, though noise from the nearby road is a trade-off. Six miles east of Nice lies Villefranche-sur-Mer, a tiny harbor village that has maintained much of its 13th-century charm despite being featured in several James Bond films. At **Hôtel Welcome** you can stay in a room formerly occupied by Jean Cocteau, Somerset Maugham, or Richard Burton.

Auberge des Arts is a good option for upscale dining. The casual **Nissa Socca** serves local specialties at great prices.

A good place to have a drink and meet English-speaking visitors and expats is **Chez Wayne**. You can try your luck at **Casino Ruhl**, which has a limited choice of games, American-style bar, and dinner theater.

July 14 is Bastille Day, France's most celebrated national holiday. Check with the concierge to find out whether there are special events in the area that may be worth a change in itinerary. To round out the picture of the Riviera, be sure to look at the Hot Sheets for both Cannes (see page 136) and Monte Carlo (see page 143).

The Hot Sheet

☎ 33/49

$ 6.1 Franc

HOTELS	DAY	ADDRESS	PH	PRICE	FX	RMS	BEST ROOMS
Château des Ollières	A	39 av. des Baumettes	215-7799	$$$$+	215-7798	8	Tower rm
Hôtel Beau Rivage	1	24 rue St-François-de-Paule	247-8282 800- 223-5652	$$	247-8283	118	Dlx sea vw
Hôtel Welcome	A	quai Courbet	376-2762	$$	376-2766	32	Sea vw
Negresco	A	37 promenade des Anglais	316-6400 800- 223-6800	$$$$+	316-6440	143	Sea vw, rms 312, 412

RESTAURANTS	DAY	ADDRESS	PH	PRICE	REC	DRESS	FOOD
Auberge des Arts	A	9 rue Pairolière	385-6353	$$$	LD	Euro	Provençal
Chez René	2	2 rue Miralhetti	392-0573	$	L/D	Kazh	Niçois
Grand Café de Turin	3	5 pl. Garibaldi	362-2952	$$	D	Euro	Seafood, Provençal
L'Escalinada	2	22 rue Pairolière	362-1171	$$	L/D	Kazh	Niçois
La Colombe d'Or	3	pl. du Gaulle, in St-Paul-de-Vence	332-8002	$$$	L/D	Kazh	French
La Mérenda	1	4 rue de la Terrasse	no phone	$$$	D	Euro	Niçois, Provençal
Le Koudou	1	33 La Croisette	387-3374	$	L/BD	Local	International, cafe
Nissa Socca	A	5 rue St-Réparate	380-1835	$	LD	Kazh	Niçois

NITELIFE	DAY	ADDRESS	PH	PRICE	REC	DRESS	MUSIC
Bar des Oiseaux	2	5 rue St-Vincent	380-2733	None	H	Euro	
Casino Ruhl	A	1 promenade des Anglais	387-9587	$$	GHF	Euro	
Chez Wayne	A	15 rue de la Préfecture	313-4699	None	MOP(F)	Kazh	Rock, British pop
L'Iguane Café	2	5 quai des Deux Emmanuel	356-8383	$	OP	Euro	Salsa
Le Mississippi	1	5 promenade des Anglais	382-0661	$$	MO	Euro	Piano bar, disco
Le Relais	1	see Negresco hotel	316-6400	None	M	Euro	Piano bar
Le Safari	3	1 cours Saleya	380-1844	None	H(F)	Euro	

SIGHTS & ATTRACTIONS	DAY	ADDRESS	PH	ENTRY FEE
Maeght Foundation	3	623 chemin Gardettes	332-8163	$
Musée d'Art Moderne	2	pl. Yves-Klein	362-6162	$
Musée du Message Biblique Marc Chagall	1	av. du Dr-Ménard	353-8720	$
Musée Matisse	1	164 av. des Arènes-de-Cimiez	381-0808	$
Bureaux d'Accueil de l'office du Tourisme		5 promenade des Anglais	214-4800	

EVENT & TICKET INFO

Nice Jazz Festival (Cimiez): One-day tickets ($31) or three-day passes ($71) should be purchased in advance by calling the *Office du Tourisme de Nice* (33/49-214-4800).

RECommendations: (Restaurants) B–Breakfast; L–Lunch; D–Dinner; T–High tea or snack
(Nitelife) G–Gaming; H–Hangout bar; M–Live music; O–Dancing (disco); P–Dancing (live music); S–Show; F–Food served
( )–Available but without recommendation. For complete explanation of Hot Sheet format, see page 34.

🕐 NYC +6   ☀ 66°/81° (19°/27°)   ✈ Nice/Côte d'Azur (NCE); 15 min./$25   🚗 Yes/No   🗣 French

The Fun Also Rises

Montreux Jazz Festival

Origin: 1967	Event ★ ★ ★ ★ ★ City	Attendance: 220,000

How does a jazz festival with relatively little jazz in a town with very little to do become one of the world's best events? The gorgeous setting on the shores of Lake Geneva (Lac Léman) certainly helps, but it's the intimacy of the venues and the world-class jam sessions until dawn that ultimately steal the show.

With the magnificent Swiss Alps as a backdrop, the *Montreux Jazz Festival*—known as the grande dame of jazz festivals—blossoms every July into 16 glorious days and nights of world-class music. From noon until dawn, music lovers and international party people move and groove between the festival's two concert halls and the three outdoor stages of the *Festival-Off*. The Auditorium Stravinski and Miles Davis Hall host more than 80 major acts, while the best college and amateur big bands and ensembles from the United States and Europe perform free at the outdoor venues. Encompassing everything from jazz, blues, rock, and soul to sounds from Brazil, Latin America, and Africa, the festival hosts the world's top artists and keeps fans continually choosing between seeing favorite groups and checking out what's new and hot on the world circuit.

The festival area is filled with stalls selling jewelry, souvenirs, and an incredible array of food. In the subtropical climate of what has been called the Pearl of the Swiss Riviera, palm and cypress trees flourish and the Quai (lakeside promenade) invites visitors to wander amid botanical gardens and stunning scenery. The main stage is set atop the Quai, and with 200,000 people passing by, it's the best place to hang out and catch the pulse of the festival.

Located in the canton of Lake Geneva, Montreux has a population of about 20,000 and is a relatively short distance from breathtaking attractions. Plentiful buses, boats, and trains allow festival-goers to explore the entire region without missing a beat of the evening festivities.

Montreux Jazz Festival

Day 1. Thu. Jul. 20, 2000
(Day 1. Thursday *July 19, 2001)*

Swiss Rail (CFF) services Montreux from the Geneva airport with a scenic one-hour ride along Lake Geneva.

11:00am Arriving in Montreux, cab to the stylish and modern **Royal Plaza Inter-Continental** hotel. Situated on the lakeside promenade next to the Congress Center (site of the festival's main stage), it's a short walk to anywhere in Montreux, and the lake view is spellbinding.

Noon Walk through the festival site to **Le Palais** (also called **Le Hoggar**), a brightly colored Middle Eastern restaurant. Like just about everything else on the menu, the hummus is delicious. A pot of fresh-brewed mint tea is a must.

3:00pm Head back toward the hotel along the Grand Rue, dropping by the Congress Center for an early look at festival activities. Follow the walkway along the terrace to one of the three lakeside ***Festival-Off*** stages—Kiosque a Musique de la Rouvenaz, Terrasse Stravinski, or Terrasse Petit Palais. Music starts every day at noon and features a selection of college and amateur bands from around the world.

6:00pm Dine on the patio of the hotel's **La Croisette**. Its light and summery atmosphere, not to mention the excellent food, make for a memorable meal. A good selection of local wines is available.

8:00pm Although concerts usually begin at 8:30 p.m., wander around the Congress Center a little early on your first night to get a feel of the ***Montreux*** magic.

1:00am Stop at **Harry's New York Bar**, the late-night haunt of celebrities. Open until 5 a.m., it's the place to be for late-night dining or just to wind down after the evening's concert.

3:00am If you don't feel like sleeping, follow the aroma of freshly baked bread to **Aux Délices**.

Day 2. Fri. Jul. 21, 2000
(Day 2. Friday *July 20 2001)*

9:00am Make your way to **Romance** for the breakfast buffet. Try the *meuslix*, but leave room for a chocolate croissant. *Café au lait* on the outdoor terrace is an invigorating way to get the day moving.

10:00am Head to the bus stop a few steps from the hotel entrance and board the bus for **Château de Chillon** (immortalized by Lord Byron's *The Prisoner of Chillon*). Castle tours provide insight into the history of the region as well as spectacular countryside views.

Noon Leaving the château, walk along the promenade to **La Terrasse de l'Eden au Lac** and have lunch in the garden. Serving specialties from the local waters, this is one of Montreux's finest restaurants and a favorite lunch spot for locals.

2:00pm Continue walking along the Quai to the outdoor stage at La Rouvenaz and listen to ***Festival-Off*** bands. Treat yourself to a Mövenpick ice cream, one of the best ice creams you'll ever taste.

3:30pm On the Grand Rue, hop a bus for the short ride to Vervey, a former home of Charlie Chaplin. The lakeside statue dedicated to his memory is the best place to begin your tour of this quaint town.

6:30pm Head to the **Montreux Palace Hôtel**. Its famous grand staircase reflects Montreux's Old World charm. Attend a free ***acoustic concert*** in the Petit Théâtre. Performances usually feature one of the festival's premier pianists. While the music plays, admire the beautiful decor and spacious sitting rooms. This is an ideal place to meet for cocktails and quiet conversation.

7:30pm Exit through the rear onto the Avenue des Alpes and walk to **La Couronne** (also called **il Brigantino**). A small Italian restaurant complete with red-and-white-checkered tablecloths, it serves traditional Mediterranean dishes. The *frutti de mere* is outstanding.

9:00pm From La Couronne it's a short walk to the acoustically perfect Auditorium Stravinski. Whatever performers are on stage, the show is sure to be magical.

Midnight To see a different side of the festival, head to the **Montreux Jazz Café** on the ground floor of the Congress Center. The crowd is young and lively, the music is loud, and there's always a party atmosphere. Performers come here to jam after their sets, so you might wind up dancing until the early hours.

2:00am Back at the Inter-Continental, **Duke's Bar** stays open until 5 a.m. and is legendary for its late-night jam sessions. This is one of the best places in Montreux to hear music or to meet people. And your room is only an elevator ride away.

Day 3. Sat.   Jul. 22, 2000
(Day 3. Saturday   July 21, 2001)

10:00am Order room-service breakfast and eat on your balcony. Then walk to the train station for a ride by cog-wheel train to Rochers-de-Naye, 6,700 feet above Montreux. The trip takes about an hour each way and the panoramic views of the region are stunning.

1:00pm Lunch at **Plein Roc** mountain restaurant. You can sample traditional dishes such as raclette (melted cheese served on a plate with boiled potatoes and sour pickles) while taking in more amazing views.

5:00pm From the deck of a ferry steamer, check out the towns along the lake on your way to Lausanne and the Beau Rivage Hôtel, one of the region's finest accommodations. Enjoy an aperitif and the sunset from the **Café Beau Rivage**. Then get set for

a true French gastronomic experience at **La Rotonde Restaurant**.

11:00pm The somewhat intimate Miles Davis Hall is just beginning to heat up for what is always a marathon ending to the **Montreux Jazz Festival**. Along with some of the world's most accomplished musicians, be sure to stay up for the grand finale—another beautiful sunrise over Lac Léman.

Alternatives

If you attend the first weekend of the festival you can ride on the **gospel**, **salsa**, or **samba boats**. Each offers a supercharged way to have fun on the lake with 2,000 other music and party lovers.

The five-star **Montreux Palace Hôtel** is the most elegant and expensive hotel in Montreux. Scenic views from its luxurious rooms, fine restaurants, and terraces make this *belle-époque* jewel as good a choice as the Royal Plaza Inter-Continental. With first-class amenities, the Victorian-style **Hôtel Eden au Lac** is a short walk from festival activities.

For fine dining away from the center of town, try **L'Ermitage**.

A number of excursions from Montreux are available by boat or train. Favorite stops include Evian (the source of the famed water), Lausanne (the Olympic Museum), and Gruyéres (as in the cheese). Each of these towns is attractive and worth a visit if time permits.

The Hot Sheet

☎ 41/21

$ 1.5 Swiss Franc

HOTELS	DAY	ADDRESS		PH	PRICE	FX	RMS	BEST ROOMS
Hôtel Eden Au Lac	A	11 rue de Théâtre		963-5151 800- 223-5652	$$$	963-1813	105	Gdn or lake vw
Montreux Palace Hôtel	A	100 Grand Rue		962-1212 800- 223-1230	$$$	962-1717	235	Lake vw
Royal Plaza Inter-Continental	1	97 Grand Rue		962-5050 800- 327-0200	$$$	962-5151	153	Lake vw

RESTAURANTS	DAY	ADDRESS	*	PH	PRICE	REC	DRESS	FOOD
Aux Délices	1	57 av. des Alpes		963-4795	$	T/B	Local	Bakery
L'Ermitage	A	75 rue du Lac, Clarens		964-4411	$$	LD	Local	International gourmet
La Couronne (il Brigantino)	2	102 av. des Alpes		963-3528	$$	D	Kazh	Italian
La Croisette	1	see Royal Plaza Inter-Continental		963-5131	$$	D/L	Euro	Gourmet
La Rotonde Restaurant	3	13 quai du Mont Blanc, Lausanne in Beau Rivage Hôtel	22	716-6666	$$	D	Euro	French
Le Palais (Le Hoggar)	1	14 quai de Casino		963-1271	$$	L/D	Kazh	Oriental, Middle Eastern
La Terrasse de l'Eden au Lac	2	11 rue de Théâtre		963-5551	$$	L/D	Kazh	Gourmet
Plein Roc	3	Rochers-de-Naye		963-7411	$	L	Kazh	Local cuisine
Romance	2	see Royal Plaza Inter-Continental		963-5131	$	B	Kazh	International

NITELIFE	DAY	ADDRESS	*	PH	PRICE	REC	DRESS	MUSIC
Café Beau Rivage	3	13 quai Du Mont Blanc, Lausanne in Beau Rivage Hôtel	22	716-6666	$	H	Euro	
Duke's Bar	2	see Royal Plaza Inter-Continental		962-5050	None	M	Kazh	Jazz, R&B
Harry's New York Bar	1	see Montreux Palace Hôtel		962-1212	None	MPF	Kazh	Jazz, R&B

SIGHTS & ATTRACTIONS	DAY	ADDRESS		PH	ENTRY FEE
Château de Chillon	2	Château de Chillon, Veytaux		966-8910	$
Montreaux Convention and Tourist Office		5 rue de Théâtre		962-8484	

EVENT & TICKET INFO

Montreux Jazz Festival: Auditorium Stravinski (Congress Center, 95 Grand Rue): The only seating is in the balcony ($65). Otherwise you must stand on the slanted main floor ($45). Miles Davis Hall (Congress Center): Tickets for orchestra seating ($45) and elevated standing-room areas ($35) are available. Seats usually sell out in advance, but tickets for standing room do not. There are usually three one-hour performances at each venue, with 30-minute intermissions.

Festival Off (all venues, including the Montreux Jazz Café and Petit Théâtre): Free

Gospel, **salsa**, and **samba boats**: Tickets ($25) sell out weeks in advance.

For tickets and information, call *Montreux Jazz Festival* (41/21-963-8282).

RECommendations: (Restaurants) B–Breakfast; L–Lunch; D–Dinner; T–High tea or snack
(Nitelife) G–Gaming; H–Hangout bar; M–Live music; O–Dancing (disco); P–Dancing (live music); S–Show; F–Food served
()–Available but without recommendation. For complete explanation of Hot Sheet format, see page 34.

NYC +6   59°/77° (15°/25°)   Geneva (GVA); 90 min./$20 (R)   No   French

The Fun Also Rises

All That Jazz

The Fun Also Rises FunGuide 100 reviews the four most fun jazz festivals in the world: the **Montréal Jazz Festival**, **Montreux Jazz Festival**, **New Orleans Jazz & Heritage Festival**, and **Nice Jazz Festival**. But there's no reason to stop there. Just about every major (and even many not-so-major) city now celebrates this musical genre.

What exactly is a jazz festival? Usually the event features multiple bands on multiple stages on multiple days, but that can vary. The **Jazz & Image Festival** in Rome has only one stage, tucked into a hill above the Coliseum, but presents jazz every summer night. Audiences sip Brunello with their pasta as they listen to the music on warm Italian evenings. In contrast, the **North Sea Jazz Festival** in Holland squeezes 68,000 audience members into the Hague Congress Center for 270 performances on 15 stages in just three days. The fare? Herring and beer, naturally. But, if the Dutch event is one of the largest and the Roman one of the longest, the smallest, briefest festival might be the one-day, one-act **Jazz in the Sangres**, presented in a tent on the town green in tiny West Cliffe, Colorado, each August.

There's no shortage of jazz holidays—from France to Finland, from Cuba to California— literally thousands of festivals celebrate the beloved American art form each year. The millions of pilgrims who attend these events attest to the prominence of jazz in 20th-century culture. Although the music sprang up in the American South, the jazz-festival tradition reaches back to jazz-mad France in 1948, when the high priests of the Hot Club of France produced the first such affair—the **Nice Jazz Festival**—headlined by Louis Armstrong. The following year, Paris hosted the Festival International du Jazz with performances by Charlie Parker and Miles Davis, among others.

In 1954, just five years after the bash in Paris, came the jazz event that would set the stan-dard for all to come—the Newport Jazz Festival, in Newport, Rhode Island (which continues today as the **JVC Jazz Festival Newport**). Since its inception, just about every jazz star has performed at Newport. Its genre-bending affairs of 30 years ago featured Frank Sinatra and Frank Zappa, alongside Duke Ellington and Sarah Vaughan. Nowadays, you can hear superstars and young lions, while soaking up a New England ambience redolent of clam chowder and lobster and full of beachfront mansions and elegant sailboats.

Two California events round out the selection of great American jazz festivals. The **Monterey Jazz Festival**, founded in 1958, takes place near the scenic coastline, 120 miles south of San Francisco, and always features the best mainstream jazz. Many world-première performances have been presented here over the years, including Duke Ellington's "Suite Thursday." The **Playboy Jazz Festival** sells out the huge Hollywood Bowl each year with stellar performers in classic and contemporary styles. Jazz fan Bill Cosby is often the master of ceremonies.

The French jazz connection has wound its way to the present-day **Antibes Jazz Festival**, commonly known as the Jazz a Juan, on the famous topless beaches of the country's southern coast. Farther north, the **JVC Jazz Festival Paris** presents concerts in classic venues such as the Théâtre Champs d'Élysées, Salle Pleyel, and Élysée Montmartre. In the Parisian early hours, you can catch a set at the New Morning jazz club. In addition to these notable events, France hosts more than 80 other jazz festivals each year!

Jazz festivals are as diverse as the music itself. Experimental and avant-garde styles are well represented at **Moers Music Festival** (Germany), while Dixieland, swing, and other early forms can be heard at **The Great Connecticut JazzFest**. But how about a festival high in the Japanese Alps? The **Newport Jazz Festival in Madarao** has been swinging Japanese audiences since 1984 on the grassy summer slopes of the Madarao ski area in Nagano, site of the 1998 Winter Olympics. Twenty-thousand-plus jazz lovers picnic on barbecued squid and *yaki soba* (fried noodles) while enjoying the festival's unique jam sessions, with musicians from different ensembles improvising together.

Romance is everywhere at the **Umbria Jazz Festival** in the hilltop city of Perugia, Italy. As you stroll through the narrow, spiraling streets, you may find a big band playing in the ruins of a medieval church, a piano solo at an outdoor restaurant, or a guitar trio beneath an Etruscan arch. For northern ambience, check out the **Pori Jazz Festival** in Finland. In a birch grove in Pori's city park, you can hear top international musicians as the sun sets—at 1 a.m.!

No legitimate review of jazz festivals could neglect New York, christened the Big Apple by swing-era musicians 60 years ago. The Apple hosts a dozen jazz fests each year, but the biggest is the **JVC Jazz Festival New York**. The event takes place at such hallowed venues as Carnegie Hall and the Lincoln Center, and also around Harlem, Greenwich Village, and Bryant Park in the heart of the city.

Salty types can dig their jazz while riding the high seas aboard the *Queen Elizabeth II*. The **QE2 Newport Jazz Festival at Sea** cruises up the Atlantic coast with world-class musicians performing on board. When the liner anchors at Newport, passengers are ferried directly to the granddaddy of them all—the **JVC Jazz Festival Newport**. Similar jazz-theme excursions abound worldwide, adding a little bit of "rock and roll" to the rich heritage of the jazz festival.

THE WORLD'S MOST FUN JAZZ FESTIVALS

Name	Location	Telephone	Month	Attendance
Montréal Jazz Festival	Montréal	888-515-0515	Jun.-Jul.	500,000
Montreux Jazz Festival	Montreux, Switzerland	41/848-800-800	Jul.	200,000
New Orleans Jazz & Heritage Festival	New Orleans	504-941-5100	Apr.-May	480,000
Nice Jazz Festival	Nice, France	33/49-214-4800	Jul.	49,000

15 MORE GREAT JAZZ FESTIVALS

Name	Location	Telephone	Month	Attendance
Antibes Jazz Festival (Juan-les-Pins)	Antibes, France	33/49-290-5300	Jul.	24,000
The Great Connecticut JazzFest	Moodus, Connecticut	800-468-3836	Aug.	17,000
JVC Jazz Festival New York	New York	212-501-1390	Jun.	82,000
JVC Jazz Festival Newport	Newport, Rhode Island	401-847-3700	Aug.	24,000
JVC Jazz Festival Paris	Paris	33/14-621-0837	Oct.	38,000
Jazz & Image Festival	Rome	39/06-580-6876	Jun.-Aug.	92,000
Jazz in the Sangres	West Cliffe, Colorado	303-794-4170	Aug.	2,000
Moers Music Festival	Moers, Germany	49/2-841-7741	May	100,000
Monterey Jazz Festival	Monterey, California	831-373-3366	Sep.	20,000
Newport Jazz Festival in Madarao	Madarao, Japan	81/33-216-2611	Aug.	23,000
North Sea Jazz Festival	The Hague, Holland	31/15-214-8900	Jul.	68,000
Playboy Jazz Festival	Los Angeles	310-449-4070	Jun.	35,000
Pori Jazz Festival	Pori, Finland	35/82-626-2200	Jul.	90,000
QE2 Newport Jazz Festival at Sea	New York	800-728-6273	Aug.	1,700
Umbria Jazz Festival	Perugia, Italy	39/75-573-2432	Jul.	200,000

Cowes Week

Origin: 1812	Event ★ ★ ★ ★ ★ City	Attendance: 30,000

"**R**ed eyes in the morning, sailors take warning!" That's the nautical maxim during *Cowes Week*, the world's largest international yacht regatta, an event that transforms the small town of Cowes on the Isle of Wight into a wild gathering of seamen and a frenzied meet market. For eight days in midsummer, a grand mix of 15,000 tourists, 4,000 boats, 200 races, 31 classes of sailboats, 10 yacht clubs, assorted royalty, fireworks, parties, and dances creates a championship presentation of wild fun.

From a line of ancient cannons, thunderous blasts reverberate each morning at five-minute intervals to mark the start of each race. The guns are fired off in front of the venerable Squadron Yacht Club, which borders the Solent—England's busiest yachting waterway and the scene of the week's racing. At day's end, the spirit of competitive camaraderie embraces the throngs and Cowes transforms into a massive party. Local pubs, restaurants, cafes, party tents, and discos all overflow with revelers. Most boats dock at Cowes Yacht Haven, where, during this week, partyers consume more beer than an average pub sells in a year. Special events include the black-tie *Cowes Week Ball* on Wednesday, lively *Crews Ball* on Thursday, and *fireworks* on Friday.

While sailors do battle on the water during the day, visitors tend to walk through the small town of Cowes watching each other watch each other. Historic treasures are scattered throughout the small Isle of Wight, which is a manageable 23 miles wide by 12 miles long. Among the more interesting finds are 120-million-year-old dinosaur fossils, Roman ruins, Carisbrooke Castle (where Charles I was kept before being beheaded), and Osborne House (Queen Victoria and Prince Albert's favorite residence). Local lore says Charles Darwin got his inspiration for *Origin of the Species* on a visit to the Isle of Wight. If that's true, it's just possible he timed his stay to coincide with the eight days of highly evolved partying of *Cowes Week*.

Cowes Week

Day 1. Wed. Aug. 2, 2000
(Day 1. Wednesday   August 8, 2001)

9:00am Start your journey (en route from London and/or London airports) in the picturesque town of Winchester. Park close to the **Winchester Cathedral**. A relic from Norman times, the famed church, which dates from 1079, includes tombs of saints, royalty, and the renowned Jane Austen.

Noon Lunch on fresh sandwiches and tea at the **King's Lounge**. Sit by the bank of windows to look at the imposing cathedral and its well-manicured grounds.

1:30pm Take in the atmosphere of Old England with a brief walk though town.

3:00pm Travel by auto to Lymington and take the **Wightlink Ferry** to Yarmouth, Isle of Wight. Car reservations are a must.

3:30pm For a refreshing spot of tea, drive a few minutes to **The George Hotel**. Weather permitting, ask to sit in the garden area at the rear of this 17th-century establishment to view the Solent (the waterway between the southern coast of England and the Isle of Wight).

4:30pm Motor along a two-lane road to the country-house-style **Swainston Manor** in Calbourne, where Old World style combines with spacious rooms and modern amenities. Rest in your room, then change into formal wear for tonight's party.

7:30pm Drive to the **Cowes Ball** for a champagne reception, dinner, cabaret show, and dancing until 2 a.m.

Day 2. Thu. Aug. 3, 2000
(Day 2. Thursday   August 9, 2001)

9:00am After breakfast at the hotel, get into the unofficial uniform of the yachting set: Top-Siders, chinos,

blue blazer (in case the weather gets cool), and a personalized polo shirt in bright nautical colors. A smashing tan will also help you fit in.

10:30am Proceed to Cowes and plan to be in town most of the day. Walk to the Squadron Yacht Club, where the signalman orders the firing of the cannons every five minutes (10:30 a.m.-12:30 p.m.) to start each race. Keep your eyes open for royalty who disembark in front of this historic center. Sit on the Green to watch the colorful yachts—15 to 50 feet long—tacking furiously on the Solent. Many of your fellow spectators will be locals. Most are talkative and filled with knowledge of boatmaking, sailing, and English yachting history.

Noon Walk to town along the Parade, which borders the waterfront along the Solent. Andean musicians add to the buzz of the crowd. Head up High Street for lunch at **The Union Inn**, where colorful old salts (and some young ones) hang out. Order the special of the day, usually a local fresh catch.

1:30pm Complete your tour of Cowes with a stroll along High Street to Cowes Yacht Haven. This is party central, with places to eat, drink, listen to music, and relax.

4:00pm The "yotties" are heading back into port. Rub shoulders with the racers as they lower sail and raise party spirits at Cowes Yacht Haven. Simply smiling and saying "hello" may get you invited to one of the boat parties.

6:30pm If you aren't up to the all-day-all-night pace, drive back to Swainston Manor for a nap.

8:30pm In your most outrageous sailing clothes, head to the **Crew Ball** at Northwood House and let your hair down along with the racing crews. The infectious spirit of team camaraderie—team members wear matching polo shirts—along with live music, decorations, and free-flowing drink, more than make up for the notoriously bad menu of beans and rolls. Fortunately, sandwiches can be bought. This party rocks and rolls—or pitches and heaves—as much as a stormy sea!

12:30am Hike into town and check out the action on High Street as well as the discos and live music at the Yacht Haven tent in the marina. Mount Gay Rum hosts a disco, which stays loud until 2 a.m. For a somewhat quieter atmosphere, try the semiprivate club above the main bar.

Day 3. Fri.   Aug. 4, 2000
(Day 3. Friday   August 10, 2001)

9:30am Breakfast at **Eegon Rodney's**, a magic shop and local hangout for comfort food. The lighthearted quips posted on the walls are sure to raise a laugh.

11:00am Drive to the Medina River, which splits the Isle of Wight in two, and take a car ferry to East Wight for a day of motoring around the area.

Noon In East Cowes, visit **Osborne House**, a favorite summer home of Queen Victoria and Prince Albert. Take a look at the private lives of this famous couple by touring the royal apartments, family rooms, and gardens.

1:30pm Lunch at **Wheatsheaf Hotel and Pub**, a 17th-century spot with 20th-century refinements in Newport, East Wight.

3:00pm Don't miss the medieval **Carisbrooke Castle**, where Charles I was briefly imprisoned before being beheaded in 1649.

4:30pm Return to Swainston Manor via a two-lane road bordered by woods, forests, and ponds. You should make it back in time for high tea.

7:00pm Put on comfortable clothes, grab a sweater, and go back into town. Park as close to the green as possible.

8:00pm Walk to the green to get a seat on the grass for the sundown *fireworks*. Rockets are launched from a floating raft anchored just off the Marine Esplanade. Almost as impressive is the light show from the brightly lit yachts bobbing up and down on the Solent.

10:00pm For dinner, go to **The Red Duster**, a place that closes when they run out of people. The restaurant is spirited and the menu is inviting, with starters such as smoked haddock or chive pancakes.

11:30pm Take one last stroll through still-partying Cowes before sailing off into the night.

Alternatives

A good hotel option is the **Villa Rothsay**, a small, family-run Victorian hotel with views of the Solent. The **New Holmwood Hotel**, located on the edge of the water at Egypt Point, has contemporary decor and comfortable rooms.

Instead of visiting Winchester Cathedral on the way to the Isle of Wight, you could have lunch at **Chewton Glen**. But be warned, Chewton Glen is one of the world's great destination resorts, so it may be tempting to stay all weekend. The **Capri Italian Restaurant** in Cowes is known for its traditional Italian fare. **Baan Thai Restaurant** is good for Thai food.

If you've got some time to spare, the outstanding natural beauty of **The Needles Pleasure Park** is worth a visit.

The Hot Sheet

☎ 44/1983

$ 0.6 Pound

HOTELS	DAY	ADDRESS		PH	PRICE	FX	RMS	BEST ROOMS
New Holmwood Hotel	A	Queens Rd., Egypt Point		29-2508	$$	29-5020	24	Dlx w/ sea vw
			800-	528-1234				
Swainston Manor	1	Calbourne, on the B3401		52-1121	$$	52-1406	20	Rms 1 and 9
Villa Rothsay	A	Bearing Rd.		29-5178	$$	29-0352	14	Sea vw

RESTAURANTS	DAY	ADDRESS	*	PH	PRICE	REC	DRESS	FOOD
Baan Thai Restaurant	A	10 Bath Rd.		29-1917	$	D	Local	Thai
Capri Italian Restaurant	A	Princess Bldg., Bath Rd.		29-5137	$	D/L	Local	Traditional Italian
Chewton Glen	A	New Milton, Hampshire	1425	27-5341	$$$	BLD	Euro	Nuvo continental
Eegon Rodney's	3	72 High St.		29-1815	$	B	Local	Homemade breakfast
The George Hotel	1	Quay St., Yarmouth		76-0331	$	T/LD	Kazh	Brasserie
King's Lounge	1	Paternoster Row, Winchester in Wessex Hotel	1962	86-1611	$	L/TD	Kazh	Traditional Italian, British
The Red Duster	3	37 High St.		29-0311	$	D/L	Kazh	Local British eclectic
The Union Inn	2	Watch House Ln.		29-3163	$	L/D	Local	Local seafood, traditional
Wheatsheaf Hotel and Pub	3	St. Thomas St.		52-3865	$	D/L	Local	Traditional British, steaks, Indian, vegetarian

SIGHTS & ATTRACTIONS	DAY	ADDRESS	*	PH	ENTRY FEE
Carisbrooke Castle	3	Newport		52-2107	$
Osborne House	3	East Cowes		20-0022	$
The Needles Pleasure Park	A	Alum Bay		75-2401	None
Winchester Cathedral	1	The Close, Winchester	1962	85-3137	$

OTHER SIGHTS, SERVICES & ATTRACTIONS

Wightlink Ferry	1		990	82-7744	$$$$+
Tourist Information		The Arcade, High St.		29-1914	

EVENT & TICKET INFO

Cowes Week (Cowes, Isle of Wight, United Kingdom): Tickets for both the **Cowes Ball** ($50, Northwood House), which includes a champagne reception, dinner, cabaret show, and dancing, and the **Crew Ball** ($34) are available by contacting the *Cowes Tourist Information Centre* (44/1983-29-1914).

RECommendations: (Restaurants) B–Breakfast; L–Lunch; D–Dinner; T–High tea or snack
(Nitelife) G–Gaming; H–Hangout bar; M–Live music; O–Dancing (disco); P–Dancing (live music); S–Show; F–Food served
( )–Available but without recommendation. For complete explanation of Hot Sheet format, see page 34.

NYC +5   55°/70° (13°/23°)   London Heathrow (LHR); 180 min./SNA
London Gatwick (LGW); 120 min./SNA   Yes   English

The Fun Also Rises

Stockholm Water Festival

Origin: 1991	Event ★ ★ ★ ★ ★ ★ ★ ★ City	Attendance: 1.1 million

Think of it as the ultimate Swedish meet ball. Although Stockholm remains the most underrated city in the world, this spectacular celebration—Sweden's largest annual event and one of the world's best festivals—is beginning to give this charming European capital the recognition it deserves. Not an alcohol-crazed shipwreck, *Water Festival* is an exuberant street party highlighted by a broad range of cultural events from around the world—a great place to meet people and have a ball.

Water is the theme—the bulk of *Water Festival*'s proceeds benefit the world's imperiled water resources—and Stockholm's pristine waterways and history as a Baltic Sea port are impressive. But it's the event's setting in the city's colorful historic center, the enchanting island of Gamla Stan (Old Town), that hooks most people.

Music is a main attraction. Local and international superstars bring music from every continent to spirited crowds—everyone from Johnny Cash to Smashing Pumpkins to King Sunny Ade has played the festival. Live theater, opera, comedy, and poetry performances also dot the schedule. One of the biggest splashes, the fireworks championships, is held over five nights—the thrilling displays are doubled by resplendent reflections in the water surrounding Stockholm.

During daylight hours, street theater crops up unexpectedly amid the festival throngs. Futuristic animals, stilt-walkers, and roving performers sometimes induct spectators into the act. Street musicians are everywhere. And don't forget the reason for all this celebrating. The Swedes use the wet stuff for inventive contests and games that never get old.

The festival is easy to negotiate. A single Water Pass grants access to all events and just about everything is in English. The only difficulty is deciding how to fit everything you want to do into your schedule. Stockholm, with an area population of about 1.5 million, is one of the world's most beautiful cities, inhabited by some of the world's most attractive people. Clean streets, well-groomed parks, endless cafes and clubs, and friendly people provide plenty of walker-friendly diversions beyond the pulsing festival areas.

Stockholm Water Festival

Day 1. Thu.   Aug. 3, 2000
(Day 1. Thursday   August 16, 2001)

10:00am Check in at the five-star **Grand Hôtel**, where Nobel prize winners have enjoyed exclusivity and elegance since 1901.

10:30am Head to nearby Gamla Stan, the old section of Stockholm. Wander through narrow alleys, old town houses, and picturesque shops.

12:15pm Watch the changing of the guards in the outer courtyard of the Royal Palace. For the best view, either follow the guards in or stand on the ledge of the first pillar on the right side of the courtyard. Check out the statue of St. George slaying the dragon in front of the cathedral.

1:00pm Walk to the center of modern Stockholm to ℞ lunch with celebrities (maybe) at chic **Lydmar**. Munch on pan-seared scallops on a bed of citrus-infused risotto in an ultramodern setting.

2:30pm Taxi to the **Vasamuseet** to see the 376-year-old battleship *Vasa*. A gargantuan salvage effort brought this ancient sunken warship to the surface and into one of Europe's most intriguing museums.

4:00pm The **Skansen** is the world's oldest outdoor museum. It details Scandinavian life through the ages with buildings that have been moved in from all over Sweden.

6:30pm People-watching—a Stockholm pastime—is great in Kungsträdgården, the royal park, which is also a hip place to hang out or get a drink. Look for the life-size chess board.

8:00pm The hottest spot in town is at the Operakällaren, ℞ the 200-year-old opera house. The trendy **Café Opera** serves international cuisine before becoming a disco at midnight.

10:15pm Walk back to the festival for music, a street performance, fireworks, or an outdoor movie. Throughout the **Water Festival**, the Stockholm Film Festival projects offbeat cinema until 3 a.m.

12:30am Return to Café Opera or move on to **Fasching**, a renowned jazz club in the city center that features international and local talent.

Day 2. Fri.   Aug. 4, 2000
(Day 2. Friday   August 17, 2001)

8:00am Start the day with coffee and apple-custard ℞ cake at **Sturekatten**, a large old landmark.

9:00am Stockholm is among the few cities in the world that allow ballooning over their airspace. **City Ballong**, one of several companies that guide visitors over the waterways and islands that make up Stockholm, supplies champagne upon setting down.

2:00pm Like an army-style canteen, the **Sturehof** ℞ restaurant has a boisterous and convivial atmosphere and serves basic international comfort food. Return later for a drink at its **O-Bar** and enjoy a partylike atmosphere with DJs and live bands.

3:30pm Visit Viking Village, a new addition to the **Water Festival** that re-creates Viking life, wenches and all.

5:00pm Head to Happening Street around Norrbro, where theater groups from around the world perform dance, music, theater, improvisation, and comedy routines. You can join the crowds that follow the acts through the streets.

8:00pm For smoked reindeer and Swedish meatballs, ℞ you can't beat the traditional cuisine at **Källaren Diana**. This cozy restaurant is nestled in an 18th-century brick-lined cellar in Gamla Stan.

10:30pm Karlsson & Co. has a German pub atmosphere, and its 27-plus door policy keeps out young raver types. **La Isla** pumps Latin music over one of the friendliest dance floors in Stockholm.

Day 3. Sat.   Aug. 5, 2000
(Day 3. Saturday   August 18, 2001)

9:00am Have a smorgasbord buffet breakfast on the hotel's glassed-in veranda while you look over the harbor.

10:00am Housed in a building designed by Rafael Moneo, the recently reopened **Moderna Museet** (Modern Art Museum) has an impressive collection of 20th-century art that includes many notable Swedish pieces.

Noon Stadshuset (City Hall), where the Nobel Prizes are handed out every year, is worth a quick visit to see the interesting mix of architectural styles. You can climb the tower for a great view of the surroundings.

1:30pm The ***Water Festival*** offers some of the best festival food anywhere. Grab lunch at one of the myriad booths.

3:00pm Stop by the blues stage for up-and-coming acts. Featuring unsigned and amateurish-but-hopeful bands, this is a good place to earn your I-saw-them-when-they-were-nobodies credentials.

5:00pm Find the ***Creative Kilometer***, a thousand meters of arts and crafts in the middle of the city.

6:00pm Ever wonder if some bands were ever small? The main stage is not the place to figure it out. Acts such as Van Morrison, Tom Jones, and B.B. King have appeared here in years past.

8:00pm For a dose of Michelin stars, try **Fredsgatan 12**. This highly touted restaurant serves innovative Swedish and mainland specialties in the same building as the Royal Academy of Arts.

10:00pm Join the enormous crowd watching either a laser-light show or fireworks—you never know what kind of over-water display you'll catch at the ***Festival***.

Midnight The noisy but trendy **Spy Bar** nightclub caters to all types of people in an apartmentlike setting. Jerry Seinfeld has been spotted at the pre-Revolutionary Cuba-inspired **Tiger Bar**. By the time you head back to your hotel, crews will be returning Stockholm to normal by dismantling what remains of the festival—in itself an impressive sight—but somehow "normal" can never describe Stockholm.

Alternatives

An alternative to the opulent Grand Hôtel is the **Berns' Hotel**, which takes a stylish but minimalist approach to decor. The antique-laden **Lady Hamilton** is a small and charming hotel in a converted house dating from 1470. Checking in at the **Lydmar Hotel** feels like checking into a chic hotel on Manhattan's Upper East Side.

Halv **Trappa Plus Gård**'s courtyard is filled with beautiful people eating international-fusion cuisine. **Nils Emil** restaurant in the Sodermalm district provides generous portions and is a favorite of royalty—Baltic herring is a house specialty. **East** serves pan-Asian food, while **Ocean** dishes out Swedish-fusion cuisine to repeat customers. Both trendy and friendly, **Biblos** is a mix of restaurant and nightclub.

The **Daily News** and the **Victoria Bar and Kitchen** are two popular nightclubs located in the royal gardens of Kungsträdgården. A great hangout and dance spot, **Berns Salonger** is closed for renovation as of press time but should reopen by 2000.

The Stockholm Metro is a tourist destination. Seventy of the 100 stations feature amazing artistic, cultural, or nature displays, which include waterfalls, mosaics, sculpture, and murals. **Nordiska Museet** (Nordic Museum) details Swedish life from the 16th century to the present.

The Hot Sheet

☎ 46/8

$ 8.1 Krona

HOTELS	DAY	ADDRESS	PH	PRICE	FX	RMS	BEST ROOMS
Berns' Hotel	A	8 Näckströmsgatan	5-663-2200 800- 223-6800	$$$	5-663-2201	65	Dlx park vw
Grand Hôtel	1	8 Södra Blasieholmshamnen	679-3500 800- 223-6800	$$$$	611-8686	307	Dlx harbor vw
Lady Hamilton	A	5 Storkyrkobriken	23-4680 800- 448-8355	$$$	411-1148	34	Triple rm, 34 or 40
Lydmar Hotel	A	10 Sturegatan	5-661-1300	$$$	5-661-1301	56	Park vw

RESTAURANTS	DAY	ADDRESS	PH	PRICE	REC	DRESS	FOOD
Biblos	A	9 Biblioteksgatan	611-8030	$$	LD	Euro	Cosmopolitan
Café Opera	1	4 Strömgatan in Operakällaren	676-5870	$$$	D/L	Euro	International
East	A	13 Stureplan	611-4959	$$	LD	Euro	Pan Asian
Fredsgatan 12	3	12 Fredsgatan	24-8052	$$$	D/L	Euro	International fusion
Halv Trappa Plus Gård	A	3 Lästmakargatan	611-0277	$$$	D	Euro	International fusion
Källaren Diana	2	2 Brunnsgränd	10-7310	$$	D	Kazh	Traditional Swedish
Lydmar	1	see Lydmar Hotel	5-661-1388	$$	L/BD	Kazh	Modern Swedish
Nils Emil	A	122 Folkungagatan	640-7209	$$	D	Kazh	Swedish
Ocean	A	76 Norr Mälarstrand	652-4090	$$$	D	Kazh	Fusion
Sturehof	2	2 Stureplan	440-5730	$$	L/D	Kazh	Comfort food
Sturekatten	2	4 Riddargatan	611-1612	$	BT	Local	Bakery, cafe

NITELIFE	DAY	ADDRESS	PH	PRICE	REC	DRESS	MUSIC
Berns Salonger	A	Berzeli Park	614-0550	None	H(F)	Euro	
Café Opera	1	see Café Opera restaurant	676-5807	$$	OF	Euro	Disco
Daily News	A	10 Västraträdgårsgatan	21-5655	$$	O	Kazh	Dance
Fasching	1	63 Kungsgatan	21-6267	$$	MP	Kazh	Jazz
Karlsson & Co.	2	56 Kungsgatan	5-451-2140	$	O	Kazh	Dance
La Isla	2	48 Fleminggatan	654-6043	$	O	Kazh	Salsa, Latin
O-Bar	2	see Sturehof restaurant	440-5730	None	H	Euro	
Spy Bar	3	20 Birger Jarlsgatan	611-6500	$	H	Euro	
Tiger Bar	3	18 Kungsgatan	24-4700	$	HO(F)	Euro	Pop, salsa
Victoria Bar and Kitchen	A	Kungsträdgården	10-1015	None	O(F)		Dance, house

SIGHTS & ATTRACTIONS	DAY	ADDRESS	PH	ENTRY FEE
Moderna Museet	3	Skeppsholmen	5-195-5200	$
Nordiska Museet	A	6-16 Djurgårdsvägen	5-195-6000	$
Skansen	1	39-41 Djurgårdsslätten at Djurgården	442-8000	$
Stadshuset	3	1 Hantverkargatan	5-082-9000	$
Vasamuseet	1	4 Galärvarvsvägen	5-195-4800	$

OTHER SIGHTS, SERVICES & ATTRACTIONS

City Ballong	2	hotel pick-up	34-5464	$$$$
Tourist Center		27 Hamngatan in Sweden House	789-2490	

EVENT & TICKET INFO

Stockholm Water Festival (various locations around Stockholm): Purchase a Water Pass ($25) for entry to all activities by calling the *Stockholm Water Festival* (46/8-459-5500).

RECommendations: (Restaurants) B–Breakfast; L–Lunch; D–Dinner; T–High tea or snack
(Nitelife) G–Gaming; H–Hangout bar; M–Live music; O–Dancing (disco); P–Dancing (live music); S–Show; F–Food served
()–Available but without recommendation. For complete explanation of Hot Sheet format, see page 34.

NYC +6 · 53°/66° (11°/18°) · Arlanda (ARN); 45 min./$50 · No · Swedish

The Fun Also Rises

July/August 2000

July/August 2001

Bridgetown, Barbados

Crop Over Festival

Origin: 1974   Event ★ ★ ★ ★ ★ City   Attendance: 100,000

Mix the excesses of Carnival, traditions of an African heritage, and bounty of an island harvest with cricket, polo, tea, and scones, and you get locals and visitors "raising cane" all over one of the most magical islands in the Caribbean. Despite Barbados' *veddy* English trimmings and left-hand driving, *Crop Over*—which celebrates the annual sugar-cane harvest—is no high-tea-and-crumpets fest.

Crop Over rocks the Caribbean's most easterly island for a full five weeks, reaching its peak in the last four days when the Calypso Monarch is crowned and **Bridgetown Market Day** washes the island with gaudy colors and spicy Barbadian aromas. On the climactic **Kadooment Day**, a national holiday and the festival's finale, masqueraders and minstrels pour through the streets of the capital, Bridgetown, for parades, dancing, drinking, and fireworks. This is the country's biggest to-do, an enthusiastic and noisy display of Caribbean culture at its best.

The names of festival events recall the days when sugar was king and the harvest cause for massive celebrations. Today, music dominates many events and revelers retreat to the island nation's plentiful beaches before and after the parades, parties, and pageants. The west coast, north of Bridgetown, is one long sand bar, studded with beach bars, snorkel sites, and sun worshipers. The south coast draws windsurfers and hipster crowds. The dramatic east coast is pounded by the Atlantic and revered by nature lovers.

Barbados' 250,000 or so residents like to call their triangular-shaped island "England in the tropics." But this sophisticated Caribbean nation drops its British reserve this weekend. *Crop Over* craziness is encouraged by local restaurant and bar promotions. The 166-square-mile island has more rum shops (bars) than churches—10 per square mile. More than likely, you'll end up sharing bar seats at local joints packed with costumed revelers, who'll set aside their feathered headdresses to throw down a Cockspur—a most appropriate way to celebrate the *Crop Over Festival*.

Crop Over Festival

Day 1. Sat.   Aug. 5, 2000
(Day 1. Saturday   August 4, 2001)

9:00am Wake at the **Royal Pavilion** in St. James. Nestled amid forests of bougainvillea, the pastel-pink resort has Moorish arches and Spanish colonial accents. Enjoy breakfast and the view from the hotel's bistro-style restaurant.

10:00am Join the throngs heading into the capital (30 minutes away) for **Crop Over**'s **Bridgetown Market Day**, a massive street fair. Food, drink, and crafts stalls line the open-air market. *Boom-a-tuk*, *boom-a-tuk* pulsates from the log drums of tuk bands, which open with waltzes, shift into military marches, and wind up with frenzied African beats.

11:00am Check out National Heroes Square near the market. The 1813 monument to Horatio Nelson is 20 years older than its London counterpart and a source of some controversy. Some Barbadians say it's a positive reminder of their colonial past; others want to replace it with a national hero. The compromise? Nelson has been turned so he no longer faces Broad Street, Bridgetown's major thoroughfare.

Noon Mount Gay Rum, the island's potent firewater has been bottled here for three centuries, despite an English archbishop's assertion that "rum is destructive to nature, wasting to vitals, and an enemy of propagation." Well, yeah, but that shouldn't stop you from checking out the **Mount Gay Rum Visitors' Centre**. It's a five-minute ride from town and has a quickie tour and tasting of the inviting intoxicant.

1:30pm Head up the west coast to Paynes Bay's golden sand beach and home of **Bombas Beach Bar and Restaurant**. Highlights are the rustic setting, casual crowd, grilled fish, and Bombaburger special.

3:00pm Drive or cab into the countryside, where the villages (and villagers) celebrate with *mucho*

gusto. Impromptu tuk bands stretch along Highway 2 from Bridgetown to the northern Scotland district.

4:00pm Seize the moment between parades and parties and go down under (via electric tram) to the subterranean limestone caverns at **Harrison's Cave**. There's a great show of waterfalls, streams, pools, and several hundred bats high above.

6:00pm Wear comfortable but festive clothes tonight—dancing is in order, but so is looking nice for dinner.

7:30pm Splurge on dinner at open-air **Carambola's**, high on the cliffs overlooking the Caribbean on the west coast. It doesn't get much better than this for an elegant setting. The fare is *haute* French cuisine with Barbadian accents.

10:00pm St. Lawrence Gap is jumpin'. At the **Reggae Lounge**, $20 gets you all you can drink from a 75-foot-long bar that stocks 1,000-plus brands of rum. The nearby **Ship Inn** pulls in a hip **Crop Over** crowd, which grooves on the large patio and small dance floor. The club stays open until the last reveler leaves.

Day 2. Sun.   Aug. 6, 2000
(Day 2. Sunday   August 5, 2001)

11:00am Book a sea-view table for brunch at the **Atlantis Hotel** on Barbados' east coast. Sample pepper pot, pumpkin fritters, fried plantains, and pickled bananas, and watch surfers conquer the Atlantic far below on Bathsheba Beach.

1:00pm The **Crop Over Bridgetown Market** is in full swing all day, but take a break and pick up shells on the sugar-soft, south-coast Crane Beach, which is long, broad, and pink. The waves are big, but lifeguards are on duty and the view is out of this world.

3:00pm Experience life on a 300-year-old sugar estate. Head inland to **Sunbury Great House**, a Barbados

The Fun Also Rises

gem rebuilt after a 1995 fire destroyed all but the two-and-a-half-foot-thick stone walls. Sip a rum and tonic or have high tea on the back patio of the ℞ **Courtyard Café**.

6:00pm *Cohobblopot*. Don't worry about pronouncing the word. Just join the throngs heading for the National Stadium for this potpourri event of costumes, calypso, and carnival. Don't plan on sitting —all the chairs have been cleared out to create one enormous dance floor.

10:00pm Hang with locals at **After Dark** or **B4 Blues** at St. Lawrence Gap. More music, more bands. For a late-night snack, hit the food kiosks at the **Oistins** ℞ **Fisheries Complex** on the main road in Oistins Town near the hotel.

Day 3. Mon.   Aug. 7, 2000
(Day 3. Monday   August 6, 2001)

8:30am Eat a big breakfast at the hotel. This is ℞ *Kadooment Day*, the biggest and the best event of *Crop Over*.

10:00am Masqueraders, musicians, and plain folk— everybody on the island—pour onto the streets of Bridgetown to parade, dance, drink, and make lots of noise. Drop your inhibitions and join one of the costume parades and wend your way from the National Stadium to the Spring Garden Highway. After the parades and celebrations, partyers take to the streets to "jump-up" and dance to the best of the soca and calypso bands.

1:00pm Upstairs at the Bridge House, overlooking The Careenage, Bridgetown's picturesque old inner harbor, cool off with an icy drink and Tex-Mex grub at ℞ the funky **Rusty Pelican**. Menus are written on brown paper bags.

2:00pm Rejoin the festivities on the Spring Garden Highway or enjoy the beach at the hotel.

8:00pm Have dinner with other merrymakers and pos-

sibly members of the festival's royal court, who ℞ come to dine at the **39 Steps Wine Bar**.

10:00pm Located in Bridgetown, **The Boatyard** is popular with locals and visitors. Dance to recorded and live music at this comfortable bar. As night wanes, Bridgetown's Baxter Road is the street that never sleeps. Great for late snacks and rum bars.

Midnight Back at the Royal Pavilion, take a moonlit champagne stroll down the beach, creating a final, sugar-sweet *Crop Over* memory of tropical perfection.

Alternatives

A half-hour's drive from Bridgetown, **Cobblers Cove** pampers at a price. The old plantation house, now a 40-suite oasis of luxury, has private terraces, a pool, restaurant, and beach bar. The **Sandy Lane** is scheduled to reopen in late 2000— this already gorgeous hotel on a perfect crescent of powdery white sand should be amazing. The **Casuarina Beach Club**, in bustling St. Lawrence Gap, has tropical gardens and rooms with a view at a reasonable price.

The **Waterfront Café** at The Careenage, in the heart of historic Bridgetown, is ideal for people-watching. Jazz and steel bands accompany flying fish, a local dish. **The Restaurant** in the Sandy Lane resort will offer fusion cuisine and outstanding desserts. **Brown Sugar** serves local (Bajan) specialties, including pepper pot, and baked breadfruit. For a romantic courtyard dinner, try **The Mews**, situated in actor Minnie Driver's old residence. Dinner and a cultural hodgepodge of song, dance, limbo, and fire-eating make for a great show at the **Plantation Restaurant and Garden Theatre** in Christ Church.

If you arrive a day early (Friday), you can catch the *Pic-O-De-Crop Finals* at the National Stadium. Musicians vie for the coveted title of Calypso Monarch. This is followed by the *Fore-Day Morning Jump-Up Parade* which gets going at 2 a.m. (Saturday) in Spring Garden near Bridgetown.

The Hot Sheet

☎ US/246

$ 2.0 Barbados Dollar

HOTELS °	DAY	ADDRESS	PH	PRICE	FX	RMS	BEST ROOMS
Casuarina Beach Club	A	St. Lawrence Gap	428-3600 800- 550-6288 ext. 2210	$$	428-1970	158	Ocean vw
Cobblers Cove	A	Road View, St. Peter	422-2291 800- 890-6060	$$$$+	422-1460	40	Colleton rm
Royal Pavilion	1	St. James	444-2000 800- 223-1818	$$$	422-3940	72	Ocean vw
Sandy Lane	A	St. James	432-1311 800- 223-6800	$$$$+	432-2954	120	Ocean vw

RESTAURANTS	DAY	ADDRESS	PH	PRICE	REC °	DRESS	FOOD
39 Steps Wine Bar	3	Chattel Pl., Hastings	427-0715	$$	D/L	Euro	Pub food, continental
Atlantis Hotel	2	Tent Bay, Bethsheba, St. Joseph	433-9445	$$	B/LD	Local	West Indian, brunch buffet
Bombas Beach Bar and Restaurant	1	Payne's Bay near Tamarind Cove Hotel	432-0569	$	L/D	Local	Bajan, burgers
Brown Sugar	A	Bay St., Aquatic Gap, St. Michael	426-7684	$	D	Local	Bajan
Carambola's	1	Derricks, St. James	432-0832	$$$	D	Kazh	Seafood, French
Courtyard Café	2	see Sunbury Great House	423-6270	$	T/LD	Kazh	High tea
The Mews	A	Second St., Hole Town	432-1122	$$	D	Kazh	Seafood
Oistins Fisheries Complex	2	Oistins Town	no phone	$	T/LD	Local	Fast-food
The Restaurant	A	see Sandy Lane resort	432-2838	$$$	D	Kazh	Modern Caribbean
Rusty Pelican	3	The Careenage, Bridgetown	436-7778	$	L/D	Local	Tex-Mex, steaks
Waterfront Café	A	The Careenage, Bridgetown	427-0093	$	LD	Local	Bajan

NITELIFE	DAY	ADDRESS	PH	PRICE	REC	DRESS	MUSIC
After Dark	2	St. Lawrence Gap	435-6547	$	P	Local	Jazz, calypso
B4 Blues	2	St. Lawrence Gap	435-6560	$	M	Local	R&B, calypso
The Boatyard	3	Bridgetown	436-2622	$	P	Yuppie	Calypso, reggae
Plantation Restaurant and Garden Theatre	A	St. Lawrence Gap	428-5048	$$$	SF	Kazh	Floor show, Caribbean
Reggae Lounge	1	St. Lawrence Gap	435-6462	$	P	Local	Reggae, calypso, R&B
Ship Inn	1	St. Lawrence Gap	435-6961	$	P	Local	Dance

SIGHTS & ATTRACTIONS	DAY	ADDRESS	PH	ENTRY FEE
Harrison's Cave	1	Hwy. 2	438-6640	$
Mount Gay Rum Visitors' Centre	1	Spring Garden Hwy.	425-8757	$
Sunbury Great House	2	St. Philip	423-6270	$
Barbados Tourism Authority		Harbour Rd., Bridgetown	427-2623	

EVENT & TICKET INFO

Crop Over (various locations around Barbados): Tickets for stadium events ($19-$44) are available from the *National Cultural Foundation* (246-424-0909). All other events are free, and participation is encouraged.

RECommendations: (Restaurants) B–Breakfast; L–Lunch; D–Dinner; T–High tea or snack
(Nitelife) G–Gaming; H–Hangout bar; M–Live music; O–Dancing (disco); P–Dancing (live music); S–Show; F–Food served
( )–Available but without recommendation. For complete explanation of Hot Sheet format, see page 34.

NYC+1   74°/87° (23°/31°)   Grantley Adams (BGI); 30 min./$20   Yes/No   English

The Fun Also Rises

Fun Destination: Ibiza/Majorca

A FunGuide 100 Destination

When it comes to island hopping in the lap of luxury, Ibiza and Majorca are still the hippest of the hip. Even with competition from international hot spots such as Mykonos, Madrid, and South Beach, Florida, no place beats these sister islands for spectacular scenery and nonstop nightlife.

These radiant Mediterranean islands exist in perfect, symbiotic splendor, with Majorca offering beautiful, hidden coves and fun day trips, and Ibiza featuring an explosive and glamorous nightlife scene. We recommend you spend two days and one night in Majorca, and one day and two nights in Ibiza. (Of course, it's always preferable to stay until your dancing shoes and suntan lotion wear out.)

Majorca, which lies 90 miles south of Barcelona, combines the passion and charm of ancient Spain with the sensuality of a Mediterranean island. Narrow streets, elegant gardens, and a colossal sandstone cathedral are the highlights of the capital city of Palma—once a prominent Spanish port between Europe and Africa. But it's the island's wooded hills, ocean crags, crystalline coves, and wild bougainvillea that create the overwhelming aura of romance and hedonism. Days in Majorca are usually spent on sandy beaches, beautiful golf courses, or in adventurous exploration. The nightlife is relatively sedate.

After dark, however, nearby Ibiza glows like a beacon on the sea calling partyers to play until sunrise. Days in Ibiza revolve chiefly around shopping—extravagant shoppers come to find fresh-off-the-runway fashions from London, Paris, and Milan in Ibiza's chic boutiques. But it's more fun to see this elegant apparel being worn after nightfall when island activity crescendos into a vogue parade through the flashy club scene. A diverse, international crowd of beautiful people converges on the bars and discos with nightly fanfare, stirring up a sexual energy that vibrates to pounding techno beats. The idea in Ibiza is to party until you can't go on, then take a seat, order another drink, and wait for your second wind.

Fun Destination: Ibiza/Majorca

Day 1. Thu.   Aug. 10, 2000
(Day 1. Thursday   August 9, 2001)

9:30am Check into **Hotel Meliá Victoria** in Palma. It has lovely gardens, cascading fountains, and sun ® terraces. Enjoy a leisurely breakfast at the hotel restaurant overlooking the busy harbor and indulge in one of their famous Bloody Marys.

10:30am Explore the labyrinthine streets and garden plazas of Palma. To celebrate the overthrow of the Moors, the 13th-century **Catedral de Palma** was built over the ruins of an Arab mosque—the modernist interior was designed by Spanish architect Antoni Gaudí. Opposite the cathedral is the impressive **Palau de l'Almudain**, which housed Moorish royalty and, later, Majorcan kings. Tours are available and definitely worth taking.

2:00pm Have lunch at **Caballito de Mar**. Soak up the ® port atmosphere on the terrace while enjoying a hearty plate of salt-baked fish.

4:00pm For Roman, Punic, and Arabic artifacts, stop by the **Museu de Mallorca**. Then wander down Pont I Vich and Pare Nadal to the **Basilica de Sant Francesc**. The imposing, Gothic structure has an astounding, cavernous interior. The odd statue outside is a tribute to Franciscan missionary Junipero Serra, founder of Monterey and San Diego, California.

7:30pm Back at the hotel, have drinks on the terrace and enjoy the sunset.

9:30pm Have dinner at **Real Club Náutico**, which ® serves fish and paella fit for a king ... one may be sitting at the next table.

Midnight Head to the town of Magaluf, home of **BCM**, the largest disco in the world, where 5,000 people fill two dance floors. The lower level is easier on

the ears. The crowd picks up at around 2 a.m. Arrive before 3 a.m. or you'll wait in line. The best scene is in the basement, called Party Zone. Back in Palma, the view of and from **Tito**'s is amazing. Take the elevator up to its three tiers of bars and caged dancers.

Day 2. Fri.   Aug. 11, 2000
(Day 2. Friday   August 10, 2001)

10:00am After a hotel breakfast, drive to the nearby vil-® lage of Valldemosa, where George Sand spent a dismal (yet somehow romantic) winter nursing a sickly Chopin back to health. From there it's only a short drive into the hills to the picturesque town of Deiá, where Robert Graves lived and wrote for years.

1:30pm Savor a gourmet lunch while enjoying the dramatic mountain views from the terrace of the ele-® gant **El Olivo** restaurant. It's located in La Residencia hotel on the outskirts of town.

3:30pm Head back to Palma, allowing plenty of time for a leisurely drive, and prepare to go to Ibiza. If you have beach time, head to the cafe-lined Andraitx (only 20 minutes from the city center) and hang out with a chic crowd of models and their wealthy friends.

8:00pm Check out of the Meliá Victoria and catch the last flight to Ibiza at 9:30 p.m.

10:30pm Check into **Pikes** hotel. Nestled into a lush hillside, it has panoramic views overlooking olive and citrus groves, impeccable service, and uniquely decorated rooms. Everyone who's someone gets a room at Pikes.

11:00pm Have dinner and drinks at stylish **Sa** ® **Capella**, a unique restaurant built inside an old chapel. Try the suckling pig and take in the regal atmosphere.

12:30am For after-dinner, preclubbing drinks, stroll along Ibiza harbor, where a cluster of popular bars will be in full swing. Brace yourself for the endless parade of competitive disco promoters assailing bar patrons with fliers and stickers touting their clubs.

2:30am Start (yes, you are starting at 2:30) at **El Divino**, the prettiest club in Ibiza, where an older and wealthier crowd hangs out. For the height of haughtiness and low couture, try **Pachá**, a renovated farmhouse across the harbor that features six rooms and 15 bars.

Day 3. Sat. Aug. 12, 2000
(Day 3. Saturday   August 11, 2001)

11:00am Order a room service breakfast and relax by the pool (a poolside massage is an option).

2:00pm Head south to Playa Es Cavallet. Before hitting the stretches of white sand, have lunch at **El Chiringuito**, conveniently located on the beach. Savor delicious Mediterranean food and a chic crowd.

3:30pm Spend the day baking in the sun. Nearby, Ses Salinas beach is equally beautiful. Es Cavallet is the official nudist beach, but topless tanning is the norm on Ses Salinas, as well.

7:30pm People don't come to Ibiza for the tourist attractions, but you should walk down the water-side walkway, pass the restaurants and bars of D'Alt Vila (Old Town), and explore the maze of alleys and footpaths. Head to **Café del Mar** in San Antonio to enjoy a drink and watch the sunset. It's the hottest spot on the island to see the close of the day, so arrive early to get a table.

10:00pm Have dinner at **Pikes** elaborate buffet, then sit on the terrace for drinks.

Midnight Try a few new bars on the Ibiza harbor and wait for the discos to fill up.

2:00am Take the Discobus (which runs every hour from all over the island) to **Amnesia**, between the town of Ibiza and San Antonio—it has a hot sound system and novel look every day of the week. Or get wet at **Eden**, formally known as Kaoos, where foam and water parties keep things wild and the state-of-the-art sound-and-light system keeps dancers grooving. **Privilege**, formally known as Ku, has a more tame but far glossier scene, and one of the steepest cover charges around. Regardless of where you go, parties rage until the sun is in the sky. Remember that a successful night in Ibiza means going to bed with your feet sore, your ears ringing, and a sudsy wig of foam in your hair.

Alternatives

On Majorca, **Son Vida** is one of the finer hotels in Spain. It's set in a 13th-century castle overlooking Palma Bay and surrounded by 1,400 acres that include Turkish baths and an 18-hole golf course. Occupying two manor houses outside of the village of Deià, **La Residencia** offers lush gardens, green lawns, and spectacular mountain views. On Ibiza, **Hotel Ocean Drive** has a sleek design and ideal location near Ibiza's hottest clubs. **Les Jardins de Palerm** hotel is more sedate, with romantic bougainvillea-laden terraces.

Majorca's **Tristan** restaurant at the harbor of Puerto Portals has the finest reputation around. On Ibiza, the lively **El Divino** serves excellent beef, duck, and seafood and has terrace views of Dalt Vila and the Mediterranean. For paella or seafood try **El Faro**, which has ocean views and serves dinner until six in the morning. Or check out the trendy **L'Eléphant**, originally a favorite in Paris, known for its fresh seafood and savory sauces.

The Hot Sheet

☎ 34/971

$ 150 Peseta

HOTELS	DAY	ADDRESS	*	PH	PRICE	FX	RMS	BEST ROOMS
Hotel Meliá Victoria	1	21 Av. Joan Miró	M	73-2542	$$$	45-0824	161	Sea vw
Hotel Ocean Drive	A	Playa de Talamanca, Aptdo. 223	I	31-8112	$$	31-2228	38	Mtn or sea vw
La Residencia	A	Camino Son Canals, Deià	M	63-9011	$$$$	63-9370	63	Rm 12 Bes
Les Jardins de Palerm	A	Aptdo. 62, San José	I	80-0318	$$	80-0453	9	Rm 1
Pikes	2	San Antonio de Portmany	I	34-2222	$$	34-2312	26	Rm 3
Son Vida	A	2 c/ Raixa	M	79-0000	$$$	79-0017	170	Supr rm w/ city vw

RESTAURANTS	DAY	ADDRESS	*	PH	PRICE	REC	DRESS	FOOD
Caballito de Mar	1	5 Paseo Sagrera	M	72-1074	$$$$	L/D	Kazh	Seafood
El Chiringuito	3	Playa Es Cavallet	I	39-5355	$$	L	Euro	Mediterranean
El Divino	A	Paseo Juan Carlos	I	19-0176	$$	D	Euro	International, Spanish, Basque
El Faro	A	at end of port	I	72-6212	$$$$	BLTD	Kazh	Seafood, paella
El Olivo	2	See La Residencia hotel	M	63-9011	$$$$+	L/D	Euro	Nouvelle, Mediterranean
L'Eléphant	A	Pl. de la Iglesia, San Rafael	I	19-8056	$$	D	Kazh	Seafood
Pikes	3	see Pikes hotel	I	34-2222	$$	D/BL	Euro	International
Real Club Náutico	1	1 Muelle San Pedro	M	71-8783	$$$$+	D/L	Euro	Paella, fish, Spanish
Sa Capella	2	Carretera Santa Inez	I	34-0057	$$$$	D	Euro	International, seafood, Spanish
Tristan	A	Puerto Portals	M	67-5547	$$	D	Kazh	International, Mediterranean

NITELIFE	DAY	ADDRESS	*	PH	PRICE	REC	DRESS	MUSIC
Amnesia	3	Carretera San Antonio	I	19-8041	$$	O	Euro	House, funk, pop
BCM	1	Av. Solivera, Magaluf	M	13-1546	$$	O	Euro	House
Café del Mar	3	San Antonio	I	34-2516	None	H	Kazh	
Eden	3	1 c/ Salvador Esprui, San Antonio	I	34-2551	$$$$	O	Euro	House
El Divino	2	Paseo Juan Carlos	I	19-0176	$$$$	O	Euro	House, techno
Pachá	2	Av. Ocho de Agosto	I	31-3600	$$$$+	O	Euro	Funk, hip-hop, salsa, house
Privilege	3	Urbanización San Rafael	I	19-8086	$$$$	O	Euro	Techno, house
Tito's	1	Paseo Marítimo	M	73-0017	$$	O	Euro	House, Latin, dance

SIGHTS & ATTRACTIONS	DAY	ADDRESS	*	PH	ENTRY FEE
Basilica de Sant Francesc	1	1 Pl. de San Francisco	M	71-2695	$
Catedral de Palma (La Seu)	1	2 Capiscolato, 1st fl.	M	72-3130	$
Museu de Majorca	1	5 c/ Portella	M	71-7540	$
Palau de l'Almudain	1	c/ Palau Reial	M	71-4368	None
Fomento del Turismo de Ibiza		4 Historiador José Clapes	I	30-2411	
Majorca Tourist Information		2 Pl. de la Reina	M	71-2216	

*I=Ibiza, M=Majorca

REComendations: (Restaurants) B–Breakfast; L–Lunch; D–Dinner; T–High tea or snack
(Nitelife) G–Gaming; H–Hangout bar; M–Live music; O–Dancing (disco); P–Dancing (live music); S–Show; F–Food served
()–Available but without recommendation. For complete explanation of Hot Sheet format, see page 34.

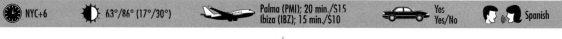

NYC+6   63°/86° (17°/30°)   Palma (PMI); 20 min./$15   Ibiza (IBZ); 15 min./$10   Yes Yes/No   Spanish

The Fun Also Rises

Discotrek

If Studio 54 was still going strong the last time you stepped onto a dance floor, you may feel a little disoriented by the techno-music revolution. Well, don't feel alone. When disco went the way of leisure suits and avocado-colored shag carpeting, many dance aficionados were left bereft of their favorite pastime.

But during the mid-1980s in Chicago and Detroit (mostly), the tradition of disco was resurrected, aurally reconfigured, and given brand-new identities as house and techno music. Drawing from the electronic instrumentation of new wave and disco's R&B-inspired vocals, house and techno were created for a familiar, age-old purpose—to give people an excuse (and a little bit of help) to shake their butts until dawn.

Today's nightclubs offer a nearly endless number of musical options. No other form of contemporary music contains as many subgenres as dance music: House, garage house, techno, techno bass, drum 'n' bass, tech-step, and trance are just a few. The youngest and most heavily pierced group of club-goers generally choose drum 'n' bass—a dark, harsh music composed of speedy beats, abrupt rhythm breaks, and gut-vibrating sub-bass levels. As you might guess, trance is a daze-inducing style that builds and builds, then builds some more, until it reaches a cathartic peak that sends dancers into a state of euphoria. Trance clubs are mainly populated by youths in glow-in-the-dark, fractal-patterned clothing.

Even normally flamboyant club-hoppers may find the scene and fashion statements at trance clubs a bit dizzying. More mainstream clubs tend to focus on house music—it's easy to dance to (imagine up-tempo disco) and usually requires less in the way of cutting-edge fashion sense. These clubs are definitely the safest bets for the casual club visitor.

Once inside a club, you may want to tackle the VIP lounge—this is normally a restricted-entry area, which is less congested and quieter than the main area. The prevailing attitude is usually one of superciliousness and superiority. VIP lounges—not all clubs have them but you might be surprised at how many do—are where you're likely to find beautiful models, *über*-cool club kids, wealthy businessmen, and party hipsters of all ages. Although there are no hard rules for getting in, often you have to buy an expensive bottle of champagne or liquor to stay.

The Fun Also Rises steers you to the best clubs around the world, places where you can be comfortable and have fun. As a rule, we recommend places where the music isn't deafening and, even if you happen to have grown up with The Beatles, you won't feel like a grandparent on the dance floor. Admission requirements vary. While the most mainstream and egalitarian clubs admit anyone who can foot the entry fee, some establishments have the velvet rope, bouncer, and guest list. Being attractive or being with someone who is almost guarantees entry. If you don't have a connection, ask your hotel's concierge to get you on the guest list. When all else fails, try tipping.

No matter what the genre, dance clubs provide entertainment (some have extraordinary technical effects), a chance to let loose, great people-watching, and, if you're lucky (or suave), great opportunities for meeting people. The seductive power of the dance floor is like no other on earth. Nonstop beats, flashing lights, and wild rhythms typically move people to drop inhibitions—or in some cases to even take on new personalities. The raw hedonism of Studio 54 may be long gone, but the butt-shaking mating ritual on dance floors will never disappear.

How Did They Get There Before Us?

It seems the only people who know where all the great events are, even before this book's author, are pan-flute musicians. And this has been going on long before the book was a twinkle in the author's eye. Take ancient Greece, for example. Even back then, Pan (the god of fields, forests, and wild animals) was piping his reed flutes in honor of a magical romantic interest.

Pan-flute artists agree their music has been handed down through the ages, but its precise origins have been lost to antiquity. Ernesto Pomareda, a pan flutist who has studied the instrument's history, suggests it may have started in the bamboo jungles of South America as a way for humans to imitate animal sounds. But while the pan flute is most closely associated with South America and the Andes mountains, it's also popular in Greece, Thailand, and the Solomon Islands.

Most pan flutes are made of bamboo. Pitch varies according to the length of the pipe. While the Kjarkas Academy in Bolivia trains and sponsors pan-flute musicians, most learn from generations of flutists in their own families or from friends or street musicians. Although there are recognizable national rhythms such as *saya* in Bolivia and *sanjuanito* in Ecuador, the music is similar no matter what part of the world you're in.

After thousands of years at local ceremonies and festivals, pan-flute music burst onto the world stage and found commercial success in the 1980s. Making a concerted effort to gain recognition for their music in the United States and Europe, several Andean groups ferreted out prime festivals and tourist areas and began playing. First-time listeners instantly loved the joyous, soulful music of groups such as Chile's Inti Illimani and Illapu and Bolivia's Los Kjarkas. From there it was a quick step to Zamfir, the American cable-TV sensation billed as Master of the Pan Flute. Zamfir's marketing campaign was cheesy, but it helped raise awareness of the ancient instrument.

The success of these artists inspired more pan-flute groups to join the international festival circuit. In France, pan flutes have become a national obsession. Pomareda estimates there are now about 1,000 pan-flute musicians playing festivals full time worldwide, with many more professionals playing on a casual basis. Huge festivals often draw several hundred thousand people, and musicians have found volume directly affects their sales. Not surprisingly, amplifiers, crowds, and sales all have gotten bigger.

With all this success, is there a dark side to the pan-flute universe? Going commercial has turned this buoyant music into an extremely competitive business. Some groups have become fiercely territorial about the festivals and locations where they play and vie to be the sole pan-flute group at each event.

How do these musicians find the world's best festivals without the help of *The Fun Also Rises*? Group managers research exhaustively, poring over event listings and making lots of phone calls to book appearances.

Pan-flute music still serves ceremonies and local festivals and there are many musicians famous only in their own countries. But commercial success has spread this music worldwide, making Pan a very busy guy.

August 2000

August 2001

Palio

(Palio di Siena)

Origin: c. 1600   **Event ★ ★ ★ ★ ★ City**   **Attendance: 50,000**

Few events in the world can hold a torch to the explosive passion and tension that surround the *Palio* in the Tuscan city of Siena, Italy. Far more than a mere horse race, the *Palio* pageant centers around the city's 17 ancient *contrade*, or districts, and contains all the Renaissance elements of rivalry, intrigue, pride, betrayal, and allegiance that defined the peak of the area's Medici era.

Deemed the most beautiful town square in Tuscany, Piazza del Campo is magically converted each year into a racing venue for 10 horses, which thunder for a minute and a half around its dirt-covered perimeter. The night before the race, speeches, songs, and toasts arouse the emotions of the 25,000 diners who have come for the fabled event. With the honor of each *contrada* at stake, rumors of secret pacts and collaborations add to tension that increases during the six trial runs. On the morning of the *Palio*, the archbishop bestows special blessings on the jockeys and horses. Then comes the *coreto storico*, a two-hour pageant of parading people and animals bedecked in costumes that replicate 15th-century designs.

The firing of the *mortaretto* signals the start of the race. Horses speed past 50,000 spectators—most of them crowded into the center of the track, some biting their nails or fighting back tears, all cheering and screaming. After the brief race, jubilant members from the victorious *contrada* wildly parade around the Campo waving the cherished victory banner, and post-race partying begins!

Siena, one of the region's most attractive cities, is renowned for its sienna-hued medieval palaces and towers. To the north, the ancient city's traditional enemy also radiates with Renaissance passion. Florence, capital of Tuscany, is filled with museums, cafes, red-tiled roofs, and a population of about one million. Still, with its combination of history, emotion, and pageantry, the most exciting and exhilarating event in Italy remains Siena's *Palio*.

Palio

Day 1. Tue.   Aug. 15, 2000
(Day 1. Wednesday   August 15, 2001)

9:00am Nestled in a verdant park, the stylish, 15th-century **Park Hotel** has modern, comfortable rooms.

10:00am After a 15-minute drive to Siena, start your walking tour at the Piazza del Duomo. In the center of the famed square, the black-and-white-striped **Duomo** cathedral is even more magnificent on the inside. Take a moment to look at the panels and statues inside the **Museo dell'Opera del Duomo**. For paintings done by the Sienese school, check out **Pinacoteca Nazionale** just off the piazza.

1:30pm Follow Casato di Sotto to the Piazza del Campo, the site of tomorrow's *Palio*. Wander this pedestrian-only zone, stopping to admire the towering Palazzo Ⓡ Pubblico. The family-run **Da Divo** serves excellent traditional meals.

3:30pm Lose yourself exploring the fascinating streets of this Gothic town. Be sure to visit a *contrada* museum—there are 17 to choose from.

5:00pm Return to the Campo for the *Palio*'s dress rehearsal. One more trial heat will be run tomorrow morning, but results of the last race today often determine strategies for the real race. You'll get a taste of tomorrow's tension.

8:00pm Joining the denizens of Siena on the ***passeggiata***—a nightly promenade through the city—is a great way to meet people and cool down in the stifling August heat.

9:00pm Have ***cena*** (dinner) with one of the *contrade*. Ⓡ Streets are closed off, flags hang everywhere, and hundreds of people sit and listen to speeches while plate after plate of Tuscan food arrives under the stars. In a centuries-old tradition, people stand on chairs to sing while others pound out rhythms on

the white-linen-covered tables. This is one of the high points of the event.

12:15am Follow the ***passeggiata*** back to the Campo. Here you can join groups getting a head start on tomorrow's partying.

Day 2. Wed.   Aug. 16, 2000
(Day 2. Thursday   August 16, 2001)

9:00am After breakfast in the hotel, head for the Ⓡ medieval town of San Gimignano, 20 minutes outside Siena. On your way, stop at the 13th-century ramparts of Monteriggioni, once part of Siena's defenses against its Florentine enemies. The imposing towers of San Gimignano shield twisting cobblestone streets. Sit in the Piazza del Duomo for great people-watching.

Noon Head back to Siena; leave the car at the hotel and taxi into town. Have a Tuscan-style lunch at **Il** Ⓡ **Campo** and watch the *Palio* preparations.

2:30pm If you haven't picked your personal *contrada*, wander through town and adopt a new family. Tie on a sash or buy a souvenir with the colors of your chosen *contrada* and find a seat.

4:00pm Horses are first marched around the Campo, then charged around the track with swords drawn. A cannon is set off and the pageantry begins.

7:00pm It seems to take forever for the *Palio* race to begin—jockeys spend the afternoon forming alliances and cutting deals—and then, after a year of preparation, it's over in less than two minutes. During and after the race, the crowds go crazy. The winning jockey is lifted onto the shoulders of the victorious *contrada* and paraded around the Campo.

8:00pm Dine at **Osteria Le Logge**. The restaurant Ⓡ is usually booked up and people are asked to share tables—try oven-baked radicchio or white-bean salad.

10:30pm Return to the Piazza del Campo and join the revelry. The winning *contrada* will party into the night—the losers are already plotting for next year.

Day 3. Thu. Aug. 17, 2000
(Day 3. Friday   *August 17, 2001*)

8:00am Take the scenic Strada Chiantigiana through Chianti to Florence. Check into the architecturally interesting **Brunelleschi**. A tower, medieval church, and more modern building were joined to create this unique hotel. Of course, ask for a room with a view.

10:00am Start your walking tour of Florence with a cappuccino at **Gilli** on Piazza della Republica in the heart of the Old City. Several blocks away you'll find the **Duomo**, Florence's most famous landmark. Climb all 463 steps to the top of the cathedral dome for a fabulous view. Next door is the octagonal **Battistero**, which dates back to at least the 6th century. Awe-inspiring mosaics are inside.

1:00pm Walk to Piazza della Signoria, the civic and social center of Florence. Lunch outside at **Rivoire Caffè**, a Florentine institution that serves typical cafe fare.

3:00pm Having made your reservation more than ten days in advance, skip the three-hour wait in line to view the world's greatest collection of Renaissance art at the **Galleria degli Uffizi**.

7:00pm Stroll from the Uffizi to the Ponte Vecchio, the last existing medieval bridge over the river Arno. Walk to the Piazza di Santa Croce and stop for a *gelato* at **Vivoli**, the best ice creamery in Florence.

9:30pm Arrive by cab for dinner at the elegant **Cantinetta Antinori**, a restaurant run by the 600-year-old wine company in central Florence. Fresh food is brought from the Antinori family's farm, but an even-bigger attraction is the city's best wine bar.

Midnight Taxi to the hottest dance club in Florence, the **Meccanò**, where you'll find a well-dressed crowd dancing and posing amid modern decor. When you're ready to return to your room with a view, sleep well, knowing you have an entire *contrada* to call your own.

Alternatives

If you can't make the *Palio* in August, it's also run on July 2.

The **Excelsior** hotel in Florence was once a neo-Renaissance palace—rooms are decorated with 19th-century antiques. Housed in an old monastery outside Siena, the **Certosa di Maggiano** has gorgeous furnishings and superior service. The large, opulent **Villa Scacciapensieri** sits on the top of a Tuscan hill. Centrally located a few blocks from the Piazza del Campo, the quaint **Piccolo Hotel il Palio** was once a 15th-century monastery.

Food is not Siena's strong suit, but there are several adequate restaurants around the Campo. **Al Mangia** serves dinner under the stars. **Al Marsili** has a gorgeous vaulted ceiling and offers a variety of pastas and excellent antipasto. In Florence, **Rose's** restaurant is a popular gathering spot for trendies, who show up between 10 and 11 p.m. for drinks. Chic **Coco Lezzone** is famous for wood-fired steaks served in a humble yet endearing *trattoria*.

Yab Yum is an often-crowded dance club in the center of Florence. In Siena, stop at the **Enoteca Italica Permanente**, a government-run wine "library." Here you can find a bottle of every known Italian vintage—most are available for sale and tasting.

The Hot Sheet

☎ 39/0577

$ 1,800 Lire

HOTELS	DAY	ADDRESS	*	PH	PRICE	FX	RMS	BEST ROOMS
Brunelleschi	3	3 Piazza Sant'Elisabetta	055 800-	2-7370 457-4000	$$$	21-9653	96	Dlx w/ cathedral vw
Certosa di Maggiano	A	82 Strada di Certosa		28-8180	$$$$+	28-8189	17	Rm 12
Excelsior	A	3 Piazza Ognissanti	055 800-	26-4201 325-3535	$$$$	21-0278	168	Dlx w/ piazza or river vw
Park Hotel	1	18 Via di Marciano		4-4803	$$$$+	4-9020	69	Supr dlx w/ vw
Piccolo Hotel il Palio	A	18 Piazza del Sale		28-1131	$	28-1142	26	Rm 234
Villa Scacciapensieri	A	10 Via di Scacciapensieri	800-	4-1441 645-3876	$$$$	27-0854	32	City or gdn vw

RESTAURANTS	DAY	ADDRESS	*	PH	PRICE	REC	DRESS	FOOD
Al Mangia	A	43-45 Piazza del Campo		28-1121	$$$	LD	Euro	Tuscan, international
Al Marsili	A	3 Via del Castoro		4-7154	$$	LD	Euro	Sienese, Italian
Caffè Vivoli	3	7 Via Isola delle Stinche	055	29-2334	$	T/L	Local	*Gelato*
Cantinetta Antinori	3	3 Palazzo Antinori	055	29-2234	$$$	LTD	Euro	Florentine, Tuscan
Coco Lezzone	A	26 Via del Parioncino	055	28-7178	$$	LD	Euro	Florentine
Da Divo	1	29 Franceosa		28-4381	$$$	L/D	Kazh	Tuscan
Gilli	3	39 Piazza della Republica	055	21-3896	$	B/LD	Local	Cafe
Il Campo	2	50 Piazza del Campo		28-0725	$$$	L/D	Local	Italian
Osteria Le Logge	2	33 Via del Porrione		4-8013	$$	D/L	Kazh	Sienese
Rivoire Caffè	3	4 Piazza della Signoria	055	21-4412	$$	L/BD	Local	Cafe
Rose's	A	2 Via Rosina	055	21-8550	$$	LD	Euro	Sushi, cocktails

NITELIFE	DAY	ADDRESS	*	PH	PRICE	REC	DRESS	MUSIC
Enoteca Italica Permanente	A	Fortezza Medicea		28-8497	None	H	Euro	
Meccanò	3	1 Viale degli Olmi	055	33-1371	$$	O	Euro	Disco
Yab Yum	A	5 Via Sassetti	055	21-5160	$$	O	Euro	Disco

SIGHTS & ATTRACTIONS	DAY	ADDRESS	*	PH	ENTRY FEE
Battistero	3	Piazza del Duomo	055	230-2885	$
Duomo	1	Piazza del Duomo		28-3048	None
Duomo	3	Piazza del Duomo	055	230-2885	$
Galleria degli Uffizi	3	6 Piazzale degli Uffizi	055	238-8651	$$
Museo dell'Opera del Duomo	1	Piazza del Duomo		28-3048	$
Pinacoteca Nazionale	1	29 Via San Pietro		28-1161	$
Azienda Promozione Turistica		16 Via A. Manzoni	055	2-3320	
Tourist Office		56 Piazza del Campo		28-0551	

EVENT & TICKET INFO

Palio (Piazza del Campo, Siena): Standing (sardine-like) in the center of the Campo is free. Tickets for the stands and balconies (approximately $250 and sold by merchants) are in short supply, but try the *Siena Tourist Office* (39/0577-28-0551). The surest (but not the cheapest) way to get good seats is to contact your hotel concierge before arrival.

Contrada cena: Tickets ($30) are available by contacting the *Siena Tourist Office* (39/0577-28-0551) or your concierge.

*055=Florence

RECommendations: (Restaurants) B–Breakfast; L–Lunch; D–Dinner; T–High tea or snack
(Nitelife) G–Gaming; H–Hangout bar; M–Live music; O–Dancing (disco); P–Dancing (live music); S–Show; F–Food served
()–Available but without recommendation. For complete explanation of Hot Sheet format, see page 34.

NYC +6   63°/83° (17°/28°)   Florence (FLR); 60 min./$50   Yes   Italian

Edinburgh Fringe Festival

(Edinburgh Festival Fringe)

Origin: 1947   Event ★ ★ ★ ★ ★ ★ ★ ★ City   Attendance: 800,000

Seven hundred performing-arts companies stage 14,000 performances of 1,300 shows in just over 20 days—and that's just the *Fringe Festival!* At this event, there's also the main stage *Edinburgh International Festival*, the *Edinburgh Military Tattoo*, and the ongoing nightlife of the city itself. That's not entertainment, that's a party!

While many great art festivals attract high-brow followings, Edinburgh's *Fringe Festival* aims at more earthbound crowds. Make no mistake, there are terrific performances here—even as an unknown, *Fringe*-alumni Emma Thompson was no slouch. But the festival's faithful followers are not a crew likely to let snotty reviews or contemptuous experts spoil their appreciation of the most important parts of this gathering—top-rate art and top-rate ale (or Scotch, if you prefer).

Performances of all types—theater, dance, music, comedy—entertain massive crowds 24 hours a day. Ranked as the world's largest arts festival by the *Guinness Book of World Records*, the *Fringe* has simply too many events for one person to see. Scattered around the city are a variety of exhibitions as well as book and film festivals. Modern music is part of the packed schedule, but traditional bands remain the favorites. Don't miss the *Edinburgh Military Tattoo* at Edinburgh Castle for an unforgettable display of military precision, bagpipes, and drums.

The Scottish capital, with a population of half a million, resembles a dramatic set situated between ocean and coastal crags. Castles, royal residences, and architecture from the ancient, medieval, Edwardian, and Victorian eras are set in a lush valley. Dining options won't disappoint gourmands eager to find authentic Scottish heritage. Haggis—minced sheep or calf innards with suet and oatmeal boiled in animal stomach—is widely available. But restaurants increasingly express Caledonian cuisine's more visitor-friendly side and many international restaurants have trickled in. Pubs are the favorite destination at night, when comparing performances and pints with the stranger on the next stool is a big part of the *Fringe* tradition.

Edinburgh Fringe Festival

Day 1. Thu.   Aug. 17, 2000
(Day 1. Thursday   *August 16, 2001)*

9:00am The Balmoral offers Edwardian splendor in the heart of the city. This former railway hotel is one of Edinburgh's finest, with great views across the city to the castle.

10:00am Walk the Royal Mile and encounter *Fringe* madness as costumed actors persuade you to visit their shows. You'll pass plenty of eateries along the way—try **Common Grounds** for a great range of coffees. Grab a copy of the festival's daily newspaper and start planning your schedule. Wander around taking in superb street performances—participatory comedy, mime, music, juggling, and much more.

12:30pm In the pretty boutique shopping area of Victoria Street, lunch upstairs in the relaxed atmosphere of **The Grain Store**. The restaurant uses fresh Scottish produce to create modern British cuisine.

2:00pm At Waverly Bridge, take the **Guide Friday** open-top bus for a tour of Edinburgh highlights. Informative guides impart some of the area's dramatic history. You can get on and off at any point, so make a stop at **Edinburgh Castle**, where you'll see the Scottish crown jewels and great views of the city.

7:30pm Located in an unlikely back alley is **Martins**, one of Edinburgh's finest restaurants. Chefs use organic and wild ingredients to superb effect, creating dishes that are light and healthy. The cheese board and wine list are extensive.

9:00pm *Fringe* venues can be as much fun as the performances. The Assembly Rooms, which offer many shows under one roof, are a scene. Put together overnight for the festival, the astounding interior of the 1920s-style Spiegeltent is a must-see.

Midnight During the festival, Club Graffiti (housed in an abandoned church) is good for late-night carousing. The outdoor beer garden is perfect for warm summer nights.

Day 2. Fri.   Aug. 18, 2000
(Day 2. Friday   *August 17, 2001)*

11:00am After breakfast in the hotel, head to Charlotte Square. **The Georgian House** shows what life was like for the wealthy in the early part of the 19th century. In the center of the square is the *Edinburgh International Book Festival*—meet the authors, buy the books!

1:30pm Elegant George Street is full of lunch options: **Est Est Est** for modern Italian, **All Bar One** for bistro-bar cuisine, or **The Dome** for lunch in an amazing Victorian banking hall.

3:00pm Up the hill is the neo-classical **National Portrait Gallery**. You'll see paintings of plenty of famous Scots, plus a fantastic building interior. Nearby, stop at the **National Gallery** to view a fine collection of impressionist, Renaissance, and Scottish works.

6:30pm Start the night with a cocktail at **Indigo Yard**, a spacious designer bar. This popular place to be seen by Edinburgh's young professionals is open until 1 a.m. nightly.

7:30pm You may decide to attend one of the world-class events at the *Edinburgh International Festival*, but if you're sticking to the *Fringe*, begin the night at **The Atrium**. Enjoy innovative modern cuisine in a visually striking atmosphere. Afterward, head upstairs to **Blue Bar Cafe**. Linger over coffee or single-malt whisky and soak up the sophisticated, minimalist atmosphere.

10:30pm On to the shows you researched earlier. A typical evening might include drama in the Assembly

Rooms, comedy in The Gilded Balloon, drinks in the lively cafe **EH1**, a late-night film première at The Cameo Cinema, and finally, Scottish beer with other film buffs in the **Cameo Bar**.

1:00am Play on at the hip North African club **Po Na Na Souk Bar**. You could finish off the night at the classy **Why Not** disco, located below The Dome restaurant.

Day 3. Sat. Aug. 19, 2000
(Day 3. Saturday August 18, 2001)

9:30am Pile on the calories with an almond croissant
® and other pastries at **Café Florentin**.

11:00am It might be a little early for your first Scotch, but not too early for the **Scotch Whisky Heritage Centre**, where you can learn all about the amber liquid of life.

12:30pm Head for the Victorian splendor of **The**
® **Abbotsford** on Rose Street. There's an authentic bar and the best pub lunch around. If you're feeling adventurous, go for the haggis. The fish and chips are good, too, and be sure to sample the good selection of real ales (beer brewed by traditional methods).

2:00pm Spend a few hours at the ***Fringe***, maybe taking in a play or a ***Book Festival*** event.

7:00pm Head to the castle and the ***Edinburgh Military Tattoo*** where massed pipe-and-drum bands put on a ceremonial exhibit of military music and prowess.

10:00pm Only flickering candlelight illuminates the room
® as you dine in **The Witchery By The Castle**'s nouveau-Gothic dining rooms. Chefs brew up modern, imaginative Scottish fare in a historic Old Town structure that was once Edinburgh's center for witchcraft.

Midnight Head for a typical ***Fringe*** finish at **Café Royal Bistro Bar**. Enjoy a fine Scotch as you reflect on the previous days of art, music, theater, writing, film, and carnival atmosphere, or just meditate on your own image in another glass of the amber magic.

Alternatives

Set amid elegant, leafy streets, **The Bonham** is a contemporary hotel with a Victorian frontage and real style in its use of colors, fabrics, and furnishings. **Malmaison Hotel**, a fashionable boutique hotel with a chic clientele, is located in Leith, a taxi ride from downtown. **The Point Hotel**, a new four-star accommodation, has a hip reputation and a walk-to-everything location.

In the heart of Old Town, the stylish **Dial Restaurant** serves modern Scottish cuisine. **Hadrian's** is part of The Balmoral—its soothing, cool colors will provide you with a change of scene without having to leave your hotel. Inside the Edwardian Caledonian Hotel is **La Pompadour**—very French, very sophisticated, very good. For breakfast or a snack, go to **Glass & Thompson**, a great coffee shop and deli. Or stop at **Valvona & Crolla**, Edinburgh's legendary Italian deli and cafe.

Try natural beer brewed by traditional methods (real ale) at **The Cumberland Bar**.

The **Museum of Scotland** has a superb international collection housed in a fantastic Victorian cast-iron building—check out the *Story of Scotland* in the much newer and very impressive extension. Have lunch in its restaurant, **The Tower**, and enjoy terrific panoramic views of the city.

EVENT & TICKET INFO
(continued from page 210)

Edinburgh International Book Festival (Charlotte Square and other locations in Edinburgh): For information, call the *International Book Festival* (44/131-624-5050).

Edinburgh International Festival (various locations around Edinburgh): For information, call the *International Festival* (44/131-473-2000).

Edinburgh International Film Festival (The Filmhouse, 88 Lothian Rd.; The Cameo Cinema, 38 Home St.; and other movie houses in Edinburgh): For information and tickets, call the *International Film* Festival (44/131-229-2550).

The Hot Sheet

☎ 44/131

$ 0.6 Pound

HOTELS	DAY	ADDRESS	PH	PRICE	FX	RMS	BEST ROOMS
The Balmoral	1	1 Princes St.	556-2414 800- 223-6800	$$$$	557-3747	186	Dlx king rm
The Bonham	A	35 Drumsheugh Gardens	226-6050 800- 323-5463	$$$	226-6080	50	Supr sea vw
Malmaison Hotel	A	1 Tower Pl., Leith	468-5000	$$$	486-5002	60	4-poster rm
The Point Hotel	A	34 Bread St.	221-5555 800- 448-8355	$$$	221-9929	95	Exec lux dbl

RESTAURANTS	DAY	ADDRESS	PH	PRICE	REC	DRESS	FOOD
The Abbotsford	3	3 Rose St.	225-5276	$	L/D	Local	Traditional pub food
All Bar One	2	29 George St.	226-9971	$$	L/D	Kazh	Bistro, modern
The Atrium	2	10 Cambridge St.	228-8882	$$$	D/L	Kazh	Modern Scottish
Café Florentin	3	8 Giles St.	225-6267	$	B/LD	Local	Cafe, French
Common Grounds	1	2-3 N. Bank St.	226-1416	$	B/LD	Local	Cafe
Dial Restaurant	A	44-46 George IV	225-7179	$$	LD	Kazh	Modern Scottish
The Dome	2	14 George St.	624-8624	$$	L/D	Euro	Scottish, Mediterranean
Est Est Est	2	135 George St.	225-2555	$$	L/D	Local	Italian
Glass & Thompson	A	2 Dundas St.	557-0909	$	BL	Local	Gourmet deli
The Grain Store	1	30 Victoria St.	225-7635	$$	L/D	Kazh	Modern Scottish
Hadrian's	A	see The Balmoral hotel	556-2414	$$	BLD	Kazh	Scottish brasserie
La Pompadour	A	Princes St. in Caledonian Hotel	459-9988	$$$$	LD	Dressy	Classic French, Scottish
Martins	1	70 Rose St. Ln. N. in Traverse Theatre foyer	225-3106	$$$	D/L	Euro	Modern Scottish
The Tower	A	see Museum of Scotland	225-3003	$$	LD	Kazh	Nuvo Scottish
The Witchery By The Castle	3	3 Castlehill	225-5613	$$$	D/L	Dressy	Nuvo Scottish, Mediterranean
Valvona & Crolla	A	19 Elm Row	556-6066	$	B/L	Local	Italian deli

NITELIFE	DAY	ADDRESS	PH	PRICE	REC	DRESS	MUSIC
Blue Bar Cafe	2	10 Cambridge St.	221-1222	$	HF	Kazh	
Café Royal Bistro Bar	3	17 W. Register St.	557-4792	None	HF	Kazh	
Cameo Bar	2	2 Home St. in Cameo Cinema	228-4141	None	H	Local	
The Cumberland Bar	A	1-3 Cumberland St.	558-3134	None	HF	Local	
EH1	2	197 High St.	220-5277	None	HF	Kazh	
Indigo Yard	2	7 Charlotte Ln.	220-5603	None	HF	Kazh	
Po Na Na Souk Bar	2	43B Frederick St.	226-2224	$	OF	Kazh	Rock, pop, house
Why Not	2	14 George St.	624-8633	$	O	Euro	Dance

SIGHTS & ATTRACTIONS	DAY	ADDRESS	PH	ENTRY FEE
Edinburgh Castle	1	top of Castlehill	225-9846	$
The Georgian House	2	7 Charlotte Sq.	225-2160	$
Museum of Scotland	A	Chambers St.	225-7534	$
National Gallery	2	The Mound off Princes St.	556-8921	None
National Portrait Gallery	2	1 Queen St.	556-8921	None
Scotch Whisky Heritage Centre	3	354 Castlehill	220-0441	$

OTHER SIGHTS, SERVICES & ATTRACTIONS

Guide Friday	1	Waverly Bridge	556-2244	$
Edinburgh & Lothians Tourist Board		3 Princes St.	473-3800	

EVENT & TICKET INFO

Edinburgh Fringe Festival (various locations around Edinburgh): Performances are priced individually. Tickets can be purchased by calling the *Edinburgh Festival Fringe Box Office* (44/131-226-5138).

Edinburgh Military Tattoo (Edinburgh Castle): Tickets ($13-30) can be purchased by calling *The Tattoo Office* (44/131-225-1188).

(continued on page 209)

RECommendations: (Restaurants) B–Breakfast; L–Lunch; D–Dinner; T–High tea or snack (Nitelife) G–Gaming; H–Hangout bar; M–Live music; O–Dancing (disco); P–Dancing (live music); S–Show; F–Food served ( )–Available but without recommendation. For complete explanation of Hot Sheet format, see page 34.

NYC +5   51°/65° (10°/18°)   Edinburgh (EDI); 30 min./$25   No   English

The Fun Also Rises

Real Swingers

The Scots have invented many things, including the Edinburgh festivals, bag-pipes, and Scotch—all of which we've covered in this book. But you'll have to agree, the world would be a lesser place without the most addictive, intriguing, and implausible Scottish invention of them all: golf.

One of the Scots' best-loved contributions to the civilized world, The British Open, the world's oldest golf tournament, remains among the sport's greatest annual events. It's been played for almost 140 years and is always contested on one of England's or Scotland's hallowed venues. Watching this tradition-filled tournament unfold in person at Turnberry, Muirfield, or St. Andrews (the birth-place of golf and host of the 2000 British Open) is an unforgettable life experience.

Even for nonplayers, professional golf tourna-ments can be fun. Some spectators plant themselves at one hole and break out their lawn chairs for the day. Others follow a favorite golfer. The surroundings are always lush, lovely, and per-fect for an invigorating walk in the park. Hospitality tents and refreshment areas present great oppor-tunities to meet people and discuss everything from missed putts to your latest merger or takeover.

With increasing media coverage, golf has become one of the most popular sports on the planet—more than 50 million people world-wide now pronounce themselves golfers. But the skill level may not have changed much since Scottish shepherds first played with sticks and stones more than 300 years ago—most of us are still woeful on the links. Yet, there's a whole lot more hacking going on these days.

Hitting a tournament is easy, with several pro tours and events all over the world. The best men players congregate on three tours: The Professional Golfers' Association Tour (PGA Tour), the Japan Professional Golfers' Association Tour (JPGA Tour), and the European Professional

Golfers' Association Tour (EPGA Tour). The best women play on the Ladies Professional Golf Association Tour (LPGA Tour), and the best players over 50 compete on the Senior Professional Golfers' Association Tour (Senior PGA Tour).

The format for most tournaments is "stroke play," which simply means that the golfer with the lowest aggregate score at the end of the designated number of holes (usually 72) wins the tournament. A "skins game" is typically played between four golfers, and each hole is worth a cer-tain number of dollars. If no one wins the hole, the value is carried over to the next hole. Particularly at televised skins games featuring a quartet of golf's biggest stars, a single hole can be worth $500,000 or more! "Match play" pits one golfer against another. Whichever player wins the most holes wins the match. This format is often used in nail-biting international competition, such as the Ryder Cup or The Presidents Cup.

The Senior PGA Tour—players more than 50 years of age—is fun to watch because many of the golfers ham it up for the crowds. Swashbuckling Chi Chi Rodriguez waves his putter around in the air like a pirate's sword after each successful putt. The "Merry Mex," Lee Trevino, drops to his knees whenever he misses a close putt. Arnold Palmer and Jack Nicklaus still battle for top honors after 40 years of competition. The players at these events are often master showmen who have as much fun as the spectators.

You can have loads of fun at the LPGA, too. At most ladies tournaments the galleries are smaller, making it easier to get close to players and hear what they're discussing with their caddies. If you want to improve your swing, pattern it after an LPGA player. The women are widely held to have the best swings in the game.

The PGA Tour is where you'll find Tiger Woods and colleagues. In 1999, there were 47 official events on the PGA Tour, with prize money totaling $131.7 million. Over the course of the year, the most successful golfers on tour pocketed more than $2 million in prize money (and even more in endorsements). Are the big-money players worth it? Could Michael Jordan dunk?

The professional tours travel from one end of the globe to the other. Each host city has its charm, and each tournament its distinct personality. Some are downright fun, such as the AT&T Pebble Beach National Pro-Am, which draws top celebrities as well as top golfers into the field. Bill Murray, Jack Lemmon, and Clint Eastwood are regulars here. Others, such as the Masters and U.S. Open—two of the four prestigious "majors" played each year—are more serious. Winning one of these tournaments boosts a golfer to a new level of respect and accomplishment.

If you've ever taken narrow stick to dimpled spheroid and tried to manipulate its course of flight toward a hole in the ground 450 yards away marked by a half-inch diameter flagpole, you know that golf is aggravating enough to make a bishop kick a hole in a stained-glass window. Par on most courses is 72; the average golfer doesn't break 100. If you were this successful in your job, you'd be fired! Once, when asked which single factor contributed most to his success, Jack Nicklaus, perhaps the greatest golfer ever to play the game, remarked, "I miss better than anyone else." The Golden Bear wasn't kidding.

But, for all its infamous aggravation, golf remains mysteriously fun. Watching a perfectly hit ball as it floats magically against a solid blue sky produces a feeling like no other. A 20-foot putt dropping exquisitely into the cup makes a

uniquely graceful sound. And a hole-in-one is like a grand slam, three-point buzzer beater, and long-bomb touchdown all rolled into one.

To enjoy watching a golf tournament, you don't have to paint your face in team colors. There's no "dawg pound" in the visiting team's end zone taunting and heckling. Golf is a civilized sport with skilled athletes playing a game of honor. See for yourself at a professional tournament and you'll be a better hacker for it.

KEEPING YOUR EYE ON THE BALL

The Majors

The Masters (April)
Ticket information: *Augusta National, 706-667-6000*

U.S. Open (June)
Ticket information: *Wide World of Golf, 800-214-4653*

The British Open (July)
Ticket information: *The Ticket Office, Royal & Ancient Golf Club, 44/133-447-8478*

The PGA Championship (August)
Ticket information: *PGA of America, 800-474-2776*

Most Fun U.S. Tournaments

The Phoenix Open; Phoenix, Arizona (January)
Ticket information: 602-870-4431

MCI Classic—The Heritage of Golf
Hilton Head Island, South Carolina (April)
Ticket information: 800-234-1107

The AT&T Pebble Beach National Pro-Am
Pebble Beach, California (February)
Ticket information: 800-541-9091

Nabisco Dinah Shore; Rancho Mirage, California (March);
Ticket information: 760-324-4546

Most Fun International Tournaments

Ryder Cup (U.S. team versus European team)
Biennial, alternating sites;
Ticket information: *Wide World of Golf, 800-214-4653*

The Presidents Cup (U.S. team versus International team)
Biennial, alternating sites;
Ticket information: *Wide World of Golf, 800-214-4653*

Notting Hill Carnival

Origin: 1965   Event ★ ★ ★ ★ ★ ★ ★ ★ City   **Attendance: 1.5 million**

The days of the British Commonwealth essentially are over. But with the end of Britain's reign has come an awesome rainbow of more than a million good-vibe citizens of the world, who show up in London's now-hippest neighborhood to party. The *Notting Hill Carnival* claims to be Europe's largest outdoor arts festival and one of the world's biggest street parties—second only to Carnaval in Rio de Janeiro.

Even though *Notting Hill Carnival*'s parade is officially the centerpiece of the event, it functions more as a combination of scenery, sound track, and lively excuse for celebrants to come together to dance, sing, and, in the parlance of the islands, "cruise." The 15,000-participant-strong parade stretches three miles and features marchers from Afghanistan, Khurdistan, Bangladesh, and the Philippines, as well as the more-expected revelers from the Caribbean, Africa, Central and South America, and Europe. One hundred costumed bands and 45 licensed sound systems keep the entire four-square-mile party area thumping and spectators dancing to reggae, samba, soul, calypso, soca, steel bands, mas bands, and sound-system mixes. Hundreds of food stands add spice to the mix, with most serving Caribbean, African, or Asian fare. Many vendors also sell alcohol, and the air is occasionally sweetened by a hint of "spliffs" (marijuana cigarettes).

Once day-jammin' is over, *Carnival*-related parties pound through the night. Clusters of hotspots around the city have inspired many European magazines to designate London one of the coolest places to be. Soho, at one time a seedy peep-show district, now provides London's greatest concentration of hip clubs, restaurants, bars, and street life. Begin a night out at one of London's trendy restaurants, with some good British food—no longer an oxymoron.

Choosing how to spend your time when not at *Carnival* from the variety of things to see and do in London can be overwhelming. This itinerary highlights one set of must-do places to go; check out the Ascot chapter (see page 155) for more possibilities.

Notting Hill Carnival

Day 1. Sat.   Aug. 26, 2000
(Day 1. Saturday   August 25, 2001)

9:00am The Metropolitan hotel is ultrachic and your ticket to its hotel bar so exclusive that out-of-towners staying elsewhere have been known to book rooms here just to gain entrance. The hotel's Donna Karan-clad staff are friendly and in-the-know.

10:30am Famous for its antiques and high prices, the Portobello Road Market bustles and haggles its way through every Saturday from 8:30 a.m. until 5:30 p.m. Even if you're not planning to lug an armoire back home, the bargaining atmosphere makes it worth a visit.

12:30pm The people-watching is as appealing as the
® Pacific Rim menu at **The Sugar Club**.

2:00pm Cab to Little Venice and board an aquatic bus that **Jason's Trip** navigates through the canal along Regent's Park, the former hunting ground of Henry VIII, to Camden Lock. The trip takes about 45 minutes and winds up amid Camden Town's wacky shops and stalls. Pick up a glittery number to wear tomorrow, but be back in time to catch Jason's last bus at 5:15 p.m.

8:30pm The fun starts at **Momo**, where the cuisine may
® be singularly North African but the mixed clientele keeps things lively. Sink into the low cushions and watch the scene unfold by lantern light.

10:30pm Hit London's biggest club—**Hippodrome**—where six bars, caged dancers, and a dramatic laser light show occupy the former opera house and theater. At **L'Equipe Anglaise** the high-energy atmosphere is worth the wait in line. By midnight, it'll be jammed, so

if you need more space to dance, check out the **Equinox Discotheque**.

3:00am At **Bar Italia**, there's singing, two-fisted drinking, and dancing to classic tunes.

Day 2. Sun.   Aug. 27, 2000
(Day 2. Sunday   August 26, 2001)

9:30am Have a room-service breakfast and prep for
® the day. Outside of actual participants, not many people attend *Carnival* in costume. Wear something light and comfortable for dancing.

10:30am Head to Hyde Park for a stroll through its well-tended greenery. The park's northeastern tip, a former site of public floggings, has become Speakers' Corner, where you can pull up a soapbox and speak your mind—barring blasphemy, libel, or obscenity. You might have trouble being heard over all the orators who compete with hecklers for airspace.

11:30am Have brunch at **Dakota**, a fun place serving
® upscale U.S. Southwestern cuisine.

2:00pm Head to the *Notting Hill Carnival*, which has been heating up for the last two hours. It's Children's Day, but this isn't kid stuff. You can follow your favorite mas band by jumping into the noncostumed section tailing each band. If you want to "check" (*Carnival*-speak for "picking up or chatting up the opposite sex"), avoid the Portobello Green and Ladbroke Grove, where crowd density makes flirting nearly impossible. Pick up a copy of *Touch* magazine, which has tips on *Carnival* and associated parties.

4:30pm If you feel "peckish"
® (hungry), try some spicy snacks at one of the hundreds of food stands.

> **Sophisticated Heckling at Speakers' Corner**
> The speaker is interrupted by two hecklers, one on either side of the listening crowd, who shout out alternately, "This–is–an–experiment–in–stereo–phonic–heckling!"

6:30pm Leave early to avoid the crowds when *Carnival* ends at 7 p.m.

8:00pm Begin the evening with cocktails—or better yet, a martini-tasting—in the **Met Bar**, the most exclusive bar in London, located in your hotel.

9:30pm The Metropolitan also houses **Nobu**, one of the ® trendiest restaurants in London. Chef Nobuyuki Matsuhisa serves exquisite Japanese cuisine. A meal here is an investment and draws a posh crowd.

11:30pm There's a livelier dinner scene at **Atlantic Bar & Grill**, where the club crowd fits the restaurant's nightclubbish decor. Some come for the scene, some for the internationally-influenced British fare, and others for the two bars that toast until 3 a.m.

1:00am The "wining" (dancing) continues at several clubs likely to host *Carnival* parties. **Bar Rumba** is the place to meet other Carnival-goers who can't stop grinding to swing and hip-hop. To hear the finest London DJs, head to **The End** and **333**—the latter has three floors of nighttime activities.

Day 3. Mon. Aug. 28, 2000
(Day 3. Monday   August 27, 2001)

9:00am At **Pâtisserie Valerie**, the mostly French crew ® serve breakfasts for bohemians. Cigarette smoke and oil paintings make your pastry and *café au lait* taste all the more French.

10:00am *Notting Hill Carnival* takes place during the two months of the year **Buckingham Palace** is open to the public. Cab to the historic residence for a glimpse of the rooms and royal furnishings the queen uses to entertain visiting heads of state. Buy tickets across the street in Green Park and be out in time to catch the changing-of-the-guard ceremony.

1:30pm Heading back to Notting Hill, stop en route on still-hip King's Road. Lunch on modern British fare at ® **Bluebird**, a bright restaurant-cum-outdoor-market.

3:00pm It's a national bank holiday, so *Carnival* rages with even more dancing and whistle-blowing. Snack on jerk chicken, a carnival classic.

7:00pm Have dinner at nearby, fun **Kensington Place**, ® which serves modern British fare in a noisy environment.

8:30pm Though *Carnival* was supposed to end at 7 p.m., it hasn't. Everyone loosens up under cover of darkness, so take in the final throes.

10:30pm The bar should be hopping at the nearby and trendy **Pharmacy Restaurant & Bar**, which features a drug-store-inspired interior.

Midnight Star DJs set the crowd into motion at the internationally famous **Ministry of Sound**, bringing your *Notting Hill Carnival* weekend to a close.

Alternatives

Close to the *Carnival* action, **The Portobello Hotel**'s unique Victorian-Middle Eastern decor and ever-open bar keep its rock-star clientele returning. **Covent Garden Hotel** features comfortable, quirky rooms (odd details include a tailor's mannequin in every room). The epitome of minimalist elegance, **The Hempel** hotel is Zen-inspired and draws a hip crowd.

The **Pharmacy Restaurant & Bar** is also an option for lunch or dinner. Most of the cool crowd at the post-mod brasserie **192** are too busy socializing and people-watching to notice the excellent cuisine (closed during *Carnival*). A fun and chic place for sushi is **itsu**.

Calypso fanatics start *Carnival* no later than Friday. North of Notting Hill, calypso monarch competitions get underway at the *London Calypso Tent*. Saturday night, the *Steelbands' Panorama and Festival* gives a taste of *Carnival*'s metal.

The Hot Sheet

☎ 44/171 $ 0.6 Pound

HOTELS	DAY	ADDRESS	PH	PRICE	FX	RMS	BEST ROOMS
Covent Garden Hotel	A	10 Monmouth St., WC2	806-1000	$$$$+	806-1100	50	Dlx
The Hempel	A	31-35 Craven Hill Gardens, W2 Hempel Garden Sq.	298-9000 800- 747-1337	$$$$	402-4666	49	Dlx
The Metropolitan	1	19 Old Park Ln., W1	447-1000 800- 637-7200	$$$$+	447-1100	155	Dlx
The Portobello Hotel	A	22 Stanley Gardens, W11	727-2777	$$$$	792-9641	24	Supr

RESTAURANTS	DAY	ADDRESS	PH	PRICE	REC	DRESS	FOOD
192	A	192 Kensington Park Rd., W11	229-0482	$$	LD	Euro	Modern British
Atlantic Bar & Grill	2	20 Glasshouse St., W1	734-4888	$$$$	D/L	Kazh	Modern European
Bluebird	3	350 King's Rd.	559-1000	$$	L/BDT	Kazh	Modern British
Dakota	2	127 Ledbury Rd., W11	792-9191	$$	L/BD	Euro	Southwestern U.S.
itsu	A	118 Draycott Ave., SW3	584-5522	$$$	LD	Kazh	Asian
Kensington Place	3	201-205 Kensington Church St., W8	727-3184	$$$	L/D	Euro	Modern British
Momo	1	25 Heddon St., W1	434-4040	$$$	D/L	Euro	North African
Nobu	2	see The Metropolitan hotel	447-4747	$$$$+	D/L	Dressy	Fusion
Pâtisserie Valerie	3	44 Old Compton St., W1	437-3466	$	B/L	Local	Bakery
Pharmacy Bar & Restaurant	A	150 Notting Hill Gate, W11	221-2442	$$$	LD	Euro	International
The Sugar Club	1	21 Warwick St., W1	437-7776	$$$	L/D	Euro	Pacific Rim

NITELIFE	DAY	ADDRESS	PH	PRICE	REC	DRESS	MUSIC
333	2	333 Old St., EC1	739-5949	$$	O	Euro	Soul, house
Atlantic Bar & Grill	2	20 Glasshouse St., W1	734-4888	None	MPF	Kazh	Jazz
Bar Italia	1	22 Frith St., W1	437-4520	None	H(F)	Kazh	
Bar Rumba	2	36 Shaftesbury, W1	287-2715	$	O	Euro	Latin, funk, house, R&B
The End	2	16A W. Central St., WC1	419-9199	$$	O	Euro	House, hip-hop, techno, jungle
Equinox Discotheque	1	Leicester Sq., WC2	437-1446	$$	P(F)		Dance, popular, R&B
Hippodrome	1	Hippodrome Crnr., WC2	437-4311	$$	OS	Euro	House
L'Equipe Anglaise	1	21-23 Duke St., W1	486-8281	$$	OF	Dressy	Techno, house
Met Bar	2	see The Metropolitan hotel	447-1000	None	OF	Euro	Funk, R&B, Latin
Ministry of Sound	3	103 Gaunt St., SE1	378-6528	$$	O	Euro	Garage, house, club classics
Pharmacy Bar & Restaurant	3	150 Notting Hill Gate, W11	221-2442	None	HF	Euro	

SIGHTS & ATTRACTIONS	DAY	ADDRESS	PH	ENTRY FEE
Buckingham Palace	3	Buckingham Palace Rd., SW1A	839-1377	$$

OTHER SIGHTS, SERVICES & ATTRACTIONS

Jason's Trip	1	opposite 60 Blomfield Rd., W9 Little Venice	286-3428	$
London Tourist Information Centre		Victoria's Station Forecourt, SW1	None	

EVENT & TICKET INFO

Notting Hill Carnival (Ladbroke Grove and Portobello Green): All official events are free, including the **London Calypso Tent** (Yaa Asentawa Arts Centre, W10) and **Steelbands' Panorama and Festival** (Hornimans Pleasance, W10). For information, contact *Notting Hill Carnival Committee* (181-964-0544).

RECommendations: (Restaurants) B–Breakfast; L–Lunch; D–Dinner; T–High tea or snack
(Nitelife) G–Gaming; H–Hangout bar; M–Live music; O–Dancing (disco); P–Dancing (live music); S–Show; F–Food served
( )–Available but without recommendation. For complete explanation of Hot Sheet format, see page 34.

🕐 NYC +5   ☀ 55°/70° (12°/25°)   ✈ London Heathrow (LHR); 45 min./$60 (R)
London Gatwick (LGW); 90 min./$75 (R)   🚗 No   👥 English

The Fun Also Rises

La Tomatina

Origin: 1957	Event ★★★★★★★★★ City	Attendance: 25,000

One hundred thirty tons of tomatoes can make a lot of soup, salad, or sauce, but at Spain's *La Tomatina*, it makes for the world's biggest, messiest food fight. On the last Wednesday of August in tiny Buñol's Plaza del Pueblo, the event lasts just sixty minutes and makes a fraternity food fight look like a formal luncheon at The Ritz.

Everyone is fair game. Individuals and makeshift platoons from the largely shirtless crowd (shirts are ripped off during warm-up festivities that pass time until dump trucks unload the tomatoes) attack and retaliate, retreat and give chase. Midway into the pulp storm, those desperate for ammo sift through the red goo for any tomato bits large enough to lob. By the end of the madness, people splash each other with purée and all of Buñol looks like a walking emergency ward. Afterward, clean-up crews provide a nearly-as-impressive sight as they return the town to normal within two hours.

Stories vary on when and why *La Tomatina* began—some cite a local political rally; others say it was during a religious procession honoring San Luís Beltrán, the town's patron saint. Whatever the reason, the event has put Buñol on the map. Before media coverage made *La Tomatina* famous in the 1990s, the only feature distinguishing the tiny Spanish town from its neighbors was its cement works. Now, *La Tomatina* pilgrims outnumber the town's 9,000 inhabitants almost 3 to 1, and the event is seen on televisions throughout the world.

Aside from the tomato toss, there's not much to do in Buñol. Luckily, cosmopolitan Barcelona (population 2 million), your *La Tomatina* headquarters and one of the world's sexiest cities, is just a short flight away. During August, cafes and restaurants move outdoors and locals dine as late as 11 p.m. before heading to the Catalonian capital's flourishing late-night (actually early-morning) entertainment districts. After a few days admiring its ancient architecture and a few nights admiring its modern beauties, everyone falls in love with Barcelona and no one ever forgets *La Tomatina*.

La Tomatina

*You can spend the night near the Valencia airport in the **Meliá Confort Azafata**, part of Spain's biggest luxury-hotel chain. Or stay in Barcelona and travel to Buñol on Day 1 by fast train (four hours) or car (three hours).*

Day 1. Wed. Aug. 30, 2000
(Day 1. Wednesday August 29, 2001)

8:30am Throw on your oldest duds and eat at the hotel buffet. If you taxi to Buñol, have the driver wait for you at the train station (about $12 an hour) as there are no cabs in Buñol.

10:30am Follow the anxious crowds to the Plaza del Ayuntamiento (City Hall). The first act—participants tearing off each other's shirts (women should wear bathing suits under their T-shirts)—is about to begin. As Act 2—townspeople throwing water on the crowd—begins, stake out your spot. Any small, narrow street is a great place to begin fighting. Another place is next to the tomato trucks near City Hall. If you don't want to be totally drenched, crouch low and head for open spaces away from the center of town. But with big red tomatoes soon flying from all sides, it's hard not to get splattered. The best plan is to grit your teeth, roll up your sleeves (assuming your shirt hasn't already been torn off), and dive in!

Noon Act 3—various lunatics climbing a greased pole and trying to grab the ham at the top—signals the beginning of the world's largest food fight (Act 4)!

1:00pm In an hour, a whistle blows marking the end of **La Tomatina** madness. Grab after-fight refreshment at the Bar de Feo, Bar de Litro, or the smaller Bar Fresnal, all near the Plaza del Ayuntamiento.

2:00pm Use a public shower and change clothes before getting back to your cab. Just don't leave without looking at the town square, now completely cleaned

as though one of the most amazing events of your life hadn't even happened.

2:30pm Lunch at **Restaurant Azafata** in the Meliá Confort Azafata hotel before catching an Iberia Airline flight to Barcelona.

8:00pm Check in to the luxurious, monochromatic, and eclectic **Hotel Claris**.

9:00pm Taxi to Barrio Xines, an otherworldly area near the Barrio Gótic, and have dinner at **Ca l'Isidre**, a small but sophisticated Catalan restaurant whose guests have included Julio Iglesias.

11:00pm Wander to **Boadas**, a 1920s cocktail-society bar. They specialize in *mojitos*, a mint-and-rum drink that Hemingway loved.

1:00am One of Barcelona's most popular bars, **Oliver & Hardy**, will be filling up about now. Famous for its strict admission policy, this is the place to see the well-heeled *gente guapa* (beautiful people) of Barcelona.

Day 2. Thu. Aug. 31, 2000
(Day 2. Thursday August 30, 2001)

9:00am Visit **Mesón del Café** for traditional breakfast pastries and superb coffee.

10:00am Pay homage to the father of Spanish art nouveau (*modernisme* in Catalonian), Antoní Gaudí. His masterpiece, the cathedral of **La Sagrada Família**, is breathtaking. Continue to Casa Milà, a bizarre structure Gaudí originally designed as an apartment building. Other modernist buildings on the same street (Paseo de Gràcia), include the Casa Lleó Morera and the Casa Batlló.

2:00pm Lunch at **La Dama**, located inside an art-nouveau mansion. The warm salad of prawns and orange vinegar is a house specialty.

4:30pm Walk up the steep hill to Gaudí's **Parc Güell**, which has been described as a surrealistic Disneyland. In the center of town, enjoy the work of 20th-century Catalan artists at the **Museu d'Art Modern**.

7:00pm Head to the Port Olímpic area. Any of the hundreds of cafes, bars, or restaurants are a good bet, but **Café & Café** is a sure thing for cocktails or coffee.

9:00pm Dine in the relaxed atmosphere of **Tinglado Moncho's**, which has attentive service and a lively crowd. Wander the length of Port Olímpic, stopping at any of the number of bars, clubs, and discos that dot the area.

Midnight Cab to the Eixample district for a club crawl. In a three-tiered former movie house, **Luz de Gas** offers quiet bar areas, live music, and wild dancing. **Nick Havanna** is great for funk, soul, and salsa dancing. Well-dressed socialites frequent the **Club Otto Zutz** disco.

Day 3. Fri. Sep. 1, 2000
(Day 3. Friday   August 31, 2001)

9:00am Head to the Barrio Gótic for breakfast at **Café de l'Opera**, an Old World-style cafe with outdoor tables.

11:00am Walk to the **Museu Picasso** to see an extensive collection of work by the museum's namesake.

1:00pm Have lunch at **Els Quatre Gats** (The Four Cats), where, as a then-struggling artist, Picasso designed the menu covers.

3:00pm Explore the narrow streets of the Gothic quarter, whose buildings date to the 12th century. The **Gothic Catedral**, which took two centuries to build, is one of the most impressive in Spain. Stroll down La Rambla. With its mix of outdoor cafes and street performers, it's the most famous (and eccentric) boulevard in Barcelona.

6:30pm Enjoy *tapas* on the bustling Plaça Reial. **Glaciar** is a hip place for people-watching.

9:00pm Also in the Plaça is the oldest flamenco *tableau* in Barcelona. **Los Tarantos** offers traditional shows and buffet dinners.

1:00am Finish at the classy **Up and Down Club** or head to the happening Aribau for **Dry Martini**, a *cocteleria*, and fashionable **Búcaro**, Barcelona's newest venue for live music, dancing, and drinks.

Alternatives

The five-star **Hotel Arts** is a 44-story skyscraper in the central city by the beach. For Old Europe charm in the center of town, try the **Hotel Majestic**. The **Ritz Hotel** always lives up to its famous reputation.

Roig Robí is one of the most popular Catalan restaurants in Barcelona. For good *cava* (sparkling wine) and *tapas*, try **El Xampanyet** (usually closed in August). **Jean Luc Figueras**, in the hip Gràcia district, serves impeccable nouveau-Catalan cuisine. **Egipte** restaurant attracts a young, hip crowd. For nouveau-Basque cuisine, dine at **Beltxenea**.

In rundown Barrio Xines, **Bar Marsella** is a beautiful turn-of-the-century bar that serves absinthe, the liqueur that prompted mad visions in Rimbaud, Gauguin, and others. **Luna Mora Club**, which doesn't close until 5 a.m., has two dance floors. Drinks are available Friday and Saturday evenings on the roof of **Casa Milà**. Grab a beer at longtime favorite **El Vaso de Oro**.

The **Museu de l'Eròtica** is a mishmash of international erotica. Worth visiting are the **Museu de Ceràmica/Museu de les Arts Decoratives**, which showcase arts and crafts. The **Fundació Joan Miró** rounds out a Catalan *modernisme* experience.

The Hot Sheet

☎ 34/93

$ 150 Peseta

HOTELS	DAY	ADDRESS	*	PH	PRICE	FX	RMS	BEST ROOMS
Hotel Arts	A	19-21 c/ de la Marina		221-1000 800- 241-3333	$$$$	221-1070	399	Dlx harbor or city vw
Hotel Claris	1	150 c/ Pau Claris		487-6262 800- 525-4800	$$$	215-7970	120	Crtyd vw
Hotel Majestic	A	68 Passeig de Gràcia		488-1717 800- 448-8355	$$$	488-1880	329	Patio vw
Meliá Confort Azafata	A	15 Autopista Aeropuerto, Valencia	96	154-6100 800- 448-8355	$$	153-2019	128	Gdn or pool vw
Ritz Hotel	A	668 Gran Vía		318-5200 800- 223-6800	$$$	318-0148	122	Supr Gran Vía vw

RESTAURANTS	DAY	ADDRESS	*	PH	PRICE	REC	DRESS	FOOD
Beltxenea	A	275 c/ Mallorca		215-3024	$$$$+	LD	Euro	Basque, international
Ca l'Isidre	1	12 Les Flors		441-1139	$$$	D/L	Kazh	Traditional Catalan
Café de l'Opera	3	74 La Rambla		317-7585	$	B/LTD	Kazh	Cafe, *tapas*
Egipte	A	79 La Rambla		317-9545	$$	LD	Kazh	Catalan
Els Quatre Gats	3	3 c/ de Monsió		302-4140	$$	L/BD	Local	Catalan
Jean Luc Figueras	A	10 c/ Santa Teresa		415-2877	$$$	LD	Euro	Nuvo Catalan
La Dama	2	423 Av. Diagonal		202-0686	$$$	L/D	Euro	Gourmet Catalan
Mesón del Café	2	16 c/ Libreteria		315-0754	$	B/T	Local	Cafe
Restaurant Azafata	1	see Meliá Confort Azafata hotel	96	154-6100	$$	L/D	Local	International
Roig Robí	A	20 Seneca		218-9222	$$$$	LD	Euro	Traditional Catalan
Tinglado Moncho's	2	Port Olímpic		221-8383	$$$$	D/L	Euro	Seafood

NITELIFE	DAY	ADDRESS	PH	PRICE	REC	DRESS	MUSIC
Bar Marsella	A	65 c/ de Sant Pau, at c/ Sant Ramon	442-4433	None	H	Local	
Boadas	1	1 c/ del Tallers, at La Rambla	318-8826	None	H	Local	
Búcaro	3	195 Aribau	209-6562	None	O	Euro	Dance
Café & Café	2	30 Moll del Mistral	221-0019	None	H(F)	Kazh	
Casa Milà	A	92 Passeig de Gràcia	484-5900	None	M	Kazh	Jazz
Club Otto Zutz	2	15 c/ Lincoln	238-0722	$$	HO	Euro	House, garage, funk
Dry Martini	3	162-6 Aribau	217-5072	None	H	Euro	
El Vaso de Oro	A	6 c/ Balboa	319-3098	None	H	Kazh	
El Xampanyet	A	22 c/ de Montcada	319-7003	None	HF	Kazh	
Glaciar	3	3 Plaça Reial	302-1163	None	HF	Euro	
Los Tarantos	3	17 Plaça Reial	318-3067	$$$	SF	Dressy	Flamenco
Luna Mora Club	A	Passeig Maritim	221-6161	$$	O	Euro	Pop, salsa
Luz de Gas	2	246 c/ Muntaner	209-7711	$$	HO	Euro	Disco, dance
Nick Havanna	2	208 c/ Rosellón	215-6591	$	O	Euro	Funk, soul, salsa
Oliver & Hardy	1	593-595 Av. Diagonal	419-3181	None	H	Dressy	
Up and Down Club	3	179 c/ Numància	205-5194	$$	HOP(F)	Euro	Disco, dance

SIGHTS & ATTRACTIONS	DAY	ADDRESS	*	PH	ENTRY FEE
Fundació Joan Miró	A	Plaça Neptú, Parc de Montjïc		329-1908	$
Gothic Catedral	3	Plaça de la Seu		315-1554	None
La Sagrada Família	2	401 c/ Mallorca, Plaça Sagrada Família		207-3031	$
Museu d'Art Modern	2	Parc de la Ciutadella		319-5728	$
Museu de l'Eròtica	A	96 La Rambla		318-9865	$
Museu Picasso	3	15 c/ Montcada		319-6310	$
Museus de Ceràmica/ de les Arts Decoratives	A	686 Av. Diagonal		280-1621 280-5024	$
Parc Güell	2	c/ Olot		424-3809	None
Buñol TIC		Pl. del Ayuntamiento in City Hall	96	250-0151	
TIC Catalunya		107 Passeig de Gràcia		238-4000	

EVENT & TICKET INFO

La Tomatina (Plaza del Ayuntamiento, Buñol): Admission is free. For more event information, contact the *Valencia Regional Tourist Board* (34/96-398-6422). For more information on Barcelona, contact the *Spanish National Tourist Office* in New York (212-265-8822).

*96=Valencia

RECommendations: (Restaurants) B–Breakfast; L–Lunch; D–Dinner; T–High tea or snack
(Nitelife) G–Gaming; H–Hangout bar; M–Live music; O–Dancing (disco); P–Dancing (live music); S–Show; F–Food served
( )–Available but without recommendation. For complete explanation of Hot Sheet format, see page 34.

🕐 NYC +6   ☽ 70°/82° (21°/27°)   ✈ Barcelona (BCN); 30 min./$25 Valencia (VLC); 30 min./$20   🚗 No   👥 Spanish

September/October 2000

September/October 2001

Munich, Germany

Oktoberfest

| Origin: 1810 | Event ★★★★★★★★ City | Attendance: 6 million |

You've made your way onto the bandstand in the center of a 3,000-person tent to lead the crowd in a rendition of "Hang On Sloopy." Welcome to the mother of all beer parties, the world's best-known folk fest.

Calling *Oktoberfest* big is like saying the Sears Tower is a tall building. Some 750,000 kegs of beer get tapped during the annual event's 16-day run. Revelers down nearly a million gallons of brew, mostly inside jam-packed tents. Hungry partyers typically wipe out 700,000 barbecued chickens, half a million grilled pork sausages, and seven dozen oxen roasted whole on the spit—plus spareribs, grilled fish, endless tubs of sauerkraut, and countless thirst-inducing pretzels.

Most of *Oktoberfest* actually covers the last two weeks of September. The event originally celebrated the 1810 wedding of Bavaria's Crown Prince Ludwig and Princess Therese von Sachsen-Hildburghausen. They tied the knot in October, hence the event's name. The action now takes place primarily on the Theresienwiese (Therese's Meadow), a vast, open space locally called the Wies'n, 20 minutes' walk southwest of downtown Munich. Visitors can simply aim toward the lights, noise, and Bavaria herself, a 60-foot bronze goddess overlooking the proceedings. On center stage in each tent, brass bands belt out Bavarian polkas. Buxom waitresses are decked out in dirndls. Trumpeters and tuba players sport lederhosen.

The Wies'n also features a full-fledged amusement park, complete with carnival midways and four dozen rides, including a mile-long roller coaster. The party kicks off with a grand entry parade on opening day, then an even bigger one—four miles of Germania—the next morning.

Munich is Germany's third-largest city (with 1.3 million residents, it's outnumbered by only Berlin and Hamburg). Ornate architecture, cultural institutions, and two palaces remind visitors that the city reigned as formerly independent Bavaria's capital for 200 years. Today, however, endless kegs and hearty smiles make the city the kingdom of all beer parties.

Oktoberfest

Day 1. Fri.   Sep. 15, 2000
(Day 1. Friday   September 21, 2001)

9:00am The **Kempinski Hotel Vier Jahrezseiten** is an elegant member of the German hotel chain, perfectly located for all the weekend festivities.

9:30am Grab a bite at **Café Glockenspiel** on the Marienplatz, Munich's hub, named after the statue of the Virgin Mary in the center. For panoramic views, ascend the historic **Frauenkirche**'s south tower. Don't miss the show at the Neues Rathaus (New City Hall) façade at 11 a.m., signaled by the glockenspiel carillon's clanging.

12:30pm The cellar of nearly every *Rathaus* in Germany has its **Ratskeller** beer garden or restaurant. Munich's is cavernous, with vaulted stone walls, flickering candles, and a sizable lunch menu and salad bar.

1:30pm Save room for dessert at old-time (since 1888) **Café Luitpold**, renowned for its rich whipped-cream pastries.

2:00pm The 171-foot hill that qualifies as a mountain in pancake-flat Munich is where World War II air-raid rubble was dumped. It's also high ground at Olympic Park, laid out for the 1972 Summer Games. Europe's speediest elevator whisks you up to the 951-foot **Olympia Tower** observatory for views of the snow-capped Bavarian Alps.

4:00pm Across the park is the Bavarian Motor Works. Generations of autos, motorcycles, and airplane engines are displayed in the **BMW Museum**.

6:30pm Have dinner at **Spatenhaus**, where huge windows overlook Max-Joseph-Platz and Munich's colonnaded National State Theater. Beer connoisseurs take note—this popular restaurant serves the Spaten-Franziskaner brand.

9:00pm Head across the Isar River to the arty Haidhausen district. Hit Kunstpark Ost, a potato-processing-plant-turned-nightlife-center with more than 18 clubs and bars, near the *Ostbahnhof*. In nearby Laim, another ex-factory has become **Nachtwerk**, where a celebrity-watching crowd congregates.

Day 2. Sat.   Sep. 16, 2000
(Day 2. Saturday   September 22, 2001)

9:30am Breakfast in a beer hall? Sure, because Saturday morning is regarded as the best time to savor Munich's little white *Weisswürst* veal sausages, slathered with a sweet mustard and accompanied—despite the early hour—by a golden-hued wheat beer. Join in at **Donisl**, a circa-1715 landmark.

11:00am *Oktoberfest* gets underway with the ceremonial *Grand entry parade* of horse-drawn brewery wagons, flower-covered floats, and marching bands. Get to the tent where, at noon, Munich's Lord Mayor taps a keg and the festival fun officially begins.

1:30pm Head back downtown. **Augustiner-Keller** is a vintage, *gemütlich Gasthaus* (genial guest house) for a lunch of Bavarian specialties, including autumn's strong bock "muscle beer." There's a courtyard out back.

3:00pm The **Deutsches Museum** is Europe's superstar science and technology museum. Its collections cover the first automobile (an 1886 Benz), old aircraft, an IMAX movie theater, and excellent displays of astronomy equipment, photography, and rocketry.

7:30pm Student-populated Schwabing, a hip enclave north of the city center, has plenty of restaurants and watering holes. With touches of alpine atmosphere, **Weinbauer** has draught beer and Bavarian and Austrian specialties on the menu.

9:30pm For more *Oktoberfest*, cab to the Wies'n. Service in the beer tents continues until 11 p.m. nightly, and the park is illuminated at night, creating a totally different atmosphere. Otherwise, take advantage of Schwabing's nightlife. **Schwabinger Podium** is a famed jazz joint. The aptly named **Skyline** dance club occupies the Hertie department store's rooftop. Outside Schwabing, **P-1** is the place to be (if you can get in). At the frenetic disco, royalty, models, and artists mix with "the little people" lucky enough to get past the eye of the doorman.

Day 3. Sun. Sep. 17, 2000
(Day 3. Sunday   September 23, 2001)

10:00am Get prepared with a buffet breakfast at the hotel because yesterday's hullabaloo was merely a warm-up.

11:30am Now comes an even bigger extravaganza: The two-hour, four-mile-long *Costume & Riflemen's Parade* features trumpeters on horseback, brewery wagons, floats, livestock, drill teams, marksmen's clubs, clowns and jesters, and Bavarian dignitaries. In all, some 7,000 participants start in the city center and make their way to the Theresienwiesen. Watch the parade from your hotel or, better yet, walk the parade route in reverse—you'll see the whole parade in half the time and get a good tour of the city.

12:30pm Expect shoulder-to-shoulder humanity on the sprawling Wies'n. You'll experience true *Oktoberfest* camaraderie in the vast brewery tents, the largest of which are roomy enough for 10,000 party animals. Pick one of these *festival halls* for lunch.

3:30pm Switch your attention to three of Europe's most esteemed art museums. Your choice: **Alte Pinakothek** (early German and European masterworks), **Neue Pinakothek** (French impressionist paintings and international art), or the **State Gallery of Modern Art** (20th-century focus, in a Hitler-era building).

5:00pm Back at the Wies'n, try the rides, shooting galleries, and numerous sideshows. Test your courage by free-falling from the tall Jumping Tower.

8:30pm At the world-famous **Hofbräuhaus am Platzl**, patrons have been emptying beer from quart-size HB mugs since 1589. The arm-in-arm, back-and-forth swaying to brass-band music takes place in the raucous main-floor halls. Hearty Bavarian meals are served upstairs, where you can converse without shouting across tables.

10:30pm The **Park Café** exemplifies Munich's late-night scene, with its large dance floor and reverberating soul, reggae, and jazz—quite *schicki-micki* (chic). Another "in" place, the **Nachtcafé**, a jazz-and-blues club, swings up to the start of another day of *Oktoberfest*.

Alternatives

Located in the heart of Munich, **Hotel Bayerischer Hof** is run by the fourth generation of proprietors. The **Hotel Rafael** is within walking distance of the Wies'n and Maximilianstrasse promenade. For proximity to the famous Hofbräuhaus beer hall, check into the recently renovated **Platzl Hotel**.

Off Munich's Marienplatz, **Dallmayr**—founded about 1700—is Germany's best-known gourmet deli. For the best in new German cuisine, try **Mark's**, in the Hotel Rafael. **Käfer's am Hofgarten** has a piano bar and fantastic lobster ravioli. Olympic Park's casual **Olympic Tower Restaurant** is good.

For more beer, check out **Schumann's**, one of Munich's most famous hangouts. **Maximilian's Nightclub** attracts the late-night crowd.

The Englischer Garten (English Garden) encompasses a lake, pavilions, pathways, four beer gardens, and, reportedly, a large collection of nudists who sometimes gather behind the Haus der Kunst art gallery. Bavarian royalty's old summer place, the baroque **Schloss Nymphenburg** (Nymphenburg Palace) is set in a 495-acre park. More movies and TV shows are cranked out in Bavaria's capital than anywhere else in Europe—the **Bavaria Filmtour** offers behind-the-scenes showbiz stuff.

The Hot Sheet

☎ 49/89

$ 1.8 Deutschmark

HOTELS	DAY	ADDRESS	PH	PRICE	FX	RMS	BEST ROOMS
Hotel Bayerischer Hof	A	2-6 Promenadeplatz	2-1200 800- 207-6900	$$$$+	212-0624	396	Promenadeplatz vw
Hotel Rafael	A	1 Neuturmstr.	29-0980 800- 223-6800	$$$$+	22-2539	73	Rms 607 or 507
Kempinski Hotel Vier Jahreszeiten	1	17 Maximilianstr.	2-1250 800- 426-3135	$$$$+	2-125-2777	316	5th and 6th fls w/city vw
Platzl Hotel	A	10 Sparkassenstr.	23-7030 800- 448-8355	$$$	2-370-3800	167	Dlx rm w/ Hofbräuhaus vw

RESTAURANTS	DAY	ADDRESS	PH	PRICE	REC	DRESS	FOOD
Augustiner-Keller	2	52 Arnulfstr.	59-4393	$$	L/BD	Kazh	Bavarian
Café Glockenspiel	1	28 Marienplatz	26-4256	$	B/LD	Kazh	International
Café Luitpold	1	11 Briennerstr.	29-2865	$	T/BL	Euro	German
Dallmayr	A	14-15 Dienerstr.	2-1350	$$$	BLT	Kazh	German
Donisl	2	1 Weinstr.	22-0184	$	B/LD	Kazh	Bavarian
Hofbräuhaus am Platzl	3	9 Am Platzl	22-1676	$$	D/BL	Kazh	Bavarian
Käfer's am Hofgarten	A	6-7 Odeonsplatz	290-7530	$$	BLD	Euro	International
Mark's	A	see Hotel Rafael	29-0980	$$$	D	Euro	Nuvo German
Olympic Tower Restaurant	A	7 Spiridon-Louis-Ring	3-066-8585	$$	LDT	Kazh	International
Ratskeller	1	8 Marienplatz	219-9890	$	L/BD	Kazh	German
Spatenhaus	1	12 Residenzstr.	290-7060	$$	D/L	Kazh	Bavarian, international
Weinbauer	2	5 Fendstr.	39-8155	$$	D/L	Kazh	German, Austrian

NITELIFE	DAY	ADDRESS	PH	PRICE	REC	DRESS	MUSIC
Maximilian's Nightclub	A	16 Maximiliansplatz	22-3252	None	O	Euro	Disco
Nachtcafé	3	5 Maximiliansplatz	59-5900	None	M(F)	Kazh	Blues, jazz
Nachtwerk	1	185 Landsbergstr.	570-7390	$	O(F)	Kazh	Soul, R&B, house, pop, oldies
P-1	2	1 Prinzregentenstr. in Haus der Kunst bldg.	29-4252	None	O	Euro	Disco, funk, soul, house
Park Café	3	7 Sophienstr.	59-8313	$	O(F)	Kazh	Jazz, reggae
Schumann's	A	36 Maximilianstr.	22-9060	None	H(F)	Euro	
Schwabinger Podium	2	1 Wagnerstr.	39-9482	$	MP(F)	Kazh	Jazz, rock
Skyline	2	82 Leopoldstr.	33-3131	$	O(F)	Euro	R&B, jazz, salsa, house

SIGHTS & ATTRACTIONS	DAY	ADDRESS	PH	ENTRY FEE
Alte and Neue Pinakothek	3	27-29 Barerstr.	23-8050	$
Bavaria Filmtour	A	7 Bavariafilmplatz	6-499-2304	$
BMW Museum	1	130 Petuelring	3-822-3307	None
Deutsches Museum	2	1 Museuminsel	2-1791	$
Frauenkirche	1	12 Frauenplatz	290-0820	$
Olympia Tower	1	21 Spiridon-Louis-Ring in Olympic Park	3-067-2414	$
Schloss Nymphenburg	A	1 Schloss Nymphenburg	17-9080	$
State Gallery of Modern Art	3	1 Prinzregentenstr. in Haus der Kunst bldg.	2-112-7137	$
Munich Tourist Office		Neues Rathaus, Marienplatz	2-233-0300	

EVENT & TICKET INFO

Oktoberfest (Theresienwiese, located southwest of downtown Munich): Admission is free. Bleacher seats are available for the **Grand entry** ($23) and **Costume & Rifleman's** ($36) parades. For more information, call the *Munich Tourist Office* (49/89-233-0300) or the *German National Tourist Office* in New York City (212-661-7200).

RECommendations: (Restaurants) B—Breakfast; L—Lunch; D—Dinner; T—High tea or snack
(Nitelife) G—Gaming; H—Hangout bar; M—Live music; O—Dancing (disco); P—Dancing (live music); S—Show; F—Food served
( )—Available but without recommendation. For complete explanation of Hot Sheet format, see page 34.

🕐 NYC +6　　☀ 36°/75° (2°/23°)　　✈ Munich (MUC); 45 min./$70 (R)　　🚗 No　　👥 German

Galway Oyster Festival

(Galway International Oyster Festival)

Origin: 1955	Event ★ ★ ★ ★ ★ ★ City	Attendance: 10,000

Stamina, and plenty of it, is required to survive Galway's celebration of the oyster, when merrymakers consume some 100,000 of the slippery shellfish and more than 30,000 pints of Guinness. The smooth, dark beer, which experts call the perfect accompaniment for oysters, provides the kicker at this event and definitely gets Irish eyes smiling.

Traditionally, people don't eat oysters unless there is a letter *R* in the name of the month, so the festival heralds the return of oyster season after the barren months of May, June, July, and August. Each year the *Oyster Festival* lures more than 10,000 visitors to Galway with infamous partying that continues day and night over the last full weekend of September. The highlight is the *Festival Gala Ball*, held on Saturday night (tickets are scarce and booking months in advance is a must).

For most locals, though, the place to be is in the *Festival*'s Grand Marquee on Saturday afternoon. Located beside Galway Bay, looking out onto the Atlantic, this is the perfect venue for an afternoon of drinking, dancing, and socializing. In front of 3,000 people, 18 national oyster-opening champions from Singapore to the United States compete in

The Guinness World Oyster Opening Championship, the winner being the first person who can open 30 of the balky bivalves to the standards set by gourmet restaurants worldwide. Meanwhile, out on the town, the city's many pubs distribute free oysters with the purchase of a Guinness.

The capital of western Ireland's Connacht region, Galway is a small, winding city of some 60,000 people, where everything happens within walking distance of the city center. Most any time of year, Galwegians dedicate a good portion of their lives to *craic* (pronounced "crack"), which simply means "having a good time." So, it's no surprise that they invest so much energy in enjoying themselves at the *Oyster Festival*, the city's final fling of the summer.

The Fun Also Rises

Galway Oyster Festival

Day 1. Fri. Sep. 22, 2000
(Day 1. Friday   September 28, 2001)

9:30am Check into the ideally located **Eyre Square Great Southern Hotel**, Galway's most elegant establishment. Its gracious Victorian dining room serves full Irish breakfasts, including porridge and puddings.

11:00am Across the street lies Eyre Square, officially titled the John F. Kennedy Memorial Park, in honor of President Kennedy's visit there in 1963. The unusual fountain with rusty sails pays homage to Galway's fishing tradition.

11:30am On Shop Street you'll discover the remains of some of the medieval buildings for which Galway was once famous. Lynch's Castle, now a bank, is one of Ireland's finest examples of a medieval town house. Down the street, you'll see the 14th-century **St. Nicholas Collegiate Church**, which Columbus is reputed to have visited in 1477 while trading in Ireland.

12:30pm No trip to Galway would be complete without stopping at **Kenny's Bookshop & Art Gallery**. This family-run business is a treasure-trove of Irish books, specializing in first editions.

1:00pm Walk through the narrow streets to Quay Street, home of the internationally renowned **McDonagh's Seafood**. Serving an enormous range of locally caught fish, McDonagh's is popular with locals.

2:30pm The small **Claddagh Ring Museum**, in the back of a jeweler's shop on Quay Street, is worth a brief look. It's dedicated to the history of a uniquely Galwegian ring, consisting of a crowned heart held by two hands meaning "may love and friendship reign."

3:00pm From the Quay Street/High Street/Cross Street area, known as Galway's Latin Quarter, follow Quay Street to the Spanish Arch, alongside the fast-flowing River Corrib. This segment of Galway's old city wall, named in recognition of the medieval trade between Galway and Spain, is now dwarfed by larger buildings but still one of the city's most important sights.

4:00pm You've waited all day—or have you?—and now it's time for a pint of Guinness. On the corner of Quay and Cross streets is **Tigh Neachtain**, a colorful pub that has been owned by the same family for more than a century. Look carefully, the name is written in Old Irish script.

9:00pm Events at the ***Oyster Festival*** kick off with the ***Friday Banquet***, an informal evening of eating, drinking, singing, and all-night partying. Where many good parties end with dancing on the tables, this one often starts that way!

Midnight If you want to leave the party early, head to **Club Cuba**, a nightclub right on Eyre Square. Expect a young crowd dancing to live jazz, rock, and salsa.

Day 2. Sat. Sep. 23, 2000
(Day 2. Saturday   September 29, 2001)

9:00am Have breakfast at **Kinsella's Bistro**. Tucked off the main street, it offers a choice of healthy gourmet meals.

10:00am Ramble toward Galway's Saturday market, held in the shadow of St. Nicholas Church. It's small but highly colorful and sells everything from carrots to crafts to chapatis.

Noon Head back to Eyre Square, where the ***Oyster Festival*** is just taking off. Saturday is the focus of the weekend, with locals involved and many of the pubs serving complimentary oysters with their Guinness. A band starts playing at noon, followed by a parade, which, although not sophisticated, is marked by enthusiasm and spontaneity.

1:30pm The *Festival's* most popular gathering is held in the Grand Marquee, by the River Corrib. Join 3,000 people crammed into an enormous tent and learn the precarious art of balancing food and Guinness while ℝ trying to manipulate the much-touted mollusk. Chowder, salmon, and brown bread are also served. There's a band, dancing, and visible signs of the reputed aphrodisiac qualities of oysters. Or Guinness. Or both.

2:00pm *The Guinness World Oyster Opening Championship* pits the Irish champion (decided on Thursday night) against international contenders.

3:00pm Cross the road to **Goya's Fine Confectionary**, ℝ where coffee and the best pastries in Galway are served by a friendly staff.

4:00pm Join the throng that moves from one pub to another, drinking Guinness and eating complimentary oysters during the *Guinness Oyster Trail Pubs*.

9:00pm The black-tie *Festival Gala Ball*, held at the Corrib Great Southern Hotel, is the festival's most exclusive event. A sprinkling of national and international politicians, businesspeople, and celebrities ℝ are always spotted at this seven-course meal. The raucous event has lots of rituals, such as parading around the participating countries' flags.

Midnight A hip nightspot is **Queen Street Club**, which features live jazz and rock bands on the weekends. It's located off Eyre Square, in the Victoria Hotel. Or visit one of Galway's hotspots, the **Quays Bar**, where there's live music upstairs every night. The club looks like a church, decorated with furnishings from old Welsh monasteries.

Day 3. Sun.   Sep. 24, 2000
(Day 3. Sunday   September 30, 2001)

Noon Haven't had enough partying? *Sunday Brunch* in ℝ the Grand Marquee features a local jazz group, as well as four other bands.

2:00pm Take a cruise on Lough Corrib, the Republic of Ireland's second-largest lake, which contains an island for every day of the year. At 2:30 p.m., the comfortable *Corrib Princess* (**Corrib Tours**) sails from Wood Quay, 20 minutes' walk from the marquee. Along the way there are ruined castles, mountain ranges, and the Corrib's famous swans.

5:00pm The best traditional-music session in town is at the **Róisín Dubh** pub on Dominick Street, where an eclectic mix of musicians hold an informal jam session, with occasional Irish folk songs thrown in.

8:00pm **The Malt House**, a favorite with Galwegians, ℝ serves classic French food using local seafood. This being oyster time in Galway, feel free to order another Guinness as soon as you sit down.

Alternatives

Jurys **Galway Inn** is one of the city's most popular hotels and is located close to the festival marquee. A mile from the city center sits the gracious **Ardilaun House Hotel**, surrounded by its own park. The Ardilaun hosts an oyster banquet on Saturday night, less formal than the official one. Thirty minutes' outside Galway lies **St. Clerans**, an exquisite Georgian manor house once owned by filmmaker John Huston—it's now a 12-room hotel.

In the heart of medieval Galway, trendy **Kirwan's Lane** offers modern European cuisine—reservations are a must. **Bridge Mills** serves a splendid high tea and good continental food, but most people come for the gorgeous view of the River Corrib. For the best in new Irish cuisine, go west to Moycullen, just outside Galway, to **Drimcong House**.

Busker **Brownes**, one of Galway's largest pubs, boasts three lively bars housed in a 400-year-old converted convent, and an adjoining restaurant. With a friendly staff, **Murphy's** occupies one of the oldest pub sites in Galway. **Taylor's** claims to fame are a barman who has pulled his two-millionth pint and an outdoor beer garden.

The Hot Sheet

☎ 353/91

$ 0.7 Irish Punt

HOTELS	DAY	ADDRESS	PH	PRICE	FX	RMS	BEST ROOMS
Ardilaun House Hotel	A	Taylors Hill	52-1433 800- 448-8355	$$$	52-1546	90	4th fl bay vw
Eyre Square Great Southern Hotel	1	Eyre Sq.	56-4041 800- 448-8355	$$$	56-6704	117	Front of hotel
Jurys Galway Inn	A	Quay St.	56-6444 800- 448-8355	$	56-8415	128	Rms by River Corrib
St. Clerans	A	Craughwell in County Galway	84-6555 800-9184-6000	$$$$	84-6600	12	Huston Rm

RESTAURANTS	DAY	ADDRESS	PH	PRICE	REC	DRESS	FOOD
Bridge Mills	A	O'Briens Bridge off Dominick St.	56-6231	$	BLDT	Local	Continental
Drimcong House	A	Moycullen in County Galway	55-5115	$$$	D	Yuppie	Modern Irish
Goya's Fine Confectionary	2	Kirwan's Ln.	56-7010	$	T/BL	Kazh	Bakery, cafe
Kinsella's Bistro	2	Upper Abbeygate St.	56-4422	$	B/L	Local	Salad, sandwiches
Kirwan's Lane	A	2-3 Kirwan's Ln.	56-8266	$$$	LD	Yuppie	Modern European
The Malt House	3	19 High St. in The Olde Malte Mall	56-3993	$$$	D/l	Dressy	Modern Irish
McDonagh's Seafood	1	22 Quay St.	56-5001	$$	L/D	Kazh	Seafood

NITELIFE	DAY	ADDRESS	PH	PRICE	REC	DRESS	MUSIC
Busker Brownes	A	Kirwan's Ln. at Cross St.	56-3377	None	H(F)	Local	
Club Cuba	1	11 Prospect Hill	56-5991	$	MP	Kazh	Jazz, rock, salsa
Murphy's	A	9 High St.	56-4589	None	H	Local	
Quays Bar	2	Quay St.	56-8347	$	MP(F)	Yuppie	Irish, pop, rock
Queen Street Club	2	Victoria Pl. in the Victoria Hotel	56-7433	$	MP	Kazh	Jazz, rock
Róisín Dubh	3	Dominick St.	58-6540	$$	M	Local	Rock, Irish
Taylor's	A	7 Upper Dominick St.	58-7239	None	H	Local	
Tigh Neachtain	1	Cross St. at Quay St.	None	None	H	Local	

SIGHTS & ATTRACTIONS	DAY	ADDRESS	PH	ENTRY FEE
OTHER SIGHTS, SERVICES & ATTRACTIONS				
Claddagh Ring Museum	1	Quay St.	56-6365	None
Corrib Tours	3	Wood Quay	59-2447	$$
Kenny's Bookshop & Art Gallery	1	High St.	56-2739	None
St. Nicholas Collegiate Church	1	Lombard St.		
Tourist Information		Victoria Pl. off Eyre Sq.	56-3081	

EVENT & TICKET INFO

Galway Oyster Festival (Grand Marquee): Tickets for Saturday events ($70, including **The Guinness World Oyster Opening Championship**) and **Sunday Brunch** ($28) can be purchased at the door.

Friday Banquet and **Festival Gala Ball** (Corrib Great Southern Hotel): Tickets ($84 and $126, respectively) should be purchased in advance by contacting the *Galway Oyster Festival* (353/91-52-2066).

Guinness Oyster Trail Pub (downtown Galway): Admission to the pubs is free.

RECommendations: (Restaurants) B–Breakfast; L–Lunch; D–Dinner; T–High tea or snack
(Nitelife) G–Gaming; H–Hangout bar; M–Live music; O–Dancing (disco); P–Dancing (live music); S–Show; F–Food served
( )–Available but without recommendation. For complete explanation of Hot Sheet format, see page 34.

🕐 NYC +5   ☀ 44°/59° (6°/15°)   ✈ Shannon (SNN); 60 min./SNA   🚗 Yes   👥 English

The Fun Also Rises

Stuttgart's Volksfest

(Cannstatter Volksfest)

Origin: 1818	Event ★ ★ ★ ★ ★ City	Attendance: 5 million

The best two reasons to go to Stuttgart are to pick up your Mercedes (which you can do any time of year) and join Stuttgarters who annually let loose at their beloved ***Cannstatter Volksfest***. This 16-day explosion of fun has become the world's second-largest beer blast, topped in attendance and consumption only by Munich's behemoth Oktoberfest (see page 221). The area's Swabians, as distinctive a Germanic group as Bavarians and Rhinelanders, are known for being as industrious at work as they are at partying.

Volksfest started as an autumn harvest celebration–even before Swabians Gottlieb Wilhelm Daimler and Karl Friedrich Benz, working separately, almost simultaneously invented the internal-combustion engine in the 1880s. The mammoth keg party takes place on a sprawling riverside meadow in Bad Cannstatt, a mineral-spa suburb of Stuttgart. Beer flows in hangar-size tents, giving visitors unlimited opportunities to test zesty regional brews such as Dinkelacker, Schwabenbräu, Stuttgarter Hofbräu Herren-Pils, and Alpirsbacher Klosterbräu—the beer generally holds up longer than the beer drinkers. Swabian pasta specialties such as *Spätzle* and *Maultaschen* accompany the liquid protein. A 78-foot *Fruchtsäule* (fruit column), symbolizing nature's harvest-season bounty, has become the festival's trademark and centerpiece. It's also a handy orientation point in case you lose your way amid the crowds.

The festival, which always starts the last Saturday of September, has wide-ranging appeal. Stuttgart is close to Germany's Black Forest, so one of the beer tents features woodsy Schwarzwald atmospherics and rustic hoedown music. A Französische village, filled with brasseries dispensing drinks and culinary goodies, celebrates nearby French territory. When you need a breather from hoisting mugs of beer or flaky pastries, you can hop a ride on the world's highest and largest transportable Ferris wheel or bump around in dodge-'em cars shaped like mini-Mercedes.

Rolling hills, one of which, the Kriegsberg, is home to a vineyard that slopes right into the city center, surround Stuttgart and its population of 590,000. There are bustling streets, palace gardens, and expanses of public greenery—all ideal places to recuperate after the historic party binges you'll experience at ***Volksfest***.

Stuttgart's Volksfest

Day 1. Fri.   Sep. 29, 2000
(Day 1. Friday   September 28, 2001)

10:00am Beside the Schlossgarten in downtown
Stuttgart, the modern **Hotel Inter-Continental** welcomes you with a beautiful lobby and comfortable,
traditional rooms. It's conveniently situated near
the main railway station and the shopping district
of Königstrasse.

11:00am Acclimate yourself to Germany's Motor City,
more than half of which is layered with public
parks and forests. This includes the palace gardens'
two miles of meandering pathways, leafy dells, and
swan lagoon. Nearby is Stuttgart's bustling, mile-
long main thoroughfare, Königstrasse, a pedestrian
zone lined with trendy stores and cafes. It passes
the spacious Schlossplatz, popular among locals
and out-of-towners as a fresh-air hangout.

Noon Württemberg wines are highly regarded by connoisseurs, and Stuttgart is loaded with hospitable
and kitschy establishments called *Weinstüben* pur-
Ⓡ veying various vintages. **Weinstube Kochenbas** is a
good choice for a hearty lunch.

2:00pm Time for a cultural double-header at Stuttgart's
fine-arts museum, the **Staatsgalerie**, with intercon-
nected *Alte* and *Neue* wings. The latter is housed in
a stunning postmodern building and holds the
largest collection of Picassos in Germany, along
with works by 20th-century luminaries such as
Marc Chagall, Wassily Kandinsky, Mondrian, Otto
Dix, Roy Lichtenstein, and Andy Warhol. In the
older, neo-classical structure, admire paintings by
Flemish, Dutch, French, and German greats.

4:30pm Take a *Kaffee und Kuchen* break at **Café**
Ⓡ **Königsbau**, an utterly Germanic, lace-curtained
pastry-and-ice-cream emporium on the second floor
of a colonnaded 19th-century building. Through the

windows, you can watch the afternoon crowds
milling around Königstrasse and the Schlossplatz.

6:00pm By now, lights are blazing on the Wasen festival
grounds, so get to Bad Cannstatt by cab or public
transport, grab a stein, and take your first swig of
Volksfest fun.

9:00pm Look skyward for a spectacular ***fireworks show***.

9:30pm Dine at high altitude in **Weber's Gourmet Im**
Ⓡ **Turm**, a stylish restaurant inside Stuttgart's 712-
foot television tower. Standing atop a tall hill, it
can't be beat for spectacular views. And the restaurant's list of Württemberg wines is among the best
in this part of Germany.

11:30pm Reserve your energy for a final round and
high-decibel music. **Perkins Park**, Stuttgart's
hottest disco, draws a 30-something crowd.

Day 2. Sat.   Sep. 30, 2000
(Day 2. Saturday   September 29, 2001)

8:30am For breakfast, stroll no farther than the hotel's
Ⓡ **Les Continents** for a pass or two at the hearty buffet.

10:00am The **Mercedes-Benz Museum**, across the
Neckar River from downtown Stuttgart, is tucked
into the automaker's manufacturing complex in
Untertürkheim, just a bit south of Bad Cannstatt's
Wasen festival grounds. Marvel at a century of mint-
condition Benzes, including racing cars, sport
coupes, and, of course, a timeline of luxury sedans.

12:30pm Head to the nearby Wasen for another binge
of ***Volksfest*** activities. This being Saturday, figure
on rubbing shoulders with an extra-large and boisterous weekend throng. Have lunch along with
Ⓡ many German beverages in one of the beer halls.

6:00pm Walk or cab into Stuttgart. The Schlossgarten includes the world-class **Carl-Zeiss-Planetarium**, named for the Stuttgart-born optics whiz. The innercity Bohnenviertel (Bean Quarter, so-called because residents used to cultivate beanstalks in front of their houses) is full of charming timber-framed cottages, wine taverns, and knickknack shops. If you're feeling fit, climb the hills via San Francisco-type stairways to reach photogenic old neighborhoods with knockout views of the urbanized valley below.

8:30pm Have dinner in the Bohnenviertel. Creative adaptations of traditional Swabian cooking distinguish ® **Der Zauberlehrling** (The Sorcerer's Apprentice).

11:30pm The weird and fun German cabaret scene is typified by downtown's **Laboratorium**, favored by the spiky-haired crowd. If that's too alternative for you, try **Longhorn** for pop and rock with occasional live acts.

Day 3. Sun. Oct. 1, 2000
(Day 3. Sunday   September 30, 2001)

9:30am For breakfast, wander Königstrasse and vicinity for a traditional *Konditorei*—a bake shop/coffeehouse, usually filled with local color. One of several ® good ones is **Café Wien**.

10:30am Depart from Bad Cannstatt for a three-hour **Neckar Boat Cruise**. Enjoy the scenic countryside, half-timbered villages, and historic sites. Don't be surprised if the ride includes live Dixieland jazz. ® Have lunch on the boat while drinking Swabian beer or Baden wine.

2:00pm Upon returning to Bad Cannstatt, either check out the *Volksfest* a last time or head to one of the mineral hot springs that has made Stuttgart famous in Germany.

8:30pm For dinner in a historic setting, hit **Alte** ® **Kanzlei**, part of Stuttgart's moated Altes Schloss (Old Castle). The castle was built in the 14th cen-

tury as an in-town residence of dukes and duchesses. This old-time restaurant specializes in *Maultaschen*, a Swabian version of ravioli, stuffed with your choice of ham or spinach.

10:30pm The beat goes on into the early hours at **Jazzothek Rogers Kiste**. DJs and live bands take turns at the equally hip, late-night **Classic Rock Cafe**. But you couldn't possibly be up for another beer, could you?

Alternatives

The posh **Steigenberger Graf Zeppelin** hotel is strategically located directly across from the *Hauptbahnhof* (main railroad station). A price notch below is the contemporary, centrally located **Hotel Ketterer**, which has spacious rooms and a restaurant that replicates a beer hall.

Another Bean Quarter restaurant winner is **Basta Weinstube**. Savor inexpensive French specialties at **Brasserie Flo** in the Breuninger shopping arcade. Wildly popular, **Schellenturm** has a unique atmosphere (it occupies an ancient prison tower) and features Swabian cuisine. For fine dining in a historic castle, try **Speisemeisterie**.

Take a rapid-transit commuter train a short distance north from downtown to the **Porsche Museum** in Zuffenhausen. The first of Ferdinand Porsche's pricey little autos came out in 1948. Fifty roadsters and racers are displayed at the museum. Travel a bit farther north by rail or Neckar River excursion boat to Ludwigsburg to see the 18th-century baroque palace, **Residenzschloss Ludwigsburg**, nicknamed the Swabian Versailles. Suburban Vaihingen's **Swabian Brewery Museum** celebrates 5,000 years of beer. In the Killesberg hills on Stuttgart's northwest outskirts, the **Weissenhof Siedlung** (Weissenhof Estate) consists of avant-garde houses designed for a 1927 exhibition by seven famous architects, notably Bauhaus big shots Walter Gropius and Mies van der Rohe.

The Hot Sheet

☎ 49/711

$ 1.8 Deutschmark

HOTELS	DAY	ADDRESS	PH	PRICE	FX	RMS	BEST ROOMS
Hotel Inter-Continental	1	30 Willy-Brandt-Str.	2-0200 800- 327-0200	$$$$	2-020-2020	276	5th fl w/ park vw
Hotel Ketterer	A	3 Marienstr.	2-0390 800- 528-1234	$$$	203-9600	103	5th fl Comfort rm w/ front vw
Steigenberger Graf Zeppelin	A	7 Arnulf-Klett-Platz	2-0480 800- 223-5652	$$$	204-8542	195	5th fl Avant Garde rm

RESTAURANTS	DAY	ADDRESS	PH	PRICE	REC	DRESS	FOOD
Alte Kanzlei	3	5A Schillerplatz	29-4457	$$	D/L	Euro	German
Basta Weinstube	A	39 Wagnerstr.	24-0228	$$	D	Kazh	German, international
Brasserie Flo	A	Breuniger Karlspassage	211-1661	$$	BLD	Kazh	German, French
Café Königsbau	1	28 Königstr.	29-0787	$	T/B	Kazh	Cafe
Café Wien	3	2 Königstr.	29-5860	$	B/LD	Kazh	Cafe, pastries
Der Zauberlehrling	2	38 Rosenstr.	237-7770	$$	LD	Euro	German
Les Continents	2	see Hotel Inter-Continental	2-0200	$$	B	Kazh	Breakfast buffet
Schellenturm	A	72 Weberstr.	236-4888	$$	D	Kazh	German
Speisemeisterei	A	Am Schloss Hohenhelm	456-0037	$$$	D	Dressy	German
Weber's Gourmet Im Turm	1	120 Jahnstr.	2-489-9610	$$$$	D/L	Dressy	Mediterranean, French
Weinstube Kochenbas	1	33 Immerhoferstr.	60-2704	$	L/D	Kazh	German

NITELIFE	DAY	ADDRESS	PH	PRICE	REC	DRESS	MUSIC
Classic Rock Cafe	3	22 Eberhardstr.	234-8858	None	MP(F)	Kazh	Rock
Jazzothek Rogers Kiste	3	35 Hauptstätterstr.	23-3148	$	M(F)	Kazh	Jazz
Laboratorium	2	147 Wagenburgstr.	46-5775	$	S(F)	Kazh	Cabaret
Longhorn	2	6 Heiligenwiesen	409-8290	None	MP(F)	Kazh	Rock, pop
Perkins Park	1	39 Stresemannstr.	256-0062	$	O	Euro	Disco

SIGHTS & ATTRACTIONS	DAY	ADDRESS	* PH	ENTRY FEE			
Carl-Zeiss-Planetarium	2	25 Willy-Brandt-Str., Mittlerer Schlossgarten	162-9215	$			
Mercedes-Benz Museum	2	137 Mercedesstr.	172-2578	None			
Porsche Museum	A	42 Porschestr.	911-6581	None			
Residenzschloss Ludwigsburg	A	30 Schlosstr., Ludwigsburg	714 118-6440	$			
Staatsgalerie	1	30-32 Konrad-Adenauer-Str.	212-4050	$			
Swabian Brewery Museum	A	12 Robert-Koch-Str.	735-7899	None			

OTHER SIGHTS, SERVICES & ATTRACTIONS

Neckar Boat Cruise	3	Anlegestelle Wilhelma	5-499-7060	$$			
Touristik-Information "i-Punkt"		1A Königstr.	222-8240				

EVENT & TICKET INFO

Cannstatter Volksfest (Wasen festival grounds in Bad Cannstatt): Admission is free. For more information, contact the *Stuttgart Marketing GmbH* (49/711-222-8223) or the *German National Tourist Office* in New York City (212-661-7200).

RECommendations: (Restaurants) B–Breakfast; L–Lunch; D–Dinner; T–High tea or snack
(Nitelife) G–Gaming; H–Hangout bar; M–Live music; O–Dancing (disco); P–Dancing (live music); S–Show; F–Food served
()–Available but without recommendation. For complete explanation of Hot Sheet format, see page 34.

NYC +6   39°/75° (3°/23°)   Frankfurt (FRA); 30 min./$30   Stuttgart-Echterdingen (STR); 30 min./$30   No   German

Athens

Flying plates, trampled flowers, screaming, sweating, kissing—no, it's not a lovers' quarrel, it's a bouzouki nightclub deep in the ancient city of Athens. Summer tourists may turn the Greek islands into a party, but the nation's capital stays in full swing all year long, with more to do by day and night.

Heralded as the birthplace of Western civilization, Athens is now a schizophrenic 20th-century metropolis that titillates all five senses. On the surface, it's a vast cityscape marked by modern apartment buildings and streets choked by traffic and smog. Beyond the sprawl, however, are warm people, charming villages, and one of the hottest, nonstop nightlife scenes around.

Life in Athens continues in many ways as it has for centuries. In the Pláka, the 19th-century pedestrian quarter that lies at the foot of the Acropolis, men play backgammon at local *tavernas* and drink ouzo in neighborhood *ouzerís*. Women sip coffee and idly chat on their geranium-decked balconies. Children run amid countless stray cats and frolic freely among the ancient ruins.

But in the middle of this timeworn setting are the world-renowned bouzouki clubs, which feature hours of continuous live music in unique interactive concerts. The unforgettable shows are surprisingly intimate, with performers encouraging individuals from the crowd to join them on stage to dance or sing. The audience flirts, dances on tables, and hurls tinfoil plates (no more dishes) of carnations through the air like wedding bouquets.

Only in Athens can you find a club scene so charged with passion and an energy so intense that it burns throughout the night. In fact, with bouzouki action rocking this city of about a million residents from 2 to 7 a.m., it's a wonder the Greek economy survives at all. But for thousands of years the country has managed, with the gray eyes of Athena keeping watch through the days, and Aphrodite taking charge of the nights.

Day 1. Thu.   Oct. 19, 2000
(Day 1. Thursday   October 18, 2001)

10:00am Check into the **Grande Bretagne** hotel, located in Constitution Square and overlooking the Parliament. With stunning antiques and ceilings that stretch to the sky, it's been a favorite of dignitaries and celebrities for more than 150 years.

11:00am After leaving the hotel, cross the square diagonally, turn to the right down Ermou Street to explore Athens' chic shopping district. Or go left on Voulis Street and stroll through the Pláka, known for its narrow streets; tiny squares; outdoor *tavernas*; and bohemian atmosphere. The **Museum of Greek Folk Art** has an interesting collection of Greek weaving, embroidery, and pottery.

1:00pm Do lunch at a Greek *taverna*, many of which lie adjacent to the antiquities. **O Platanos** is among the best. Try grilled sausage, fish, pork, or skewered lamb kebabs.

3:00pm After lunch, stop by the **Centre for Folk Art and Tradition** on Hatzimichali Street to see an interesting array of traditional Greek crafts.

6:00pm Head up to the quaint neighborhood of whitewashed houses known as Anafiotika—the area was built by stonemasons from the island of Anáfi. The views from most of the vicinity's many *tavernas* are outstanding.

7:00pm Take an indirect route back to the hotel by passing Hadrian's Arch, an ancient Roman structure, and walk through the cool oasis of the National Gardens.

9:00pm For Mediterranean cuisine, taxi to **Koutí** overlooking the Agorá. Or, for Mediterranean food and views of the Acropolis, try **Pil Poul** in the adjacent area of Thesseio.

Midnight Go to a *rembetika* club, where singers perform the Greek soul music that resembles Portuguese *fado* and American blues. **Stoa Athanáton** in the Central Market and **Frangosyriani** in the Exarchia are highly recommended—both go until 6 or 7 a.m.

Day 2. Fri.   Oct. 20, 2000
(Day 2. Friday   October 19, 2001)

9:00am Have breakfast at the popular **GB Corner** in the Grande Bretagne hotel. Throngs of Athenians gather here to sip strong coffee.

10:30am No trip to Athens would be complete without a visit to the awe-inspiring **Acropolis** complex that dominates the city skyline. Pay homage to Athena, the city's patron goddess, in the Doric-columned Parthenon that dates to 438 B.C. Hit the **Acropolis Museum** to see many of the striking marble sculptures and other objects that once adorned the sacred site.

1:30pm Taxi to Kolonáki Square, Athens' most stylish area and a great place for people-watching. Lunch at **Kafenion**, where young, hip Athenians have traditional *mezédhes* food in a fashionable setting.

3:30pm Spend time in Kolonáki's expensive shops or visit the nearby **Mousío Benáki**, which has an interesting collection of ancient Greek ceramics, jewelry, textiles, and artifacts.

6:30pm Take the funicular railway to the top of Lycavittós Hill, where you'll find the Chapel of St. George's, the modern open-air Lycavittós theater (sometimes spelled Lycabettus), a few *tavernas*, and a panoramic view of the city.

8:00pm Enjoy drinks and backgammon on the top of the hill at **Dionyssos**, a *taverna* with magnificent views of Athens.

10:00pm For a dinner of international *haute cuisine*, ® taxi to **Symposio**, a favorite among the Athenian elite. With a jovial bar, Symposio's unique menu of Italian- and Greek-inspired dishes changes weekly.

Midnight The time has come for bouzouki! Watch modern pop stars perform traditional folk tunes while the audience goes mad, throwing flowers on stage, jumping on table tops to bump, grind, and excite each other—sans touching! Located at the seaside during the summer and in central Athens during the winter, **Romeo** is the quintessential bouzouki club. **Asteria** is a more upscale place where audience and performers alike know how to put on a show.

Day 3. Sat.   Oct. 21, 2000
(Day 3. Saturday   October 20, 2001)

10:00am Breakfast at **Everest**, one of many good cafes ® in Constitution Square.

11:00am Visit the renowned **National Archeological Museum**, which houses an outstanding collection of Cycladic, Minoan, Mycenaenan, and classical Greek art.

1:00pm Via the Metro, head to Piraeus, Athens' harbor area. Linger over a traditional, 16-course Greek ® meal at **Vassilenas**, a fabulous 70-year-old restaurant that has served the likes of Aristotle Onassis and Sir Winston Churchill.

5:30pm After wandering around the waterfront area, go back to the hotel for the essential disco nap.

8:30pm Head to the hip neighborhood of Psirí, 15 minutes on foot from the Pláka and home to a bar scene so popular that partyers on the street blur the lines between venues. While all of the bars are great, **Astron** is the trendiest.

10:00pm Cab to the ultrachic **AristeraDexia** restaurant. The modern stainless-steel interior, fusion food, and extensive wine list have made this spot a popular, albeit out of the way, dining destination.

Midnight Kick off the evening with drinks at **Stádio**, where sophisticated Athenians meet for live music.

2:00am Taxi to the seaside and hit megadiscos such as **Tango** or **Privilege**, where, according to the doormen, it's an honor just to get in. In the birthplace of democracy, however, everyone has the right to sing and dance, so find a place on a dance floor (or better yet, a table top) and enjoy the party—after all, beyond the history, antiquity, and philosophy, that's what Athens is all about.

Alternatives

The most modern hotel in Athens is the **Athenaeum Inter-Continental**, located outside the city center. If you're looking for luxurious accommodations, try the **Astir Palace Resort** complex of three hotels near the coast—it has great pools and a small beach area. The boutique **Andromeda Athens Hotel** has artistic touches, such as gold-flecked mirrors and Raphael reproductions.

The unique **Ta Kioupia** restaurant in Glyphada serves old Greek recipes. There's no menu; instead you get to sample dozens of *tapas*-style dishes prepared that day. **Varoulko** is known for its fresh seafood and large wine cellar. While in the Kolonáki, have lunch at **Lykóvrysi** and watch beautiful people parade by. Walk from the Pláka to **Strophi** in the Makriyiánni neighborhood—it's set on a rooftop terrace from which you can watch the **Sound and Light Spectacle** held on Pnyx Hill outside the Acropolis.

In summer, the islands of Mykonos and Santorini are hot vacation spots. Mykonos has been a popular holiday destination for both the counterculture and economic elite since the 1960s. Everyone here, gay and straight, drops their inhibitions (and sometimes their clothes), especially at Paradise and Super Paradise beaches. Santorini, thought by some to be the actual site of Atlantis, has an infamous nightlife scene (drawing a younger crowd) that has created a mythology of its own. Both islands are accessible by short flight from Athens.

The Hot Sheet

☎ 30/1

$ 300 Drachma

HOTELS	DAY	ADDRESS	PH	PRICE	FX	RMS	BEST ROOMS
Andromeda Athens Hotel	A	22 Timoléontos Vássou St., Mavili Sq.	643-7302 800- 525-4800	$$$	646-6361	30	Front rm
Astir Palace Resort	A	40 Apollo St., Vouliagméni	896-0211 800- 888-1199	$$$	896-2582	503	Aphrodite sea vw rm
Athenaeum Inter-Continental	A	89-93 Syngroú Ave.	920-6000 800- 327-0200	$$$$	924-3000	520	Club rm
Grande Bretagne	1	A-1 Vasileos Georgiou	323-0251 800- 325-3535	$$$$	322-8034	364	5th fl Acropolis vw

RESTAURANTS	DAY	ADDRESS	PH	PRICE	REC	DRESS	FOOD
AristeraDexia	3	3 Andronikou St.	342-2380	$$$	LD	Euro	Fusion
Everest	3	Constitution Sq.	no phone	$	B/LD	Local	Cafeteria
GB Corner	2	see Grande Bretagne hotel	323-0251	$	B/LTD	Local	Cafe
Kafenion	2	26 Loukianou St.	722-9056	$$	L/D	Kazh	Greek
Koutí	1	23 Adrianoú	321-2836	$$$$	L/D	Kazh	Mediterranean
Lykóvrysi	A	Plateía Kolonakiou	361-6712	$	LD	Kazh	Greek, contintental
O Platanos	1	4 Diogenous	322-0666	$	L/D	Local	Traditional Greek
Pil Poul	1	51 Apostólou Pávlou St.	342-3665	$$$$+	L/D	Euro	Mediterranean
Strophi	A	25 Roberto Galli St.	921-4130	$$$	D	Euro	Greek
Symposio	2	46 Erechthoiu	922-5321	$$$$	D	Dressy	International, seafood
Ta Kioupia	A	50 Metaxa St.	894-3146	$$$$	D	Local	Greek
Varoulko	A	14 Deligeorgi	411-2043	$$$	D	Euro	Seafood
Vassilenas	3	72 Etolikoú	461-2457	$$$	L/D	Local	Traditional Greek

NITELIFE	DAY	ADDRESS	* PH	PRICE	REC	DRESS	MUSIC
Asteria	2	2 Gr. Labraki	894-4558	$$	M	Kazh	Greek
Astron	3	3 Taki St.	93 295-6013	None	H	Euro	
Dionyssos	2	43 Roberto Galli St.	923-3182	None	H	Kazh	
Frangosyriani	1	57 Arachovis	380-0693	$$	M	Euro	*Rembetika*
Privilege	3	Akrotiri, Agios Kosmas	985-2995	$	O	Euro	Disco, pop, house
Romeo	2	4 Kallirrois Ave. 1 Elinikou St. (Summer season)	922-4885 894-5345	$	M	Euro	Greek
Stádio	3	1 Márkou Mousoúrou St.	923-7109	$	O	Euro	Disco, pop
Stoa Athanáton	1	19 Sofokleous in Central Market	321-4362	$$	M	Euro	*Rembetika*
Tango	3	4 Alkyonidon Ave.	895-6577	$	O	Euro	Rock, pop

SIGHTS & ATTRACTIONS	DAY	ADDRESS	PH	ENTRY FEE
Acropolis	2	Acropolis	321-0219	$
Acropolis Museum	2	see Acropolis	323-6665	$
Centre for Folk Art and Tradition	1	6 Hatzimichali St.	324-3987	None
Mousío Benáki	2	1 Koumbari	361-1617	$
Museum of Greek Folk Art	1	17 Kythathinaíon St.	321-9031	$
National Archeological Museum	3	44 Patissíon	821-7717	$
Sound and Light Spectacle	A	Pynx Hill opposite Acropolis	322-1459	$
Tourist Office		2 Amerikas St.	327-1301	

RECommendations: (Restaurants) B–Breakfast; L–Lunch; D–Dinner; T–High tea or snack
(Nitelife) G–Gaming; H–Hangout bar; M–Live music; O–Dancing (disco); P–Dancing (live music); S–Show; F–Food served
()–Available but without recommendation. For complete explanation of Hot Sheet format, see page 34.

NYC +7   60°/74° (16°/23°)   Athens(ATH); 30 min./$20   Yes/No   Greek

The Fun Also Rises

Pushkar Camel Fair

(Pushkar Mela)

Origin: 1976 **Event ★ ★ ★ ★ City** **Attendance: 200,000**

L ong, shapely legs flash across the runway. Heavy silver jewelry clinks. The brightly dyed fur is unmistakably a custom design. And she can be yours for a bagatelle, perhaps $1,000 for a best of breed.

The Paris runways? No, this is desert country, where camels are as crucial as pickup trucks in Appalachia. The humped ruminants have been reliable beasts of burden to desert dwellers for thousands of years, so it's only just, that each year in Pushkar they take center stage.

In honor of the beloved Bactrian, the holy city of Pushkar in northwest India hosts the world's largest camel festival, the *Pushkar Mela*, a boisterous gathering of traders, drivers, buyers, gawkers, and tourists. With a normal population of 13,000, the small town of Pushkar literally overflows with 50,000 camels, horses, and cattle— the animals are bought, sold, decorated, paraded, and raced—as well as 200,000 visitors. Luckily for attendees, a local company offers tents and information, plus banking, dining, and medical facilities.

Hundreds of vendors peddle dazzling wares, including mirrored saddles, bangles, and brassware. An encampment among the sand dunes outside of town throbs with bold colors, smells, and sounds. Camels wear bells, pom-poms, and ankle bracelets; musicians, jugglers, and fire-eaters work overtime.

At night, oil lamps float upon green leaves on Pushkar Lake. About 400 ninth-century temples surround the lake, and 52 stone steps allow pilgrims and ascetics to bathe. Pushkar is a vegetarian, dry town, with no meat, eggs, milk, or liquor allowed. But beware of the *bhang lhassi*, a mildly hallucinogenic local beverage that can knock your socks off.

The journey to Pushkar begins in Jaipur, the capital of Rajasthan and home to 1.8 million people. Long a fixture on the Indian must-see list, the Pink City, so called for the orange-pink hue of its ancient buildings, is a treasure-trove of palaces, shrines, bazaars, and unforgettable sunsets. But nothing can prepare you for Pushkar's incomparable sojourn in the sand.

Pushkar Camel Fair

Day 1. Thu. Nov. 9, 2000
(Day 1. Wednesday   November 28, 2001)

9:30am Check into the **Rajvilâs**, a 32-acre Rajasthani-style hotel inspired by the palaces of the Rajput princes. You'll feel as if you're a star in a Merchant-Ivory film, but with much better room service.

10:30am Take a private car and driver to **Amber Fort**, a superb example of Rajput architecture begun in 1592 by Raja Man Singh. Set high on a rugged hilltop overlooking a lake where elephants bathe, the fortress/palace served as the ancient capital of the Jaipur state. Ride one of the pachyderms up to the extensive, walled fort, which displays beautiful decorative details—*repoussé* silver doors, glittering mirrored ceilings, and intricate stonework. If it all seems familiar, perhaps you saw the movie *The Far Pavilions*, which was filmed here.

1:30pm Stop for lunch at **Niro's** in the old city of Jaipur. The restaurant's attentive staff serve excellent kebabs and Rajasthani dishes. There's a good selection of vegetarian fare as well.

3:00pm Explore the Pink City of Jaipur. For a magnificent view of the environs, climb up **Hawa Mahal**, otherwise known as The Palace of the Winds, a five-story façade with delicately honeycombed sandstone windows built so the women of the royal household could watch everyday life without being seen. On to the **City Palace** complex in the center of the Old City—it has a museum displaying royal costumes and Benares silk saris. Across the way is the 18th-century observatory, **Jantar Mantar**, which has an assortment of astronomy contraptions, including the world's largest sundial, still used by astronomers.

6:00pm Polo season is in March, but you can partake of the social ambience at **The Polo Bar** in the Rambagh Palace. Once a maharajah's home, the palace has been a luxury hotel since 1957.

7:00pm Stay for an Indian dinner at **Suvarna Mahal** in the Rambagh Palace. Here you'll find latticed windows, airy pavilions, hanging balconies, and gardens filled with peacocks.

8:30pm Nightlife is not a concept in Jaipur, but locals do love the cinema. This is where you'll find the crowd. Take in a movie at the opulent **Raj Mandir** theater, an attraction in its own right. Hindi films are kitschy, but they're fun.

11:00pm Return by taxi to the Rajvilâs for cocktails at **Rajwada**, the hotel's Burmese teak-lined bar.

Day 2. Fri. Nov. 10, 2000
(Day 2. Thursday   November 29, 2001)

7:00am Begin your morning with yoga and meditation at the spa. You'll be given a white cotton pajama set to wear—yours to keep—as you join a limber young Indian who leads exercises in the pavilion overlooking the pool. Then head back to your room for a fruit-and-yogurt breakfast.

10:00am Jaipur is famous as the center of India's semiprecious stone-cutting and -polishing market. See maharajah jewels at **The Gem Palace** (a museum upstairs showcases extravagant pieces owned by royal families). Peek around the back of the shop to see the owner's collection of vintage Bentleys and Jaguars.

11:00am Johari Bazaar is the gem cutters' center, a must-see for local atmosphere, semiprecious gems, and kundan jewelry (cabochon stones set in gold and enamel work.) Serious shoppers should explore the adjacent alleys of Haldion ka Rasta and Gopalji ka Rasta.

Noon Before packing for Pushkar, lunch at **Surya Mahal** in your hotel. Dine on European or Asian cuisine in an open-air courtyard near a gorgeous mirrored pool.

2:00pm Hire a private car and driver and depart for the *Mela*. The trip takes about three hours.

5:30pm Once you arrive in Pushkar, settle into your executive tent, then head out for a one-hour trek to the Savitri hilltop temple. Take in the magnificent sight of the hundreds of thousands of pilgrims who have journeyed to this holy site for the celebration.

8:00pm Return to camp for dinner. Rajasthani special-
® ties include spiced vegetable curry and chickpea dumplings. Try Indian *thali*, a range of spiced vegetables, soup, pickles, and dal served in small bowls with a variety of breads.

9:30pm Stroll around the campfires, where people will be singing Rajasthani folk songs. Alcohol is forbidden, but a hallucinogenic drink that goes by the names *bhang lhassi*, *thandayi*, and Special Lassi is readily served. It consists of yogurt, ice water, and *bhang*, the local marijuana, and delivers a powerful kick.

Day 3. Sat. Nov. 11, 2000
(Day 3. Friday   November 30, 2001)

9:00am Have breakfast brought to your tent over-
® looking the dunes. The deluxe tents are positioned somewhat away from the teeming village that will materialize almost overnight on the sandy landscape.

10:00am Wander through the bazaars, where peddlers gathered beneath canopied booths sell silver jewelry, beads, silk saris, carpets, slippers, brasswork, spices, mangoes, ornaments, and tons more.

Noon Lunch at the restaurant in the tent city. Choose
® from Western-style fare or eat traditional Indian food with your hands.

2:00pm Check out the camel lots—purchase is optional, of course. The amphitheater is the site of cultural programs, dances, and the official camel race. At

the fairgrounds just west of town, you can see fire-eaters, jugglers, acrobats, musicians, and dancers.

4:00pm Explore the narrow, winding streets of Pushkar. Find the red spire—it belongs to the only temple in India devoted to the Hindu god Brahma.

6:00pm Watch the procession of pilgrims on their way to Pushkar Lake, the most sacred lake in India. According to legend, it appeared after Lord Brahma dropped a lotus flower (*pushpa*) onto the site. The lake is perfectly round and surrounded by 400 temples from the 9th century, whose bells sound at nightfall.

7:00pm For a traditional Indian buffet dinner, walk to
® the **Hotel Pushkar Palace** on the lakefront. Watch as banana-leaf boats filled with candles and flower petals are floated across the lake in the moonlight.

9:00pm Devotional chants will lull you to a peaceful sleep beneath the awesome spectacle of a desert full moon.

Alternatives

The **Rambagh Palace** in downtown Jaipur is a grand building that began as a four-room pavilion in 1835 and expanded into the maharajah's palace. Expansive gardens and an in-house astrologer make the fantasy complete. Located in the middle of a man-made lake in nearby Udaipur, the **Lake Palace Hotel** was once an 18th-century royal pleasure retreat. The **Hotel Pushkar Palace**, with a fantastic location on Pushkar Lake, is a one-time palace with a fine-dining restaurant.

Surbhi, on the road from Jaipur to Amber, offers Rajasthani cuisine along with a cultural show that features dancing and puppetry. **LMB** in the Johari Bazaar is the best vegetarian restaurant in town. **Handi** serves the area's finest Mogul-style grilled meats.

The Hot Sheet

☎ 91/141

$ 43 Rupee

HOTELS	DAY	ADDRESS	*	PH	PRICE	FX	RMS	BEST ROOMS
Hotel Pushkar Palace	A	Pushkar on Pushkar Lake	145	7-2001	$$	7-2226	30	Lake vw
Lake Palace Hotel	A	Pichola Lake, Udaipur	294 800-	52-7961 448-4471	$$$	52-8700	81	Lake facing rm
Rajvilâs	1	Goner Rd.	800-	64-0101 562-3764	$$$$	64-0202	71	Luxury tent rm
Rambagh Palace	A	Bhawani Singh Rd.	800-	38-1919 448-8355	$$	38-1098	113	Dlx

RESTAURANTS	DAY	ADDRESS	*	PH	PRICE	REC	DRESS	FOOD
Handi	A	opposite post office		36-4839	$	LD	Local	Grilled meats
Hotel Pushkar Palace	3	see Hotel Pushkar Palace	145	7-2001	$	D/BL	Local	Indian buffet
LMB	A	in Johari Bazaar		56-5844	$	LD	Local	Vegetarian
Niro's	1	Mirza Ismail Rd.		37-1874	$	L/D	Local	Indian, Chinese, continental
Surbhi	A	Amber Rd.		63-5954	$$	LD	Local	International
Surya Mahal	2	see Rajvilâs hotel		64-0101	$$	L/D	Euro	Rajasthani, continental
Suvarna Mahal	1	see Rambagh Palace		38-1919	$$	D/L	Euro	Indian, Rajasthani, continental

NITELIFE	DAY	ADDRESS	PH	PRICE	REC	DRESS	MUSIC
The Polo Bar	1	see Rambaugh Palace	38-1919	None	H	Euro	
Raj Mandir	1	Panch Batti Crossing, Mirza Ismail Rd.	37-9372	$	S	Local	Cinema
Rajwada	1	see Rajvilâs hotel	64-0101	None	H	Euro	

SIGHTS & ATTRACTIONS	DAY	ADDRESS	PH	ENTRY FEE
Amber Fort	1	Amber Rd. about 7 mi. from Jaipur center	53-0293	$
City Palace	1	Pink City, within the Old City	60-8055	$
The Gem Palace	2	Mirza Ismail Rd.	37-4175	$
Hawa Mahal	1	Main st. of Pink City	66-8862	$
Jantar Mantar	1	next to entrance of City Palace	66-0494	$
Tourist Office		Platform 1, Railway Station	31-5714	

EVENT & TICKET INFO

Pushkar Camel Fair (in the desert, west of Pushkar): All events are free. For more information, contact the *Government of India Tourist Office* (800-953-9399).

TENT RESERVATIONS

The Rajasthan Tourism Development Corporation operates a tented camp, with a 24-hour coffee shop, dining hall, tourist information center, foreign currency exchange, post office, and medical facility. Royal tents are offered by the Royal Durbar a k a The Maharaja of Jodhpur. Tents should be reserved in advance through a travel agent or by contacting the *Rajasthan Tourism Development Corporation* (100 Jawajarial Nehru Marg, Jaipur 302004, Rajasthan, India).

RECommendations: (Restaurants) B–Breakfast; L–Lunch; D–Dinner; T–High tea or snack (Nitelife) G–Gaming; H–Hangout bar; M–Live music; O–Dancing (disco); P–Dancing (live music); S–Show; F–Food served ()–Available but without recommendation. For complete explanation of Hot Sheet format, see page 34.

NYC +10 　 56°/82° (13°/27°) 　 Jaipur (JAI); 30 min./$15 　 No 　 English, Rajasthani, Hindi

The Fun Also Rises

Macau Grand Prix

Origin: 1954	Event ★ ★ ★ City	Attendance: 20,000

In November, the only thing around Macau moving faster than the visiting Formula 3 race cars is the money changing hands at the city's bustling casinos. The local passion for all-night gambling—most Macau casinos operate 24 hours a day—is nearly matched each fall by an intense devotion to motor sports of all kinds.

The **Macau Grand Prix** is the world's only "mixed" circuit race, with events for Formula 3 autos, motorcycles, and international touring cars. The attraction for most visitors, however, is Macau, one of the world's most densely populated cities and the only stop on the racing tour where fans can take in Christian churches from the 1600s, Cantonese cuisine from the ages, and pagan discos from the millennium (this one).

Inspired by the Monaco Grand Prix, four motor-racing enthusiasts dreamed up the race in the coffee shop of Macau's old Riviera Hotel in 1954. The city has since grown into a mecca for the motor-sports world. Race weekend includes cultural events, a fireworks show, and musical performances. When the racing is over, visitors can choose between gambling in Macau's numerous casinos, racetracks, and jai alai courts, partying in its many restaurants and clubs, or strolling along its cobblestone lanes, plazas, and gardens.

About 40 miles from Hong Kong, Macau was founded more than 400 years ago by Portuguese colonists. Like Hong Kong in 1997, Macau reverts to Chinese control on December 20, 1999. But the city will continue to host the **Grand Prix** every third weekend in November.

Though 95 percent of its 350,000 residents are Chinese, Macau is dotted with baroque architecture, Victorian theaters, and historic citadels. Today, the city thrives mainly on tourism and gambling. The weekend throngs of Hong Kongers who come over to Macau are as likely to race to baccarat tables (Macau's most popular game) or slot machines (known locally as "hungry tigers") as to the Macau Grand Prix Museum.

Macau Grand Prix

Day 1. Fri.   Nov. 17, 2000
(Day 1. Friday   November 16, 2001)

9:00am Check into the opulent but tasteful **Mandarin Oriental** hotel. Rooms are decorated with Portuguese fabrics and teak furniture—an appropriate mix of multiculturalism in exotic Macau.

10:00am Although there's race activity (trial heats) in town today, spend the day exploring the literally thousands of restaurants, shops, and attractions in nearby Hong Kong. Pick your favorites from suggestions in the Chinese New Year itinerary (see page 51) and have the concierge help you arrange transportation—you can go to Hong Kong by jetfoil, hydrofoil, hover ferry, jet ferry, and even something called a Jetcat (a jet-propelled catamaran).

Day 2. Sat.   Nov. 18, 2000
(Day 2. Saturday   November 17, 2001)

9:00am Have a lazy breakfast on your hotel room balcony this morning.

10:00am The *Macau Grand Prix* is special because of its mix of motorcycles and Formula 3 race cars. Today is the finale of the two-wheeled speed demons. The motorcycle race takes place entirely within the city limits, so grab a spot by the racecourse or purchase seats at a raised grandstand near any of the big downtown hotels.

11:00am Begin your tour of downtown. Watch out for competing race cars as you stop to look at the colonial Leal Senado, the neo-classic legislative building. Walk through Largo do Senado (Senate Square) and the historic center of Macau.

12:30pm Near the Leal Senado, have lunch at **Afonso III**, a cozy place that could fool you into thinking you were in Portugal.

2:00pm Walk to **São Domingos** church and museum. An enormous 17th-century building, the church is Macau's most spectacular example of baroque architecture. Then head for the Ruinas de São Paulo, an old colonial church façade that once housed a Jesuit order but was destroyed by fire in 1602.

3:00pm Take a quick tour of the **Macau Museum**. Situated on dilapidated fortress grounds, it's devoted to the fascinating and variegated history, culture, and traditions of the region.

4:00pm Grab a taxi for drinks on the terrace of the **Pousada de São Tiago** hotel atop Barra Hill—you'll get magnificent views of downtown Macau. On your descent from the hill, admire the Temple of the Goddess A-Ma, the deity for which Macau is named.

6:00pm Near the temple, have an early dinner at **A Lorcha**. Popular dishes include African or tomato-and-onion-stewed chicken.

7:30pm Continue on to ***Shining Night by the Waterfront***, a fireworks show sponsored by local businesses. The waterfront has become a popular destination spot for tourists and locals to meet, drink, and hang out. New restaurants and bars seem to be opening weekly. **Opiarium** is an opium-den-style rendezvous with drinks, light snacks, and live music. The sleek **Casablanca Cafe** has indoor and outdoor seating and serves wine and beer imported from Portugal. Macau is home to many fireworks factories, so no matter from where you watch, the display over the harbor should be magnificent.

Midnight Gambling in Macau differs slightly from that in Las Vegas. Games are mostly Chinese games of luck, drinks aren't free, and slot machines don't come with comfy chairs. The **Mandarin Oriental Hotel Casino** features the most luxurious environs, while the **Lisboa Hotel Casino** is designed according to the principles of *feng shui*—the ancient Chinese practice of "arrangement"—to channel positive energy toward the gamblers. Keep in mind, however, that *feng shui* is generally intended to benefit the owner of the house. Some things aren't any different from Las Vegas.

Day 3. Sun.   Nov. 19, 2000
(Day 3. Sunday   November 18, 2001)

9:00am Head to the Largo do Senado area for breakfast
® at **Bolo de Arroz Patisserie**, a fine choice for coffee, pastries, and baked goods.

10:00am Finally, someone's figured out a safe way to combine drinking and driving: The same ticket that grants you entry to the **Grand Prix Museum** also gets you into the **Wine Museum**. The first place chronicles everything about speeding cars and motorcycles, the second contains reams of information about the red stuff.

11:00am The first leg of the ***Macau Grand Prix*** consists of 15 laps and should just be getting underway. Top drivers from the international field of Formula 3 racers often use this race to move up the ranks to prestigious Formula 1 racing. Between legs of the main event, highly entertaining local, amateur, and saloon-car races are staged.

1:00pm Break for lunch and some exhaust-free air at
Fat Siu Lau, the oldest Macanese restaurant in
® Macau. This local institution serves Chinese as well as Portuguese food in simple, nostalgic surroundings. Roast pigeon is on the menu, but you can also get good seafood.

2:30pm The final laps of the ***Macau Grand Prix*** should be in full throttle. From your grandstand seat, watch as the racers take hairpin turns, charge down the straightway, and speed toward the finish that decides this world-class race.

3:30pm Head to Hac Sa (Black Sand) beach on the adjacent island of Coloane. While the black sand makes the beach appear dirty, it's actually fine for swimming or windsurfing and popular with locals and tourists.

8:00pm Nearby, the ever-popular **Fernando's** restau-
® rant is housed in a pleasant, albeit nondescript, shack but it turns out some of the best Macanese food available.

Midnight Return to central Macau, where the finale of the Grand Prix should heat up the Mandarin Oriental's stuffy **Embassy** bar. Or make a triumphant last lap through Macau, making sure to hit the chic waterfront area for drinks and people-watching.

Alternatives

Set into the crumbling Barra fortress walls, the **Pousado de São Tiago** hotel features period-style rooms overlooking the sea. The **Westin Resort** on the island of Coloane, a 20-minute shuttle ride from downtown Macau, is a luxurious retreat with views of the South China Sea. Only ten minutes by shuttle from Macau, the first-class **Hyatt Regency** on Taipa Island houses guests in stylish, comfortable rooms that look out over the panorama of downtown Macau.

For interesting Portuguese food and a gregarious proprietor, **Carlos Restaurant** can't be beat. Authentic Portuguese cuisine and atmosphere at **Litoral** make it a local favorite. **Moonwalker Restaurant** on the waterfront serves California cuisine in a fashionable setting until 10 p.m. and stays open for drinks until 4 a.m.

The floating **Macau Palace** is an intricately carved and ornately decorated casino that is moored in the Inner Harbour. Head out with the Europeans who frequent the **Fortuna** nightclub in the Fortuna Hotel, where you can dance to a live band and rotating DJs.

The Hot Sheet

☎ 853 $ 8.0 Pataca

HOTELS	DAY	ADDRESS	PH	PRICE	FX	RMS	BEST ROOMS
Hyatt Regency	A	2 Estrada Almirante Marques Esparteiro, Taipa	83-1234 800- 233-1234	$$$	83-0195	326	10th fl rm w/ harbor vw
Mandarin Oriental	1	956-1110 Av. da Amizade, Outer Harbour	56-7888 800- 526-6566	$$$	59-4589	435	Mandarin rm w/ balc
Pousado de São Tiago	A	Av. da República, Fortaleza de S. Tiago da Barra	37-8111 800- 448-8355	$$$	55-2170	24	Vista rm w/ balc
Westin Resort	A	1918 Estrada de Hac Sa, Coloane	87-1111 800- 228-3000	$$$	87-1122	208	Dlx beach or ocean vw

RESTAURANTS	DAY	ADDRESS	PH	PRICE	REC	DRESS	FOOD
A Lorcha	2	289 Rua do Almirante Sergio	31-3195	$	D/L	Kazh	Portuguese
Afonso III	2	11A Rua Central	58-6272	$	L/D	Kazh	Portuguese
Bolo de Arroz Patisserie	3	11 Tr. de São Domingos	33-9089	$	B/LT	Local	Bakery, sandwiches
Carlos Restaurant	A	28 Rua Bispo Medeiros	52-2027	$	LD	Kazh	Portuguese, Macanese
Fat Siu Lau	3	64 Rua da Felicidade	57-3580	$	L/D	Local	Macanese, Portuguese
Fernando's	3	9 Praia Hac Sa, Coloane	88-2264	$$	D/L	Kazh	Portuguese, Macanese
Litoral	A	261-A Rua do Almirante Sergio	96-7878	$$	LD	Kazh	Macanese, Portuguese
Moonwalker Restaurant	A	13 Av. Marginal da Baia	75-1326	$	LTD	Kazh	Italian, bar food

NITELIFE	DAY	ADDRESS	PH	PRICE	REC	DRESS	MUSIC
Casablanca Cafe	2	Av. Marginal da Baia, Edf. Vista Magnifica Court	75-1281	None	H(F)	Kazh	
Embassy	3	see Mandarin Oriental hotel	56-7888	None	M(F)	Kazh	Easy listening
Fortuna	A	63 Rua de Cantão in Fortuna Hotel	78-6333	$	O	Local	International
Lisboa Hotel Casino	2	2-4 Av. de Lisboa	57-7666	None	GH	Euro	
Macau Palace	A	in Inner Harbour	72-7928	None	GH	Euro	
Mandarin Oriental Hotel Casino	2	see Mandarin Oriental hotel	56-7888	None	GH	Euro	
Opiarium	2	Av. Dr. Sun Yat-sen, Edf. Vista Magnífica	75-0975	None	M(F)	Kazh	International
Pousado de São Tiago	2	see Pousada de São Tiago hotel	37-8111	None	H		

SIGHTS & ATTRACTIONS	DAY	ADDRESS	PH	ENTRY FEE
Grand Prix Museum	3	Rua Luís Gonzaga Gomes	798-4108	$
Macau Museum	2	112 Praceta do Museu de Macau, Monte Fort	35-7911	$
São Domingos	2	Largo de São Domingos	36-7706	None
Wine Museum	3	Rua Luís Gonzaga Gomes	798-4188	$
Macau Government Tourist Office		9 Largo do Senado	31-5566	

EVENT & TICKET INFO

Macau Grand Prix (downtown Macau, China): Watching the event curbside is free. Bleacher seats in front of various hotels ($40-$70) are available by calling the *Macau Government Tourist Office* in Macau (853/31-5566).

RECommendations: (Restaurants) B–Breakfast; L–Lunch; D–Dinner; T–High tea or snack
(Nitelife) G–Gaming; H–Hangout bar; M–Live music; O–Dancing (disco); P–Dancing (live music); S–Show; F–Food served
()–Available but without recommendation. For complete explanation of Hot Sheet format, see page 34.

🕐 NYC +13 ☀ 77°/86° (25°/30°) ✈ Hong Kong (HKG); 90 min./$NA Macau (MSM); 30 min./$10 🚗 No 👥 Cantonese/ Portuguese

The Fun Also Rises

Acapulco, Mexico

Fun Destination? Acapulco

A FunGuide 100 Destination

All night, the bright lights of crowded bars and flashy *discotecas* twinkle and glow along the gentle arc of the bay. Since the inception of its fame in the 1950s, Acapulco has been known as a party town. But after reigning over sun-seekers, beach bums, and mind-blowing nocturnal fiestas for more than four decades, Acapulco, the glamour queen of the Pacific, was finally due for a facelift. An extensive revitalization project has now put sexy Acapulco back on the map.

Bordered by the verdant Sierra Madre mountains on the east and the crystal waters of Acapulco Bay on the west, this coastal paradise is a vision from all directions. With a rapidly growing population of two million, Acapulco is quaint yet cosmopolitan, a place that offers everything you could want from a beach town— quiet escape, raucous parties, sun-soaked siestas, water-sport adventure. But one thing it doesn't offer is a trendy carbon copy of home. Despite its historic popu-larity among American jet-setters, Acapulco never stopped being Mexican. Unlike the gringo-saturated scenes in Cancún and Cabo, Spanish still dom-inates the streets here, and traditional eateries and mar-kets prevail in Acapulco's Old Town.

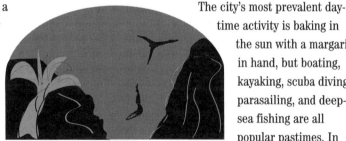

Though the high season explodes from December to March, Acapulco rocks any time of the year. The city's most prevalent day-time activity is baking in the sun with a margarita in hand, but boating, kayaking, scuba diving, parasailing, and deep-sea fishing are all popular pastimes. In a spot where more than 360 days of the year are sunny and clear, simply taking in the beauty of the beaches can be a full-time occupation.

The languor of the day dis-solves after sunset, when tanned, scantily dressed vacationers flock to nightclubs with names like Baby 'O and Enigma. There's no need to hurry. Acapulco's nightlife doesn't start until after 11 p.m.—and of course there's always *mañana*.

Fun Destination: Acapulco

Hotels

Most of Acapulco's recent hotel development and revitalization has been along Diamond Acapulco (from Las Brisas to the airport) where Acapulco's swankiest hotels and resorts are found. The largest of the luxury resorts, the **Acapulco Princess** has more than 1,000 rooms on 480 lush acres, as well as several fabulous swimming pools and one of the best beach scenes around. Sharing the beach with the Princess is its sister resort, the somewhat more exclusive and quieter **Pierre Marques**. The **Hyatt Regency**, located in town, also has a great beach with private *palapas* (palm-thatched beach huts) for guests, and an ongoing party around its giant pool. For more subdued, private accommodations, try **Las Brisas**, set high on a hill, or the stunning **Camino Real Acapulco Diamante**, which has its own small private beach.

Restaurants

Each of the recommended hotels has restaurants that are consistently good and convenient. When you're ready to venture out, your first choices should be **El Olvido**, whose nouveau-continental cuisine is served on an open-air patio overlooking the beach, and **Restaurante Kookaburra**, which specializes in seafood, steaks, and ceviche. Also good is the Italian cuisine at **Ristorante Casanova** and **Spicey**'s exotic amalgamation of flavors from Asia, Africa, India, and Mexico. If you feel like exploring the distant reaches of Acapulco, try **La Cabaña** on Caleta Beach for good seafood in a vivacious atmosphere.

Nighttime Entertainment

Nightlife action centers in two areas: the southern end of the bay's hotel zone and the La Vista area, on the way to the Marques and Princess hotels. In the hotel zone, two clubs reign. The elaborately designed **Andromeda's**, which has two aquariums, a stage for big-name acts, and a small swimming pool with an exotic mermaid show, is the current rage. **Baby 'O** lacks the dramatic decor of Andromeda's but more than makes up for it with a faithful following and always-crowded dance floor. In the bustling La Vista area, **Enigma** (formerly Extravaganzza) attracts a slightly older crowd with house and techno beats in one room and a piano bar in another. It's hard to miss the sexy shaking at the **Palladium** next door, where passersby get a look at dancers through a giant glass wall.

If you need a breather from the club scene, try **Pepe's Piano Bar**, which attracts an uninhibited, upbeat crowd that vies for the microphone in piano sing-alongs. In the same complex, **Señor Frog's** has a college-age crowd, group-party atmosphere, and casual, funky design.

Other Attractions

The torch-wielding cliff divers at **La Quebrada** are a sight to behold. These courageous, buff men make crucially timed dives from a 135-foot precipice into the rising surf. Sunset or evening is the most dramatic time to view these plunging Adonises. **La Perla Restaurant** (for a drink or dinner) at Hotel El Mirador Plaza Las Glorias is the best place to watch them—it's just a 15-minute walk up the hill from the middle of town.

Before the arrival of tourists, life in Acapulco centered around Old Town, with its narrow, winding streets filled with charming shops and strolling musicians. By contrast, the *zócalo*, a k a Plaza Juan Alvarez, in the heart of town bears testament to Acapulco's less-than-traditional past. Nearby is the interesting **El Fuerte de San Diego**, a fort built in 1616. Today it contains a museum dedicated to Acapulco's history.

The Hot Sheet

☎ 52/74

$ 9.5 Peso

HOTELS	ADDRESS	PH	PRICE	FX	RMS	BEST ROOMS
Acapulco Princess	Playa Revolcadero	69-1000 800- 223-1818	$$	69-1012	1019	Dlx ocean vw w/ balc
Camino Real Diamante	Baja Catita	66-1010 800- 722-6466	$$	66-1111	156	Supr rm w/ balc and ocean vw
Hyatt Regency	1 Av. Costera Miguel Alemán	69-1234 800- 233-1234	$$	84-3087	644	21st fl w/ ocean vw
Las Brisas	5255 Carretera Escénica Clemente Mejía	69-6900 800- 223-6800	$$$$	84-6071	265	Royal Beach rm, 4th level
Pierre Marques	Playa Revolcadero	66-1000 800- 223-1818	$$	66-1046	344	4th fl w/ ocean vw

RESTAURANTS	ADDRESS	PH	PRICE	REC	DRESS	FOOD
El Olvido	Pl. Marbella, Costera Miguel Alemán	81-0214	$$$	D	Euro	French, international
La Cabaña	Caleta Beach, Lado Oriente	83-7121	$	BLD	Local	Seafood
Restaurante Kookaburra	Carretera Escénica, Las Brisas	84-1448	$$$	D	Kazh	International, seafood
Ristorante Casanova	5256 Carretera Escénica	84-6815	$$$$	D	Euro	Italian
Spicey	Carretera Escénica, Fracc. Marina de Las Brisas	81-1380	$$	D	Kazh	International, Asian, fusion

NITELIFE	ADDRESS	PH	PRICE	REC	DRESS	MUSIC
Andromeda's	Av. Costera Miguel Alemán, Lomas de Costa Azul	84-8815	$$$	MOP	Euro	Pop, techno, house, Latin
Baby 'O	22 Av. Costera Miguel Alemán	84-7474	$$$	O	Euro	Disco, pop, Latin
Enigma	Carretera Escénica, Las Brisas	84-7164	$$$	OM	Euro	House, techno, Latin, piano bar
La Perla Restaurant	74 c/ La Quebrada in El Mirador hotel	83-1155	None	HF	Euro	
Palladium	Carretera Escénica	81-0300	$$$	O	Euro	Techno, pop, house, Latin
Pepe's Piano Bar	28 Carretera Escénica in La Vista center	84-8060	None	M(F)	Kazh	Piano
Señor Frog's	28 Carretera Escénica in La Vista center	84-8020	None	O	Local	Disco

SIGHTS & ATTRACTIONS	ADDRESS	PH	ENTRY FEE
El Fuerte de San Diego	c/ Hornitos y Morelos, Colonia Centro	82-3828	$
La Quebrada	c/ La Quebrada	83-7228	$
Secretary of Tourism Office	4455 Av. Costera Miguel Alemán, Lower fl. in Convention Center	84-1168	

RECommendations: (Restaurants) B–Breakfast; L–Lunch; D–Dinner; T–High tea or snack
(Nitelife) G–Gaming; H–Hangout bar; M–Live music; O–Dancing (disco); P–Dancing (live music); S–Show; F–Food served
( )–Available but without recommendation. For complete explanation of Hot Sheet format, see page 34.

🕐 NYC -1   ☀ 74°/89° (23°/31°)   ✈ Acapulco (ACA); 45 min./$20   🚗 Yes/No   👥 Spanish

Hogmanay

(Edinburgh's Hogmanay)

Origin: 1993	Event ★★★★★★★★★ City	Attendance: 400,000

If you've ever felt there must be more to New Year's Eve than just waiting for the countdown to midnight, the place to be is the New Year's Eve party in Edinburgh, the capital of Scotland and the home of Europe's largest winter celebration. Despite frigid temperatures, you'll see plenty of kilts and hearty Scots celebrating their favorite holiday.

Edinburgh hosts festivals throughout the year, including the Edinburgh Festival Fringe (see page 207), but Scotland's best-known traditional event is *Hogmanay*, a December 31 national obsession that has only recently exploded onto the world stage. As the centerpiece of *Hogmanay* celebrations, the Edinburgh party engulfs the whole city for four days, making it one of the coolest (literally and figuratively) and biggest street parties in the world. The amazing backdrop of ancient Edinburgh Castle is illuminated by spectacular fireworks. This feast of innovative international street performers; Celtic, classical, and rock music; torchlight processions; specialty food stands; and parties to suit all tastes confirms Edinburgh's international reputation as The Festival City.

The word *Hogmanay* is thought to come from a northern-dialect French word, *hoginane*, meaning "a gift at new year."

The event has links to ancient pagan celebrations that marked the passing of midwinter and has always been a time to party for the Scots. And if you think New York City has more New Year's tradition, remember it was Scottish poet Robert Burns who wrote *Auld Lang Syne* in 1789.

During the day, visitors can see Edinburgh Castle, the home of Scotland's crown jewels. From there the Royal Mile sweeps through the medieval Old Town, a warren of narrow lanes and historic buildings. City-center art galleries, stylish cafes, bars, and cozy pubs are equally irresistible. With a population of about 450,000 people, Edinburgh is one of the world's most beautiful cities, nominated as a World Heritage Site by UNESCO. The real beauty of the place, however, is found among the people, whose knack for New Year's celebrating can't be matched anywhere in the world.

Hogmanay

In lieu of an itinerary, see the Edinburgh Fringe chapter (page 207) for to-do suggestions. You'll have to plan about six months ahead of time to get hotel reservations for **Hogmanay**.

For a complete listing of street entertainment and festival activities, pick up a copy of the *Hogmanay* program. Although the schedule of hundreds of activities changes from year to year, the highlights listed below remain at the heart of the festival.

A dramatic *Torchlight Procession* and *Fire Festival* officially launch the celebration. Purchase a torch and join the magical parade from Parliament Square to Carlton Hill. The parade culminates with fireworks. There should be time to see a music, comedy, or theater performance, or join one of the parties going on around town. Don't miss the opportunity to attend a traditional *ceilidh*, a Scottish version of a square dance with a large shot of Scotch thrown in.

Screams of pleasure and flashing lights come from the *Hogmanay Carnival* at the east end of Princes Street, where you can test your courage on white-knuckle rides, eat candy floss, and try to win a tartan bear—this is Britain's largest winter fairground. The *Hogmanay Food Fair* in George Street's Assembly Rooms is a good place to sample gourmet delicacies such as shortbread, whisky, and smoked salmon. Both of these events run for the entire festival.

Only (!) 200,000 passes are given out for the *New Year's Eve street party*, but that attracts enough body heat to keep everyone warm. At least three public stages, presenting a wide range of dance music, compete for attention, as do scores of partyers in wild costumes. Everything from salsa rhythms to Celtic rock can be heard, often on the same street. After the street party and its breathtaking midnight fireworks display, join the *New Year Revels* in the Assembly Rooms.

Part of The Witchery restaurant, **The Secret Garden** is an enchanting restaurant hidden in the Old Town, close to the castle. Lit entirely by candles and furnished with antiques, this romantic dining spot is located on a converted school playground. An amazing wine list plus stylish cuisine make it a great party spot. Reservations are essential. Street theater and live music are just outside. Watch the fantastic fireworks and enjoy the party atmosphere or step into the crowd and watch live bands playing throughout the city.

EVENT & TICKET INFO

Hogmanay (Edinburgh, Scotland): Tickets are free, but must be requested in advance by writing the *Hogmanay Box Office* (The Hub, Castle Hill, Royal Mile, Edinburgh EH1 2NE, Scotland U.K.) or calling the *Info Hotline* (44/131-473-2000).

☎ 44/131   ⊕ NYC +5   ◐ 35°/44° (1°/6°)   ✈ Edinburgh (EDI); 30 min./$25   🚗 No   🗣 English   💲 0.6 Pounds

---

JUNO: ABOUT NEW YEAR'S

(continued from page 250)

Despite the hype, however, it's the millennium for only a third of the world's population. The majority of people on the planet mark time in a different way. For example, the Christian calendar year 2000 spans the Islamic years 1420-21. The Chinese will be observing the years 4697-98, while Jews consider it to be the years 5760-61. Which may explain why, with the exception of Hong Kong and Singapore, the major millennium celebrations will take place in the South Pacific, North and South America, and Europe. But over time, even the grandeur of these events will fade. Maybe we should start socking away a dollar each year so that we can enjoy the big one—getting away from Earth for a few days for some really wild billennium events!

But What Are You Doing for the Billennium?

If you've been thinking about the millennium, you've been thinking too small. For a real blowout party, set your sights on Earth's billionth anniversary coming up in just 240 million years. If, however, you're one of those types who lives more in the moment, there's always the current millennium, which you could celebrate twice—New Year's Eve 1999, the symbolic end of the century, and New Year's Eve 2000, which suits those who care about precise numeric details ... or who just want another excuse to stay up late.

No matter which New Year's Eve you're celebrating, the biggest, boldest, and brightest blowouts will take place in the major cities traditionally famous for New Year's extravagance—Edinburgh, London, Paris, Rio de Janeiro, Hong Kong, Tokyo, Sydney, Las Vegas, and, of course, New York in Times Square. If the changing of the calendar puts you in a more contemplative mood, celebrate the dawn of time by heading to some of civilization's oldest locales such as the Great Wall of China, the Acropolis, Stonehenge, Machu Pichu, or Istanbul. Romantics may want to follow their hearts to destinations such as the Taj Mahal, the Château of Versailles, Marrakesh, or any number of European castles.

Those who always need to be first should head for Tonga or a volcano on Fiji (where the new century will make its first landfall), or in Gisborne, New Zealand (the new year's first city). Cruisers can have it both ways by heading east over the international dateline, thereby popping the cork on the new year's first bottle of champagne and later sneaking in the last first-kiss of the year.

If twice still isn't enough, several Concorde airplanes will begin the year with a midnight toast at the international dateline. They'll outpace the date, touching down for replays at up to three more locations, the last being Hawaii. If being a mile high for the big moment doesn't float your boat, so to speak, you can join a wet and wild party on the bottom of the sea in Belize, where an underwater New Year's party for gay and lesbian divers will include champagne in squeeze bottles. Rio de Janeiro, host of the largest celebration in the world, also ranks high among the sweat-and-wild events. Three million people dressed in white are expected to samba all night at Copacabana beach while fireworks light up the sky. New York City, with its famous countdown in Times Square, fireworks all over the city, and big parties in its Convention Center, Rainbow Room, and sky-high Windows on the World, won't let anyone challenge its standing as New Year's Eve central. But Las Vegas is trying. The slot machines don't pay any better on New Year's Eve, but the city may throw in a hotel demolition to excite crowds.

Never mind if you missed the best events of New Year's Eve 1999 or want to do the whole millennium party again. Many countries, including Canada, Australia, and Singapore, are using New Year's Eve 1999 as the kickoff for a year's worth of festivities and special events. Travel operators are counting on travelers making grand trips throughout the year to celebrate the change of millennium. The year 2000 is calculated by the Christian calendar, so it's no surprise that Vatican City will be celebrating Holy Year 2000—millions of religious wayfarers are expected to visit the Holy See this year. The same boom in travel is also expected in Palestine and Israel.

(continued on page 249)

Any one of the destinations in this book makes for a great trip, but some dates and locations make it possible to double or even triple your fun and minimize your travel hassles with back-to-back events at nearby locations. Some indefatigable readers are figuring out ways to attend all 100 events in *The FunGuide 100* (yahoo!), but if that's not possible, combining just two could turn a great vacation into an unforgettable epic.*

1. **Latin Fire:** February 19-March 7
   Viña del Mar Song Festival (59), ***Vendimia*** (75), ***Carnaval Rio*** (89)
   Sing and dance in Santiago (with a quick visit to Buenos Aires), get to Mendoza in time for wine, then fly to Rio de Janeiro for *Carnaval*.

2. **Carnival:** February 29-March 6
   Vienna Opera Ball (67), ***Venice Carnival*** (79), ***Karneval*** (83)
   Start in Vienna, then take the spectacular train ride through the Dolomites to Venice for the first weekend of the *Carnival*. Then fly to Köln in time for a German-style *Karneval*. In the process, your wardrobe will change from white tie to Renaissance costume to clown suit!

3. **Down (and Out) Under:** March 2-13
   Sydney Gay and Lesbian Mardi Gras (71), ***Moomba*** (97)
   There couldn't be a better time to visit Australia —its two biggest events take place back to back.

4. **Asia Wet and Wild:** April 7-15
   Fertility Festival (109), ***Songkran Water Festival*** (113)
   Cherry blossoms won't be the only thing you'll admire in Tokyo, a fun stop on the way to Thailand and the wildest water fight you've ever seen.

5. **Riviera Style:** May 18-June 12
   Cannes Film Festival (136), ***Monaco Grand Prix*** (143), ***Féria de Nîmes*** (147)
   Start in Cannes, take the short drive to Monaco, and then back to the heart of Provence.

6. **Jazz and Pizzazz:** July 13-22
   Bastille Day (170), ***Nice Jazz Festival*** (175), ***Montreux Jazz Festival*** (179)
   Take a circular trip that includes fireworks in Paris and jazz and magnificent scenery on the French Riviera and in Montreux.

7. **British Street Theater:** August 21-28
   Edinburgh Fringe Festival (207), ***Notting Hill Carnival*** (213)
   In one very packed week you can go from a huge arts festival in Edinburgh to Europe's largest street festival in London (one-hour flight).

8. **Spanish Fiesta:** August 25-September 1
   Ibiza/Majorca (197), ***La Tomatina*** (217)
   Ibiza and Majorca are a short flight from Valencia (and Barcelona), making it easy to combine an island hop with a trip to Buñol for its wild tomato fight.

9. **Hedonism:** various
   Hedonism II (63)
   If going to one of the Caribbean events isn't enough pleasure-seeking for one trip, you can easily make a stop at the legendary resort before or after ***Junkanoo*** (36), ***Calle San Sebastián*** (47), ***Trinidad Carnival*** (93), ***Sailing Week*** (127), or ***Crop Over Festival*** (193).

* Suggested travel dates are for the year 2000; page numbers for each event are listed in parenthesis.

Tourist Information for Destination Countries

 ust in case you'd like more information on the countries you'll be visiting, here are the phone numbers for their tourist information offices in the United States.

Antigua	.888-268-4227	Italy	.212-245-4822
Argentina	.212-603-0443	Jamaica	.800-233-4582
Australia	.805-775-2000	Japan	.212-757-5640
Austria	.212-944-6880	Macau	.877-622-2800
Bahamas	.800-422-4262	Mexico	.800-446-3942
Barbados	.800-221-9831	Monaco	.800-753-9696
Brazil (Rio de Janeiro)	.310-643-2638	Netherlands	.888-464-6552
Chile	.800-244-5366	Philippines	.212-575-7915
China (Hong Kong)	.800-282-4582	Portugal	.212-354-4403
Denmark (Scandinavia)	.212-885-9700	Puerto Rico	.800-223-6530
France	.410-286-8310	South Africa	.800-723-7458
Germany	.212-661-7200	Spain	.888-657-7246
Great Britain	.800-462-2748	Sweden (Scandinavia)	.212-885-9700
Greece	.212-421-5777	Switzerland	.212-757-5944
India	.800-953-9399	Thailand	.212-432-0433
Ireland	.800-223-6470	Trinidad	.888-595-4868

Note: We have provided toll-free numbers (800 or 888) wherever available. You can access each destination city's Web site through our Web site at www.funrises.com

JUNOS

(p. 193) (p. 136) (p. 155) (p. 83) (p. 79) (p. 109) (p. 67)

Alan S. Davis, Author

Alan is a needy person. He's spent his life taking on nearly impossible tasks in the hopes of gaining sympathy. Apparently it didn't work. But then what made him think that spending five years traveling to the world's most fun events is deserving of sympathy? Alan, an entrepreneur, philanthropist, publisher, and lecturer, began traveling professionally as a tour representative in 1967. This career path was interrupted by the pursuit of politically correct endeavors, but a fortune cookie set him back on the right path: "Preserve wild life—throw more parties."

Chuck Thompson, Editor

Alan Davis met Chuck Thompson while both were on assignment at Carnival in Trinidad. How Davis convinced Thompson to give up such extraordinary assignments to spend six months in front of a computer is a mystery for the ages, but great fortune for the readers of this book. Thompson is a contributing editor for *American Way* and *Escape* magazines. A senior travel editor for *American Way* magazine until 1997, he has worked on assignment for a variety of magazines in more than 15 countries.

THE **FUN**GUIDE 100
THE 100 MOST FUN PLACES TO BE IN THE WORLD AT THE RIGHT TIME

The FunGuide 100 is the smartest—and only—place to go for answers to your toughest travel questions ...

- Where should I go for the best-ever birthday or anniversary celebration?
- Where is the most fun place to be on *St. Patrick's Day, Memorial Day, Fourth of July, Labor Day, Halloween, New Year's Eve?*
- Where can I find the most fun *music, performing-arts, food,* and *film festivals*?
- Where (and when) should I go on my next vacation?

The FunGuide 100 includes **annual calendars** (there is something to do every week of the year!), a **chronological index**, and a **geographical index** keyed to maps.

Essential information for all 100 events is provided, including: popular and official name, a thumbnail description, location, official events dates, our recommendations for the best three days to be there, the event attendance and date of origin, and our ratings for both the event and the city.

Detailed **itineraries** and **Hot Sheets** for the 50 international destinations begin on page 35.

The North American destinations are described in the companion edition, *The Fun Also Rises Travel Guide North America*, available at bookstores and on the Web.

Find out how to have the best time at events such as **Mardi Gras** in New Orleans, the **Kentucky Derby**, the New Age **Burning Man** festival, the **Sundance Film Festival**, San Francisco's **Halloween**, and 45 more!

Be sure to check out our Web site at www.funrises.com. Not only can you order books, but it has links to homepages for all the events and destinations listed on *The FunGuide 100!*

And let us know if you think we've done something wrong (or right)—we'd love to hear from you. But most importantly: Go have fun!

INTL9912